ISABELLA LUCY BIRD (1831–1904), the daughter of a clergyman, grew up in Tattenhall, Cheshire. Early in life she suffered from a spinal complaint and in 1854 she was sent by her doctor to America and Canada to improve her health. She published *The Englishwoman in America* in 1856 and *Aspects of Religion in the United States* in 1859. In 1860 her father died, and Isabella, with her mother and sister Henrietta, moved to Edinburgh. From there she made several excursions to the Outer Hebrides, writing articles on the island crofters and on subjects ranging from the poetry of John Donne to ragged schools. She continued to suffer from back trouble, insomnia and depression until, at the age of forty, she set off for Australia, continuing to Hawaii where her health miraculously improved. She wrote *Six Months in the Sandwich Islands* (1875) and climbed the world's largest volcano, Mauna Loa.

In 1873, Isabella Bird set off for the Rocky Mountains; her 'Letters from the Rocky Mountains' were published in the magazine *Leisure Hour* in 1878 and later published as *A Lady's Life in the Rocky Mountains* (1879). After a period at home she set off once more, this time to the northern Japanese Island of Hokkaido and to the Native States of Malaya. As a result of these two journeys she published *Unbeaten Tracks in Japan* (1880) and *The Golden Chersonese* (1883).

In 1881 Isabella Bird married Dr John Bishop. He died in 1886, and three years later she set off on her travels to western Tibet and Ladakh, the deserts of Persia and Kurdistan, the Korean peninsula and the remote interiors of China. These remarkable expeditions were recorded in *Journeys in Persia and Kurdistan* (1891), *Among the Tibetans* (1894), *Korea and Her Neighbours* (1898) and *The Yangtze Valley and Beyond* (1899).

Isabella Bird returned from the Far East in 1898; making her final journey at the age of seventy, she visited Morocco, touring the country on a black stallion given her by the Sultan. She died in Edinburgh in 1904.

TIBETAN LAMAS MASKED FOR A RELIGIOUS DANCE.

THE
YANGTZE VALLEY
AND BEYOND

AN ACCOUNT OF JOURNEYS IN CHINA,
CHIEFLY IN THE PROVINCE OF SZE CHUAN
AND AMONG THE MAN-TZE OF THE
SOMO TERRITORY

ISABELLA BIRD

WITH A NEW INTRODUCTION BY
PAT BARR

Virago

Published by Virago Press Limited 1985
41 William IV Street, London WC2N 4DB

First published by John Murray 1899

Virago Press edition reproduced from the John Murray edition

Introduction copyright © Pat Barr 1985

British Library Cataloguing in Publication Data
Bird, Isabella L.
  The Yangtze Valley and beyond.
  1. China—Description and travel—To 1900
  I. Title
  915.1'043   DS709
  ISBN 0-86068-790-2

Printed in Great Britain by
St Edmundsbury Press at Bury St Edmunds, Suffolk
and bound by Anchor Brendon Ltd., at Tiptree, Essex

PREFACE

THESE journeys in China [concluding in 1897], of which the following pages are the record, were undertaken for recreation and interest solely, after some months of severe travelling in Korea. I had no intention of writing a book, and it was not till I came home, and China came very markedly to the front, and friends urged upon me that my impressions of the Yangtze Valley might be a useful contribution to popular knowledge of that much-discussed region, that I began to arrange my materials in their present form. They consist of journal letters, photographs, and notes from a brief diary.

In correcting them, and in the identification of places, not an easy matter, I have been much indebted to the late Captain Gill's *River of Golden Sand, The Gorges of the Yangtze*, by Mr. A. Little, three papers on "Exploration in Western China," by Mr. Colborne Baber, in the *Geographical Journal of the Royal Geographical Society*, and very specially to the official reports of H.B.M.'s Consuls at the Yangtze ports. I have denied myself the pleasure of reading any of the recent literature on China, and it was only when my task was done that I glanced over some of the later chapters in *The Break Up of China*, and *China in Transformation*. For a great part of my inland journey I have been unable to find any authorities to refer to, and as regards personal observation I agree sadly with the dictum of Socrates— "The body is a hindrance to acquiring knowledge, and sight and hearing are not to be trusted."

I cannot hope to escape errors, but I have made a laborious effort to be accurate, and I trust and believe that they are not of material importance, and that in the main this volume will be found to convey a truthful impression of the country and its people. The conflicting statements made on every subject by well-informed foreign residents in China, as elsewhere, constitute a difficulty for a traveller, and homogeneous as China is, yet with regard to very many customs, what is true in one region is not true in another. Even in the single province of SZE CHUAN there is a very marked unlikeness between one district and another in house and temple architecture, methods of transit, customs in trade, and in much else.

I have dwelt at some length on "Beaten Tracks"—*i.e.*, treaty ports and the Great River—though these have been described by many writers, for the reason that each one looks at them from a different standpoint, and helps to create a complete whole. The illustrations in this volume, with the exception of the reproductions of some Chinese drawings, and nine which friends have kindly permitted me to use, are from my own photographs. The spelling of place names needs an explanation. I have not the Chinese characters for them, and in many cases have only been able to represent by English letters the sounds as they reached my ear ; but wherever possible, the transliteration given by Consul Playfair in his published list of Chinese Place Names has been adopted, and with regard to a few well-known cities the familiar but unscholarly spelling has been retained. To prevent confusion the names of provinces have been printed in capitals.

I am painfully conscious of the many demerits of this volume, but recognising the extreme importance of increasing by every means the knowledge of, and interest in, China and its people, I venture to ask for it from the public the same kindly criticism with which my former records of Asiatic travel have been received, and to hope that it may be accepted as an honest attempt to make a contribution to the data on which public opinion on China and Chinese questions must be formed.

ISABELLA L. BISHOP

October, 1899.

CONTENTS

CONTENTS

LIST OF ILLUSTRATIONS

LIST OF ILLUSTRATIONS

INTRODUCTION

". . . I am too old for hardships and great exertions now," wrote Isabella Bird to her publisher John Murray in the summer of 1893. It seemed a reasonable enough conclusion for a sixty-three-year-old woman who, according to her doctors, was suffering from "fatty degeneration of the heart", an affected lung, rheumatic gout and recurrent spinal weakness. Nevertheless, Murray, who knew her well having published all her books, beginning with the zestful *Six Months in the Sandwich Islands* in the 1870s to her most recent *Journeys in Persia and Kurdistan*, perhaps had his doubts on that score. More especially so as Isabella also mentioned that, in spite of her sorry condition, she was vaguely considering a little trip to Japan and even Korea the following winter. And certainly Murray must have hoped her travelling days were not over, for all her works were now immensely popular and were earning both publisher and author considerable sums of money.

And of course Isabella had not finished travelling. After consulting several specialists about her health, she proceeded to ignore their diagnosis and her estimate of her own strength and spent the rest of that year quietly preparing for another prolonged and arduous journey in the East, while also fulfilling a large number of public-speaking engagements on behalf of Christian missions overseas.

Her fervent advocacy of the missionary cause at this later stage in her life was rooted in her early upbringing. She was born in 1831 into a highly respectable clerical family quite closely related to the Wilberforces, and had grown up in an atmosphere of good causes. (Her aunts refused sugar in their tea as a protest against slave-grown products. "Oddly enough," comments Anna Stoddart, Isabella's first biographer, "although they daily mourned its absence, they took sugarless tea long after the emancipation in the West Indies.") The freedom-loving, adventure-seeking side of Isabella's nature eventually rebelled against the mental and physical restraints of her social background and her early books are more exuberant and liberal-spirited as a result.

However in 1880, soon after her first expedition to Japan, her beloved younger sister Henrietta died. She was "the centre of my world," wrote Isabella and, according to those who knew her, a sweet, kind and virtuous lady. While still in a state of shock and grief Isabella married a long-standing admirer, Dr John Bishop who was also, in her opinion, ". . . a pure, saintly, heroic, unworldly, unselfish" man. Conscientiously, she devoted herself to the normal domestic and social rounds of middle-class life which always reduced her to "nervous prostration" more quickly than any perils and discomforts in foreign climes. But within a year of their marriage John Bishop fell seriously ill and died in 1886, leaving her doubly bereft. Weighed down from then on with a sorrow that seldom left her, she determined to preserve the precious memories of both sister and husband by trying to follow in their footsteps and by supporting missionary endeavours in which they had fervently believed. In a revealing letter to a close friend, Lady Middleton, written in 1892, she explains that since these bereavements she has "nothing any more to hope for . . . no personal projects." Yet she feels bound to continue her chosen path of duty because "I must make the best of myself, I must bear an active part in life, I must follow their examples."

The strongly conflicting traits in Isabella Bird's character were never completely resolved, and those which were to the fore in the autumn of 1893 have little appeal for most of us nowadays. See her, for instance, one November afternoon on the platform of Exeter Hall, London — a short, plump, earnest gentlewoman addressing the annual gathering of the Gleaners' Union on the theme of "Heathen Claims and Christian Duty." She is an accomplished public speaker and her low, firm tones are persuasive with true conviction as she tells her audience that her conversion to the cause of foreign missions has resulted from her own travels in Asia. "*There* is sin and shame everywhere", she claims. Buddhism and Mohammedanism are corrupt, false doctrines that "degrade women" and stimulate "the worst passions of human nature". She speaks of barbarous oriental punishments, official corruption, the "gross superstition of the masses" and urges her listeners to give up the "unnecessary luxuries of home life" and carry Christ's word to the heathen.

This address was widely circulated by the Church Missionary Society and apparently exercised great influence on the public. But had only that note of single-minded missionary zeal been sounded in the two books Isabella was to write about her last great eastern journey, they would surely have been left undisturbed among the piles of worthy, unreadable "missionary literature" of the period. Fortunately however, Isabella sounded many other notes, and some were joyous songs in praise of travelling through the remotest wilds of the world that burst from her almost in spite of herself, and are present in this last full-length book she wrote, as in all her others.

By this stage in her exceptional career honours were beginning to accumulate round the doughty Mrs Bishop. Since her return from Persia in 1890 she had dined with Prime Minister Gladstone (they had discussed the Nestorian heresy) and been presented to Queen Victoria; she was a well-known lecturer at gatherings of the British Association and the Royal Geographical Society and a respected contributor to various learned journals; she numbered many prominent politicians, clerics and diplomats among her friends. All this had given her an air of poised dignity and quiet authority which, according to Anna Stoddart, greatly impressed and charmed all who met her. But she remained an essentially modest woman and, as she once wrote, "cared little for fame or fortune". In fact she *did* take a certain legitimate pride in this belated recognition of her talents, but always felt they counted for little compared to the selfless, devotedly Christian lives of her now-deceased relatives. And as to fortune – she had no family to support, no extravagant tastes to satisfy, was quite incapable of settling down and furnishing a home of her own, and spent most of the "munificent cheques" she was now receiving from her publishers on the establishment of mission hospitals overseas.

To report on the work of Asian missions was the principle avowed motive for returning to that iniquitous continent, for which she embarked in January 1894. She went as "God's Ambassador to the East" according to pious Anna Stoddart, but she soon overstepped the boundaries of this demanding role, exercising instead those qualities of shrewd observation, tireless perseverance, enthusiastic and objective curiosity, resourcefulness and sheer courage which made her such an excellent traveller and perceptive writer.

Her first port-of-call was Korea, a frail, troubled country whose precarious political and social state soon fascinated her. When China and Japan declared war that summer, with Korea as their first cockpit, she was obliged to leave, going first to Mukden in Manchuria, then to parts of Russian Siberia. Eventually, after another long visit to Korea during its occupation by the Japanese, she reached Shanghai in the summer of 1895 – from which she soon fled, for she never could abide the claustrophobic society of foreign settlements.

As her book relates, she went from there to Hangchow and then by boat to Shao Hsing where (though she doesn't mention it) she stayed with one Rev. Gilbert Walshe who later wrote vividly and admiringly of the impression she made on him. "Her absolute unconsciousness of fear was a remarkable characteristic", he wrote. "Even in the face of the largest and noisiest crowds, Mrs Bishop proceeded with her photography and her observations as calmly as if she were inspecting some of the Chinese exhibits in the British Museum." She was, he continued, "very anxious to conciliate the natives of whatever country she passed through, and when travelling in the interior of China she generally adopted a costume which was designed to fulfil the Chinese canons of good taste. The principal feature of it was a large, loose jacket, or mantle, of 'pongee' which effectually disguised the figure of the wearer, but which, unlike Chinese garments generally, was furnished with most capacious pockets in which she carried all sorts of travelling paraphernalia, including some articles of her own design. Amongst other things, she used to produce from one of the pockets a portable oil lamp, ready for use at a moment's notice, and it seemed rather remarkable that the oil did not leak. If I remember rightly, she carried a loaded revolver in another pocket as a protection against robbers."

The pursuit of photography to which Walshe refers incidentally had recently become a great enthusiasm of hers. She had taken a course in developing and printing her own films before leaving England and was rather proud that she could soon print "with a highly enamelled surface like a professional." Indeed the results were very good by the standards of the time and make excellent illustrations for her last two books.

After that initial foray into the Chinese interior, Isabella returned to Shanghai, spent the summer in Japan and embarked on her truly spectacular adventure up the Yangtze Valley in January 1896. In the course of it she pushed herself to the very limits of her own courage and endurance, and in the whole of her eventful life she was probably never in greater danger than when racketting up and down the Yangtze rapids in sundry fragile craft, when she was almost torn limb from limb by a howling Chinese mob, when she crossed the Pass of Tsa-ku-shan in a snowstorm, sinking in drifts up to her throat. We can but remember with awe that the survivor of these and the many other hazards and hardships she describes was an English lady of sixty-four with numerous physical disabilities including a weak heart! Yet she did survive, though personally I've always imagined that her secret, probably unacknowledged desire was to die quickly and cleanly in the wild mountain passes of the Chinese frontier among people who, as she said, had never even heard of Britain. But that was the country in which her duty lay; God spared her to return to it and, after a three-year absence, she did so.

The remaining years of Isabella's life were mentally productive though not particularly joyous. The first book to result from her Asian journey was *Korea and Her Neighbours* which appeared to considerable acclaim in 1898. But the publication of *The Yangtze Valley and Beyond* the following year was initially overshadowed by the outbreak of the Boer War which focused public attention exclusively on South Africa. Nonetheless, reviewers quickly appreciated its considerable merit – as one of the most vivid and thoroughly documented accounts of late nineteenth-century China ever written – and sales soon picked up. By that time though Isabella was otherwise occupied – with further rounds of speaking engagements, with moving restlessly from one house to another in a fruitless attempt to make a real home for herself, and, in her seventieth year, with one last overseas fling. She went to Morocco for several months where, she wrote to a friend, she once rode "astride a superb horse in full blue trousers and a short full skirt with great brass spurs belonging to the generalissimo of the Moorish Army". Oh that she had turned her camera on herself . . .

Soon after returning to England her health broke down

completely and she was confined to bed for much of her last two years of life. Her many faithful friends visited her frequently bringing offerings of flowers and tempting delicacies, for she had finally lost the capacity to digest all and every kind of food which had stood her in such good stead on her travels. Anna Stoddart quotes from several of her last letters. My favourite is this, written to a long-standing Scottish friend and evidence that her straightforward, practical commonsense and kindliness never deserted her: "I am enjoying your bun. I like rich things and it is the first I have had for months. . . . I cannot write and must content myself this day with sending a little parcel containing a Shetland vest for you and an electric flashlight for Maggie to see her watch with at night. It should be good for a thousand flashes. The packet tied with a string is a refill."

After Isabella's death in Edinburgh in 1904 doctors speculated in medical journals on the mysterious contradictions of her physical and psychological constitution. "The invalid at home and the Samson abroad do not form a very usual combination, yet in her case the two ran in tandem for many years," wrote one. He went on to suggest that Mrs Bishop was one of those individuals "dependent to the last degree upon their environment to bring out their possibilities."

There is much truth in that and it helps to explain the chameleon-like nature of her life's pattern, her appetite for constant change and novelty, her totally absorbed response to many alien lands and cultures and the intense immediacy of her travel writing. Perhaps it also casts light on why she never fully understood herself and why she was never capable of assessing the value of her own talents or forgiving herself for her insufficiencies. To the end she aimed at goals for which she was temperamentally unsuited and was never satisfied with the great deal she actually accomplished. This was due not only to her psychological make-up of course, but to the influences of her strictly Christian upbringing and the restrictions imposed on middle-class women in male-dominated Victorian society. We can only surmise that she may have accomplished even more had she been freed from such restraints; we can only marvel that she ventured as far as she did beyond them.

Pat Barr, Isle of Coll, 1985

THE YANGTZE VALLEY

CHAPTER I.

GEOGRAPHICAL AND INTRODUCTORY

THE events which have rendered the Yangtze Valley literally a "sphere of interest" throughout the British Empire lie outside the purview of these volumes. Few people, unless they have been compelled to the task by circumstances or interests, are fully acquainted with the magnitude and resources of the great basin which in the spring of 1898 was claimed as the British "sphere of influence," and I honestly confess that it was only at the end of eight months (out of journeys of fifteen months in China) spent on the Yangtze, its tributaries, and the regions watered by them that I even began to learn their magnificent capabilities, and the energy, resourcefulness, capacities, and "backbone" of their enormous population.

Geographically the Yangtze Valley, or drainage area, may be taken as extending from the 90th to the 122nd meridian of east longitude, and as including all or most of the important provinces of SZE CHUAN, HUPEH, HUNAN, KIANGSI, NGANHUI, KIANGSU, and HONAN, with considerable portions of CHE KIANG, KUEI-CHOW, and YUNNAN, and even includes the south-eastern drainage areas of KANSUH, SHENSI, and SHANTUNG. Geographically there can be no possible mistake about the limits of this basin.* Its area is estimated at about 650,000 square miles, and its population, one of the most peaceable and industrious on earth, at from 170,000,000 to 180,000,000.

---

* Politically, as H.M.'s Under-Secretary of State for Foreign Affairs defined it in the House of Commons on May 9th, 1899, it is "the provinces adjoining the Yangtze River and Honan and Che Kiang."

The actual length of the Yangtze is unknown, but is believed not to exceed 3000 miles. Rising, according to the best geographical information, almost due north of Calcutta, its upper waters have been partially explored by Colonel Prjevalsky and Mr. Rockhill up to an altitude in the Tang-la mountains of 16,400 feet, and as far as lat. 34° 43′ N. and long. 90° 48′ E.*

It has thus been ascertained that the Great River, though not tracked actually to its source, rises on the south-east edge of the Central Asian steppes, and, after draining an extensive and little-known basin, pursues a tempestuous course under the name of the Chin Sha, hemmed in by parallel ranges, and raging through gigantic rifts in YUNNAN and South-western SZE CHUAN, which (culminate in grandeur at the Sun Bridge, a mountain about 20,000 feet in altitude, "which abuts on the river in a precipice or precipices which must be 8000 feet above its waters" (Baber).

It is not till these savage gorges are passed and the Chin Sha reaches Ping Shan, forty miles above Sui Fu, that it becomes serviceable to man. In long. 94° 48′ Colonel Prjevalsky describes it as a rapid torrent, with a depth of from five to seven feet, a bed, upwards of a mile wide, covered in summer, and a width in autumn of 750 feet at about 2800 miles from its mouth. In travelling from its supposed source to Ping Shan, a distance roughly estimated at 1500 miles, its fall must be fully 15,000 feet (assuming that the altitude of its source is 16,400 feet),† while for the same distance (again roughly estimated) from Ping Shan to Shanghai the fall is only 1025 feet, and from Hankow to the sea, a distance of 600 miles, only an inch per mile.

The Min or Fu appears to have its source in the Baian Kara range, called in Tibetan Maniak-tso,‡ and joins the Chin Sha at Sui Fu. While the Chin Sha is only navigable for about forty miles above this junction, the Min is navigable to Chengtu, about 266 miles from Sui Fu, and by another branch to Kuan Hsien, forty miles higher. I descended the Min from Chengtu to Sui Fu in a fair-sized boat at the very lowest of low water. As being navi-

---

* The lowest latitude which it is believed to reach is 26° N., east of its junction with the Yalung at its great southerly bend, and its junction with the ocean is in lat. 31° N.

† *The Geographical Journal*, September, 1898, p. 227 : "The Yangtze Chiang," W. R CARLES, H.B.M.'s Consul at Swatow.

‡ *Land of the Lamas*, p. 218.

gable for a far greater distance, the Chinese geographers regard the Min as the true "Great River," the superior length of the Chin Sha not being taken into account. It should be noted that the Chinese only give their great river the name of Yangtze for the two hundred miles of its tidal waters.*

After the River of Golden Sand and the Min unite at Sui Fu, the Great River asserts its right to be regarded as the most important of Asiatic waterways by furnishing, by its main stream and the tributaries which thereafter enter it, routes easy of navigation through the rich and crowded centre of China, with Canton by the Fu-ling, with only two portages, and with Peking (Tientsin) itself by the Grand Canal, which it cuts in twain at Chin Kiang.

It is only of the navigable affluents of the Yangtze that mention need be made here. The raging and tremendous torrents foaming through rifts as colossal as its own, and at present unexplored, lie rather within the province of the geographer.

In estimating the importance of these affluents it must be remembered that the Yangtze, of which they are feeders, is not *an* outlet, but *the* outlet, for the commerce of SZE CHUAN, which, owing to its size, population, wealth, and resources, may be truly termed the empire-province of China.

On the north or left bank the Min, before uniting with the Chin Sha at Sui Fu, receives near the beautiful trading city of Chia-ling Fu the Tung or Tatu, a river with a volume of water so much larger than its own as to warrant the view taken by Mr. Baber and Mr. von Rosthorn that it ought to be considered the main stream, and the Ya, which is navigable for bamboo rafts up to Ya-chow, the centre of the brick tea trade with Tibet. After this the Yangtze at Lu-chow receives the To, which gives access to one of the richest regions of the province, and at Chungking, the trading capital, the Chia-ling.

This is in itself a river of great importance, being navigable for over 500 miles, actually into the province of Kansuh. It receives

---

* It is the Mur-usu ("Tortuous River") in Tibet, the Chin or Kin Sha where it is the boundary between Tibet and China, and from the junction of the Yalung to Sui Fu the Chin Ho. Between Sui Fu and Wan Hsien it is called the Ta Ho ("Great River") and the Min Chiang. At and below Sha-shih it is the Ching Chiang, and below Hankow for 400 miles it is called the Chiang, Ch'ang Chiang ("Long River"), or Ta-Kuan Chiang ("Great Official River").

several noble navigable feeders, among the most important of which are the Ku, entering it a little above Ho-chow, the Honton or Fu, and the Pai Shui. It passes for much of its course through a rich and fertile region, and through a country which produces large quantities of salt, and it bisects the vast coalfields which underlie Central SZE CHUAN. On the right or south bank above the gorges, at the picturesque city of Fu-chow, the Fu-ling, which has three aliases, enters the Yangtze. This is an affluent of much commercial importance, as being the first of a network of rivers by which, with only two portages, goods from the Far West can reach Canton, and as affording, with its connections the Yuan Ho and the Tungting lake, an alternative route to Hankow, by which the risks of the rapids are avoided.

After the Yangtze enters the gorges, which at one point, at least, narrow it to a width of 150 yards, there are no affluents worthy of special notice until Ichang is passed, when the Han, navigable for cargo-boats for 1200 miles of north-westerly windings from its mouth at Hankow, takes the first place, followed by the Yuan, Hsiang, Kan, Shu, and others, which join the Yangtze through the Tungting and Poyang lakes. These rivers, specially the Han, are themselves swelled by a great number of navigable feeders, which east of Sha-shih, in the Great Plain, are connected by a vast network of navigable canals, the differences in level being overcome by the ingenious contrivance called the *pah*. These natural and artificial waterways are among the chief elements of the prosperity of the Yangtze Valley, affording cheap transit for merchandise, land carriage in China, mile for mile, costing twenty times as much as water carriage.

The time of the annual rise and fall of the Great River can be counted on with tolerable certainty. With regard to the rise, from what I saw and heard I am inclined to attach more importance to the swelling of its Yunnan affluents during the south-west monsoon than to the melting of those snows which, as seen from the stupendous precipice of Omi-shan, are one of the grandest sights on earth—the long and glittering barrier which secludes the last of the hermit nations.

The rise of the Yangtze is from forty feet or thereabouts at Hankow to ninety feet and upwards at Chungking. During three months of the year the rush of the vast volume of water is so tremendous that traffic is mainly suspended, and even in early June many hundreds of the large junks are laid up until the autumn in quiet reaches between Chungking and Wan Hsien. The annual rise of the river as well as the rapids have to be taken into consideration in the discussion of the question as to whether steam navigation on the Upper Yangtze can be made commercially profitable.

The actual rise, which is more reliable than that of the Nile, begins late in March, is at its height early in August, and then gradually falls until December or January. Late in June, when I descended the Great River, its enormous submerged area presented the same appearance on a large scale as the limited Nile valley—an expanse of muddy water, out of which low mounds, probably of great antiquity, rise, crested with trees and villages, with boats moored to the houses.

The country in the neighbourhood of Shanghai is a fairly good example of the characteristics of the Great Plain. In ordinary dry weather the surface of the soil is not more than five feet above the water-level, and as seen from any pagoda the whole country, with the exception of the two or three low Tsing-pu hills, which are seldom visible, presents the aspect, familiar to dwellers in the fens, of a cultivated dead level, intersected by numerous canals and creeks and by embankments for the preservation of the fields from inundation. Much the same sort of view in winter may be seen from any elevated point for hundreds of miles, modified by a few ranges of hills of somewhat higher elevation, wider creeks, and shallow marshy lakes.

It is not solely by deposits of rich alluvium brought down by the annual rise of the river that the soil of the Great Plain is gradually raised. The agency of dust-storms is an important one, and these occur extensively throughout Northern and Central China, moving much material from place to place. I saw a dust-storm at Kueichow which lasted for seven hours, burying some hovels and much agricultural country, and even producing a metamorphosis of the rocky bed of the Yangtze. Such storms have been observed as far east as Shanghai, but their occurrence at Kueichow shows that their area is not limited to the Great Plain or even to the region east of the mountain barrier between HUPEH and SZE CHUAN.

It is not till the Yangtze reaches Sha-shih that its character completely changes. The first note of change is a great embankment, thirty feet high, which protects the region from inundation. Below Sha-shih the vast river becomes mixed up with a network of lakes and rivers, connected by canals, the area of the important Tungting lake being over 2000 square miles. The Han alone, with its many affluents and canals, disperses goods through the interior for 1200 miles north of its mouth at Hankow, but there are some difficult rapids to surmount. The Hsiang and the Yuan, uniting with the Yangtze at the Tungting lake, are navigable nearly as far to the south. The Kan, which unites with the Yangtze through the Poyang lake, which has an area of 1800 square miles, is navigable to the Mei-ling pass, near the Kwantung frontier.

The delta of the river is indicated below Wu-sueh by even a greater labyrinth of tributaries, lakes, and canals, the area of the Tai Hu and the other lakes in the southern delta being estimated at 1200 square miles, and the length of the channels used for navigation and irrigation at 36,000 miles. In summer, after the spring crops have been removed, the whole region is under water. The population migrates to mounds, and the temporary villages communicate by boats.

At Chinkiang the Grand Canal enters the Yangtze from Hangchow, and leaves it on the left bank, some miles away, for Tientsin. On that north bank engineering works, extending over a vast area of country, have been constructed, evidencing the former energy and skill of the Chinese.

These have diverted the river Huai, which with its seventy-two tributaries form important commercial routes to North An Hui and Honan, from its natural course to the sea, and have compelled the bulk of its waters to discharge themselves into the Yangtze through openings in a large canal which runs nearly parallel with it for 140 miles. By means of innumerable artificial waterways, the excavation of some lakes, and the enlargement of others, the Huai no longer has any existence as a river east of the Grand Canal, most of this work having been carried out to prevent undue pressure on the bank of that great waterway at any one point south of the old course of the Hoang Ho.

North of the canal, and parallel with the Yangtze, lies a parallelogram the extent of which is estimated by Père Gandar at 8876 square miles, and is one of the most productive rice-fields in China. This is below the water-level. It has immense dykes protecting it from the sea, pierced by eighteen drainage canals, but its chief drainage is into the Yangtze. Waterways under constant and careful supervision intersect this singular region. For the remaining distance the mighty flood of the Yangtze rolls majestically on through absolutely level country, in which in winter embankments and waterways are everywhere seen. The influence of the tide is felt for about 200 miles.

There is an ancient Chinese proverb regarding the mouth of the Great River: "Lo, this mighty current hastens to its imperial audience with the ocean." But opaque yellow water and mud flats, extending as far as the eye can reach, leave the imperial grandeur to the imagination.

Tennyson's description of the work of rivers as being "to sow the dust of continents to be," applies forcibly to the Yangtze, which, after creating the vast alluvial plains which stretch from Sha-shih for 800 miles to the ocean and endowing them in its annual overflow with sufficient fresh material to keep up an unsurpassed fertility, has yet enough to spare to discharge 770,000 feet of solid substance every second into the sea, according to scientific estimates. The Yangtze has done much to create, within comparatively recent years, at least the eastern portion of the province of Kiang Su and the island of Tsungming near Shanghai, capable of supporting a population of considerably over 1,000,000 souls. Another marked instance of its power to create is shown near the treaty port of Chinkiang. The British fleet ascended the Yangtze, so recently as in 1842, by a channel south of the beautiful Golden Island. Now, instead of the channel, there is an expanse of wooded and cultivated land sprinkled with villages.

Nearly a mile wide 600 miles from its mouth, nearly three-quarters of a mile at 1000, and 630 yards at 1500, with a volume of water which, at 1000 miles from the sea, is estimated at 244 times that of the Thames at London Bridge, with a summer depth of ninety feet at Chungking and of ten feet at its few shallow places at Hankow when at its lowest winter level, with a capacity for a rise of forty feet before it overflows its banks, with an annual rise and fall more reliable than those of the Nile, with navigable tributaries penetrating the richest and most populous regions of China, navigable in the summer as far as Hankow for the largest ships in the world, and during the whole year to Ichang, 400 miles farther, for fine river steamers carrying large cargoes, even the Upper Yangtze, that region of grandeur, perils, and surprises, is traversed annually by 7000 junks, employing a quarter of a million of men.   During my own descent of the Min and Yangtze from Chengtu to Shanghai, a distance by the windings of the river of about 2000 miles, I was never out of sight of native traffic, and those who, like myself, have waited for two or three days at the foot of the great rapids for the turn to ascend, can form some idea of how vast that traffic is.

The navigable portion of the Yangtze, as regarded from the sea, naturally divides itself into three stretches, the first, of 1000 miles, rolling as a broad turbid flood, traversed by several lines of steamers, through the deep grey alluvium of some of the richest and most populous provinces of China, mainly its own creation ; the second, the region between Ichang and Kueichow Fu, through which hitherto goods have been carried by junks alone, in which it cleaves the confused mass of the HUPEH ranges by a series of magnificent gorges and tremendous cataracts; and the third, the long stretch of rapids and races between Kueichow Fu and Sui Fu at its junction with the Min.

It is not possible to exaggerate the sublimity and risks of the navigation of the Upper Yangtze, especially at certain seasons. Of the vast fleet of junks which navigate its perilous waters, five hundred on an average are annually wrecked, and one-tenth of the enormous importation of cotton into Chungking arrives damaged by water.   Yet so ample are the means of transport, and so low the freight considering the risks, that, according to Mr. von Rosthorn, of the Chinese Imperial Maritime Customs, foreign cottons are sold in SZE CHUAN at a barely appreciable advance on their price at Ichang, to which point they are brought by steam from the coast in eight days.

The *Chinese Gazetteer* notifies one thousand rapids and rocks between Ichang and Chungking, a distance of about 500 miles ; and in winter this does not seem an outlandish estimate, but in early summer, with the water twenty-four and thirty feet higher, many of the vigorous rapids, alternating with smooth stretches of river only running three knots an hour, disappear, along with boulder-strewn shores, rocks, and islets, giving place to a broad and tremendous volume of water, swirling seawards at the rate of seven, eight, and ten knots an hour, forming many and dangerous whirlpools.

Of the magnitude of the native traffic on the Lower Yangtze, undiminished by the various steamboat lines which keep up daily communication with Hankow, it is scarcely needful to write. In ascending it is evident to the traveller by the time that Chin-kiang, the port of junction with the Grand Canal, is reached, that, broad as the river is, there is none too much " sea room " for the thousands of junks of every build, from every maritime and riverine province, fishing and cargo boats of every size and rig, rafts, lorchas, and cormorant boats, which throng its waters.

The open ports of Wuhu and Kiu-kiang, each with its fleets of junks, and trade worth several millions sterling annually, and big cities such as Nanking, Yangchow, and Nganking, each with its highly organised mercantile and social life, and trade guilds and charities, are important and interesting ; and it is seen in a rapid glance that large villages with numerous industries, rice, cotton, and silk culture predominating, abound, that everything is utilised, that every foot of ground capable of cultivation is bearing a crop, and that even the reed-beds of the irreclaimable swamps furnish materials for houses, roofs, fences, and fuel. It is seen that elaborate and successful engineering works have reclaimed large tracts of country and keep them drained, that a network of irri-gating and navigable canals spreads over the whole level region, and that the traffic on these minor waterways is enormous.

So ceaseless are the industries by land and water, that it is hardly a surprise to find them culminating 600 miles from the ocean in the " million-peopled " city of Hankow (Han Mouth), the greatest distributing centre for goods in China, with miles of craft moored in triple rows along the Han, itself navigable for 1200 miles.

The empire province of SZE CHUAN, with the great navigable tributaries of the Yangtze, by which goods are conveyed at small cost to countless towns and villages, will be treated in some detail farther on. It is enough to remark here that it has about the area of France, that it has a population estimated by the Chinese census authorities at 70,000,000, and by none at less than 50,000,000 ; that it has a superb climate, ranging from the temperate to the sub-tropical ; a rich soil, much of which, under careful cultivation, yields three and even four crops annually of most things which can be grown ; forests of grand timber, the area of which has not even been estimated ; rich mineral resources, and some of the most valuable and extensive coal-fields in the world. It cannot be repeated too often that for its export trade, estimated at £3,300,000, and its import trade, estimated at £2,400,000, the Yangtze is the *sole* outlet and inlet.

Such an exhibition of Chinese energy, industry, resourcefulness, and power of battling with difficulties is not to be seen anywhere to the same extent as on the Upper Yangtze, where the enormous bulk of the vast import trade has to be dragged up 500 miles of hills of water by the sheer force of man-power, at two or three of the worst rapids a junk of over one hundred tons requiring the haulage of nearly four hundred men.

Waterways take the place of roads, which are usually infamous, throughout the Yangtze basin, but the bridges are marvels of solidity, and in many cases of beauty. The annual inundations on the Great Plain partly account for the badness of the roads, and constitute an expensive difficulty in the way of the forthcoming railroads.

To write of the Yangtze Valley, the British " sphere of influence" (a phrase against which I protest), without any allusion to such an important factor as its inhabitants, would be a mistake, for sooner or later, in various ways, we shall have to reckon with them.

The population throughout, from the ocean to the unexplored rifts of the Chin Sha, is homogeneous, that is Chinese, with the exception of certain tribes of the far west : the Sifan, Mantze, and Lolo. The Tartars or Manchu, who have supplied the throne with the present dynasty, whose fathers drove the Chinese before them like sheep, and who still garrison the great cities, have mainly degenerated into opium-smoking loafers, the agent in their downfall being hereditary pensions.

Throughout this vast population, perhaps not over-estimated at 180,000,000, with the exception of spasmodic and local rebellions now and then, law and order, prosperity (except in such disasters as floods or famines) and peace prevail, and that security for the gains of labour exists without which no country is great. The system of government, the written language, and the education are uniform, and the "three religions"—Confucianism, Buddhism, and Taoism—are so mixed up together that there is little antagonism between them.

The organisation of this valley population, social and mercantile, is a marvel, with its system of trade, trade guilds, trade unions, charities, banking and postal systems, and powerful trade combinations.

In much talk about "open doors" and "spheres of influence" and "interest," in much greed for ourselves, not always dexterously cloaked, and much jealousy and suspicion of our neighbours, and in much interest in the undignified scramble for concessions in which we have been taking our share at Peking, there is a risk of our coming to think only of markets, territory, and railroads, and of ignoring the men who, for two thousand years, have been making China worth scrambling for. It may be that we go forward with "a light heart," along with other European empires, not hesitating, for the sake of commercial advantages, to break up in the case of a fourth of the human race the most ancient of earth's existing civilisations, without giving any equivalent.

In estimating the position occupied by the inhabitants of the Yangtze Valley, as of the rest of China, it is essential for us to see quite clearly that our Western ideas find themselves confronted, not with barbarism or with debased theories of morals, but with an elaborate and antique civilisation which yet is not decayed, and which, though imperfect, has many claims to our respect and even admiration. They meet with a perfectly organised social order, a system of government theoretically admirably suited to the country, combining the extremes of centralisation and decentralisation, and under which, in spite of its tremendous infamies of practice, the governed enjoy a large measure of peace and prosperity, a noteworthy amount of individual liberty and security for the gains of labour, and under which it is as possible for a peasant's son to rise to high position as in the American Republic.*

---

* Lest it should be supposed that I am taking an unduly favourable view of the position of the Chinese, and especially of the Chinese of Sze Chuan, under their government, I fortify my opinion by quoting that of Mr. Litton, British acting consul at Chungking. He writes in his official report to our Foreign Office, presented to both

Western civilisation finds itself confronted also by a people at once grossly material and grossly superstitious, swayed at once by the hazy speculations and unintelligible metaphysic which in Chinese Buddhism have allied themselves with the most extravagant and childish superstitions, and by the dæmonism of Taoism, while over both tower the lofty ethics and profound agnosticism of Confucius. It finds a classical literature universally held in profound reverence, in which, according to all testimony, there is not a thought which could sully the purest mind, and an idolatry puerile, superstitious, and free from grand conceptions, but in which bloody sacrifices and the deification of vice have never had a part, or immoral rites a place.

The human product of Chinese civilisation, religion, and government is to me the greatest of all enigmas, and so he remains to those who know him best. At once conservative and adaptable, the most local of peasants in his attachments, and the most cosmopolitan and successful of emigrants—sober, industrious, thrifty, orderly, peaceable, indifferent to personal comfort, possessing great physical vitality, cheerful, contented, persevering—his filial piety, tenacity, resourcefulness, power of combination, and respect for law and literature, place him in the van of Asiatic nations.

The Chinese constitute an order by themselves, and their individuality cannot be read in the light of that of any other nation. The aspirations and modes of thinking by which we are ruled do not direct their aims. They are keen and alert, but unwilling to strike out new lines, and slow to be influenced in any matters. Their trading instincts are phenomenal. They are born bargainers, and would hardly think half an hour wasted if through chaffering they gained an advantage of half a *cash*, a coin forty of which are about one penny. They are suspicious, cunning, and corrupt; but it is needless to run through

Houses of Parliament in May, 1899, thus:—" The government, though obstructive and unintelligent, is not as a rule actively oppressive; one may travel for days in West China without seeing any signs of that reserve of force which we associate with the policeman round the corner. The country people of Sze Chuan manage their own affairs through their headmen, and get on very well in spite of, rather than because of, the central government at Chengtu. So long as a native keeps out of the law courts, and does not attempt any startling innovations on the customs of his ancestors, he finds in the general love of law and order very fair security that he will enjoy the fruit of his labour." This general disposition towards law and order, though it may have something to do with race, is undoubtedly on the whole the result of the teachings of Confucius.

the established formula of their vices. Among the things which they lack are CONSCIENCE, and such an enlightened public opinion as shall sustain right and condemn wrong.

Matthew Arnold has said that Greece perished for want of attention to conduct, and that the revelation which rules the world is the "pre-eminence of righteousness." It may be that the western powers are not giving the Middle Kingdom a very desirable object-lesson.

On the whole, as I hope to show to some extent in the following pages, throughout the Yangtze valley, from the great cities of Hangchow and Hankow to the trading cities of SZE-CHUAN, the traveller receives very definite impressions of the completeness of Chinese social and commercial organisation, the skill and carefulness of cultivation, the clever adaptation of means to ends—the existence of provincial patriotism, or, perhaps, more truly, of local public spirit, of the general prosperity, and of the backbone, power of combination, resourcefulness, and independence possessed by the race. It is not an effete or decaying people which we shall have to meet in serious competition when it shall have learned our sciences and some of our methods of manufacturing industry. Indeed, it is not improbable that chemistry, for instance, might be eagerly adapted by so ingenious a race to the perpetration of new and hitherto unthought-of frauds! But if the extraordinary energy, adaptability, and industry of the Chinese may be regarded from one point of view as the "Yellow Peril," surely looked at from another they constitute the Yellow Hope, and it may be possible that an empire genuinely Christianised, but not denationalised, may yet be the dominant power in Eastern Asia.

The Chinese are ignorant and superstitious beyond belief, but on the whole, with all their faults, I doubt whether any other Oriental race runs so straight.

The Yangtze Basin is a magnificent sphere of interest for all the industrial nations for fair, if not friendly, rivalry, and to preserve the "open door" there, and throughout China, is a worthy object of ambition. To strengthen instead of to weaken the Central Government is undoubtedly the wisest policy to pursue, for in the weakness of the Peking Government lies the weakness and possible abrogation of all treaty obligations. It is its strength and capacity to fulfil its treaties which alone make them worth anything. In the weakening of the Central Government, and the disintegration of the empire, our treaty rights in the Yangtze Valley, for instance, would be worth as much as our sword could secure, and it cannot reach above Ichang, while if the integrity of the empire be preserved, and it is aided along judicious paths of reform, this vast basin, with its singular capabilities, and its population of 180,000,000, may become the widest arena for commercial rivalries that the world has ever seen.

CHAPTER II.

"THE MODEL SETTLEMENT"

THOSE of my readers who have followed me through all or any of my eleven volumes of travels must be aware that my chief wish on arriving at a foreign settlement or treaty port in the East is to get out of it as soon as possible, and that I have not the remotest hankering after Anglo-Asiatic attractions. Nor is Shanghai, "The Model Settlement of the East," an exception to the general rule, though I gratefully acknowledge the kindness and hospitality which I met with there, as everywhere, and recall with pleasure my many sojourns at the British Consulate as the guest of Mr. and Mrs. Lowndes Bullock.

But as the outlet of the commerce of the Yangtze Valley, and as a foreign city which has risen on Chinese shores in little more than half a century to the position and importance of one of the great trading centres of the world—its exports and imports for 1898 being of the value of £37,680,875 sterling*—it claims such notice as I can give it, which is chiefly in the shape of impressions.

I have reached Shanghai four times by Japanese steamers, three times in coasting steamers of American build, once in one of the superb vessels of the Canadian *Empress* line, once from Hankow in a metamorphosed Dutch gunboat, and the last time, after nearly three and a half years of far eastern travel, in a small Korean Government steamer, her quaint, mysterious, and nearly unknown national flag exciting much speculation and interest as she steamed slowly up the river. Of these vessels, the *Empress of China* alone discharged her passengers and cargo at Woo-sung, a railroad terminus twelve miles below Shanghai, and that not necessarily.

---

* For Shanghai and the other open ports, it is the gross value of trade, exports and imports, including re-exports, which is given in this volume.

Many hours before reaching port, the deep heavenly blue of the Pacific gradually changes into a turbid yellowish flood, well named the Yellow Sea, holding in suspension the rich wash of scarcely explored Central Asian mountain ranges, the red loam of the "Red Basin" of SZE CHUAN, and the grey and yellow alluvium of the Central Provinces of China, all carried to the ocean by the "Great River," according to a careful scientific estimate, to the extent of 6,428,858,255 cubic feet a year, solid stuff enough to build an island ninety feet in depth and a mile square annually.

Countless fishing - boats roll on the muddy waste; sailing vessels, steamers, and brown-sailed junks of every build show signs of convergence towards something, and before long a blink of land is visible, and a lightship indicates the mouth of the Yangtze Kiang and a navigable channel. It is long even then before anything definite presents itself, and I confess to being disappointed with the first features of the Asiatic mainland—two long, thin, yellow lines, hardly more solid-looking than the yellow water stretching along the horizon, growing gradually into low marshy banks, somewhat later topped with uninteresting foliage, through which there are glimpses of what looks like an interminable swamp. Then Woo-sung appears with its new railroad, godowns, whitewashed buildings, and big ships at anchor discharging cargo into lighters and native boats, and then the banks of the narrowing Huang-pu, the river of Shanghai, are indicated by habitations and small fields and signs of small industries.

Within four miles of Shanghai the vivacity of the Huang-pu and its banks becomes overpowering, and the West asserts its ascendency over the slow-moving East. There are ranges of great godowns, wharves, building yards, graving docks, "works" of all descriptions, filatures, cotton mills, and all the symptoms in smoky chimneys and a ceaseless clang of the presence of capital and energy. After the war with Japan there was a rapid increase in the number of factories.

The life and movement on the river become wonderful. The channel for large vessels, though narrow, shifting, and intricate, and the subject of years of doleful prophecies as to "silting up" and leaving Shanghai stranded, admits of the passage of our largest merchantmen, and successful dredging enables them to lie alongside the fine wharves at Hongkew. American three and four-masted and other sailing vessels are at anchor in mid-stream, or are proceeding up or down in charge of tugs. Monster liners under their own steam at times nearly fill up the channel, their officers yelling frantically at the small craft which recklessly cross their bows; great white, two-storeyed paddle arks from Ningpo and Hankow, local steamers, steam launches owned by the great firms, junks of all builds and sizes, manageable by their huge rudders, *sampans*, hooded boats, and native boats of all descriptions, lighters, and a shoal of nondescript craft make navigation tedious, if not perilous, while sirens and steam whistles sound continually. "The plot thickens." Foreign *hongs*, warehouses, shipping offices, and hotels are passed in Hongkew, the American settlement, and gliding round Pu-tung Point, the steamer anchors abreast of the bund in a wholesomely rapid flow of water 2000 feet wide.

I arrived in Shanghai the first time on a clear, bright autumn day. The sky was very blue, and the masses of exotic trees, the green, shaven lawns, the belated roses, and the clumps of chrysanthemums in the fine public gardens gave a great charm to the first view of the settlement. Two big, lofty, white hulks for bonded Indian opium are moored permanently in front of the gardens. Gunboats and larger war-vessels of all nations, all painted white, and the fine steamers of the Messageries Maritimes have their moorings a little higher up. Boats, with crews in familiar uniforms, and covered native boats gaily painted, the latter darting about like dragon-flies, were plying ceaselessly, and as it was the turn of the tide, hundreds of junks were passing seawards under their big brown sails.

On landing at the fine landing-stage, where kind friends received me and took me to the British Consul's residence in the spacious grounds of the Consulate, I was at once impressed with the exquisite dress of the ladies, who were at least a half of the throng, and with the look of wealth and comfort which prevails.

All along the British bund, for at least a mile from the Soochow Creek, which separates it from Hongkew, to the French settlement, are banks, hongs, hotels, and private houses of the most approved and massive Anglo-Oriental architecture, standing in large, shady gardens, the Hong Kong and Shanghai Bank, the "P. & O." office, the Canadian-Pacific Railroad office, the fine counting-house and dwelling-house of the old and famous firm of Jardine, Matheson & Co., and the long façade of the British Consular buildings, with their wide sweep of lawns, being prominent.

The broad carriage-road and fine flagged side-walk are truly cosmopolitan. Well-dressed men and women of all civilised nations, and of some which are not civilised, promenade gaily on the walk and in the garden. Single and two-horse carriages and buggies, open and closed, with coachmen and grooms in gay and often fantastic cotton liveries, dash along the drive. Hackney victorias abound, and there are *jinrickshas* (from which foreigners drop the first syllable) in hundreds, with Chinese runners, and Shanghai wheelbarrows innumerable, some loaded with goods or luggage, while the coolies of others are trundling along from two to four Chinese men or women of the lower classes, seated on matted platforms on either side of the wheel, facing forwards.

I was not prepared for the Chinese element being so much *en evidence* in the foreign settlement. It is not only that clerks and compradores dressed in rich silks on which the characters for happiness and longevity and the symbols of luck are brocaded are in numbers on the bund, and that all the servile classes, as may be expected, are Chinese, but that Chinese shops of high standing, such as Laou Kai Fook's, are taking their places in fine streets which run back from the bund, that some of the handsomest carriages on the bund and the Bubbling Well Road, the fashionable afternoon drive of Shanghai, are owned and filled with Chinese, that Chinese ladies and children richly dressed drive in the same fashion, and that of late, specially, wealthy Chinese have become keen competitors for British houses, and have even outbid foreigners for them. Is Shanghai menaced by the "Yellow Peril" as Malacca, Singapore, and Penang have been?

A great trading Chinese city, with an estimated population of 200,000, has grown up within the foreign boundary, subject to foreign municipal laws and sanitary regulations, but so absolutely Chinese, that were it not for the wide streets and the absence of refuse-heaps and bad smells, one might think oneself in one of the great cities of the interior. The Chinese are quite capable of appreciating the comfort and equity of foreign rule, and the various advantages which they enjoy under it. They pay municipal taxes according to their rating, and "feu duty" for their land, which it is usual for them to hold in the name of a foreigner. They are under the jurisdiction of the Chinese Government, but civil cases in which foreigners are concerned and breaches of the peace are tried in what is known as the "Mixed Court," an apparently satisfactory and workable arrangement, and serious criminal cases belong to the Chinese Shanghai magistrate.

I soon began to learn why Shanghai is called, or calls itself, "The Model Settlement," and to recognise the fitness of the name. The British and American settlements are governed by a Municipality elected by the ratepayers, consisting of nine gentlemen, who, assisted by a secretary and general staff, expend the sums provided by the ratepayers to the general satisfaction, arranging admirably for the health, security, comfort, and even enjoyment of the large foreign community, as well as for the order and well-being of the constantly increasing Chinese population, showing to the whole East what can be accomplished by an honest and thoroughly efficient British local administration. This body is, as it deserves to be, grandly housed.

The more important streets are lighted with electricity, the others with gas. Mounted Sikh police patrol the suburban roads, and a mixed force of Europeans, Sikhs, and Chinese preserves order and security in the settlement by day and night. An expensive but successful drainage system keeps Shanghai sweet and wholesome. Water-carts are always at work in dry weather, and scavengers' carts cleanse the streets three times daily. Water-works three miles from city pollutions supply pure water abundantly, and keep up a very high pressure unfailingly. The band of thirty performers, which plays in the public gardens every afternoon in winter, and three evenings a week in summer, attracting nearly the whole foreign community to lounge under the trees or stroll on the smooth gravel walks, is the creature of the Municipality.

Shanghai has two telegraph lines embracing London ; daily papers well conducted, the *North China Daily News* specially maintaining a deservedly high reputation ; several magazines, and communication with Europe always once a week, and usually

oftener, by well-appointed mail steamers of four lines.   Tele-
graphic news from all parts of the world appears simultaneously
in London and Shanghai; it is thoroughly in touch with Europe
and America, and European politics and events in general are
discussed with as much intelligence and almost as much zest as at
home.   Excellent libraries, and the large book-store of Messrs.
Kelly & Walsh, cater for the intellectual needs of the population,
but it is likely that the depressing climate in spring and summer,
and the whirl of society and amusements in winter, indispose most
of the residents for anything like stiff reading.

The tremendous energy with which Shanghai amuses itself
during seven months of the year is something phenomenal.   It
is even a fatigue to contemplate it.   Various causes contribute
to it on the part of the ladies.   There is the Anglo-Saxon vitality
which must find some outlet.   Then there is the absence of household cares owing to the efficiency of Chinese cooks and "boys,"
and ofttimes the absence of children also, owing to the need for
home education ; and there is also the lack of those benevolent
outgoings among "the poor" which occupy usefully a portion
of the time of leisured women at home.   Then, owing to the
imitative skill of Chinese tailors, who can construct the most
elaborate gowns from fashion-plates for a few shillings, it is
possible for women to have the pleasure of appearing in an infinite
variety of elegant toilettes at a very small expense, and dress is
certainly elevated into a fine art in Shanghai.

Of the men I write tremblingly !   Chinese tailors seem as
successful as Chinese dressmakers, and the laundrymen equal
both, no small matter when white linen suits are in question.
May it be permitted to a traveller to remark that if men were
to give to the learning of Chinese and of Chinese requirements
and methods of business a little of the time which is lavished on
sport and other amusements, there might possibly be less occasion
for the complaint that large fortunes are no longer to be made in
Chinese business.

For indeed, from ignorance of the language and reliance on that
limited and abominable vocabulary known as "Pidgun," the British
merchant must be more absolutely dependent on his Chinese compradore than he would care to be at home on his confidential clerk.
Even in such lordly institutions as the British Banks on the bund

it seems impossible to transact even such a simple affair as cashing a cheque without calling in the aid of a sleek, supercilious-looking, richly-dressed Chinese, a *shroff* or *compradore*, who looks as if he knew the business of the bank and were capable of running it. It is different at the Yokohama Specie Bank, which has found a footing in Shanghai, in which the alert Japanese clerks manage their own affairs and speak Chinese. May I be forgiven?

An extraordinary variety of amusements is crowded into every day. Then the community is most hospitable, as every visitor to Shanghai knows, and the arrival of every ship of war and eminent globe-trotter is the signal for a fresh outbreak of gaiety. Home diversions are reproduced, and others are superadded, such as paper hunts in the adjacent cotton-fields, house-boat picnics and pleasure excursions, and house-boat shooting excursions, lasting from three days to a week, for which special advantages exist, as the inland cotton-fields during the winter are alive with pheasants, partridges, quail, woodcock, and hares, while the water-courses abound with wild fowl. Pony races are a leading institution, with gentlemen riders of course. The morning gallops extract people from their beds at unwonted hours, and in spring and autumn the prospects of the stables make great inroads on conversation. But I will not go further. The very imperfect list given below gives some idea of the diversions which the community provides for itself.* Amateur theatricals are "the rage" in the winter, the amateur company providing several performances in a theatre built by a subscription of £5000, and holding over eight hundred persons, and the Fine Art Society gives an annual exhibition.

The continual presence of strangers imparts a needed element of freshness to society, and a zest to amusements which might pall, and gives people an excuse, if any were needed, for enjoying themselves. Shanghai has become the metropolis of gaiety for the Far East, and a week at the Astor House, the great recreation looked forward to not only by the dwellers in the

* Yachting Club, Golf Club, Athletic Club, Lawn Tennis Club, Polo Club, Volunteer Club, Boating Club, Bowling Club, Swimming Club, Cricket Club, Blackbird Club, Drag Hound Club, Steeplechase Club, Racquet Club, Racing Club, Rifle Club, Fives Court, Gymnasium, Fire Flies Society, Lurderfatel Society, Amateur Dramatic Company ; and of a graver cast, the Philharmonic and Photographic Societies, the Royal Asiatic Society, the Fine Art Society, etc., etc. (List by W. S. Percival, Esq.)

treaty ports of China and Japan, but by those who roast and dissolve on the rock at Hongkong, and its delirious whirl attracts people even from Singapore.

But it would be quite an error to suppose that amusement crowds out the kindlier emotions. Europeans fall into distress constantly, some from misfortune, and some from fault, and many widows and orphans are left penniless. One may safely say that there is never a case of distress arising from any cause which is not immediately and amply relieved and planned for; and benevolence never wearies, the Ladies' Benevolent Society doing a ceaseless good work. There is a Sailors' Home and Rest in a very efficient and flourishing condition, with musical evenings frequently, at which ladies and gentlemen play and sing; and, without going further into detail, it may be said that the various useful organisations which our civilisation considers essential for a large community, from a fine general hospital downwards, have their place in Shanghai.

Church accommodation is ample for the church-goers. The Protestant cathedral, a really beautiful edifice, built from the designs of Sir Gilbert Scott, is one of the greatest adornments of the settlement, and is the finest ecclesiastical building in the Far East.

From the early days of Shanghai many Protestant missions, both European and American, have had mission houses in the settlement, the most important being the large, appropriate, and substantial headquarters of the China Inland Mission, the gift of Mr. Orr Ewing, with a home for a hundred missionaries, a hospital, goods and business departments, and postal arrangements. Dr. Muirhead, of the L.M.S., whose missionary zeal is unchilled in the winter of his age, and Dr. Edkins, of the same Society, whose Chinese scholarship and researches among things Chinese have won him a European fame, are well known to, and are much respected by, the foreign community. There is also a large Roman mission. British and American Bible Societies, and the English Religious Tract Society and others also have agents and depôts there, and much translation is done by missionaries, and by agencies which have for their noble object the diffusion of pure and useful western literature among the Chinese, and their elevation mentally and morally.

There is a North China branch of the Royal Asiatic Society in Shanghai, with a fine library, regular meetings, and a journal, which gathers up a great deal of very valuable matter. If the size and material of the audience on the night when I had the honour of reading a paper before the Society may be regarded as an indication of the interest in its objects, it must be flourishing indeed.

The topography of this metropolis is fully dealt with in various official and other volumes. The salient points which impress a newcomer are Hongkew, the American settlement, with its commercial activity, the Soochow creek, with its fine bridge, the handsome buildings of the British Consulate, the British Bund, with its fine retaining wall, the long line of handsome private and public buildings, and the glimpses of broad and handsome streets full of private residences which run from the bund towards the boundary.

The French Bund is a continuation of the British; but the French settlement is small, markedly inferior, and gives one an impression of arrested development, the only noteworthy buildings being the Consulate, the Town Hall, and the large but plain Roman cathedral. As some compensation, the fine wharves at which the big Yangtze steamers load and discharge their cargoes are in this settlement, as well as the handsome and commodious premises of the Messageries Maritimes, beyond which stretch, far as the eye can reach, the crowded tiers of the Chinese shipping. The French boundary is an undesirable creek, running past the east gate of the native city, between which and the Huang-pu are crowded and unsavoury suburbs.

It is apparent that France regards her concession as a colony rather than a settlement, and she has lately urged her claims for an extension of it in a most selfish and indefensible manner. The settlement has been frequently in very hot water, and a serious disagreement with the Chinese occurred so recently as 1898. Its Municipal Board was once forcibly dissolved by the French Consul for a difference of opinion, and some of its members were imprisoned.

The English settlement makes a proud display of the wealth of the insular kingdom in the number of its stately buildings, the Consulate, the cathedral, the municipal buildings, the four-storeyed and elaborately-designed club house, the banks and shipping offices, and the massive mansions of historic firms, standing in their secluded grounds; though of the magnates of eastern commerce in the days of the rapid making of great fortunes almost none remain. British, too, in design, architecture, and arrangement, in all indeed but cost, is the magnificent pile of buildings in which the Imperial Maritime Customs and the new Post Office, under the same management, are housed.

Shanghai in every way makes good her claim to be metropolitan as well as cosmopolitan, and, in spite of dark shadows, is a splendid example of what British energy, wealth, and organising power can accomplish.

To us the name Shanghai* means alone the superb foreign settlement, with all the accessories of western luxury and civilisation, lying grandly for a mile and a half along the Huang-pu, the centre of Far Eastern commerce and gaiety, the "Charing Cross" of the Pacific—London on the Yellow Sea.

But there was a Shanghai before Shanghai—a Shanghai which still exists, increases, and flourishes—a busy and unsavoury trading city, which leads its own life according to Chinese methods as independently as though no foreign settlement existed; and long before Mr. Pigou, of the H.E.I.C., in 1756, drew up his memorandum, suggesting Shanghai as a desirable place for trade, Chinese intelligence had hit upon the same idea, and the port was a great resort of Chinese shipping, cargoes being discharged there and dispersed over the interior by the Yangtze and the Grand Canal. Yet it never rose higher than the rank of a third-rate city.

It has a high wall three miles and a half in circuit, pierced by several narrow gateways and surrounded by a ditch twenty feet wide, and suburbs lying between it and the river with its tiers of native shipping as crowded as the city proper. This shipping, consisting of junks, lorchas, and native craft of extraordinary rig, lies, as Lu Hew said, "like the teeth of a comb."

---

* Situated a few miles from the junction of the Huang-pu with the Yangtze, in lat. 31° 10′ N. and long. 121° 30′ E., nearly on the same parallel as Charleston and Alexandria, the port is the great outlet of the commerce of the rich and populous provinces of Central China, and the sole outlet of that of Sze Chuan, besides communicating by waterways with Hangchow, Soochow, and other great cities on the Grand Canal, and with cities innumerable by canals innumerable.

To mention native Shanghai in foreign ears polite seems scarcely seemly; it brands the speaker as an outside barbarian, a person of "odd tendencies." It is bad form to show any interest in it, and worse to visit it. Few of the lady residents in the settlement have seen it, and both men and women may live in Shanghai for years and leave it without making the acquaintance of their nearest neighbour. It is supposed that there is a risk of bringing back small-pox and other maladies, that the smells are unbearable, that the foul slush of the narrow alleys is over the boots, that the foreigner is rudely jostled by thousands of dirty coolies, that the explorer may be knocked down or hurt by loaded wheelbarrows going at a run; in short, that it is generally abominable. It is the one point on which the residents are obdurate and disobliging.

I absolutely failed to get an escort until Mr. Fox, of H.M's Consular Service, kindly offered to accompany me. I did not take back small-pox or any other malady, I was not rudely jostled by dirty coolies, nor was I hurt or knocked down by wheelbarrows. The slush and the smells were there, but the slush was not fouler nor the smells more abominable than in other big Chinese cities that I have walked through; and as a foreign woman is an every-day sight in the near neighbourhood, the people minded their own business and not mine, and I was even able to photograph without being overborne by the curious.

Shanghai is a mean-looking and busy city; its crowds of toiling, trotting, bargaining, dragging, burden-bearing, shouting, and yelling men are its one imposing feature. Few women, and those of the poorer class, are to be seen. The streets, with houses built of slate-coloured, soft-looking brick, are only about eight feet wide, are paved with stone slabs, and are narrowed by innumerable stands, on which are displayed, cooked and raw and being cooked, the multifarious viands in which the omnivorous Chinese delight, an odour of garlic predominating. Even a wheelbarrow—the only conveyance possible—can hardly make its way in many places. True, a mandarin sweeps by in his gilded chair, carried at a run, with his imposing retinue, but his lictors clear the way by means not available to the general public.

All the articles usually exposed for sale in Chinese cities are met with in Shanghai, and old porcelain, bronzes, brocades, and embroideries are displayed to attract strangers. Restaurants and tea houses of all grades abound, and noteworthy among the latter is the picturesque building on the Zig-Zag Bridge, shown in the illustration. The buildings and fantastic well-kept pleasure grounds of the Ching-hwang Miao, which may be called the Municipal Temple, the Confucian Temple, the Guild Hall of the resident natives of Chekiang, and the temple of the God of War, with its vigorous images begrimed with the smoke of the incense sticks of ages of worshippers, its throngs, its smoke, its ceaseless movement, and its din are the most salient features of this native hive.

Yamens, of course, exist, and *yamen* runners, for Shanghai has the distinction of being the residence of a Taotai, or Intendant of Circuit, and a magistrate, in whose hands the administration of justice is placed, involving responsibility for the interests of over 560,000 Chinese, the estimated native population of the city and the settlements, the total population being estimated at 586,000.

On returning to the light, broad, clean, well-paved, and sanitary streets of foreign Shanghai, I was less surprised than before that so many of its residents are unacquainted with the dark, crowded, dirty, narrow, foul, and reeking streets of the neighbouring city.

ZIG-ZAG BRIDGE AND TEA HOUSE, SHANGHAI.

CHAPTER III.

HANGCHOW*

A JOURNEY of 150 miles to visit friends in the ancient city of Hangchow required no other preparations than the hire of a boat and the engaging of a servant, who I was compelled to dismiss a few days later for gross dishonesty. 2755 steam launches, owned and run by Chinese, towing 7889 passenger boats, carrying 605 foreign and 125,000 native passengers, entered and cleared in 1897 between Hangchow, Shanghai, and Soochow.

Every evening one of these launches, towing a long string of native boats, leaves the Soochow creek below the British Consulate for the new treaty ports, opened as such only in 1896. My small bamboo-roofed boat, in which I could just stand upright, much decorated in the tawdry style of Chinese fourth-class fancy, and through which irremediable draughts coursed friskily, was the contemptible final joint of a tail of nine quaint and picturesque passage junks and family houseboats, a varnished procession of high-sterned, two-storeyed, many-windowed arks, squirming and snaking along at the stern of a noisy, asthmatic tow-boat. There were red flags flying, gongs crashing out dissonance, crackers exploding, poles with clothes drying on them pushed out of windows, incense sticks smouldering, and reports of firearms ; and with this cheerful din, the usual accompaniment of Chinese movement, we started in the red twilight.

---

* Hangchow, though not geographically in the drainage area of the Yangtze, as the capital of Chekiang, which has been declared officially to be within our "sphere of interest" in the Yangtze Valley, is treated of here as being specially interesting. Of Ningpo, Wenchow, and Soochow, open ports in the same province, merely the *net* value of their total net trade for 1898 is given, along with that of Hangchow :—

Ningpo	.	.	.	.	.	£2,162,780
Wenchow	.	.	.	.	.	215,669
Soochow	.	.	.	.	.	229,113
Hangchow	.	.	.	.	.	1,199,022

I paid six dollars for my boat with three men, and five dollars fifty cents for towage, about 23s.

All day long the life on the two-storeyed open-sterned boat in front of mine was exposed to view. It was occupied by three generations, nine souls in all, under the rule of a grandmother. They rose early, lighted the fire and their incense sticks, kotowed to an idol in a gilded shrine, offered him a small bowl of rice, and cooked and ate their morning meal. The smell of their cooking drifted for much of the day into my boat, and " broth of abominable things was in their vessels." The man sat in the bow smoking and making shoes. The grandmother lived below in blissful idleness and authority. The wife, a comely, healthy, broad-shouldered woman, with bound feet, worked and smoked all day, and contrived to steer the boat as she stooped over the fire or the wash-tub by holding its heavy tiller under her arm or chin or pressing her knee against it. Four young children lived a quiet life on a broad high shelf, from which they were lifted down for meals. A girl of thirteen helped her mother slightly. Cooking, washing, mending, eating, and watching my occupation with far less interest than I watched theirs, filled up their day. Evening brought fresh kotowing and burning of incense sticks, the opium lamp was lighted, the man passed into elysium, and they wrapped themselves in their wadded quilts and slept till sunrise.

I learned their habits and knew their few "plenishings," and perhaps, as they stared persistently at me, they were wondering how much I earned a day by writing and sewing, a question of much speculative interest to the Chinese.

The country looked inviting in the first flush of early spring, although, like our own fens, it is a dead level. Houses, villages, mulberry plantations, temples, groves, large farmhouses, shrines, and *Pai fangs* succeeded each other rapidly. Great lilac clusters of wistaria bloom hung over the water from every tree, the beans were in blossom, and the greenery was young and fresh. At times our curiously twisting procession passed through ancient water-streets of large cities, with the inevitable picturesqueness given by deep eaves, overhanging rooms and balconies, steep flights of stone stairs, and rows of armed junks full of soldiers or river police in brilliant, stagey uniforms. Several times we were delayed for an hour or more by the difficulty of getting through the crowded river streets *en route*.

I have since learned by experience that China is a land of surprising bridges, but at that time it amazed me that we entered nearly every city under a fine arch, from fifteen to thirty feet in height, formed of blocks of granite cut to the curve of the bridge, the roadway attaining the summit by thirty-nine steps on each side. Or there are straight bridges, the piers being monoliths thirteen feet high, and the roadway massive blocks of stone thirty feet long.

Part of the route is along the Grand Canal, that stupendous work, wonderful even in its dilapidation, which connects Hangchow with Tientsin. This part of it, which connects Imperial Hangchow with the flourishing port of Chinkiang on the Yangtze, was cut in 625 A.D., but never mapped till the work was undertaken by our own War Office in 1865.

If the "nine thousand barks conveying tribute to the emperor," as described by an ancient writer, no longer crowd its waters, I can testify that at the points where I touched it, such as Chinkiang, the laden fleets were so vast as to leave only a narrow lane of water available for traffic, and that on arriving at Tientsin from Tungchow my boat took two days and a half to make its way through the closely-jammed mass of cargo and passage boats at the terminus.

The neighbourhood of the Grand Canal, which suffered terribly in the Taiping Rebellion, has recovered itself, and is again yielding its great harvests of rice and silk, the inexhaustible fertility of the Great Plain having effaced every trace of destruction. If the Grand Canal since the dilapidation caused by the outbreak of the Yellow River in 1851 is far less valuable for through traffic than it was, it is still of immense importance as an artery for the commerce of the great provinces through which it passes. Lu Yew, a much-travelled mandarin of the twelfth century, the translated account of whose journey from Shanjin near Ning Po to Kueichow on the Upper Yangtze is a fascinating bit of literature, writes that at the sluice gates "the concourse of vessels was packed together like the teeth of a comb," and so it is still in certain places. The bridges which span this canal are among the most striking and beautiful in all China—single arches, sometimes 220 feet in span and 30 feet in height, piles of massive masonry, with massive decorations wherever any deviation has been permitted from the ordinary stately simplicity.

Seven centuries ago Lu Yew commented on the remarkable industry of the population of this region, and noted that "both banks near the villages are covered with waterwheels pumping up the water, women and children alike exerting all their efforts, cattle in some cases being also at work." The heredity of industry is still manifest. Not an idler was to be seen along river or canal. Every agricultural operation of the season was being carried on vigorously, even children of seven years old were carrying agricultural burdens on their shoulders. Women with robust infants strapped on their backs had their hands busy with the distaff, while working the waterwheels with their feet; and all along the waterways fishermen were busy with their great bamboo plunge nets. Lu Yew mentions the women as employed with both waterwheel and distaff in the twelfth century.

On the morning of the second day from Shanghai the steam launch cast off her tail at the mouth of a narrow canal overarched with trees, up which my boat moved silently as far as a "lock," by which we mounted into a broad waterway leading direct into Hangchow, encircling it on three sides and connected with other navigable canals, spanned by picturesque stone bridges, and giving easy access to most parts of the interior of the city.

That which I have called a "lock," properly a *pah* or "haulover," is an ingenious contrivance by which the difficulty of "negotiating" different levels in the same boat is skilfully adjusted. The illustration shows the principle and the mode of applying it in Chekiang, but various methods are adopted. The essential parts of the contrivance, as shown here, are a smooth stone slide, from the higher to the lower level, the middle of which is thickly coated with moist mud, two stout and tall uprights, two rude wooden windlasses, and stout bamboo ropes with strong iron hooks. In ascending, the boat is wound up to the higher level by a number of men at the windlasses, and in going down she is drawn to the verge and tipped over, descending with great velocity by her own impetus, the restraining rope at her stern scarcely moderating the violence of the plunge with which she takes a header into the water below, when everything not securely fastened breaks adrift, and a lather of foaming water surges round the surprised passenger's feet. A few *cash* are charged for the transfer.

I thought the canal entrance to Hangchow grand, although below the high blank walls of large private residences the grassy

A *PAH*, OR HAULOVER.

slopes are the resort of unpleasantly active pigs searching, and not vainly, for offal. The gunboats, or police junks, with their striped blue and white canopies and brilliant crews, and the lofty bridges are pleasing to the eye. At one of the latter Dr. Main, for eighteen years a C.M.S. missionary doctor in Hangchow, met me, and I was carried through a populous and dirty quarter, through a door in a high wall, and under a trellis from which hundreds of lilac wistaria clusters were hanging, into a large enclosure, partly lawns and partly rose borders, with an old-fashioned English house on one side, and on the other two the fine two-storeyed buildings of two of the crack hospitals of the East, with their outgrowths of leper hospitals for men and women, a home for leper children, and an opium refuge. It was a bewildering change from the crowds, dirt, and sordid bustle of the lower parts of a Chinese city to broad, smooth, shaven lawns, English trees and flowers, English buildings with their taste and completeness, and the refined quiet of an English home.

This most ancient city, situated on the left bank of the shallow Ch'ien T'ang river, of which a magnificent description is given by Marco Polo under the name of Kinsai, though it has not fully recovered from the destruction wrought by the Taiping troops, is still handsome and dignified, and to my thinking, with its lovely environs, is the most attractive of the big Chinese cities.

It is certainly one of the most important, as the capital of the rich and populous province of Chekiang, the centre of a great silk-producing district, and of the manufacture of the best silks, the sole source of the silk fabrics supplied to the Imperial House-hold, the southern terminus of the Grand Canal, and a great centre of Chinese culture and literature. It possesses the Ting Library, the finest private library in China, appropriately housed in buildings adjoining the "palace" of the Ting family. The arrangements for the storage and classification of books are admirable, and a very gentlemanly and intelligent son of the enlightened possessor is the enthusiastic and capable librarian. The treasures of this library are open freely to anyone who introduces himself by a card from an official. The collection of zoological and botanical books, superbly illustrated in the best style of Chinese wood engraving, is in itself a noble possession. Every part of a plant is figured, and the illustrations are almost photo-graphically accurate, leading one to hope that the letterpress accompanying them has equal scientific merit!

Hangchow is also important as a "residential" city, the chosen home of many retired merchants and mandarins. The homes, frequently palaces, of men of leisure and local patriotism adorn its streets, but their stately proportions and sumptuous decorations are concealed from vulgar view by high whitewashed walls, in which heavily - barred and massive gates give access to the interiors. The mansion of the Ting family, in which I took "afternoon tea," with its lofty reception-rooms, piazzas, and courts, must cover two acres of ground. It is stately, but not comfortable, and the richly-carved blackwood chairs with panels of clouded grey marble for backs and seats, and table centres of the same, seem only fitted for the noon of a midsummer's day. Besides

WEST GATE, HANGCHOW

the dwellings of the "leisured class" there are those of high officials, bankers, and wealthy tea and silk merchants, many of them extremely magnificent, the cost of one built by a wealthy banker being estimated at £100,000.

I wrote of dirt and sordid bustle. This is chiefly by the water-side, and is not surprising in a city of three-quarters of a million of inhabitants. The "west-end" streets are, however, broad, light, well flagged, and incredibly clean for China. Hangchow impresses one with a general sense of well-being. I did not see one beggar. The people are well clothed and fed, and I understood that except during epidemics there is no abject poverty. It is the grand centre for the trade of a hundred cities, and much of the tea and silk sold in Shanghai and Ningpo passes through it.

Everything in the city and neighbourhood suggests silk. In all the adjacent country the mulberry tree is omnipresent, planted in every possible place along the creeks, on the ridges separating the fields, in plantations, acres in extent, and near villages, in nurseries each containing several thousand shoots, in expectation of a greatly increased demand for this staple product. There are 7000 handlooms for the weaving of silk in Hangchow, employing about 28,000 people, and 360 of these looms under the inspection of an Imperial Commissioner work exclusively for the Imperial Household.

Some of the silk shops rival that of Laou Kai Fook at Shanghai. In them are rich self-coloured silks in deep rich colourings and the most delicate shades, brocaded washing silks in various shades of indigo dyeing, and delicate mauves and French greys, which become more lustrous every time they are washed, heavy and very broad satins, plain and brocaded, and, what I admire more than all, heavy figured silks in colourings and shades unknown to us sold for Chinese masculine dress, and brocaded with symbolical bats, bees, spiders, stags' heads, dragons for mandarins' robes, and the highly decorative characters representing happiness and longevity. These quaint and beautiful fabrics are not exported to Europe, and are not shown to Europeans unless they ask for them. Fans exported to all parts of the empire are another great industry, and provide constant work for many thousand people. Elaborate furniture, silk and gold embroidering, and tinselled paper money for burning, to supply the dead with the means of comfortable existence, are also largely manufactured in this thriving capital.

The situation of Hangchow is beautiful, separated only by a belt of clean sand from the bright waters of the Ch'ieng T'ang river. The south-western portion is built on a hill, from which broad gleams of the sea are visible ; and to the west, just outside the walls, is the Si Hu [Western Lake], famous throughout China, a lovely sheet of water, surrounded by attractive country houses, temples, and shrines, studded with wooded islands connected by ancient and noble causeways, the islands themselves crowned with decorative pavilions, some of which are Imperial, and are surrounded by the perfection of Chinese gardening, as in the case of the beautiful Imperial Library, with its ferneries, rockeries, quaint ponds, and flowering shrubs. This lovely lake, with its deep, wooded bays and inlets, its forest-clothed hills and ravines, its gay gondolas and pleasure boats, and its ideally perfect shores, which I saw over and over again in the glorious beauty of a Chinese spring, mirrors also in its silver waters a picturesque range of hills, bare and breezy, close to the city, on which stands, in an imposing position, a very ancient pagoda, while the lower hill-slopes are clothed with coniferous trees, bamboo, plum, peach, cherry, camphor, azalea, clematis, roses, honeysuckle, and maple. Near the lake is a deep, long dell, the cliffs of which are recessed for stone images, and which contains several famous temples, one the temple of the " Five Hundred Disciples," who, larger than life-size, adorn its spacious corridors. The temples and shrines of this beautiful glen are visited daily by crowds from Hangchow, and have such a reputation for sanctity and efficacy as to attract 100,000 pilgrims annually. The dell is guarded by two colossal figures, under canopies, the gods of Wind and Thunder, very fine specimens of vigorous wood carving, and by an antique pagoda.

Hangchow is also famous for the phenomenon of the " Hangchow bore," seen at its best at the change of the monsoon, when an enormous mass of tidal water, suddenly confronted by the current of the river, uplifts its foaming crest to a height of from fifteen to twenty feet, and with a thunderous roar and fearful force rages down the narrow waterway as fast as a horse can gallop, affording a welcome distraction to the sightseers of Shanghai.

PAVILION IN IMPERIAL GARDEN, SI-HU.

GOD OF THUNDER, LIN-YANG.

Hangchow is enclosed by a wall faced with hewn stone, about thirteen miles in circumference, from thirty to forty feet high, from twenty to thirty feet broad, and pierced by ten large gateways with massive gates. The houses are mainly two-storeyed. The business streets blaze with colour; the principal street is five miles long. The population, estimated at 700,000, cruelly diminished during the Taiping Rebellion, is rapidly increasing. The officials, merchants, and common people are unusually friendly to foreigners, who, before the recent opening of the port, were all missionaries. The cry "Foreign devil!" is never heard. Mr. Sundius, our consular officer, considers that these very satisfactory relations are due to the greater prosperity of the people, in consequence of the increased foreign demand for silk, and to the success of the exertions of the missionaries to win their respect and esteem.

The new general and Japanese settlements are in an excellent position on the Grand Canal, four miles from the city wall. They are nearly a mile in length by half a mile in depth, and have a fine road and a bund sixty feet wide, hereafter to be turfed. The Japanese, who opened the port with their swords, have not been in any hurry to occupy it. It will be interesting to see how far foreigners will take advantage of the opening, and settle in this, one of the friendliest and most attractive of the Chinese cities. There is a well-known Chinese proverb, "Above is heaven, below are Hangchow and Suchow."

CHAPTER IV.

THE HANGCHOW MEDICAL MISSION HOSPITALS

THE hospitals, and the dispensaries attached to them, are too important as a feature of Hangchow, and as an element in producing the remarkable goodwill towards foreigners which characterises it, to be dismissed at the tail of a chapter.

These beneficent institutions treat between them over 14,000 new patients annually, afflicted with all manner of torments. The services of Dr. Main and his coadjutor, Dr. Kimber, are in request among officials, from the highest to the lowest. Mandarins of high rank, attended by their servants, are treated in the paying wards, and occasionally leave donations of 100 dollars in addition to their payments. Officials of every rank in the Chekiang province send to the British doctors for advice and medicines. Among the many marks of the approval with which the Viceroy and other highly-placed officials regard the medical work is their recent donation of an acre and a half of land in an excellent position for the site of a branch hospital. It is no disparagement to the work of Bishop Moule, who was absent during my visit, and the other British and American clerical missionaries, to express the opinion that the tact, *bonhomie*, and devotion of Dr. Main during the last eighteen years, are one cause of the friendliness to foreigners, the Chinese being as accessible to the influence of personality as other people are.

The men's and women's hospitals, of which the illustration only shows portions, are of the latest and most approved European type. They are abreast of our best hospitals in lighting, ventilation, general sanitation, arrangement and organisation, and the facility of obtaining the celebrated Ningpo varnish, really a lacquer, which slowly sets with a very hard surface, reflecting much light and bearing a weekly rub with kerosine oil, greatly aids the sanitation. The purity of walls, floors, and

C.M.S. MISSION HOSPITAL, HANGCHOW.

bedding is so great as to make one long for a speck of comfortable dirt !

The men's hospital buildings consist of four roomy and handsome general wards, eleven private paying wards, holding from one to three each, a range of rooms for the ward assistants, who are practically male nurses, students' rooms, rooms for the three qualified assistants, a lecture-room with an anatomical [in lieu of the unattainable human] subject which cost a thousand dollars, a reception-room for mandarins with appropriate Chinese furniture, Dr. Main's private room and medical library, a fine consulting-room and operating theatre, bathrooms, a room for patients' clothing done up in numbered bundles after it has been washed, wardrobes for the clothing which is lent to them while in hospital, a cashier's office, a large bottle-room, extensive storage, and an office for out-patients.

On the street side and connected with the hospitals is a fine lofty room where any non-patient passers-by, who are either tired or curious, can rest and smoke, amusing themselves meantime with the transactions of the other half of the hall, a large and attractive "drug store," fitted up in conventional English style, where not only medicines, but medical requisites of all kinds can be procured both by non-patients and foreigners. It has been remarked by Consuls Carles and Clement Allen in their official reports, that missionaries unconsciously help British trade by introducing articles for their own use, which commend themselves to the Chinese ; and this drug store has created a demand for such British manufactures as condensed milk, meat extracts, rubber tubing, soap, and the like, condensed milk having "caught on" so firmly that several of the Chinese shops are now keeping it on sale.

This rest room is also a street-chapel for preaching and discussion, and an office for inquiries of all kinds. There is also a large and handsome waiting-room for out-patients, decorated with scripture pictures, in which patriarchs and apostles appear in queues and Chinese dress, and an opium refuge—a mournful building full of bodily torment and mental depression. In the opinion of the doctor, "the cure" is seldom other than temporary, and could only be effected by building up the system for six months after leaving the refuge by tonics and nutritious diet.

Besides these buildings there are large kitchens, storehouses, and a carpenter's shop.

The women's hospital, the great central ward of which, with its highly-varnished floor, flowers, pictures, tables, chairs, and harmonium, looks like a pleasant double drawing-room in a large English mansion, is specially under Mrs. Main's charge, and has head and junior nurses and a dispenser trained by herself. It is equally efficient and admirable.

Besides the hospital staff of twenty-six persons, there are three native catechists who, along with Dr. Main, give Christian instruction in the hospital to those who are willing to receive it, one of them looking after patients in their homes, who, having become interested in Christianity, have returned to their villages within a radius of one hundred and fifty miles. Recently a patient, who had been for some weeks in the hospital, recounted what he had there heard of Christianity with such effect that over forty of his fellow-villagers, after some months, gave up their heathen practices and became Christians ; and this after he had been beaten for his new beliefs on first going home.

The hospital is also an efficient medical school, where the usual medical and surgical courses are given, along with clinical instruction, during a period of five years. This school has helped largely to win the favour of the mandarins, who have learned to appreciate Western surgery from the cures at the hospital. Some of these students, after graduation, have taken good positions in Shanghai and elsewhere. A few in going into practice in the province have somewhat dropped European medicine, and have resorted to Chinese drugs and the method of using them, but all adhere to Western surgery, the results of which in Chinese eyes are little short of miraculous, but possibly their mode of carrying out antiseptic treatment would hardly come up to Lord Lister's standard ! It is frequently believed by Chinese patients that the object of this treatment is to prevent devils from gaining entrance to the body by means of surgical wounds !

Dr. Lu, a refined and cultured man, Dr. Main's senior qualified assistant, a graduate of the hospital school, would anywhere be a remarkable man in his profession, first as a brilliant operative surgeon, and then for insight and accurate diagnosis. He has won the confidence of the resident foreigners. He is a skilful medical photographer, and his microscopic and physiological drawings are very beautiful and show great technical skill.

The clock tower is a decorative feature of the building, and everything within moves with clockwork regularity. The hospital is in a high state of efficiency and spick-and-spanness, such as I have seldom seen equalled abroad, and never exceeded.* Such work, done with skill, love, and cheeriness, has an earthly reward, and Dr. Main is on most friendly terms with the leading mandarins, who have it in their power to help or hinder greatly. The hospital blazes with their red and gold votive tablets, and I doubt if they would refuse him anything which he thought it wise to ask. Almost the latest additions to a work which is always growing are convalescent homes in the finest position outside the city, on the breezy hill above the Si Hu [Western Lake].

I have heard some grumbling at home at the expense at which this hospital is carried on, but perfection is not to be attained without outlay, and in my opinion the Hangchow hospital is a good investment. It is most desirable that Western methods of healing should be exhibited in their best aspects in the capital of this important province, and also that the medical school should be as well equipped as is possible. The benefit of this and similar schools is incalculable. The linked systems of superstition and torture, which enter largely into Chinese medical treatment, are undermined, and rational Western surgery is demanded by the people. European treatment also assails the degrading belief in sorcery and demonism in its last resort—the sick-bed—showing processes of cure which work marvels of healing, altogether apart from witchcraft and incantations.

Of the Medical Mission Hospital as a Christian agency I need scarcely write, as its name is significant of its work. I believe in medical missions, because they are the nearest approach now possible to the method pursued by the Founder of the Christian faith, and to the fulfilment of His command, " Heal and preach." It is not, as some suppose, that the medical missionary takes advantage of men in their pain and distress to " poke at them " the

* Another of the crack mission hospitals of the East, of which I had lengthened opportunities of judging, is Dr. Christie's hospital at Mukden, Manchuria, which has been largely instrumental in bringing about similar results in the friendliness of the officials and people.

claims of a foreign religion, though if he be an honest Christian he recognises that the soul needs enlightenment as much as the body needs healing. I have never seen a medical mission among the forty-seven that I have visited in which Christianity was " poked " at unwilling listeners, or in which, in the rare cases of men declining to hear of it in the dispensary waiting-room, it was in the very smallest degree to their disadvantage as patients.

A fee of twenty-four *cash* is charged for admission to the dispensary to foster a spirit of independence, and the charge in the paying wards is from two to ten dollars per month. Crowds of out-patients marshalled like an army, carefully trained assistants knowing and doing their duty, catechists, ward assistants, cashiers, photographers, cooks, gardeners, artisans, make up the crowd which in all the morning hours swarms over the staircases of the hospital and round the great entrance. The dispensary patients present a sorry spectacle, owing to the prevalence of skin diseases, superficial sores, and cavernous abscesses, from which the plasters with which the Chinese doctors had hermetically sealed them have been removed. Young and old, maimed, deaf, blind, loathsomely disfigured persons, meet together, and there are often cases of gunshot wounds, elephantiasis, and leprosy in the throng.

But, wretched as the patients are, they are capable of being amused by Dr. Main's jokes, and on one occasion when I was photographing four soldiers of the Viceroy's guard in the hospital grounds the hilarity burst all bounds, and the distempered mass yelled with enjoyment. When I photographed the backs of the soldiers they shouted, " She pictures their backs because they ran away from the *wojen* " (dwarfs); and when Dr. Main displayed their brawny legs, they nearly danced with the fun of it, yelling, " Those are the legs they ran away on." Not that the Viceroy's guard had encountered the Japanese, but these people were near enough to Shanghai to have heard of the figure the Chinese troops had cut. A Chinese loves a joke, and, as I have often experienced, if he can only be made to laugh his hostility vanishes.

One of these men, picturesquely uniformed in blue and crimson, was brought back an hour later at the point of death from opium, having attempted his life, not because he had been laughed at, but because of a tiff with his superior officer.

As is well known, suicide is appallingly common in China; and in the great cities of Swatow, Mukden, and Hangchow, as a guest at medical mission houses, I have come much into contact with its various methods. In Mukden a frequent mode of taking life, specially among young wives, is biting off the heads of lucifer matches, though the death from phosphorus poisoning is known to be an agonising one. Swallowing gold leaf or chloride of magnesium, jumping down wells or into rapid rivers, taking lead, cutting the throat, and stabbing the abdomen have been popular modes of self-destruction. But these are rapidly giving place to suicide by opium owing to the facility with which it can be obtained, the easy death which results from it, and the certainty of its operation in the absence of the foreign doctor, his emetic, and his stomach-pump. Medical mission hospitals in China save the lives of hundreds of would-be suicides every year.

So far as I have been able to ascertain, the causes of suicide in China are, not as in Europe, profound melancholia, heavy losses, or disappointment in love, but chiefly revenge and the desire to inflict serious injury on another. Suicide enables a Chinese to take a truly terrible revenge, for he believes that his spirit will malignantly haunt and injure the living; and the desire to save a suicide's life arises in most cases not from humanity, but from the hope of averting such a direful catastrophe. If a master offends his servant or makes him "lose face," or a shopkeeper his assistant or apprentice, the surest revenge is to die on his premises, for it not only involves the power of haunting and of inflicting daily injuries, but renders it necessary that the body should lie where death occurs until an official inquiry is made, which brings into the house the scandal and turmoil of a visit from a mandarin with a body of officials and retainers. It is quite common for a man or woman to walk into the courtyard of a person against whom he or she has a grudge, and take a fatal dose of opium there to ensure these desirable results!

Among common incentives to suicide are the gusts of blind rage to which the Chinese of both sexes are subject, the cruelty of mothers-in-law, quarrels between husband and wife, failure to meet payments at the New Year, gambling losses, the desire to annoy a husband, the gambling or extravagant opium smoking of a husband, imputation of theft, having pawned the clothes of another and being unable to redeem them, being defrauded of money, childlessness, dread of divorce, being sold by a husband, abridgment of liberty, poverty, and the like. Opium, from the painless death it brings, is now resorted to on the most trivial occasions, and has largely increased the number of suicides. Though the reasons which I have given for self-destruction apply mostly to women, yet where statistics are obtainable men are largely in the majority, and revenge and the desire of inflicting injury are their great motives.

Of course, there are very many risks and difficulties in the treatment of out-patients. Chinese medicines are administered bulkily, a pint or a quart at a time, and patients do not understand our concentrated and powerful doses. Hence dangerous and grotesque mistakes are continually made, such as the following :—

Patient—" Doctor, when I took the medicine you gave me yesterday it made me very sick ; it has given me diarrhœa and a severe pain in the stomach ; my fingers and toes also feel very numb."

Dr. Malcolm (looking at the bottle)—" Why, you have already almost finished the eight days' medicine" (arsenic) " that I gave you yesterday. The wonder is that you are alive at all."

Patient No. 2 enters—" Where is the old boss of this shop? I want some foreign devil medicine to cure malaria."

D.—"Allow me to tell you I am not a devil. You had better go home ; and when you can come and ask respectfully for medicine we will give it you."

P. No. 3 enters, holding out her hands and asking the doctor to find out her disease by " comparing her pulses."

D.—" Tell me what is the matter with you."

P.—" My bones and muscles are sore all over."

D.—" What was the cause of your trouble ? "

P.—" It was brought on by a fit of anger."

D.—" How long have you had it ? "

P.—" From the time the heavens were opened, and the earth was split " (*i.e.* a very long time).

The arms and shoulders of this woman were covered with pieces of green plaster, given her by the Chinese doctors. She proposed to throw these away and " to publish the doctor's name abroad " if he cured her. So she received medicine with very full directions about taking it; these were not enough. She asked a string of questions such as if she must heat it before taking it, if she must keep the bottle tightly corked, if she must take it along with anything else, and lastly—

P.—" Shall I abstain from eating anything? "

D.—" No."

P. (greatly disappointed).—" What! shall I not forbid my mouth anything at all? "

D. (jokingly).—" Yes. Do not talk too much; do not revile your neighbours; do not smoke opium; do not scatter lies."

The doctor getting worried, reiterates plain directions regarding the medicine, tells her they are very busy, and that she must not ask any more questions, and shows her out.

P. (returning after a few minutes).—" Is the medicine to be taken inwardly, or rubbed on the outside? "

Or a man comes in and describes " chills," and a dose of quinine is prepared for him, when he smiles serenely and says, " To tell you the truth, it is not I that take the chills; it is my mother."

Another comes in, and describes with great minuteness and self-pity his symptoms, which are those of malarial fever. He will not take a dose of quinine in the dispensary, but wants to take it home, saying he will not " shake " till the next day. He is feigning sickness, in order to get quinine and sell it. Or an operation for cataract has been performed in one of the hospital wards, and the son of the patient comes to the doctor, begging him to go to his father, who says that his eye pains him so that he cannot stand it. The doctor finds that the bandage has been removed, and reproaches the son, who said that some friends came in to see if he could really see after being blind for so many years, and took off the bandage. The patient had rubbed the eye, the wound had burst open and was suppurating, and the man was blind for life.

Some patients come to a hospital out of impudence, some in the hope of getting drugs to sell, others out of curiosity to see how the " foreign devil doctor " works, others to steal the clothes which are lent to in-patients, and others for a lark, pretending to have various diseases, but with these the Chinese assistants occasionally indulge in a lark on their own account, and turn on them a pretty vigorous current from the electric battery.*

With so much vexatious expenditure of time, so much imposition and greed, and so many disappointments regarding interesting cases owing to the gross ignorance of the patients and their friends, there are many drawbacks in the life of a missionary doctor, and even in such long-established work as that at Hangchow, and with such admirable equipments and assistance, it cannot always be easy to preserve the courtesy, gentleness, patience, and forbearance which are among the essentials of success.

Of the patients treated in Hangchow last year one thousand were in-patients. "Discharged cured" might be written against the great majority of their names, and those who were incurable were greatly benefited, as in the case of the lepers, whose "grievous wounds" are closed and healed, and whose pains are subdued.

Certainly this great hospital is one of the sights of Hangchow, and no one could become acquainted with it without recognising that those who work it and support it are following closely in the footsteps of Him who came "not to destroy men's lives, but to save them."†

* In a paper called *Medical Missions at Home and Abroad* for 1898, p. 70, the reader will find such experiences very graphically told by Dr. Malcolm.

† These hospitals and dispensaries under the care of Dr. Main and Dr. Kimber treated 47,000 patients in 1898, of which number 1000 were in-patients, and besides these 187 would-be suicides received back the unwelcome gift of life. These benevolent Christian institutions comprise hospitals for men and women, an opium refuge, three leper hospitals, two convalescent homes, and a home for the children of lepers.

CHAPTER V.

SHANGHAI TO HANKOW (HANKAU)

FROM Hangchow I made a very interesting journey by canal and river to the important and historical city of Shao Hsing, with its beautiful environs, and from thence by inland waterways to Ningpo and its lovely lakes, passing through a region of great fertility, beauty, and prosperity. I must put on record that I made that journey without either a companion or servant, trusting entirely to the fidelity and goodwill of Chinese boatmen, and was not disappointed. At Ningpo the Commissioner of Customs kindly lent me the Customs tender, a fast-sailing lorcha, for a week, and engaging a servant, I visited the Chusan Archipelago in glorious weather, spending three days on the remarkable island of Putu, the Island of Priests, sacred to Kwan Yin, the goddess of mercy, and two at Tinghai, on the island of Chusan, where the graves of the four hundred British soldiers who died there during our occupation present a melancholy spectacle of neglect and disrepair. The region beyond Shao Hsing technically belongs to another drainage area than that of the Yangtze, and is therefore passed over without further remark. I returned from Ningpo to Shanghai by sea.

The difficulties of getting a reliable interpreter servant who had not previously served Europeans and who was willing to face the possible risks and certain hardships of the journey I proposed were solved by the kindly intervention of friends, and I engaged a tall, very fine-looking, superior man named Be-dien, who abominated "pidgun," spoke very fairly correct English, and increased his vocabulary daily during the journey. He was proud and had a bad temper, but served me faithfully, was never out of hearing of my whistle except by permission, showed great pluck, never grumbled when circumstances were adverse, and never deserted me in difficulties or even in perils.

My other preparations consisted chiefly in buying an open bamboo armchair to be carried in, plenty of tea and curry powder, and in discarding most of my few possessions.* As nobody in Shanghai had travelled in the region which I hoped eventually to visit, there was no information about it to be gained, and I left for my journey of six or seven months remarkably free from encumbrances of every kind.

Several foreign and one Chinese company own the eighteen fine steamers which keep up daily communication between Shanghai and Hankow, and dissipate the romance of travel by their white enamel, mirrors, gilding, and electric light. The *Poyang*, by which I was a passenger, and the only one, as far as Chinkiang, resembles most of the others, being of an American type, about 2000 tons burden, luxurious to a fault, and officered by efficient and courteous gentlemen.

Sailing at night, the lumpy sea which is apt to prevail in the estuary of the Yangtze is got over comfortably, and by the following morning it is possible to believe that the expanse of muddy water is actually a river, for there are hazy outlines of brown shores.

The first day on the river was cold and raw, as, indeed, were the days which followed it; the damp-laden air wrapped one round in its dismal chill. White enamel and mirrors were detestable. The only things which harmonised with the surroundings were the stove and the thick woollen carpet. Yet the mercury was at 45°—not bad for mid-winter!

After passing Silver Island, a wooded rock, on which is a fine temple, we reached Chinkiang, the first of the treaty ports on the Yangtze, and well situated at the junction of the Grand Canal with the river. On my two visits I thought it an attractive place. It has a fine bund and prosperous-looking foreign houses, with a British consulate on a hill above; trees abound. The concession†

---

* In China the necessaries of existence, food, clothing, shoes, waterproofs, and travelling-trunks and baskets are always to be procured, and there, as everywhere, if a traveller uses native arrangements, he has much less difficulty in getting them handled or repaired.

† Concession is not, as is supposed by many, a synonym for settlement. A concession is a piece of land leased by the Queen's Government and let to Western merchants, a stipulation being made that the land is not to be sub-let to Chinese, while a settlement is an area within which Europeans may lease land directly from the native proprietors. In both cases the Queen's Government stipulates for the right of policing and controlling the land, and delegates it to a council of resident merchants.

roads are broad and well kept. A row of fine hulks connected by bridges with the shore offers great facilities for the landing of goods and passengers. Sikh police are much *en evidence*, the hum of business greets one's ears, traffic throngs the bund, the Grand Canal is choked with junks, and the rule regarding sub-letting to Chinese being honoured only in the breach, the concession is covered with go-downs and Chinese residences, and judging from appearances only, one might think Chinkiang a busier port than Hankow, the great centre of commerce in Central China. The gross value of the trade of this port is, however, only about £4,000,000 sterling annually, but is advancing. One great export is ground-nut oil, which is carried and shipped in baskets lined with paper. Another, which accounts for nearly one-fourteenth of the value of the exports, is the dried perianth of certain lily flowers (*Hemerocallis graminea* and *Hemerocallis flava*), which is greatly esteemed as a relish with meats, specially with pork.

As tokens of the increasing prosperity of Chinkiang, it is interesting to note that recently two filatures, owned and managed by Chinese, were opened, the machinery in one of them being of Chinese manufacture, while the factory was erected without foreign aid. The hands employed are women, who work twelve hours daily, at 10½d. a day, Sunday being a holiday. The success of this, under native management, was considered dubious. A distillery, for distilling spirit from rice, is another sign of progress (or retrogression?), and our German rivals have done a very "neat thing" in starting an albumen factory, in which the albumen, dexterously separated from the yolks of the eggs, is made into slabs, which are sent to Germany for use in photography, the preparation of leather, and the printing of cotton, etc. The eggs are ducks' eggs solely. The yolks undergo some preservative treatment, and after being packed in barrels are exported for use in confectionery and bar-rooms. My informant, Consul Carles, is silent on the use to which they are then applied, but doubtless it is well known to frequenters of such establishments.

The workmen in out-of-doors trades, such as masons and carpenters, seem to comport themselves much like our own, at all seasons of the year drinking tea, resting, and smoking whenever it pleases them, taking a long siesta in summer, and in winter not beginning work till nine. The building trade is a guild,* and there are five large guilds in Chinkiang, with guild funds for the relief of widows and orphans of former members. There are various missions in Chinkiang, and some general stir, which may be expected in a city of 140,000 souls.

The next day, which was raw and grim, and made the stove-side a magnet, we reached Wuhu, the ugliest, if I may be allowed to say so, of all the Yangtze ports, but its trade is not unprosperous, having more than doubled in the last ten years, its gross value as to the principal articles of export and import being now nearly £2,000,000 sterling a year.†

There again the Germans have started an albumen factory, which employs fifty women and ten men. It takes 7000 eggs to produce 100 pounds of albumen. Feathers to the amount of £23,000 for the last year of returns were also exported to Germany for the making of feather beds.

The most interesting export of Wuhu to the general reader is, however, " China ink," which is largely produced in the province of NGANHUI. The small, black sticks, decorated with Chinese characters in gold, are known and appreciated by us all. From Wuhu it goes to all parts of China and of the world. In 1895 *two tons* of it were exported from Shanghai to foreign countries. Nearly the whole of the writing done in the vast Chinese empire, as well as in Japan, Korea, Tonquin, and Annam, is done with this beautiful ink, which is rubbed down on a stone ink-slab, and applied with a sable brush. This is altogether apart from its value to the water-colour art of all nations. It is made from the oil expressed from the large seeds of the *Elæococca verrucosa*, sesamum oil, or colza oil, varnish, and pork fat, burned, the resulting lampblack being of various degrees of fineness according to the process adopted; gold leaf and musk are added. There are a dozen different grades, and the price varies from 2s. to 140s. per pound, a pound containing about thirty sticks.

Various industries, including a steam flour mill, have been started by the Chinese in Wuhu, and it is a city of 80,000 people, but to a mere passer-by it is most uninteresting, and its busy streets had neither novelty nor picturesqueness enough to repay me for a struggle through the slush.

---

* A specimen of guild rules is given in Appendix A.
† For brief statistics of the trade of the Yangtze open ports see Appendix B.

That night, while we were dining, there was a tremendous bump, a crash, and a stoppage. The junk we cut into went down like a stone with all hands. Not a shout or cry was heard. Boats were lowered, and we hung about for an hour ; it was not very dark. A Frenchman brutally remarked, "Good ! there'll be some yellow skins fewer." That was all.

The next day we reached Kiu-kiang, another treaty port, with a pretty, shady bund, and pleasant foreign houses in shady gardens, but it has a sleepy air for a city of 55,000 souls and a trade worth two millions and a quarter a year.

Totally destroyed during the Taiping Rebellion in 1858–59, it has been rebuilt, is surrounded by a defensive wall six miles in circumference, and has regained more than its former prosperity, its imports having increased steadily for the last five years.

I have mentioned only the treaty ports, but from Chinkiang westwards the great cities on or near the bank divide attention with the engineering works and the singular vagaries of build and rig in the countless craft on the river. Among the cities on or near the river are Yang Chow Fu, Nanking, the southern capital, with its ruined splendours and picturesqueness, Taiping Fu, the great and prosperous city of Nganking Fu, and many others, besides countless villages, which are apt to lead an amphibious existence. After leaving Kiu-kiang, the most prominent objects of interest are the Great and Little Orphans, picturesque rocks about 300 feet in height, rising direct from the bed of the river, and appropriated, as all picturesque sites are, by the Buddhists for religious purposes. The Great Orphan is near Hu-kow, a bluff on the river crowned by an inaccessible-looking building, half temple, half fortress, close to the junction of the important Poyang lake with the Yangtze, which is effected by a short, broad stream.

A city on a dead level can scarcely be imposing, and Hankow is not impressive from the water. Some chimneys of Russian brick tea factories rise above the greenery of the bund, and on the right bank of the broad Yangtze, above a squalid suburb of Wu-Chang, appear some tall chimneys belonging to a Chinese cotton factory under native management, but differing from those at Shanghai in that no women or girls are employed, the Viceroy considering that such occupation for women is opposed to good morals and Confucian principles! On an elevation there is also a camp with crenelated walls, an abundance of fluttering silk banners, and various antiquated engines of war.

The day was damp and grim, but the kindly welcomes, cordial hospitality, and big blazing fires at the British Consulate, where I was received, made amends for the external chill, and my visit to Hankow is among my many pleasant memories of China. Later in the day Dr. Griffith John called on me, the veteran missionary of the L.M.S., great as an evangelist, a Chinese writer and translator, and as an enthusiast. The L.M.S. has its mission buildings, which include a church, dispensaries, and hospitals, and the houses of its missionaries, in some of the pleasant shady streets which intersect the settlement. They have various agencies at work, and are full of hope as to the result. I understand that Dr. Griffith John, who has devoted his life to China and means to die there, partly from his devotion and partly from his literary gifts, is much respected by many of the official and upper classes, and has much influence.

CHAPTER VI.

THE FOREIGNERS—HANKOW AND BRITISH TRADE

HANKOW or Hanmouth, Wu-Chang Fu, the capital of HUPEH, and Han Yang would be one city were they not bisected by the broad, rolling Yangtze, nearly a mile wide, and its great tributary the Han. Hankow and Han Yang are on the north bank, and Wu-Chang on the south. The "congeries of cities," as the three have been aptly termed, is about 600 miles from Shanghai. Till 1863 Hankow was an open city, but the dread of an attack by northern banditti that year led the Government to enclose it with a stone wall, four miles in circuit and thirteen feet in height, raised by a brick parapet to eighteen feet.

Hankow considers that it has the finest bund in China, and I have no wish to dispute its assertion. In truth its length of 800 yards, its breadth of 80, its lofty and noble river wall and fine flights of stone stairs, ascending 40 feet from low water, its broad promenade and carriage-way and avenue of fine trees, with the "palatial" houses, very similar to those of Shanghai and Singapore, on the other side in large gardens and shaded by exotic trees, make it scarcely credible that the first authentic visit of Europeans to the city was that made by Lord Elgin in H.M.S. *Furious* in 1858, and that the site for this stately British settlement was only chosen in 1861, the year in which the port was opened to foreign trade.

Among the principal buildings are the British and French Consulates, the residence of the Commissioner of Customs, and the Municipal Buildings. There is a Municipal Council charged with the same functions as that at Shanghai, and Sikh policemen make a goodly show. Dead levels are not attractive unless they are bounded by the living ocean, and the bund is dull and gives one the impression that the British settlement has "seen better days."

The foreign community consists of the consuls and their staffs, the *employés* of the Chinese Maritime Customs, a very few professional men, a large number of British and American missionaries, and the members of British and other European mercantile firms, Russians taking a very prominent position. The residents have carried their amusements with them, and amuse themselves on a small scale after the fashion of those at Shanghai. There is a popular club which welcomes passing visitors, and combines social attractions with a library, reading-room, and billiard-room, keeping in touch with the world by frequent telegrams. There is a creditable newspaper—the *Hankow Times*, which has papers on Chinese, social, and other subjects—an episcopal service, a hotel, a livery stable, and other necessaries of the British exile's life. Kindness and cordial hospitality to strangers are not less characteristic of Hankow than of the less frequented ports.

The climate is not an agreeable one. The summers, lasting from May till the middle of September, are hot and damp, and severe cases of malarial and typhoid fever are not unusual. The atmosphere is thick and stagnant, and there are swarms of mosquitoes. Some of the men residents pass the hottest summer nights on the bund to get the little air stirring on the river, and the Chinese sleep on their roofs and in the streets. The autumn months are very pleasant, the mercury falls to the freezing point in January, and after light frosts there is a damp, raw period till warm weather sets in again.

Neither Hankow nor its neighbours have any special features of interest except their gigantic trade. The populations are not openly unfriendly; but Consul Carles, his wife, and I, although attended, had mud thrown at us at Han Yang.

The glory of Hankow, as well as its terror, is the magnificent Yangtze, nearly a mile wide even in winter, rolling majestically past the bund, lashed into a dangerous fury by storms, or careering buoyantly before breezes; in summer, an inland sea fifty feet deep. In July and early August Hankow is at its worst, and the rise of the river is watched with much anxiety. The bund is occasionally submerged, boats ply between houses and offices, the foundations of buildings are softened, exercise is suspended, gardens are destroyed, much business stands still, frail native houses are swept away—as many of those perched on piles were, with much loss of life, in the summer rise of 1898—and thousands are deprived of shelter and livelihood, and when the water falls widespread distress and a malarious film of mud are left behind. The appearance of the SZE CHUAN water, the red product of the "Red Basin" of Richthofen, indicates to the Chinese intelligence the approaching subsidence of the water, and points to a fact of some scientific interest. During the ordinary summer rise the whole region, viewed from Pagoda Hill, has the dismal aspect of a turbid, swirling inland sea, above which many villages with trees appear, built on mounds, probably of ancient construction.

Hankow is the most westerly port in which the Mexican dollar is actually current, and even in its back country copper *cash* are preferred to either coined or uncoined silver. For western travel, over and above any amount of cash which the traveller can burden himself with, "sycee" silver is necessary, which can be obtained from the agency of the Hong Kong and Shanghai Bank, as well as "good paper"—Chinese drafts on Chinese merchants of repute in the far west. Silver "shoes," as the uncouth lumps of silver obtained from the banks are called, are worth about fifty taels, but the tael itself is not of fixed value, the Haikwan tael, in which the Customs and some other accounts are kept, varying from the Shanghai tael, and that again from the Hankow tael, and so on.

Nor is this all. The silver itself is unfortunately of variable quality. Hankow sycee is of 2½ per cent. higher "standard" than Shanghai sycee, and SZE CHUAN silver is of higher standard than that of Hankow, so that the traveller is subject to frequent losses on his bullion, besides suffering a good deal from delays and annoyances consequent on weighings and occasional testings, though the trained eye alone can usually detect the inferior "touch" of his silver. "Confusion worse confounded" describes the currency system, if "currency" is an applicable word, when once the simplicity of the Mexican dollar is left behind, and I ceased to be surprised at the employment of Chinese "shroffs" by foreign firms, for what but an Oriental intellect could unravel the mysteries of "touch," the differences in the value of taels, the soundness and genuineness of *cash*, and the daily variations and entanglements of the exchanges?

In a treaty port which has been open for thirty-nine years, and which in 1898 had a net import trade of £3,422,669, and a net export trade of £4,643,048, and of which, so far as the import of foreign goods is concerned, the British share is one-half, the stranger naturally expects to find British merchants piling up big fortunes, and the size and stateliness of the houses on the bund gives colour to this expectation.

But, in fact, while the British firms in Hankow are merely branches of houses in Shanghai, their Chinese rivals, who have driven them out of the import trade, are Hankow merchants with branches in Shanghai. There are about eleven of these big native firms which supply the Hankow market with British cotton goods, and which have risen on the ruins of British competitors. These wealthy firms, dealing wholesale, supply the up-country merchants and local shopkeepers, buying goods through their branches in Shanghai, which employ Chinese brokers speaking "pidgun" English to buy the particular goods they want from the foreign importers. They keep well up to date regarding Shanghai auction sales, of which they get catalogues in Chinese, and are quick to seize on every small advantage. The British merchant was shortsighted enough totally to neglect to open up direct business relations with the up-country merchants, and was content to deal entirely with the Hankow native importer, to whom he left all the advantages of local connection and knowledge.*

This unfortunate state of things does not seem likely to improve either in Hankow or elsewhere. Our methods of doing business are frank and open, and the Chinese merchants have become as well acquainted with foreign trade methods as are Europeans themselves, while of their customs in trade and their arrangements among themselves for conducting business we know scarcely anything, and have no organisations equivalent to those centred in the guilds. Whether it is too late to stem the tide which is gradually sweeping business out of foreign into native hands I know not, but though actual British trade may not suffer, the openings for young men in mercantile houses in China are diminishing yearly, unless capital, push, a preference for business over athletics, a working knowledge of the Chinese language and business methods, and a determination to succeed, should develop the trade and

---

* For minor causes of the loss of the import trade see *Trade of Central and Southern China*, BOURNE, Foreign Office, May, 1898.

traffic of the Tungting lake, and turn to account the great possibilities for Lancashire trade in HUNAN, even though the ground lost in other directions can never be recovered.

As to the trade of Hankow, naturally an interesting subject, I shall make very few remarks, the first being that in the year 1898, 550,000 tons of British shipping entered the port, against 60,624 of all other nationalities, exclusive of the Chinese, Japan taking the lead among them with 32,099. Hankow has lost much of her once enormous tea trade, owing to deterioration in quality and the change of fashion in England.* Russian merchants now have the tea trade in their hands; they have factories for the production of "brick tea" at both Hankow and Kiu-kiang, while in 1898 five of the big steamers of the Russian Volunteer Fleet loaded tea direct for Odessa, and one steamer for St. Petersburg.

German and Austrian firms have started several albumen factories in Hankow, the best of the product being used in photography; the Japanese are now running two steamers a week between it and Shanghai, and will not improbably " cut in " ahead of others for the trade and traffic of the lake and inland rivers. Numbers of these alert traders have come up the Yangtze, and in their practical way are spreading themselves through the country, finding out the requirements and tastes of the people, and quietly pushing their trade in small articles, while Japan is also going ahead with her larger exports, the quantity of her cotton yarn imported into Hankow having risen from 150 cwt. in 1895 to 260,332 in 1898, displacing Indian yarn to a considerable extent. Japanese merchants, like the German, do not despise *littles* in trade, and are content with small profits, and most of what is known as the "muck and truck" trade is in their hands, in extending which they will prove formidable competitors of each other. Nor ought the competition of Japan in the larger branches of trade to be ignored by us, for to extend her markets is an absolute necessity of her existence, and the markets of China are a fair field for her commercial ambition.

* In 1868 the average consumption of tea per head of the population of the United Kingdom was 3·52 lbs., of which 93 per cent. was Chinese tea, and 7 per cent. Indian. Since that date the consumption has risen to an average of 5·73 per head of the population, but only 11 per cent. is Chinese tea, while the tea grown in India and Ceylon is 89 per cent.

I cannot omit all mention of kerosene oil, the import of which increases "by leaps and bounds," American taking the lead, and which is greatly diminishing the production of the native illuminating oils. This kerosene oil, imported from Russia, America, and Sumatra, to the quantity, in 1898, of 16,055,000 gallons, goes from Hankow through six provinces. It is one among the agents which are producing changes in the social life of China. I have seen the metamorphosis effected by it in the village life of the Highlands of Scotland and Korea, where the saucer of fish oil, with its smoky wick, and the dim, dull *andon* have been replaced by the bright, cheerful "paraffin lamp," a gathering point for the family, rendering industry and occupation possible. Chinese rooms are inconceivably dark, and smoking, sleeping, and gambling were the only possible modes of getting rid of the long winter evenings among the poorer classes till kerosene oil came upon the scene.

Hankow has eight regular guilds, which are banks and cash shops, rice and grain dealers, clothiers and mercers, grocers and oilmen, ironmasters, wholesale dealers in copper and metals, dealers in KIANGSI china, and wholesale druggists, Hankow having one of the largest and best drug markets in China. It would be well if we realised the extreme importance of these and similar trade organisations. We may talk of spheres of interest and influence, and make commercial treaties giving us the advantages of the "most favoured nation" clause ; but till we understand the power of the guilds, and can cope with them on terms of equality, and are "up to Chinese methods of business," we shall continue to see what we are now seeing at Hankow and elsewhere, which I have already alluded to. There is much that is admirable in these guilds, and their trades-unionism, combinations, and systems of terrorism are as perfect as any machinery of the same kind in England. In any matters affecting the joint interests of a trade, the members or their delegates meet and consult. The rules of guilds are both light and severe, and no infringement of them is permitted without a corresponding penalty ; these penalties vary from a feast and a theatrical entertainment being inflicted on the guilty person to expulsion from the guild in a flagrant case, which means the commercial ruin of the offender.

CHAPTER VII.

CHINESE HANKOW (HANKAU)

IT is a short step from the stately dulness of the bund to the crowds, colour, and noise of the native city—the "Million-peopled City," the commercial centre of China, the greatest "distributing point" in the empire, the centre of the tea trade, which has fallen practically into Russian hands, and the greatest junk port in China.

The city wall is imposing, with a crenelated parapet, forts at the corners, and tunnelled under double-roofed gate-towers for heavily bossed gates, which are closed from sunset to sunrise. The unpaved roadways are usually foul quagmires owing to the perpetual passage of water carriers; where big dogs of the colour of dirty flannel, with pink patches of hairlessness, wrangle over offal. The streets are from ten to twelve feet wide. The houses are high. Matting or blue cotton is stretched across from opposite roofs in summer to moderate the sun's heat and glare; so the traffic is carried on in a curiously tinted twilight, flecked now and then by a vivid ray gleaming on the red and gold of the long, hanging shopboards, lighting up their flare and glare, and giving them a singular picturesqueness.

The shape of the signboard and the different colours of the letters and face of the sign indicate different trades. The devising of a signboard is a very important matter; it may affect the luck of the shop. The name of the shopkeeper comes first, but in the case of a firm a word of good omen is substituted for the names, with a character signifying union. In both cases the top characters are followed by words of good omen, suggesting wealth, prosperity, and increase.

Gold platers of ornaments use salmon-coloured boards with green characters, druggists gilded boards frequently traced with many lines, and large standard tablets which remain in their sockets at night, and there are a few other combinations of colour used by different traders for the sake of easy distinction ; and on some signboards the articles sold within are carefully pictured, but black and gold and carnation-red and gold largely predominate, the gold being used for the highly decorative characters, the writing of which is a lucrative trade. An old signboard is a valuable piece of property, and if the business is sold fetches a high price, like the good-will of a long-established business at home. An old-established druggist's sign has sold for as much as 3000 taels, about £450. In the winter, with the streets so decorated, with the overhead screens removed, the narrow strips of bright blue sky above, and the slant sunbeams touching gold and colour into marvellous brilliancy, Chinese cities, especially Canton and Foochow, have a nearly unrivalled picturesqueness.

Of the crowded and semi-impassable state of such streets no adequate idea can be given. Though on my first visit to the native city the British Consul was walking beside me with an attendant, and my bearers wore the red-plumed hats and well-known liveries of the Consulate, I was often brought to a halt, more or less ignominious, or was roughly shaken by the impact of the burden of some hurrying coolie, while the chairmen threaded their way with difficulty through thousands of busy, blue-clad Chinese, all shouting or yelling, my bearers adding to the din by the yelling in chorus which is supposed to clear a passage for a chair.

Among the meaner cotton-clad folk there were not wanting rich costumes of heavy brocaded silks and costly furs, worn probably by compradores and shopkeepers, who in the treaty ports are coming to vie with the highest officials in the splendid expensiveness of their dress. Occasionally yells louder than usual, and an attempt on the part of the crowd to pack itself to right and left, denoted the approach of a mandarin in a heavy, coloured and gilded official chair, with eight bearers, and many attendants in heavily plumed hats and red and black decorated dresses ; the official himself sitting very erect within his chair, nearly always very pale and fat, with a thin moustache of long curved hairs, and that look of unutterable superciliousness and scorn which no Oriental of another race is equally successful in attaining.

The principal streets are flagged ; the others are miry ways

A STREET IN HANKOW.

cut into deep ruts by wheelbarrows. "Ancient and fish-like smells" abound, and strong odours of garlic, putrid mustard, frizzling pork, and of the cooking of that most appetising dish, fish in a state of decomposition, drift out of the crowded eating-houses. If of the lower class, the culinary operations of restaurants are visible from the street, the utensils consisting of a row of pans set into brickwork, one or two iron pots, and a few earthen-ware dishes. Not a tipsy man or a man noisy with drink was to be seen. The Chinese have the virtue of using alcoholic liquor in great moderation, and almost altogether with their food.

Oil in earthenware jars, each large enough to contain a man, or freshly arrived in the paper-lined wicker baskets in which it is shipped from SZE CHUAN, denotes the oil shops; parcels of tea done up in oiled paper, built up to a great height with surprising regularity, slabs of brick tea, and sacks of sugar denote the grocers; while rolls of carefully packed silk, which one longs to investigate, proclaim the prince of retail shopkeepers, the dealer in silks.

There are bean cakes, melon seeds, dates, and drugs from the north and west, brought in by the great junks, with huge sweeps and Vandyke-brown sails, which crowd the Han. There are idol-makers with every sort and size of idol for home use and export, some of which find their way to Tibet and Turkestan, and receive perpetual worship in the homes and *gonpas* of Ladak and Nubra; but none of them are treated with even scant respect until the ceremony takes place which invests them with the soul, represented by silver models of the "five viscera," which are inserted at a door in the back. In the same quarter are dealers in the manifold paraphernalia of idol worship, in the tinsel, gold, and silver shoes burned in ancestor worship, and in the very clever and in some cases life-size representations of elephants, tigers, horses, asses, cows, houses, carts, and many other things which are burned at funerals, adding to their great costliness, the sons of a merchant of average means often spending a thousand dollars on these mimicries.

But while there are dealers in everything which can minister to the luxury or necessities of the "Million-peopled City," many of the shops give a piteous notion of the poverty of their customers. And everywhere in these crowded streets not a thing is sold, from a valuable diamond down to a straw shoe, without the deafening din of bargaining, no seller asking what he means to take, and no purchaser offering what he eventually means to give, the poorest buyers, to whom time is money, thinking an hour not misspent if they get a reduction of half a *cash*. As all the bargaining, except in the case of the great shops, is done at the shop fronts, and the bargainers are men, and Chinese men, specially of the lower orders, shout at the top of their voices, the Babel in a Chinese commercial street is inconceivable.

Enormous quantities of goods are everywhere waiting for transit, for Hankow is the greatest distributing centre in China, and the big steamers lying at the bund, or at anchor in the stream, and the thousand junks which crowd the waterways, seem barely sufficient for her gigantic commerce

Among the ghastly curiosities of Hankow, as of all big Chinese cities, are the coffin shops, which usually herd together in special quarters and are apt to use portions of the streets for their timber-yards. In them are seen the great cumbrous coffins, at times ten and even twelve feet in length, which Chinese custom demands, of all grades and prices, from highly polished lacquer with characters raised or incised in gold to the roughly put together shell in which the tired coolie takes his last sleep. Many of the more costly are ordered as filial gifts from children to parents, and from grand-children to grandparents, and take their lugubrious place, set up on end, among the decorations of the lofty vestibule by which rich men's houses are entered, and where they may rest for years. As a body may remain for months or years unburied, waiting for the decision of the geomancers as to an auspicious place and date for the interment, the coffins are very carefully constructed, and are either lacquered or treated with the celebrated Ningpo varnish, which is practically impermeable both to air and moisture.

The varnishers and lacquerers also herd together, and their trade, which is based on the *Rhus vernicifera*, is a very import-ant one. The eating-houses—and from the number of them and the crowds which frequent them it might be supposed that nobody eats at home—the tobacconists, and the opium shops are scattered broadcast through the city, and each has its special *clientèle*.

Possibly there may have originally been a plan on which the

COFFINS AWAITING BURIAL.

HANKOW FROM HAN YANG.

Hankow streets were built, but it must have been outgrown for some centuries, and at present there is little suggestion of design; streets and alleys intersect each other in singular confusion, and only a practised hand can find any given point without irksome and delaying tergiversations. On the whole there is a tendency to arrive at the top of the river bank, where at low water (winter) a singular spectacle presents itself.

The Han, an opaque, yellow, rapid flood, 200 yards wide, lies from forty to sixty feet below. Its summer rises have carried away its banks on the Hankow side, and the dense mass of ill-looking houses which formerly stood, as is the wont of houses, on the ground, have been undermined, and are now propped up on what it would be flattery to call piles, for they are only slender and casual poles lashed together till the requisite length is gained, some leaning one way, some another, while the dwellings they upbear owe their continued existence to their involuntary mutual support, and to the pestilent habit which such ramshackle buildings have everywhere of hanging together. Thousands of the poorer class of coolies live in these precarious abodes, which, however, are less unsavoury than some, for they have fresh air below and innumerable holes in the floors for the easy disposal of refuse. In the summer of 1898 a great many of these dwellings were carried away with much loss of life.

Almost below these, on the mud slope above the river, are hundreds of mat huts, which have to be removed as the water rises. These are the miserable, peripatetic kennels of the very lowest dregs of the Chinese humanity of a large city. It is difficult to say how this large population lives. Doubtless the "odd jobs" which support it are mostly connected with junks, for below each house is moored some rotten leaky thing capable of floating, to which descent is made by iron spikes driven into the strongest of the piles. Here are the men who on these "odd jobs" perpetuate lives which are not worth living—the beggars, blind and seeing, with malformed and loathsome bodies; lepers with gaping sores and fingers and toes dropping off; the unsightly and unnatural who rely for their living on revolting the feelings of the passers-by; suffering women old and friendless, who prefer the free Bohemianism of beggary to the almshouse or refuge provided by Chinese charity; and hosts of others, the pariah *débris* of Hankow.

These wretched beings have one solace in life—the opium pipe—
and they starve themselves to procure it.

Flights of stone stairs, one of them at least of magnificent width
and appearance, always crowded with water carriers splashing the
contents of their pails, with coolies carrying burdens, and with
passengers hurrying to and from the ferries, lead from the bank to

FEMALE BEGGAR IN MAT HUT.

the water. Through every opening in the dilapidations the river
traffic is seen.

At least three miles of junks* and other craft lie two, three, and
four deep (to quote Lu Hew again), "like the teeth of a comb," of
all sizes, colours, and builds, having but two features in common : a

---

* "There is no harbour in the world where one may see so many craft as at Hankow.
Anchored in several rows, they reach for miles along the river banks."—Consul BULLOCK,
The Geography of China.

prominent eye on each side of the bows and sterns considerably higher than the bows. Every maritime province of China is represented on that crowded waterway. One could never weary of the spectacle. It represents the extent, the enterprise, the industry, and the conservatism of China, and with an unrivalled variety and picturesqueness.

No junks interested me more than the great passage and salt boats, from seventy to one hundred tons burthen, with their lofty, many-windowed sterns like the galleys of Henry IV., their tall single masts and their big brown-umber sails of knitted cane or coarse canvas extended by an arrangement of bamboo, looking heavy enough to capsize a liner, and with hulls stained and oiled into the similitude of varnished pine, as coming from that Upper Yangtze for which I was bound. There were huge junks from the Fukien province, bringing to me recollections of Foochow and the Min river, piled high with bamboos and poles, and extended to a preposterous width by masses of the same lashed on both sides, the buoyancy of the cargo permitting as little as five inches of freeboard, gaily painted and decorated junks from Canton, with rows of carefully tended plants on their high sterns, sombre craft from Tientsin and the north, junks from the Po-yang and Tungting lakes, nondescript craft from inland streams and canals, alert tenders to the big junks, lorchas, some of them foreign-owned, doing homage to Chinese nautical experience by their Chinese rig, rafts, with their inhabitants, *sampans* of all sizes, and huge junks heavily laden, crawling slowly down stream with their great sweeps, and the wild melancholy wail of the oarsmen— the Argonauts of Swatow or Ningpo.

People who think it witty to ridicule everything Chinese poke fun at these junks and their "pig-tailed," long-coated crews, but the handling of them is masterly; in emergencies there is no confusion, every man obeys orders, and the ease with which these apparently ungainly craft tack, with their complicated arrangement of bamboos stiffening their vast sails, is absolutely beautiful.

The streets of Hankow, like those of most of the large trading cities, present a perpetual series of dramas. In them hundreds of people eat, sleep, bargain, gamble, cook, spin, and quarrel, while they are the sculleries, sinks, and sewers of a not inconsiderable portion of the population. They are the playgrounds of the children, if that can be called play which consists merely in rolling and tumbling over each other after the manner of puppies, the elder among them watching with greedy eyes the bargains of their seniors, eager cupidity and ofttimes precocious depravity written on faces which should be young.

Itinerant barbers pursue their essential calling, carrying their apparatus on their backs, and perambulating the streets with a curious cry. Their business is an enormous one in China, where

A TRAVELLING RESTAURANT.

hair is regarded as an enemy to be battled with. Once a week at least, the Chinese, however poor, must have the front and middle of his head smoothly shaven, or he looks like a convict, his face, I cannot say his beard, and his eyebrows, if he has any, trimmed, when he emerges from the barber's hands a respectable member of the community. All these operations are conducted publicly under the eaves and gateways and at the street corners, with much shampooing, and dexterous manipulation of oddly shaped razors, which scrape rather than cut, the face of the client nevertheless wearing a look of serene contentment. The fees of the barber are an important item in the expenditure of a Chinese coolie.

Many other industries are carried on in the streets, and the Government is lenient to all encroachments, so long as a mandarin's chair and retinue can pass unhindered. Government is represented in this *congeries* of cities by *yamens*, with picturesque curved roofs, and gateways with a certain stateliness, and courtyards usually filled with petitioners and their agents, prisoners awaiting trial, *yamen* runners, who, from three to six hundred or more in number, hang about official residences; while clerks and writers carrying papers and dressed in expensive brocaded silks move haughtily among the common herd. The inner court is concealed by a plastered brick screen, on which is emblazoned in brilliant colouring a bold representation of the dragon of the Dragon Empire.

Government in its military aspect is made apparent by a number of soldiers, usually in picturesque but stagey and unserviceable uniforms, in which blue and carnation-red predominate, who are encountered in the streets hanging round opium or tobacco shops, or gambling for *cash*, or attached slightly to some procession, or lounging at the city gates, or swaggering at the great entrance to the *yamen*, under the curse of abounding leisure. Their somewhat mediæval military equipments are supplemented with additions laughably grotesque, long fans attached to their girdles, and big paper umbrellas, occasionally gaudily decorated with mythical monsters, but oftener with proverbs or Confucian maxims.

Hurry, crowds, business, the absence of the feminine element, and noise, are common to all Chinese cities. Drums and gongs are beaten, cymbals are clashed, bells ring, muskets are fired, crackers are exploded everywhere, beggars wail, there are street cries innumerable, the din of bargaining tongues rises high, and the air is full of the discordant roar of a multitude.

In the centre of such surroundings, within hearing of the ceaseless din, and within smelling of the foul and ancient odour which pervades the city, the colony of English Wesleyan missionaries has placed itself in close contact with its medical missionary hospitals and dispensaries for men and women, its home and school for the blind, and its other missionary agencies, and not far off in a Chinese house, and living and dressing as a native, was one of the noblest and most sympathetic missionaries who ever sought the welfare of the Chinese, the Rev. David Hill, who died of typhus fever shortly after my first visit, genuinely mourned by those for whom he had sacrificed himself.

CHAPTER VIII.

HANKOW TO ICHANG

I LEFT Hankow, without seeing a gleam of sunshine upon it, by the deck-over-deck, American-built, stern-wheel steamer *Chang-wo*. She had some hundreds of Chinese and two China Inland missionaries on board below, and her very limited saloon accommodation was taken up by four Canadian missionaries returning to SZE CHUAN, and the inevitable baby. They had fled nearly a year before, after the destruction of their houses in the riots. I was greatly indebted to two of them. I had a cabin directly over the boiler. The floor was very hot, and even with the window open I could not get the temperature below 74°, and they gave me their cool room in exchange.

The captain was kind and genial. He let me tone unlimited photographic prints in the saloon, ignoring the dishes and buckets involved in the process, and the engineer provided an unlimited supply of condensed water, free both from Yangtze mud and from the alum used to precipitate it. But he had a unique affluence of bad language, which neither the presence of clergy nor women sufficed to check, and which was brought out with slow, thrilling, and emphatically damnatory deliberation on the many occasions on which we ran on shoals.

I had abundant occupation in writing, printing and toning photographs, learning a little from Mr. Endacott of the region for which I was finally bound, taking walks below past the Chinese cabins, where the inmates were reclining in the bliss of opium smoking, the faint, sickly smell of the drug drifting out at the open doors, or on the upper deck to watch the fleets of strange junks through which the *Chang-wo* steamed, howling and bellowing. Lumbering, unhandy craft they look, but they are handled with consummate skill.

The Great River was at its lowest winter level, and its shores, so far as one could see them under these circumstances, were most monotonous, and then it was midwinter. We steamed for hours between high, grey mud-banks, ceaselessly eaten away by the rush of the current, gaining little beyond an idea of the vastness of the level country, the depth of the grey alluvium, and the extent of the commerce of which the Yangtze is the highway. To get deep water we were often close under the right bank, and had the *divertissement* of being pelted with mud and with such names as " foreign devils " and " foreign dogs," an amusement which one would have supposed would have palled upon the peasants in the years during which these steamers have been running.

Our progress was not rapid, owing to shoals and changes in the channel, and the *Chang-wo* anchored at night. Then, during the day, there was the frequent grinding sound of running on gravel, or the thud of touching a bank, or the buzz of a whirlpool created by ourselves in steering clear of a junk. All day long resounded the melancholy note of the Chinese leadsman calling out the soundings, varied by the sharp " Hard a-port ! " or " Hard a-starboard ! " of a European officer as some peril presented itself, or the low and terrible maledictions of the captain on all and sundry, as far back as the builders of the ship. The grounding was exasperating, losing us two hours at times. Quick as thought at every touch on shoal or mud-bank down clattered the anchor, and various skilled operations followed, which invariably resulted successfully, but at one time the navigation was so intricate, and the water shoaled for such a long distance, that, after getting off a bank after two hours' tedious work, the steam launch was lowered to sound ahead, and direct us by signal flags.

Still it was hard to get up any excitement over these mishaps, even though the captain enlarged on the risk of losing the wheel or the rudder. Very little diversified the monotony of the winter voyage, but when I returned in summer, and could look over the banks, a vast population and innumerable industries were to be seen.

Yo-chow, a fortified monastery on a high promontory, once a place of considerable domination, and Yo-chow Fu, a large city near the junction of the Tungting Lake with the Yangtze, are the chief features of the featurelessness. This lake, a vast but imperfectly known sheet of water, surrounded by towns and villages, is of very great importance to the trade of the rich HUNAN province.

The farther route lies among embanked watercourses, great flats of muddy land receiving alluvial accretions from each summer's floods, and shallow meres with a wealth of wild fowl I never saw equalled, and abounding in fish, both fish and fowl being snared in great numbers by the nearly amphibious inhabitants, by many ingenious devices born of Chinese poverty.

Among the many varieties of boats are pairs of large *sampans*, lashed together, and at once kept apart and connected by platforms, on which reeds are piled to the height of a haystack, the lowest part of the centre of the load being recessed and shored up for a sleeping and cooking place. These reeds, which are a speciality of the Yangtze for 900 miles from its mouth, and attain a height of fifteen feet and over, are as invaluable to the people of this region as are the vast reed beds of the Liao to those of Southern Manchuria, furnishing them with building, roofing, and fencing material, as well as with fuel. Quite a large part of the internal freighting business of this low-lying level is the transport of these reeds on sledges over the marshy ground, on four-wheeled wooden trucks, which might be called "trollies" if they had rails to run on, some dragged by men, and others by the quaint, appropriate water buffalo, as well as loaded on coupled boats.

In the late afternoon of the third day from Hankow we anchored in the rushing mid-stream of the Yangtze, abreast of the treaty port of Sha-shih (Sand Market), opened by the treaty of Shimonoseki in 1895, and, as was fitting, first occupied by the Japanese. I was not prepossessed with the city either on the upward or downward journey. Communication with the shore is tedious, difficult, and not free from risk. Several of the boats which attempted to reach us were unable to "catch on," and even a lighter, failing to make fast, was carried far astern and did not work her way back till the next morning.

At low water Wan-cheng Ti, the great dyke, averaging 150 feet in width at the bottom, and twenty-five at the top, twenty feet high on the river side, and forty on the land side, which follows the Yangtze for twenty-five miles to the west of

Sha-shih and thirty to the east, effectually conceals the town from view, only a seven-storeyed pagoda and the curved roofs of temples and *yamens* appearing above the heads of the crowds which throng the roadway on the dyke-top.

China must have been a greater country when this great public work was constructed than she is now, for this dyke where it protects Sha-shih is a noble, three-tiered, stone-faced construction, on the top of which are remnants of a stone balustrade; and broad, stately flights of stairs are let into the stonework at intervals, each tier of stairs being about twelve feet high. It must have been fully as impressive as the superb walls on the Chia-ling at Paoning Fu, which still remain a thing of grandeur and beauty.

Sha-shih is pre-eminently and abominably dirty; and on this fine embankment dirt is in the ascendant, and dirt and bad smells assail the traveller on landing. Much of the refuse of the crowded city at the back is thrown over the river wall, accumulating in heaps which at low water conceal half of it. Steep steps lead up these vile mounds, and appear to be preferred to the stone stairs covered with slippery, black ooze. Below the heaps lie from one to two thousand junks with crews on an average of ten men each, and frequently the junkman's wife and family in addition, giving an average floating population of 10,000.

Beggars' huts encroach on the top of the embankment; and when I write that hosts of gaunt, sore-eyed, mangy dogs, and black pigs each with a row of bristles standing up along his lean, curved back, and beggars, one mass of dirt and sores, are always routing and delving in the heaps, the reader will not be surprised that I did not find Sha-shih prepossessing. It has always had the reputation of being hostile to foreigners, which hostility expressed itself unpleasantly in a riot in May, 1898, when the China merchant's, S. N. Co.'s premises ashore and afloat, the new buildings of the Imperial Customs, and the Japanese Consulate were destroyed. The three steamship agencies in 1898 practically withdrew their agencies from the port, the British Consulate was withdrawn, Japan has taken no steps towards occupying her concession, foreign trade and passenger traffic have fallen off materially, and so far the port must be pronounced a failure.

A noisy and dirty rabble follows a stranger; mud is thrown—and, as is the fashion of mud, some of it sticks—bad names are bandied about freely; the foreigner is conscious of a ferment which may or may not result in more active annoyance, and, after being nearly suffocated by the ill-mannered and malodorous crowd in a fruitless attempt to see the lions of the city, he retreats not reluctantly to his steamer, which, in my case, was detained by heavy fog until noon of the next day.

But Sha-shih, though unprepossessing and unlikely to fulfil

CHINESE SOLDIERS.
(*From a Chinese Drawing.*)

the expectations formed of it as a treaty port, is one of the most important cities on the Yangtze; nor is its importance a thing of yesterday. Two miles above it lies the *Fu*, or prefecture, of Ching-chou, of which it may be regarded as the trading suburb. All around are the remains of fortresses and cities, mounds, earthworks, and look-out terraces, ancient in the days when our fathers were painted savages, marking the sites of the strongholds and capital of the powerful kings of Ch'u in the early days of Chinese authentic history.

Ching-chou Fu is grandly fortified, and is surrounded by a wide canal of great depth. It is the seat of a *taotai*, or intendant of a circuit, which includes Ichang, eighty miles off, and though not a provincial capital, is of such importance that it has a Manchu garrison of 12,000 men (?), the largest Manchu force south of Peking, the Manchu military colony numbering 40,000 souls. The whole organisation of this colony is military, and it

MILITARY OFFICER.
(*From a Chinese Drawing.*)

is kept separate from the civil population. Otherwise it has no interest, except that the women have unbound feet and wear long outer dresses, and that the men look lazy and demoralised. Besides this large garrison there are river and lake police, and a small body of militia under the command of a provincial general, and a thousand HUNAN "braves" trained in the rudiments of drill under a brigade-general. "Braves" are fighting mobile troops, whose superior qualities command superior pay. They receive four or five taels a month, while the common provincial soldier only gets one tael fifty cents. Now, as formerly, Ching-chou is regarded as one of the most important strategical positions in China.

It has an estimated Chinese and Manchu population of 100,000, and Sha-shih an estimated population of 80,000, a temporary one averaging 8000, and a boating one (as mentioned before) of, at the very least, 10,000, nearly 200,000 in all. The distance to Ichang is 80 miles by land and 100 by water. To Hankow, with which the great trade of Sha-shih is done, it is 300 miles by water, and would be 135 by land, if there were land! No land carriage is possible, except in seasons of drought, much of that which poses as *terra firma* on the maps being meres, relapsed agricultural lands, morasses, shallow lakes, fens, watercourses, and reed swamps, most productive wherever areas are drained and embanked.

Among the interesting features of Sha-shih are a ninth century seven-storeyed pagoda, with eight faces, each face recessed on each storey, and containing a stone image of Buddha, and a dark and foul staircase, leading to a remarkable view from the top, and the imposing halls of the trade guilds, of which I failed to see the superb interiors, owing to the clamour and pressure of the rabble. In Sha-shih, as everywhere else, these guildhalls serve the purposes of banqueting halls, temples, and even theatres at times. They number thirteen, named from the provinces or cities of which their members are natives, and each has its patron deity. There are several charitable institutions, including two orphanages, one of which receives 220 orphans annually, and boards them out until the age of sixteen.

Benevolence was considerably strained in the winter of 1896–97, when thousands of refugees flying from famine in SZE CHUAN received unwholesome and insanitary shelter in mat sheds outside Sha-shih, where a terrible and uninvestigated epidemic broke out, and was carried into the city and neighbourhood, so that during the spring and summer it was estimated that 17,000 perished in the city only. Nearly all the refugees, after being kept alive chiefly by the charitable, died, and were decently buried by those societies which in every Chinese city undertake this sacred duty for the bodies of strangers, and for those of the very poor. I am always glad to call attention to Chinese charities, for the continual reiteration of facts on the other side only tends to produce an unfair and one-sided impression of the Chinese character.

Superstition had its say regarding this baleful epidemic, which unfortunately never came under skilled observation. It was attributed to a malignant black bird, of vast size, which was said to hover over the city. It had ten heads, but one had been cut

A FISHERMAN AND PLUNGE NET.
(*From a Chinese Drawing.*)

off, and the severed neck bled profusely and continuously, and wherever the blood fell disease and death followed. A day was set apart for the propitiation of this malignant fowl, and fire crackers were burned before the door of every house.*

The fish market is an excellent, though an uncleanly one, nets, angling, cormorants, lines with hooks, and great frame nets lowered and raised by pulleys, all being employed. Sturgeon, weighing from 500 to 700 pounds, are caught off the port. There

* Foreign Office Report No. 2086, May, 1898.

are no unusual articles of diet to be seen, except Japanese sea-weed, which is largely consumed in the belief that it counteracts the bad effects of the sulphur fumes proceeding from coal fires!

The Roman Catholics and three Protestant missions hold property in the town, but mission-work has to be conducted very cautiously owing to the strongly anti-foreign feeling. There are seventeen foreigners, including the Japanese consul, but not one foreign merchant, though two or three foreign firms have agencies.

Foreign articles, few of which find any place in the customs returns, are to be bought in the shops. Very many of them are Japanese, owing to the energy or, as our merchants call it, the peddling and huckstering instincts of the Japanese traders, who through their trained Chinese-speaking agents find out what the people want and supply it to them. The cotton gins largely used in the neighbourhood are of Japanese make, and cheap clocks, kerosene lamps, towels, handkerchiefs, cotton umbrellas, cheap hardware, soaps, fancy articles of all descriptions, and cotton goods are poured into Sha-shih by that alert empire. Among English goods are rugs, blankets, and preserves and tinned milk and fruits. Most of the dealers in "assorted notions" are Cantonese.

Cotton cloth, raw cotton, silk fabrics, and hides are the staple export of Sha-shih. There are few local industries besides the weaving of cotton. Pewter, "hubble bubbles," household pewter ware, long bamboo pipes, not fashionable "down the river," coarse silk twist for plaiting into the ends of queues, boiling salt out of old salt bags, a smoky and smelly process carried on owing to the monstrous price of Government salt, brick and tile making, and furniture-making, specially of carved and gilded bedsteads and cabinets, showy but somewhat trashy, I think exhaust the list. The annual export of raw cotton is estimated at 9,000,000 pounds. Enormous quantities of it arrive to be woven at Sha-shih into a strong, durable, white cloth, fifteen and twelve inches wide, which I saw all over SZE CHUAN, and of which at least 20,000,000 pounds are annually exported. Samples of this make and of English cottons were frequently shown to me by the women in SZE CHUAN villages, with a scornful laugh at the expense of the latter.

Sha-shih is called "The Manchester of China." In it this comparatively indestructible cloth is graded, packed, and shipped away, the adjacent country being the greatest centre of weaving in the empire. There are 110 dealers in raw cotton in the city, and 114 shops deal in native cotton cloth, and there is a daily market for its sale in the early mornings. Silks, both plain and figured, are also produced in great quantities, and satin bed-covers, which are used all over China. Rich satins are also woven for altar cloths, bed and door hangings, and cushions.

Sha-shih was the first point on my journey at which I encountered the money difficulties which press so severely on the traveller in China. My broken silver was of little use, and my dollars of none, copper *cash* and *cash* notes forming the entire currency of the port. The merchants and shopkeepers calculate silver in Sha-shih taels, which vary from 6 to 11 per cent. from the standard Haikwan, Hankow, and Shanghai taels, and the exchange between *cash* and silver varies daily. There are about 130 *cash* shops in the town, nearly all of them issuing notes. Notes for 1000 *cash* abound, mostly issued by small Manchu shops in Ching-chou, for which change can hardly be obtained in Ching-chou itself. The *cash* shops issue notes for 1000, 5000, and 10,000 *cash*, but though those issued by the banks and pawnshops are current for thirty miles round, they are worthless at Ichang, as I found to my inconvenience. Each hundred *cash* being strung separately on a wisp of straw or paper, and every string having to be counted over and examined for small or spurious *cash*, the purchase of 10,000, or about 23s. 3d., is a weighty matter in various senses, and is apt to take from two to three hours, including the time spent in bargaining about "the touch" of sycee silver procured at Hankow.

I have dwelt so long, albeit so superficially, on Sha-shih because it is the most important of the treaty ports opened since the war, and because nothing is known of it by the general reader. Certainly the *couleur de rose* expectations of an outburst of foreign trade have not been realised, nor, I think, are likely to be, unless the methods of commerce on the Yangtze undergo a radical change. The total trade for 1898 was only £24,444 in value, against £47,509 in 1897, but these figures only apply to the exports and imports passing through the Imperial Maritime

Customs. For Sha-shih has not only one, but several, "back doors" through which her enormous commerce is poured, the principal one being a canal to Hankow, called at its western end the Pien-Ho, and which is not only free from the risks of the river, but is from sixty to seventy miles shorter. Altogether several routes to Hankow are practicable, either wholly by canal and lake, or partly by road and partly by canal, the water route being available during the whole year.

The Chinese are rigid conservatives. Junks are always obtainable, and wait the convenience of their hirers, and their freight and passenger charges are much lower than those of the steamers. Certainly if I had not been hurried I should have preferred a junk! The canals pass through towns which offer facilities for both trading and dawdling, so that, although there are two *likin* stations on the canal route to Hankow, the native trader finds that the junk has many advantages over the steamer. *Likin* is charged on all goods landed at Sha-shih, and the Imperial Customs duty is, in fact, only an additional tax levied on goods conveyed by steamer. These inland routes are of the greatest commercial importance.

Besides the canal and lake routes to Hankow, the great delta between the Yangtze and the Han is spotted with lakes connected by waterways, and in other directions there are available roads connecting Sha-shih with important trading cities. Among these are the great southern highway from SZE CHUAN, and the great north road leading by the Han and over the mountains to the capital of SHENSI, from which mule carts and mule litters, conveyances hardly known in Central China, descend into the Yangtze plain.

All that region lies below the summer level of its rivers, and it is a problem on which no light is likely to be shed why a country so oddly circumstanced should have become a populous and powerful kingdom at a very early date, and why its chief city has continued to be one of the most important of military positions and of commercial centres in the Chinese Empire.

Returning to the river voyage, after passing Yungtze, the western mountains appeared for the first time. The scenery changed rapidly. The river narrowed; some of its promontories were boulder-strewn; low, wooded knolls appeared above pleasant

agricultural country, green with young wheat; and hills of conglomerate and limestone replaced the grey alluvium through
which we had been steaming for nearly 1000 miles.   Although
much detained by fogs, we reached the Tiger Teeth gorge, ten
miles below Ichang, in the early afternoon of the fifth day from
Hankow.   This gorge, which hardly deserves so thrilling a name,
is a channel two miles long and about 700 yards wide, in the
easternmost of those ranges through which the Yangtze has
forced itself on its way to create the Great Plain.   This range,
rising to a height of 2600 feet, is broken up into peaks, one of
which is crowned by an inaccessible-looking Buddhist monastery,
this building, a fine pagoda, and great masses of conglomerate
being the only noteworthy features until we reached Ichang in the
glorifying light of a late afternoon sun.

CHAPTER IX.

ICHANG

UNLIKE Sha-shih, the first view of Ichang, opened to foreign trade in 1887, is very attractive. At low water it stands high on the river bank, on a conglomerate cliff above a great level sandbank, but in summer it loses whatever dignity it gains by height, and is nearly on the river level. A walled city of 35,000 people, gate towers, and temple roofs rise above the battlements and the mass of houses. Between the city and the river is a straggling suburb fairly clean, composed of small retail shops. On the river bank are the buildings and go-downs of the Imperial Customs, including the Commissioner's house and large garden, dainty dwellings for the staff of twelve Europeans, and a tennis ground, with a fine bund and broad flight of stone stairs in front. Near these are the large houses of the Scotch Church Mission, and beyond a new plain building put up by the China Inland Mission. The Roman Catholic buildings are the first to attract attention from the water. There are a few foreign hongs and godowns, and a customs pontoon moored in the stream. Behind the British Consulate, a substantial new building with a tennis lawn used for weekly hospitalities, breezy hills, much covered with grave mounds, roll up towards a mountainous region, and below, the Yangtze, with its perpetual rush and current, swirls in a superb flood half a mile wide.

At the time of my first visit a British gunboat, a wholesome and not unneeded influence, lay at anchor opposite the town.

The imposing feature of Ichang to my thinking is its multitude of junks of every build and size, lying closely packed along its shore for a mile and a half, their high castellated sterns making a goodly show. There lay in hundreds big SZE CHUAN junks, strongly built for the rapids, their stained and oiled woodwork looking like varnished pine, the junks bound up the river with their masts erect, the masts of those which had come down lashed along their sides. Big passenger boats there were too, for all passengers, as well as cargo, bound up the Yangtze must "change" at Ichang.

On the opposite side are cliffs along the river front, backed by hills and fine mountains, among which are fantastic peaks and pyramids, one of them known as Pyramid Hill, exactly resembling the Great Pyramid in shape, and said to have the same height and area as its prototype. Its peculiar position and form were supposed or believed by the local geomancers to interfere with that mystery of mysteries the FUNG SHUI, and thus to act injuriously on the prosperity of Ichang, so the powers that were, it is said, built a monastery opposite, on the Ichang side of the river, at great expense, the priests of which have as their special business to pray that the disastrous influences of Pyramid Hill may be warded off from the city.

The dead who people the hillsides far outnumber the living, and their abodes having the aspect of exaggerated mole-hills, lack the frequent stateliness of Chinese places of interment in some of the other provinces, being mostly circular mounds of earth and sod kept together by stones rudely built into them.

Just before I arrived many of these stones had served a sinister purpose, and had been used as ammunition. On entering the house of Mr. Schjöltz, the Commissioner of Customs, who was my host at Ichang and later at Chungking, I was surprised to see cairns of stones which were nearly as big as a human head both in the hall and outside it, which had been collected in the dining and drawing-rooms after their windows had been smashed in an anti-foreign riot a few days before. During some festivities the Chinese cook of the gunboat *Esk* accidentally shot a very popular Chinese officer. On this there was naturally a great ebullition of fury, specially as the cook was not given up to the Chinese authorities when they demanded him. The Customs buildings were guarded by Chinese soldiers, but the staff, who are all efficiently drilled, did sentry duty at night. This was the least serious of the many riots which have occurred in the treaty ports on the Yangtze in recent years.

There are now about forty-five foreigners in Ichang, about

THE TABLET OF CONFUCIUS.

twenty of them being missionaries. It is to be supposed that all of these have a sufficiency of serious occupation. Their amusements consist chiefly in tennis, shooting, and boating picnics to some of the picturesque ravines and rock temples off the main river, and to the Ichang gorge. The British Consul, Mr. Holland, and Mr. Woodruff, the Commissioner of Customs, throw their spacious gardens open constantly, and by the exercise of much hospitality do their best to alleviate what, it must be confessed, is the great monotony of life in a small and isolated foreign community.

Unless people are students or specialists or hobbyists of some description, as I think every man and woman should be who goes to live in so very foreign a country as China, amusements are apt to pall. The winter evenings are long and dull, and those of summer hot and mosquito-infested. People soon gauge the mental and social possibilities of new-comers, and know exactly what their neighbours think on every subject which can arise, and have sounded their intellectual depths and *shallows*, and the arrival of a stranger and of the mail boat and the changes in the customs staff are the chief varieties in life. That this and several other of these small communities "get on" with little apparent friction is surely much to their credit. Some say that it is because they are chiefly masculine!

In summer large vessels can make fast under the bund, but at low water they anchor in mid-stream, and how to get goods with due regard to economy from the steamers to the godowns when there is an average difference of forty feet between the summer and winter levels of the river is somewhat of a problem. Though in itself only a comparatively poor town in a mountainous country, the total value of the trade of Ichang for 1898 amounted to £2,298,437. All goods going west have to be transhipped at this port, and nearly all goods bound east, so that it is one of the busiest places on the river. It is a curious fact that, with enormous coal-fields only three or four days away, the river steamers 1000 miles from the sea are burning Japanese coal!

Ichang is the headquarters of a large Roman mission. Its head, Bishop Benjamin, with whom I had the pleasure of spending one afternoon, has been sixteen years in his present position without even a visit to Shanghai. His large, lofty room, though furnished with all absolute necessaries, is bare and severe, and

contains nothing on which the eye can pleasurably rest. The
Bishop is a most genial elderly man, with much charm of manner,
thick iron-grey hair, and an unclerical moustache. As we walked
down the lanes to the orphanage numbers of Chinese children,
unmistakably delighted to see him, ran up to him, kissing his hands
and struggling for positions in which they could hold on to his
robe.

With him I visited the orphanage and hospital, both under the
charge of French and Belgian sisters, comely women with much
grace and geniality of manner, in which the loving, all-embracing
maternal instinct finds its winning expression. The hospital, which
is on the ground floor, was crowded, indeed overcrowded, and, as
is usual in Roman hospitals in China, the doctor and much of the
medical treatment were Chinese, the aid of the foreign doctor (a
medical missionary) being called in in surgical cases.

The orphanage is a large building, with very lofty, well-ventilated
rooms, constructed for four hundred, but there were only eighteen
girls in it, who are instructed in the Christian faith, and in em-
broidery and other industrial occupations. The Bishop told me
that the Chinese do not, as formerly, bring orphans and foundlings
in numbers to their keeping ; indeed, I gathered that in Ichang at
least the day for this is past. I can only hazard a guess at the
reasons. These may be the anti-foreign spirit which has been
laboriously stirred up recently ; the increasing competition of
orphanages founded by charitable Chinese ; the partial disappointment with the temporal results of conversion ; and perhaps,
above all, the excessive mortality which prevails in these institutions, very much owing to the fact that the infants are brought to
them in great numbers either dying or suffering from disease,
or in such a feeble and emaciated state that they are unable to
assimilate their food. This mortality seems a matter of thankful-
ness rather than regret to the pious sisters, one of whom elsewhere,
in speaking to me of a mortality of 1600 in the late summer, said
with emotion, " So many, thank God, safe."

Besides the Bishop and his priest secretary there are French
and Chinese fathers, a French professor, and a seminary with eight
students, who study the Chinese classics and philosophy for ten
years and theology for seven. These Roman missionaries appear
to rely for the conversion of adults chiefly on native agency. A

Belgian priest, who called on me, claimed 3000 converts in a region above the gorges, where he had worked for eleven years. It is well known that one cause of the successes of the Roman missionaries is the assistance given by them to litigants, and the pressure brought to bear upon magistrates at the instance of the French Minister in Peking in legal cases in which his co-religionists are concerned. This Catholic priest mentioned to me, as among the many trials of his missionary vocation, the case of a village in which nearly all the inhabitants placed themselves under Christian instruction with a view to baptism. These villagers had a suit against another village in which the possession of a certain piece of land was the point in dispute. French influence was brought to bear, and they gained their case, let us believe justly, after which they returned *en masse* to their idolatrous practices.

My Belgian visitor, in very vivid language, depicted the sufferings of educated men from the deprivations of their lives, and specially from the absolute solitude in which he and others are placed, living in one room of low-class Chinese houses. He was obviously a man of much culture and refinement, and felt the whole life acutely—the dark and filthy houses, the dirty food, the unceasing noisy talk in a foreign tongue, the lack of real privacy and quiet, the ingratitude of the Chinese, and, more than all, his own failure to love them. This, though my first, was not my last glimpse of the anguish of loneliness which these Roman missionaries endure. " Madness would be the certain result," my visitor said, " but for the sustaining power of God, and the certainty that one is doing His work."

As I shall not return to the subject of Roman missions, I will refer briefly to four of the causes, in my opinion, of their undoubtedly growing unpopularity in SZE CHUAN and elsewhere, in spite of the assistance given to Christian litigants previously referred to.

1. The exorbitant indemnity, out of all proportion to the losses sustained, demanded and obtained by M. Gerard, then French Minister at Peking, for damage done to mission property during the riots in SZE CHUAN in 1895.

2. The claim of the Roman hierarchy [now conceded] to be placed on a level in position with the higher mandarins as to the number of their chair-bearers, etc., and the amount of per-

sonal reverence exacted by the clergy from a people essentially
democratic.

3. The non-admission of the heathen into Roman churches
during the celebration of mass and other services, while the
secrecy which attends the administration of the last rites of the
Church is undoubtedly obnoxious to the lower orders among the
Chinese, who have no conception of privacy.

4. The opposite methods pursued by the Protestants of all
denominations since their settlement in the far west a few years
ago are doubtless working against the practices of the Roman
missionaries.

On the other hand, it is but just to say that the Chinese appreciate the celibacy, poverty, and asceticism of the Roman clergy.
Every religious teacher, with one notable exception, who has made
his mark in the East has been an ascetic, and when Orientals
begin to seek after righteousness, rigid self-mortification is the
method by which they hope to attain it.

Wherever I have met with Roman missionaries I have found
them living either like Bishop Benjamin and Bishop Meitel
of Seoul, and like the sisters in Seoul, Peking, Ichang, and elsewhere, in bare, whitewashed rooms, with just enough tables and
wooden chairs for use, or in the dirt, noise, and innumerable discomforts of native houses of the lower class, personally attending
on the sick, and in China, Chinese in life, dress, style, and ways,
rarely speaking their own language, knowing the ins and outs
of the districts in which they live, their peculiarities of trade, and
their political and social condition. Lonely men, having broken
with friends and all home ties for the furtherance of Christianity,
they live lives of isolation and self-sacrifice, forget all but the
people by whom they are surrounded, identify themselves with
their interests, and have no other expectation but that of living
and dying among them.

It must be admitted that the Chinese contrast this life of self-
surrender with that of large numbers of Protestant missionaries
living in comfortable, and what seem to them wealthy, homes in
the treaty ports, surrounded by as many of the amenities of life
as are usual in the simpler homes in foreign settlements, and with
wives, children, friends, and society, not very often, as in the case
of the Wesleyan missionaries at Hankow, living in the native cities

among the Chinese, and going home with their families for a year or more once in five or seven years.*

While admiring the self-denial and devotion of the Roman missionary priests, I do not express any opinion as to rival methods and merits, but only state facts which are forced upon every traveller, and purpose to return to the subject of Protestant missions later.

* It is usual for the missionaries of the China Inland Mission and for those of the SZE CHUAN mission of the C.M.S. to live in Chinese houses actually among the city populations, a course which is considerably criticised on grounds of health and safety.

CHAPTER X.

THE UPPER YANGTZE

I WAS very impatient to be off on my western journey, but after the boat was engaged, the tracking ropes examined by experts at the customs, and my few stores—tea, curry powder, and rice—had been bought, I had four days of "hanging on." The boatmen made various excuses for delay. One day it was that the *lao-pan*, or master, had not advanced them money wherewith to buy stores; another was a feast day; a third must be spent in paying debts or they would be detained; and on the fourth they said they must visit certain temples and make offerings for the success of the voyage! The weather was raw, grim, and sunless. I had had a fire day and night in my room at the customs, and a fireless, draughty boat was a shivery prospect, but things usually turn out far better than either prophecies or expectations, and this voyage was no exception.

I was fortunate in being able to take as far as Wan Hsien Mr. Owen Stevenson, of the China Inland Mission, who had had ten years' experience in Yunnan, accompanied by Mr. Hicks, a new arrival; and they engaged the boat for the next stage to Chungking, which gave Mr. S. some little hold on the *lao-pan*, who was a mean and shifty person, coerced into evil ways by a terrible wife, a virago, whose loud tongue was rarely silent, who had beaten her eldest boy to death a few months before, and of whom the remaining boy—a child of eight—lived in piteous terror, lest he should share the same fate. This family of five lived in the high stern cabin, but were apt to run over into parts of the boat which should have been *tabu*. The crew consisted of a pilot who is responsible for the navigation, a steersman, a cook, and sixteen trackers and rowers.

The boat itself was a small house-boat of about twenty tons, flat-bottomed, with one tall mast and big sail, a projecting rudder,

and a steering sweep on the bow. Her "passenger accommodation" consisted of a cabin the width of the boat, with a removable
front, opening on the bow deck, where the sixteen boatmen rowed,
smoked, ate, and slept round a central well in which a preter-
naturally industrious cook washed bowls, prepared food, cooked
it, and apportioned it all day long, using a briquette fire. At
night uprights and a mat roof were put up, and the toilers, after
enjoying their supper, and their opium pipes at the stern, rolled
themselves in wadded quilts and slept till daybreak. Passengers
usually furnish this cabin, and put up curtains and photographs,
and eat and sit there ; but I had no superfluities, and my "furniture" consisted only of a carrying-chair, in which it was very
delightful to sit and watch the grandeurs and surprises of the
river. But gradually the trackers and the skipper's family came
to over run this cabin, and I constantly found the virago with her
unwelcome baby girl, or a dirty, half-naked tracker in my chair,
and the eight-year-old boy spent much of his time crouching in a
corner out of reach of his mother's tongue and fist.

Abaft this were three small cabins, with windows "glazed" with
paper, and a passage down the port side from the stern to the bow,
on which I cannot say they "opened," for they were open (!), and a
partial privacy was only obtained by making a partition with
a curtain. Abaft these was the steersman's place, which was also a
kitchen and opium den, where my servant cooked, and where the
pilot and most of the crew were to be seen every night lying
on the floor beside their opium lamps, passing into felicity. Abaft
again, at a greater height, the skipper and his family lived. On
the roof there were hen coops and great coils of bamboo rope
for towing.

It was an old boat, and the owner was not a man of substance.
The paper on the windows was torn away; the window-frame
of the cabin in which I slept, ate, and carried on my various
occupations, had fallen out, the cracks in the partitions were half
an inch wide ; and as for many days the sun seldom shone and
the mercury hung between 38° and 43°, and hugging a charcoal
brazier was the only method of getting warm, and that a dubious
one, the earliest weeks were a chilly period.

On the afternoon of January 30th I embarked from the customs
pontoon much exhilarated by the prospect before me, but we only

crossed the river and lay all night in a tremendous noise among a number of big junks, the yells of the skipper's baby being heard above the din. This man excused this last delay in starting by sending word from the shore that he was waiting for the mandarin's permit, and would be ready to leave on the following daybreak.

I was up at daybreak not to lose anything, but hour after hour passed, and no *lao-pan* appeared, and at ten we started without him to meet him on the bank a few miles higher, when there was a tremendous row between him and the men. We were then in what looked like a mountain lake. No outlet was visible; mountains rose clear and grim against a dull grey sky. Snowflakes fell sparsely and gently in a perfectly still atmosphere. We cast off from the shore; the oars were plied to a wild chorus; what looked like a cleft in the rock appeared, and making an abrupt turn round a high rocky point in all the thrill of novelty and expectation, we were in the Ichang Gorge, the first and one of the grandest of those gigantic clefts through which the Great River, at times a mile in breadth, there compressed into a limit of from 400 to 150 yards, has carved a passage through the mountains.

The change from a lake-like stretch, with its light and movement, to a dark and narrow gorge black with the shadows of nearly perpendicular limestone cliffs broken up into buttresses and fantastic towers of curiously splintered and weathered rock, culminating in the " Pillar of Heaven," a limestone pinnacle rising sheer from the water to a height of 1800 feet, is so rapid as to bewilder the senses. The expression "*lost* in admiration" is a literally correct one. At once I saw the reason why the best descriptions, which are those of Captain Blakiston and Mr. A. Little, have a certain amount of "fuzziness," and fail to convey a definite picture.

With a strong, fair wind our sail was set; the creak and swish of the oars was exchanged for the low music of the river as it parted under our prow; and the deep water (from fifty to a hundred feet), of a striking bottle-green colour, was unbroken by a swirl or ripple, and slid past in a grand, full volume. The stillness was profound, enlivened only as some big junk with lowered mast glided past us at great speed, the fifty or sixty

ENTRANCE TO ICHANG GORGE.

men at the sweeps raising a wild chant in keeping with the scene. Scuds of snow, wild, white clouds whirling round pinnacles, and desolate snow-clothed mountains, apparently blocking further progress, added to the enchantment. Crevices in the rocks were full of maidenhair fern, and on many a narrow ledge clustered in profusion a delicate mauve primula, unabashed by the grandeur and the gloom. Streams tumbled over ledges at heights of 1000 feet. There are cliffs of extraordinary honeycombed rock, possibly the remains of the "potholes" of ages since, rock carved by the action of water and weather into shrines with pillared fronts, grottoes with quaint embellishments—gigantic old women gossiping together in big hats—colossal abutments, huge rock needles after the manner of Quiraing, while groups of stalactites constantly occur as straight and thick as small pines, supporting rock canopies festooned with maidenhair. Higher yet, surmounting rock ramparts 2000 feet high, are irregular battlemented walls of rock, perhaps twenty feet thick, and everywhere above and around are lofty summits sprinkled with pines, on which the snow lay in powder only, and "the snow clouds rolling dun" added to the sublimity of the scenery.

It was always changing, too. If it were possible to be surfeited with turrets, battlements, and cathedral spires, and to weary of rock phantasies, the work of water, of solitudes and silences, and of the majestic dark green flow of the Great River, there were besides lateral clefts, each with its wall-sided torrent, with an occasional platform green with wheat, on which a brown-roofed village nestled among fruit trees, or a mountain, bisected by a chasm, looking ready to fall into the river, as some have already done, breaking up into piles of huge angular boulders, over which even the goat-footed trackers cannot climb. Then, wherever the cliffs are less absolutely perpendicular, there are minute platforms partially sustaining houses with their backs burrowing into the rock, and their fronts extended on beams fixed in the cliff, accessible only by bolts driven into the rock, where the small children are tied to posts to prevent them from falling over, and above, below, and around these dwellings are patches of careful culture, some of them *not larger than a bath towel*, to which the cultivators lower themselves with ropes, and there are small openings occasionally, where deep-eaved houses cluster on the flat tops of rocky spurs among the exquisite plumage of groves of the golden and green bamboo, among oranges and pommeloes with their shining greenery, and straight-stemmed palms with their great fan-like leaves. Already in these sheltered places mauve primulas were blooming amidst a profusion of maidenhair, and withered clusters and tresses showed what the glory of the spring had been and was yet to be when the skirts of these spurs would be aflame with azaleas, and clematis, and great white and yellow roses, and all the wealth of flowers and trailers of which these were only the vestiges.

Another feature was boats large and small, and junks, some laboriously tracked or rowed like my own, when the wind failed, against the powerful stream, or descending, keeping the necessary steerage headway by crowds of standing men on the low deck, facing forwards, vigorously working great sweeps or *yulows*, five or ten at each, the gorge echoing all along its length to the rise and fall of the wild chants to which the rowers keep time and which are only endurable when softened by distance. After some hours of this region of magic and mystery, near sunset we emerged into open water, with broken picturesque shores, and at dusk tied up in a pebbly bay with glorious views of mountain and woodland, not far from the beautiful village of Nan-to, and the "needle" or "pillar" of heaven, well known to the dwellers in Ichang. The Ichang gorge is about twelve miles long; the Niu-kan, grander yet, about three; the Mitan about three and a half; the Wushan about twenty; and the Feng-hsiang, or "Wind Box," the last of the great gorges, about four. These are the great gorges.

I halted for Sunday in this lovely bay, an arrangement much approved of by the trackers, who employed the holiday in washing their clothes, smoking a double quantity of opium, and making a distracting noise, aggravated by the ceaseless yells of the boat baby, yells of an objectionable heredity and undisciplined naughtiness, which at first imposed on my ignorant sympathies. Nevertheless I luxuriated in the quiet which one can obtain when a babel is unintelligible.

In the afternoon the air was keen and bracing, the sky very blue, and the sunshine, after three weeks of gloom, had the charm of novelty. By the narrowest of paths I climbed a cleft down

THE AUTHOR'S BOAT.

which a crystal rivulet fell in leaps, pausing to rest now and then in deep pools fringed with a profuse growth of maidenhair. Minute plots for rice rose in steps along it; its banks were masses of ferns, roses, and clematis, the beautiful "Connecticut running fern" being as common as is the *Filix mas* with us. Higher rose the steep path; more glorious were the mountain views, more marvellous the forest of spires and pinnacles, more graceful the slender-stemmed palms, finer the contorted *Pinus sinensis*, more lush the dense foliage, bluer the sky above—not the China we picture to ourselves, of water, quaint bridges, curled roofs, and flat, formal gardens, but a Chinese Switzerland, sub-tropical, an intoxication, a dream!

In such scenery it was appropriate to come upon a deep-eaved *chalêt* of brown wood, with surroundings, models of cleanliness, shady with magnificent bamboo and orange groves, through which were seen far below deep ravines and picturesque brown villages, and the broken sparkle of the Great River, with snowy mountains on the other side, and from the junks on its broad breast the rowers' chant floated up harmoniously, and from the farmhouse, where the people seemed to be leading a rural, domestic life with guests about them, a man came out speaking politely, and hauled off a fierce dog, decidedly hostile to foreigners.

CHAPTER XI.

RAPIDS OF THE UPPER YANGTZE

O N inquiring of Mr. Endacott, at Ichang, his ideas of occupation on the upward voyage, his reply was, "People have enough to do looking after their lives." Certainly the perils of the rapids are great, and few people of whom I have heard have escaped without risks to life and loss or damage to property, either, like Consul Gardner, finding their boats disappear from under them, or like a missionary, who, coming down with his wife's coffin, came to grief, the coffin taking a lonely and ghastly voyage to a point far below, or like many others whom I met who reached their destinations minus their possessions in whole or in part. Signs of disaster abounded. Above and below every rapid, junkmen were encamped on shore under the mats of their junks, and the shore was spread with cotton drying. There were masts above water, derelicts partially submerged in quiet reaches, or on some sandy beach being repaired, and gaunt skeletons lay here and there on the rocks which had proved fatal to them. The danger signal is to be seen above and below all the worst rapids in the shape of lifeboats, painted a brilliant red and inscribed with characters in white: showy things, as buoyant as corks, sitting on the raging water with the vexatious complacency of ducks, or darting into the turmoil of scud and foam where the confusion is at its worst, and there poising themselves with the calm fearlessness of a perfect knowledge of every rock and eddy.

I have found that many of the deterrent perils which are arrayed before the eyes of travellers about to begin a journey are greatly exaggerated, and often vanish altogether. Not so the perils of the Yangtze. They fully warrant the worst descriptions which have been given of them. The risks are many and serious, and cannot be provided against by any forethought. The slightest error in judging of distance on the part of the pilot, any hampering of the

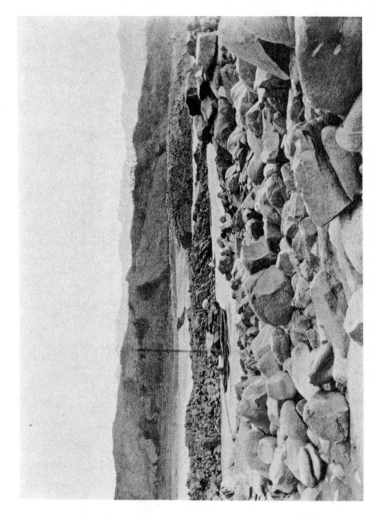

BED OF THE YANGTZE IN WINTER, TA-TAN RAPID.

bow-sweep, a tow-rope breaking, a submerged boulder changing its place, and many other possibilities, and life and property are at the mercy of a raging flood, tearing downwards at the rate of from seven to eleven miles an hour. I have no personal perils to narrate. A rock twice knocked a hole in the bottom which took a day to repair, and in a collision our bow-sweep was fractured, which led to a severe quarrel lasting half a day; this was all. I never became used to the rapids, and always felt nervous at the foot of each, and preferred the risk of fracturing my limbs among the great boulders and shining rock faces of the shores to spending hours in a turmoil, watching the fraying of the tow-ropes.

Before starting my boat's crew made offerings and vows at their favourite temples, and on the first evening they slew a fowl as an offering to the river god, and smeared its blood over the bow-sweep and the fore part of the boat. My preparations were to pack my plates, films, and general photographic outfit, journals, a few necessaries, and a few things of fictitious value, in a waterproof bag, to be carried by my servant, along with my camera, at each rapid where we landed.

The night at Lao-min-tze was too cold for sleep, and before dawn I heard the wild chant of the boatmen as great cargo boats, with from fifty to ninety rowers, swept down the stream. We untied at daylight, and, after passing the lovely village and valley of Nan-to, admired and wondered all day. It was one long glory and sublimity. A friend lately asked me if I whiled away the time by "walking on the river banks," thinking, doubtless, of the level towing paths of the meadows of the Thames and Ouse. The accompanying illustration shows the banks of the Yangtze below Wan Hsien at their best, and the pleasant possibilities for strolling!

The river-bed, there forty feet below its summer level, is an area of heaped, contorted rock-fragments, sharp-edged, through which one or more swirling streams or violent rapids pursue their course, the volume of water, even at that season, being tremendous. At its highest level these upper waters are practically non-navigable. Cliffs, mountain spurs, and noble mountains rise from this chaotic river-bed, and every sharp turn reveals some new beauty. The dark green pine is but a foil to the feathery foliage of the golden bamboo on the steep, terraced sides of tumbled heights; pleasant brown farmhouses are half seen among orange groves and orchards; grand temples, with noble specimens of the *Ficus religiosa* in their grounds, lighten hill and glen sides with their walls of imperial red. Then suddenly the scene changes into one of Tibetan grandeur and savagery, and the mountains approach the river in stupendous precipices, walling in almost fathomless water. We tied up the second night in the last crimson and violet of the sunset, where the river narrowed and progress looked impossible, and crags and pinnacles, snow-covered, rose above the dark precipices.

On that afternoon a red lifeboat suggested the first rapid, the Ta-tan, rather a *chipa* or race than a rapid, though I believe sufficiently perilous at half high water. I landed and scrambled up to the top for a three hours' wait, while three junks, each dragged up by fifty men, came up before mine, boats having to take their turn without favour. Even that ascent was an anxious sight, for sometimes the boat hung, ofttimes slipped back, and several times it looked doubtful whether the crowd of men attached to the tow-rope could get her up at all. This was the first sight of the trackers' villages, which are a marked feature of the Yangtze. Each boat carries enough men to pull her up against the strong stream, but at a rapid she needs many more, and during the navigation season coolies from long distances migrate to the river and put up mat huts as close to it as possible, to which dealers in food, tobacco, *samshu*, and opium at once gravitate, along with sellers of bamboo tow-ropes. Nor are rough amusements wanting. Rough, dirty, noisy, these temporary settlements are. Their population is from forty or fifty to over 400 men. When the river rises the huts are removed, and the coolies return to other avocations. At the Hsin-tan rapid my little boat required seventy men, and some of the big junks took on 300 in addition to their crews of 120.

The following day, after being hauled up the Kwa-tung rapid and enjoying superb scenery for some hours, a turn in the river revealed walls of perpendicular rock rising to a colossal height, estimated at from 1000 to 2000 feet, the stupendous chasm of the Niu-kan gorge, to my thinking the grandest and most imposing of all, though a short one, and the same afternoon, in exquisitely

THE HSIN-TAN.

brilliant sunshine, we arrived at the foot of the Hsin-tan rapid, then at its worst.

This Hsin-tan in winter is the great bugbear of the Yangtze, the crux of forthcoming steam navigation, a waterfall with a boiling cataract below, a thing of awe and majesty, where the risks, turmoil, bargaining, and noise of the Upper River are centred. This great obstacle, which I wonder that any man even thought of surmounting, was formed about two hundred and fifty years ago by the descent of a rocky mountain-side into the river. It consists of what are three definite falls in the winter-time, the first caused by a great fan-shaped mass of big boulders deposited malignantly by a small stream which enters on the left bank, and the two others by great barriers of rock which lie athwart the river, above the higher of which, as is seen in the illustration, is a stretch of deep, calm water in peaceful contrast—the Ping-shu gorge. The cataracts extend for over a mile, and the fall is estimated at twenty feet.

Above the Niu-kan gorge the mountains open out, and where their sides are broken up into spurs, and where the spurs are most picturesque, the romantic villages of Hsin-tan and Yao-tsai are scattered on carefully terraced heights and bold, rocky projections, villages with good houses and fine temples, and a pagoda among oranges and loquats. Many of the houses have such handsome curved roofs that one can scarcely tell which is house and which is temple, all looking as if some of the best bits of the shores of Como had been dropped down in HUPEH.

Hsin-tan is a wild and beautiful village, and has an air of prosperity. Many junk owners have retired there to spend their days, and the comparative cleanliness and good repair are quite striking. One orange-embowered village on a spur has a temple with a pagoda built out over the edge of the cliff, without any obvious support. A village which might claim to be a town, at a height of fully 400 feet, is not only piled up on terraces, but the houses are built out from the cliff on timbers, and the flights of steps leading from terrace to terrace are so steep that I made no attempt to climb them. The colonnades in the street of shops and eating-houses which projects over the cliff reminded me of Varenna; indeed, there was a suggestion of Italy throughout, under an Italian sky.

I sat on a ledge for two hours, every minute expecting to see my boat move up to the foot of the cataract, but she was immovable. Then we went into a low restaurant, and got some fourth-class Chinese food, and after long bargaining three live fowls and three eggs. Crowds, more curious than rude, pressed upon us, everywhere choking up the balconies and entrances of the eating-house, and asking no end of questions. The men asserted, as they did everywhere on the river, that with my binoculars and camera I could see the treasures of the mountains, the gold, precious stones, and golden cocks which lie deep down in the earth; that I kept a black devil in the camera, and that I liberated him at night, and that he dug up the golden cocks, and that the reason why my boat was low in the water was that it was ballasted with these auriferous fowls, and with the treasures of the hills! They further said that "foreign devils" with blue and grey eyes could see three feet into the earth, and that I had been looking for the root which transmutes the base metals into gold, and this, though according to them I had the treasures of the hills at my disposal! They were quite good-natured, however.

The whole of a brilliant afternoon was spent on that height, which looks down on the deep-water channel by which big cargo boats ascend the rapids, small junks and native house-boats like mine taking a channel on the south side. During four hours, only two junks, which had partially discharged their cargoes, effected the ascent, though each of them was dragged up by 400 men. One big junk, after getting half-way up in three hours, jibbed, and though the trackers were stimulated by gongs and drums beaten frantically, she slowly slipped back to the point from which she started, and was there two days afterwards.

At sunset, taking a boat across the still, strong water above the fall, after having a desperate scramble over boulders of great size, we reached my boat, which was then moored at the side of the cataract in an eddy below the opposite village. The *lao-pan* said we should go up at daylight; and so we did, but it was the daylight of the third morning from that night, and I had ample opportunities for studying the Hsin-tan and its ways.

Miserable nights they were. It was as bad as being in a rough sea, for we were in the swell of the cataract and within the sound of its swish and roar. The boat rolled and pitched; the great rudder creaked and banged; we thumped our neighbours, and they thumped us; there were unholy sounds of tom-toms, the weather relapsed, the wind howled, and above all the angry yells of the boat baby were heard. The splash of a "sea" came in at my open window and deluged my camp bed, and it was very cold.

The next two days were disagreeable, even in such majestic and exciting surroundings. The boatmen turned us and our servants out at 10 a.m., and we stood about and sat on the great boulders on the bleak mountain-side in a bitterly cold, sunless wind each day till nearly five, deluded into the belief that our boat would move. A repulsive and ceaseless crowd of men and boys stood above, below, and behind us, though our position was strategically chosen. Mud was thrown and stuck; foul and bad names were used all day by successive crowds. I am hardened to most things, but the odour of that crowd made me uncomfortable. More than 1200 trackers, men and boys, notoriously the roughest class in China, were living in mat huts on the hillside, with all their foul and ofttimes vicious accessories. The crowds were coarse and brutal. Could these people ever have come "trailing clouds of glory"? Were they made in the image of God? Have we "all one Father"? I asked myself.

A glorious sight the Hsin-tan is as seen from our point of vantage, half-way up the last cataract, a hill of raging water with a white waterfall at the top, sharp, black rocks pushing their vicious heads through the foam, and above, absolute calm. I never saw such exciting water scenes—the wild rush of the cataract; the great junks hauled up the channel on the north side by 400 men each, hanging trembling in the surges, or, as in one case, from a tow-rope breaking, spinning down the cataract at tremendous speed into frightful perils; while others, after a last tremendous effort, entered into the peace of the upper waters. Then there were big junks with masts lashed on their sides, bound downwards, and their passage was more exciting than all else. They come broadside on down the smooth slope of water above, then make the leap bow on, fifty, eighty, even a hundred rowers at the oars and *yulows*, standing facing forwards, and with shrieks and yells pulling for their lives. The plunge comes; the bow and fore part of the deck are lost in foam and spray, emerging but to be lost

again as they flash by, then turning round and round, mere play-
things of the cataract, but by skill and effort got bow on again
in time to take the lesser rapid below.   It is a sublime sight.
Wupans and *sampans*, making the same plunge, were lost sight
of altogether in clouds of foam and spray, but appeared again.
Red lifeboats, with their smart turbaned crews, dodged in the
eddies trim and alert, crowds of half-naked trackers, struggling
over the boulders with their 1200 feet of tow-rope, dragged,
yelled, and chanted, and from each wild shore the mountains
rose black and gaunt into a cold, grey sky.

At this great cataract pilots are necessary.   They are competent and respectable, licensed by the authorities, and their
high charges, half a dollar for the half-hour which my small boat
occupied in going up the fall, and a dollar for the five minutes
taken by a big junk on the descent, enable them to live comfortably, and many of the pretty whitewashed houses of Hsin-tan in the
dense shade of orange groves are theirs.   They deserve high pay,
for it is a most perilous business, involving remarkable nerve and
sleight of eye, for a single turn too much or too little of the great
bow-sweep, and all would be lost.   Every junk which took the
plunge over the rock barrier into the furious billows of the cataract
below looked bound for destruction.   A curious functionary came
on board my boat, a well-dressed man carrying a white flag, on
which was written, " Powers of the waters, give a lucky star for
the journey."   He stood well forward, waving this flag regularly
during the ascent to propitiate the river deities, and the cook
threw rice on the billows with the same object.   The pilot was
a quiet, well-dressed man, giving orders by signals which were
promptly obeyed.   Indeed, the strict discipline to which these
wild boatmen submit in perilous places is remarkable.   The
lao-pan trusted neither his life nor his money to the boat, and
he even brought the less valuable possessions of wife and children
on shore.

My boat had the twenty-fifth turn, and on the third day of
detention she went up with seventy men at the ropes.   It was
an anxious half-hour of watching from the rocks, but there
was no disaster, and I was glad to escape from the brutal crowd,
as foul in language as in person, to the quiet of my cabin and the
twilight stillness of the Ping-shu gorge.   The whole ascent of

PING-SHU GORGE, HSIN-TAN.

the Hsin-tan rapids took my boat five hours and forty-five minutes.

No description can convey any idea of the noise and turmoil of the Hsin-tan. I realised it best by my hearing being affected for some days afterwards. The tremendous crash and roar of the cataract, above which the yells and shouts of hundreds of straining trackers are heard, mingled with the ceaseless beating of drums and gongs, some as signals, others to frighten evil spirits, make up a pandemonium which can never be forgotten.

CHAPTER XII.

RAPIDS AND TRACKERS

A STRONG, fair wind took us swiftly and silently up the gorge of the "Military Code and the Precious Blade," in which the water is said to be 1200 feet deep (?), and with some tracking up minor rapids, and some working round corners with poles armed with steel hooks which are inserted into the crevices of the rocks, we passed through the sublime Mitan gorge into a comparatively open reach abounding in vicious-looking reefs and rocks, among very rocky mountains, villages on heights, and superb temples on crags, and at sunset made fast below the picturesque and nobly situated town of Kueichow, the first walled city on the Upper Yangtze.

The Upper Yangtze is remarkable for the picturesque beauty of its cities at a distance, and their situations, almost invariably on irregular heights, backed by mountains, and with fine gardens and trees within their crenelated stone walls, which follow the contour of the site invariably, with one or more lofty pagodas denoting the approach, and with *yamen* and temple roofs dominating the mass of houses are very imposing.

One is only slowly convinced by experience that the interiors are not worth investigating. Dangerous reefs run out from below the walls of Kueichow, and as the river, if not an actual rapid, was at that time at least a *chipa*, it was not surprising not to find a single boat or junk there. Very few people came to our moorings, and the place looked dead.

The next day we ascended one of the worst rapids, the Yeh-tan, of evil fame at certain seasons, the Niu-kau-tan, nearly as bad, the Heng-liang-tze, a minor rapid, and many *chipa*, only making ten miles in eleven hours. At times the cliffs and rocks were quite impracticable for people in European shoes, and I had reluctantly

THE MITAN GORGE.

to stay in the boat during ascents, but the *lao-pan* declined to carry passengers up the dreaded Yeh-tan.

Above Kueichow there is a comparatively open reach with steep hills 1000 feet high, cultivated in patches to their summits, then tinged with green, small villages with wooded surroundings occurring frequently. Though not called a gorge, even that part of the Yangtze has high cliffs with lateral openings, and there are numbers of small coal "workings" in the hills, mere holes, shored up with timber, about three feet high, out of which the glass showed strings of women and children creeping, with baskets of coal dust on their backs. From this reach onwards the people make "patent fuel" by mixing the coal dust with loam and clay and forming it into small cakes. The boatmen made great use of it from that point, and added clouds of smoke to the malodorousness of their cooking.

Again I admired the resourceful energy which has surmounted the difficulties of the rapids. Narrow, steep flights of steps are in many places cut in the rock to facilitate tracking, as well as rock paths a foot or so wide, some only fifteen or twenty feet above the river, others at a giddy height on which the trackers looked no bigger than flies. The reader must bear in mind that all difficulties of getting up and down are largely increased by the river varying in height forty, fifty, and even sixty feet at different seasons, and there are water lines even seventy feet above the winter level. When I came down many of these paths and stairs were submerged several feet. On all of these, and indeed for much of the upward journey, the life of the tracker is in continual peril from losing his foothold owing to the slipperiness of the rock after rain, and from being dragged over and drowned by the backward tendencies of a heavy junk tugging at the end of 1200 feet of a heavy bamboo hawser as thick as an arm.

The river at low water is thoroughly vicious above Kuei, and the pilot's task is a severe one, even before reaching the Yeh-tan. At low water this is not so bad as the Hsin-tan; still, the hill of furious breakers with a smooth, narrow channel in the centre and a fierce whirlpool at the foot looked awful enough. The whole shore above the boulders, and indeed upon them, is covered with the mat huts of trackers and those who supply boats with provisions and bamboo ropes. A great bank covered with frightful boulders projects from the north shore, narrowing the river to a width of 150 yards. Mr. A. J. Little estimates the rush of the current round the point of that bank at from eight to ten knots an hour. Forty big cargo junks lay below it waiting their turn to ascend; and a thousand trackers were filling the air with their yells, while signal drums and gongs added to the din.

My attention was occupied by a big junk dragged by 300 men, which in two hours made hardly perceptible progress, slipping back constantly, though the drums were frantically beaten and the gangers rushed madly along the lines of struggling trackers, bringing their bamboo whips down on them with more sound than force. Suddenly the junk shivered, both tow-ropes snapped, the lines of trackers went down on their faces, and in a moment the big craft was spinning down the rapid; and before she could be recovered by the bow-sweep she flew up into the air as if she had exploded, a mass of spars and planks with heads bobbing about in the breakers. Quick as thought the red life-boats were on the spot; and if the drowning wretches as they scrambled over the gunwales did not bless this most efficient of the charities of China, I did most heartily, for of the fourteen or fifteen souls on board all were saved but three. This was one of two fatal disasters that I saw on the Yangtze, but, to judge from the enormous quantity of cotton drying at the Yeh-tan and the timbers wedged among the rocks, many a junk must have had a hole knocked in her bottom. Our own ascent, which took three hours, was successfully made.

I had then had this boat for my home for a week, and various disagreeables grew apace. The *lao-pan*, the virago's old husband, a small, fearfully lean man, with the leanest face I ever saw, just like very old, yellow, mildewed parchment strained over bones, sunken eyes, no teeth, and in the bitterly cold weather clad only in an old blue cotton garment, always blowing aside to show his emaciated form, was craftiness, greed, and avarice personified. Though "sair hodden doun" by his vigorous wife, he was capable of an attempt to repudiate his contract. He bargained and battled with the trackers at the rapids for hours to save a few *cash*, though by the delay he lost more than he saved; he ground the boatmen down, and gave them inferior rice; he would not spend a few *cash* on patching his ragged sail; and at sunset near

TEMPLE NEAR KUEICHOW.

Kueichow he put in mysteriously to a creek where he mysteriously met a man with two big sacks, the contents of which were transferred with much mystery and secrecy to the shallow hold in which our luggage was kept. It turned out to be an investment in spurious *cash*, on which, if he got it safely to SZE CHUAN, he might make a puny profit; and for this he ran the risk, relying on a boat carrying foreigners not being searched at Kuei Fu. His hawk-like face was a study of pure avarice.

The *tai-kung* was a splendid fellow till he collapsed towards evening with the pangs of the opium craving. With his eyes fixed on the perils ahead, he never left the great bow-sweep except for the three meals a day, gave his orders tersely and quietly, and was master of the crew and the lean *lao-pan*. The trackers, who were troublesome from the first, broke out into rebellion, using violent language forcing themselves into the front room, refusing to let us land (a breach of contract), and being insolent. Some of them looked too low to be human, just such men as would wreck and loot foreigners' houses with violence. Mr. Stevenson was powerless with them, I think because they mistook his quietness and perfect self-control for weakness. They were absolutely masters, and decided about everything with and without motive. In that week I never saw a kind or good trait of character in them, and they misused a frail old man who was working his passage up. New faces appeared daily, till the number on board rose from sixteen to thirty-four (another breach of contract), but I could not grudge the *lao-pan* the few dollars he made by it.

The trackers would not take the trouble to put a plank for me to land by, which compelled me to land on a pole, and on one day this spar turned over, and I fell into the water between the boat and the shore, being extricated to live in wet clothes for the day in a windy temperature of 38°. I must add, however, that by the end of three weeks they became considerably humanised, so that I was able to show them my photographs taken on the Yangtze. They recognised their own boat with yells. They said pictures could only be seen with one eye, so they used one hand for holding down one eyelid and made a tube of the other. I told them not to touch, and they actually obeyed! To the end I landed over the swift water on a pole, but latterly they held a bamboo for a rail and gave me a rough haul when I got in!

Poor fellows! I learned to pity them very much. Their ignorance and superstitions keep them in dread and terror of they know not what. They are so piteously poor, and work so hard even to keep body and soul together, and when the twelve hours day of dragging and risk is done there is nothing for them on a winter voyage on the bitterly cold nights but sleeping out of doors literally on a "plank bed." They are rough and brutal, yet I admit, and that not reluctantly, that not one of them was ever drunk, that they worked hard, and that the cambric curtain which was my only partition from the passage was never pulled aside.

After the great Yeh-tan, with its crowds and excitements, we ascended various ugly rapids and had some minor disasters. The big junks are attended by fine, smart tenders, in which they land and re-embark their trackers, an operation which may be necessary thirty times a day, but my small boat made up to the rocks for this purpose, the *lao-pan* being too penurious to spend two or three *cash* in hiring the punts which are available. We were landing the trackers at the foot of the "Cross Beam" rapid when a heavy cargo boat, unmanageable in the strong wind, came upon us and forced the bow-sweep, which projected twenty feet over the bow, among the rocks, where it snapped short off, the side hamper of the two boats at the same time locking them in an unwilling embrace.

Both crews seized the iron-spiked bamboos used for poling, and with fearful yells and execrations and every sign of mad rage began a free fight, but Mr. Stevenson succeeded in preventing actual bloodshed, and after a delay of some hours the other boat repaired our steering spar for the time. A Chinese fight is apt to be nothing more than "much cry." But our men insisted on going to law at the first convenient opportunity, so for two or three days we were always following that junk, hoping to be avenged on her at Kuei Fu.

The following day was decidedly what the Chinese call an "unlucky day." In China everything is ruled by a rigid etiquette. There are four things to be attended to on getting into a cart, and rigid rules govern the getting into a chair or boat. It is not only that one is regarded as an unmannerly boor for breaking them, but one draws down the vengeance of gods and demons. The day before I came off from the shore in a punt, and just as I was getting into my own boat, and had one foot on her and the other on the punt, the swift current carried the punt away, and in the scramble which followed I violated one of these rules.

The first thing which happened was that the *lao-pan's* three-year-old daughter fell overboard, and was carried fast away by the current. The tender of a junk was being towed up astern of us, and a tracker, a strong swimmer, jumped over, and after a hard struggle saved the child and wrapped her in the clothes he had thrown off, warm with his vital warmth, going naked himself in the biting air. The virago went into one of those paroxysms which are common among the Chinese, and in which they occasionally die. She stamped, jumped, beat everyone within reach, execrated, raved, and foamed at the mouth.

Scarcely had this excitement subsided, when as we were sailing up with a stiff breeze we struck on a rock, knocking two holes in the bottom of the boat, and, as she began to fill, she was run ashore on a sandy beach, and the rest of the day was spent in repairs. Miserable repairs they were, owing to the stinginess of the *lao-pan*, and consisted chiefly in ramming cotton wool and tallow into the holes and coating the mixture with clay. After this, before she could be properly repaired, as it was the Chinese New Year holidays, it took four men baling night and day for forty-eight hours to keep the leakage down, and not only that, but as the deck on which the crew slept had to be taken up, I had to admit the trackers with their vermin and opium pipes into the " front room " next to mine.

In this leaky condition we went up a very severe rapid, which took us four hours of desperate dragging. Sitting shivering for that time on a big boulder, I saw one of the many vicissitudes to be encountered in ascending the Great River. A great cargo junk was being hauled up with two hawsers, over 200 trackers, and the usual enormous din, the beating of drums and gongs, the clashing of cymbals, and the incessant letting off of crackers to intimidate the spirit of the rapid, when both ropes snapped, the trackers fell on their faces, and four hours' labour was lost, for in a flash the junk was at the foot of the rapid, and the last sight I had of her was far below twirling round in a whirlpool with a red lifeboat in attendance.

CHAPTER XIII.

LIFE ON THE UPPER YANGTZE

A T this point, before entering on the empire province of SZE CHUAN, it is desirable to give a few facts and impressions regarding life on the Upper Yangtze, my experiences of which extended over five weeks altogether.

The Upper River, with all its peculiarities, lies above Ichang. It must never be forgotten that it is the *sole* highway for the vast commerce of the richest province of the Chinese Empire, with an area about the size of that of France, and a population estimated at from 50,000,000 to 70,000,000. The nature and risks of this highway may be gathered from these and other descriptions of it. Except in the gorges and some few quiet intervals, it is a series of rapids and races, which at present are only surmounted by man force. Mr. A. J. Little's success in 1898 in getting a large steam launch up to Chungking proves that a steamer can ascend, but not that steam navigation can be made commercially profitable, or that if it were it would be the ruin of junk navigation.

A large up-river junk is from 80 to 120 feet long, from nine to twelve broad, and from 40 to over 100 tons burden.

They are all alike in that they have low square bows, lofty sterns, flat bottoms, and single masts from thirty to forty feet high, carrying huge oblong sails, with which they can only sail with the wind aft. They are very frequently built at Wan of a cypress which abounds in its neighbourhood, and being stained with orpiment and oiled over that with the oil procured from the *Aleurites cordata*, they look like varnished pine, and have a very trim as well as picturesque appearance. The planking is about an inch thick. The holds are only from three to seven feet deep. A junk to carry fifty tons of goods can be built at Wan complete for £125, and a first-class junk to carry 100 tons or more for £200, about 2500 strings of *cash*. The holds are in compartments.

The forward part is uncovered in the daytime, and the cook does his unceasing work in a well in the middle with a clay stove in it. At night a framework covered with bamboo mats is erected, under which the crew sleep. The high stern cabin is usually occupied by the *lao-pan* and his family. A junk of 120 tons carries a crew of 120 men.

In passage junks the open space forward is diminished as much as possible, most of the deck being housed over, but in cargo junks less than half is covered. In the big junks a sponson runs along each side, which is used both for poling and communication. Junks carry a spare mast and sweeps lashed outside. The helmsman stands inside, with his head and shoulders protected by a raised "wheelhouse," in which he works with much skill and infinite patience a very long and clumsy tiller attached to a huge rudder, which often projects four feet from the stern. The roof of the housed portion is used for the monstrous coils of bamboo rope, ofttimes three inches in diameter and 1200 feet in length, which are used in tracking, and are coiled and uncoiled continually. These ropes only last one voyage.

The lofty stern is frequently much decorated, and in all cases has a fascinating picturesqueness. Its square windows are of ground oyster-shell or paper, or even of stained glass. Occasionally it has a carved gallery with flowering plants in pots. Altogether a SZE CHUAN junk is an ingenious and noble construction, and the owners take great pride in them. Their stately appearance and apparently large size are deceptive as to their carrying capacity, which is small. I believe that no junk on the Upper Yangtze draws over seven feet, which necessarily gives a shallow hold, and the freeboard is of startling scantiness. The large tenders smartly handled, which land and re-embark the trackers, are really big *sampans*, and often have a curious rig —two masts like sheers, forty feet high amidships, with the width of the deck between them, the spar which carries the sail running on both.

We call the junks "lumbering craft," but no craft anywhere are more skilfully handled ; none run such risks ; no crews are better disciplined to act together and at a second's notice in cases of emergency ; no men work so desperately hard on such small pay and with such poor food ; and it remains to be seen if vessels of any other build and management can supplant them in the carrying trade of the Upper Yangtze.

Large fortunes are not made in junks ; the losses are too heavy. But, judging from the comfortable houses of retired junk owners in many a pleasant place, a moderate competence for old age is in sight of all except the very unlucky. The wife and family usually live on board, and these wives seem to have a speciality of strident and powerful voices, which are heard above the roar of the rapids and the yells of the crews.

As to the risks, the Chinese say that one junk in twenty is annually lost, and one in ten is stranded. Consul Bourne * states that one-tenth of the foreign goods shipped at Ichang arrives damaged by water, and Mr. A. J. Little estimates the loss of junks and merchandise since the formation of the Hing-lung-t'an, or " Glorious Rapid," in 1896 as eight per cent. † Consul Bourne, writing in December, 1896, says, "A hundred junks and 1000 lives have been already lost, we are told, i.e., since September 28th of the same year at that rapid." Both the upward and downward passages are full of tremendous risks. On the upward passage in February I counted forty-one junks stranded at different points between Ichang and Wan Hsien, some breaking up, others being repaired, and all having to discharge their cargoes ; and when I came down like a flash on high water towards the end of June, though it was impossible to count the stranded junks, they must have been nearly half of that number, even with the much-reduced summer traffic, and I saw one big junk strike a rock while flying down a rapid and disappear as if she had been blown up, her large crew, at the height of violent effort the moment before, with all its frantic and noisy accompaniments, perishing with her.

Besides junks of various sizes, there are native house-boats, like mine, and others running up to four times its size, which carry passengers only, and *wupans* and *sampans*—undecked boats with hooped bamboo roofs ; these carry passengers or cargo. I have already described the arrangements of a house-boat. If the Upper Yangtze junks number from 7000 to 8000, the men employed on them at the lowest estimate must be a quarter of a million, in

---

* Diplomatic and Consular Reports, No. 458, China, Foreign Office, May, 1898.

† *Through the Yangtze Gorges*, A. J. LITTLE, p. 246.

addition to many thousands working in house-boats and smaller craft.

Junks never anchor, and, indeed, carry no anchors, and choosing a mooring ground is a most important matter—not that there are not very many nooks and bays untouched by the current, but because of the caprices of the river, which often rises or falls, as I experienced, six or seven feet in a night, so that a careful watch must be kept in order to pay out or haul in line according to circumstances.

Big junks sound their way towards the bank, rig out great wooden fenders fore and aft to prevent their sheering into shoaler water than they draw, and one of the "water trackers" plunges into the water with a line, which he makes fast to a stake on shore, the fenders, which are really massive poles or straight young pines, also being lashed to rocks or stakes.

Junks bound west keep as close in shore as they can on the side freest from rocks and easiest for the trackers. When the wind is fair and strong they can stem the ordinary current with their huge sail only, and they take their trackers on board; but if the fair wind is light, it only gives the trackers an easier haul. At all rapids, races, and rocky points, the tow-line is in requisition. Eastward-bound junks lash their mast alongside at Chungking, and are rowed down, being steered by a prodigious bow-sweep. It is absolutely necessary that their speed should be in advance of that of the current, and at every rapid frantic efforts are required from the crew.

Junks carry trackers in proportion to their tonnage, but a *lao-pan*, or skipper, usually part owner, the steersman, the *t'au-t'ai-kung*, or pilot, the *tai-kung*, or bowsman, the cook, and the *t'au-lao*, or head tracker, are indispensable. The pilot and steersman never leave the bow-sweep and rudder, except for meals, while the junk is in motion. The skipper's functions are chiefly to buy food, bargain for extra trackers, pay wages, and stimulate the crew to frantic efforts in dangerous places by yells and gesticulations.

The bowsman, or *tai-kung*, acting also as pilot in my small boat, is the most important man in a junk. I never ceased to admire mine, a tall, broad, well-made fellow, the personification of knowledge and carefulness, silent, alert, never flurried, hand and head steady, all that a pilot should be, until the moment when he collapsed with the opium craving, after which he might nightly be seen in a state of blissful vacuity lying beside his opium lamp. The work of the *tai-kung* is to lead with his skilled touch the eight or ten men who, in a big junk, work the bow-sweep, a timber, from thirty to forty feet long, projecting over the bow, without which no boat could ascend or descend rapids and races in safety. When this great spar is not in use he stands at the bow sounding with a long iron-shod bamboo pole, giving the junk a sheer-off from upstanding points or rocks, and signalling to the steersman in which direction sunken rocks lie, which his trained eye discovers by the eddies in the river. His responsibility for life and property is enormous, and he bears it nobly. The sweep is used to shoot the junk out into the current, and enable her to clear rocks which cannot be avoided by the steersman and rudder.

Having slightly sketched the junks and the manner of navigating the Great River, I will conclude with a brief description of the "inhuman work" of the trackers, by far the worst of which is in the region of the gorges and the most severe of the rapids, extending for a hundred miles west of Ichang. Captain Blakiston, Captain Gill, and more lately Mr. A. J. Little in his delightful book, *Through the Yangtze Gorges*, have all expressed both sympathy with these men and their wonder at their hardihood, industry, and good-nature, and with my whole heart I endorse what these writers have said, and regard this class as typifying that extraordinary energy of the Chinese which has made and kept China what it is, and which carries the Chinese as thrifty and successful emigrants to every part of Eastern Asia and Western America.

The crews, which in big junks number 120 men, are engaged at Ichang. For the upward voyage, lasting from thirty to fifty days, they get about four shillings and their food, which is three meals a day of rice, with cabbage fried in a liberal supply of grease, and a little fish or pork on rare occasions, and for coming down, which rarely takes more than ten days (I did it in a *wupan* in a little over four), about eighteenpence and food, and indeed many crews work their passage down for food only. For this pittance these men do the hardest and riskiest work I have seen done in any country, "inhumanly hard," as Consul Bourne calls it, week after week, from early dawn to sunset. The opening of Chungking

TRACKERS HOUSES.

as a treaty port and various other causes have tended however to raise their wages.

The larger number of these trackers are usually on shore hauling, being directed from the junk either by flag signals or drum beat, under the *tai-kung's* direction; a proportion remain on board to work the huge bow-sweep, at which I have seen as many as fifteen straining. A few attend the trackers to extricate the tow-rope from the rocks, in which it is constantly catching, and two or more *tai-wan-ti*, or water trackers, specially expert swimmers, and without clothing, run ahead of the tow-rope ready to plunge into the water and free it when it catches among rocks which cannot be reached from the shore. If tracking and sailing are both impossible, the trackers propel the junk by great oars, each worked by two men, twenty at a side, who face forwards, and mark time by a combined stamp and a wild chant.

In descending, in order to keep steerage way on the junk in a current running from six to twelve knots an hour, every agency of progression is brought into play. The slinging of the mast alongside gives a lumbering, ungainly look. The deck is literally crowded with men, naked in summer, and in winter clothed in long blue cotton coats. Some are rowing face forwards; fifteen or more are straining for life at the bow-sweep; others are working the huge oars called *che* (wheel), each of which demands the energies of ten men; others are toiling at *yu-lows*, big broad-bladed sculls, worked over the stern or parallel to the junk's side—even women and children take part in the effort—the *lao-pan* grows frantic, he yells, leaps, dances; drums and gongs are madly beaten, and yet, with all this frantic effort, it is all the junk can do to keep steerage way enough to clear the dangerous places, and not always that, as I saw on two occasions junks fly down rapids, strike rocks, and disappear as unconnected masses of timbers, as if exploded by dynamite.

I saw over eighty big junks descend the great rapids, and it was such an exciting sight, with its accompaniments of deafening din, that I not only never wearied, but would have been glad to see eighty more.

Where it is impossible to sail—and even with a fair wind there are few reaches except the gorges where it is possible—the trackers prefer the "inhuman work" of tracking to the slow headway made by the severe and monotonous toil of rowing, or of hugging the bank, and hooking the junk along by seizing with hooks on rings with staples driven into the rock for this purpose, or keeping her off with stout fenders while they pole her along with iron-spiked bamboo poles, which they drive into holes which have been made by this process in the course of ages in the hard conglomerate or granite.

In small house-boats like mine the trackers are landed from the boat, but in junks from the attendant *sampan*. Except the *tai-wan-ti*, they wear short cotton drawers, and each man has a breast strap. The huge coil of plaited bamboo, frequently a quarter of a mile long, is landed after being passed over the mast-head, a man on board paying out or hauling in as is required. Small boats pass under the loftier tow-ropes of big ones, which often saves time, and often leads to noisy quarrels and entanglements. The trackers uncoil the rope, each man attaching it to his breast strap by a hitch, which can be cast off and rehitched in a moment.

The drum beats in the junk, and the long string of men starts, marking time with a loud yell—" *Chor-chor*," said to mean " Put your shoulder to it." The trackers make a peculiar movement ; their steps are very short, and with each they swing the arms and body forward, stooping so low to their work that their hands nearly touch the ground, and at a distance they look like quadrupeds.

Away they go, climbing over the huge angular boulders of the river banks, sliding on their backs down spurs of smooth rock, climbing cliff walls on each other's shoulders, or holding on with fingers and toes, sometimes on hands and knees, sometimes on shelving precipices where only their grass sandals save them from slipping into the foaming race below, now down close to the deep water, edging round a smooth cliff with hardly foothold for goats, then far above, dancing and shouting along the verge of a precipice, or on a narrow track cut in the rock 300 feet above the river, on which narrow and broken ledge a man unencumbered and with a strong head would need to do his best to keep his feet. The reader must sympathetically bear in mind that these poor fellows who drag our commerce up the Yangtze amidst all these difficulties and perils, and many more, are attached to a heavy junk by a long and heavy rope, and are dragging her up against the force of a tremendous current, raging in billows, eddies, and whirlpools ; that they are subject to frequent severe jerks; that occasionally their burden comes to a dead stop and hangs in the torrent for several minutes ; that the tow-rope often snaps, throwing them on their faces and bare bodies on jagged and rough rocks ; that they are continually in and out of the water ; that they are running many chances daily of having their lives violently ended ; and that they are doing all this mainly on rice !

Their work is indicated from the junk either by the rapid beating of drums and gongs when they are to haul hard, or a slow rat-a-tat when they are to cease hauling, or by flag signalling, one man being told off on shore to watch the signals and communicate them to the trackers. An error would be as fatal as if within a ship's length of a reef ahead an engineer were to mistake the order " Full speed astern " for " full speed ahead."

Occasionally rough steps help the men up and down spurs, and rock paths made by the pickaxe occur frequently. Many of these were thirty feet above the river when I went up, and were submerged when I came down. There is, however, one noble rock path, four feet broad, running for many miles at an even height, built, I believe, by a private individual as an act of benevolence to the trackers and for the " accumulation of merit."

At some points where the rapids are bad and the shores are big broken rocks, only fitted for goats to climb, and the junks hang or slip back, and the men give way, and several big junks, each with from 200 to 300 trackers, are all making the slowest possible progress, gongs and drums are beaten frantically ; bells are rung ; firearms are let off ; the hundreds of trackers on all-fours are yelling and bellowing ; the overseers are vociferating like madmen, and rush wildly along the gasping and struggling lines of naked men, dancing, howling, leaping, and thrashing them with split bamboos, not much to their hurt. A tow-rope breaks, and the junk they are tugging at gyrates at immense speed to the foot of the rapid, the labour of hours being wasted in two or three minutes, if there is not a worse result.

Among the many perils encountered by junks and trackers are the *chipa* or races, which are usually caused by a projecting point or spur of rock below which there is a smooth eddy. Arrived at the point and landing the trackers, the *tai-kung* throws the boat's head out into the current to get her clear of the point, with the bow-sweep, and with the strongest line in use, seventy or eighty trackers haul on it with all their force, men work with long poles to fend her off the rocks, and with her head on to the current the water foams and rages under her bow, but if all goes well, after a period of suspense she is dragged by main force round the point into smooth water, and then it is often the case that the cliffs are inaccessible; the trackers come on board and "claw" the junk along in deep water with claws on long boathooks, which they hook into the rocks, others fending her off.

Things do not always go smoothly. I went up these races in my boat many times, and such small incidents happened as thumping a hole in the bottom on a small rock, the rope catching on a rock in the water and a bold swimmer having to go overboard to detach it, and the tow-rope holding fast round some point of rock or getting entangled in a crevice which looked inaccessible. It was horrible to see the poor fellows climb with bare feet up apparently smooth precipices, "holding on with their eyelids," while the drum beat "Cease hauling," and the junk hung tugging and quivering in the torrent and fraying the rope which was her one salvation. On two occasions where there was absolutely no foothold for a cat, a man was let down over the precipice by a rope under his arms to free the fast-fraying tow-line. These lines, hardened by the silica in the bamboo, have cut channels two, three, and four inches deep over many of the points, neat, smooth grooves in which they run easily.

There is much more to be said about the trackers and their work, but the reader is weary, and I forbear. No work is more exposed to risks to limb and life. Many fall over the cliffs and are drowned; others break their limbs and are left on shore to take their chance—and a poor one it is—without splints or treatment; severe strains and hernia are common, produced by tremendous efforts in dragging, and it is no uncommon thing when a man falls that his thin naked body is dragged bumping over the rocks before he extricates himself. On every man almost are to be seen cuts, bruises, wounds, weals, bad sores from cutaneous disease, and a general look of inferior rice.

These trackers may be the roughest class in China—for the work is "inhuman" and brutalising—but nevertheless they are good-natured in their way ; free on the whole from crimes of violence ; full of fun, antics, and frolic ; clever at taking off foreigners; loving a joke ; and with a keen sense of humour.

Those who crowd in hundreds to the great rapids in the season for the chance of getting a few *cash* for a haul are a rougher lot still.   They bargain for the price of haulage with the *lao-pan* through gangsmen, and very often where there is much competition, as at the Hsin-tan, get only about a penny for four hours' hard work.   Their mat camps are very boisterous at night.   At the lesser rapids the *lao-pan* goes ashore, dangling strings of *cash*, and as there is usually a village close by, he secures help, after some loud-tongued bargaining and wrangling, engaging even women and boys to tug at his ropes, and occasionally a woman with a baby on her back takes a turn at the dragging !

That so vast a traffic is carried on under such difficulties is a marvel.   Many of these are created on the upward passage by the necessity which hauled junks are under of taking the shallow inshore water, with its rocks, obvious and sunken, reefs, broken water, and whirlpools.   Full - powered steamers, with suitable steering arrangements, ascending the smooth deep-water channel used in the descent, might escape the majority of the risks run by junks ; but then a complete survey of the Upper Yangtze is required.   So far as I could judge of the Great River between Sui Fu, at the junction of the River of Golden Sand and the Min, and Ichang, leaving out the gorges, there are very few reaches in which rapids, races, and rocky broken water are not to be met with.   Indeed, it may be said that there is no tranquil water, and Admiral Ho, the superintendent of police for the Upper Yangtze, is probably not exaggerating when in his official *Yangtze Pilot* he enumerates about a thousand perils to navigation.   When I returned I realised that Mr. Endacott's remark concerning occupation had much truth in it : " You 'll have enough to do looking after your life." *

* Consul Bourne " risks " an estimate of the value of goods exported from Sze Chuan by this route at £3,300,000 annually, while imports coming up the rapids and passing through the Imperial Customs amounted to £1,776,586 in 1897.   The freight on cotton goods from Ichang to Chungking is estimated at £3 8s. 6d. per ton, a scarcely appreciable increase in cost on every yard after a transit of 500 miles.

CHAPTER XIV.

THE YANGTZE AND KUEI FU

ON February 7th we entered the solemn Wushan gorge, twenty miles long, a grand chasm from 330 to 600 yards in width, and walled in by perpendicular cliffs ofttimes 1000 feet in height, with lofty mountain spires and pinnacles then touched with snow above them. The "Witch's Mountain Great Gorge" is uncanny, and the black gloom of a winter day, clouds swirling round the higher summits, and the long yells with which the boatmen besought the river god for a wind, with many vows and promises to pay, did not enliven it. Nor does the name "Iron Coffin Gorge," given to a reach above, where iron chains are bolted into the cliffs fifty feet above the winter level of the river for the use of the junks bound west, cheer the situation.

We were two days in this "dowie den," and tied up for a third on Sunday, near the last inhabited village in HUPEH, Nan-mu yurh, "Cedar Garden," situated on both sides of a deep glen apparently closed by a high mountain, a covered bridge connecting the two halves. It is a romantic place, quite worth the toilsome ascent of 517 steep stone steps which form the terraced street. The houses are surrounded by loquats, orange, and pomegranate, their dark, shining foliage with a background of snow. The people of this mountainous province are said to be poor, hardy, and industrious. A respectable merchant asked if we had heard when peace was going to be made? Such ignorance was phenomenal on this great highway of commerce! Some boatmen asked ours what we were doing tied up there when there was such a good wind, and the reply was that they had foreign devils as passengers, who, though they did no work and were always eating, must sleep one day in seven!

Above this glen the walls of the gorge approach again; they are still of limestone with sandstone above, caverned at great heights, worn in places into colossal terraces, and singularly fluted by means of deep, vertical potholes, the outer halves of which have given way. Two narrow glens on each side of the river are the boundary between HUPEH and SZE CHUAN, but it was not till some hours later that we passed the first village of the empire province, Pei-shih, "Back to the Rock," a long, straggling street, on an imposing limestone ledge, and possessing a fine Taoist temple. There is a small but nasty rapid below it, which took two hours to ascend. While scrambling along the shore I picked up a piece of pink granite, which at once raised a clamour, the people saying that a foreigner with blue or grey eyes not only sees three feet into the ground, but can look inside the stones, and that I had seen a jewel in this one. I threw it down, and they broke it open ; and then, not finding anything, said that I had spirited it out of the stone by foreign magic.

The current at the upper end of the Witch's Gorge produced so much tedious delay that I was glad when we reached Wushan, the first city in SZE CHUAN, to which, for a considerable distance, we were *clawed* along by hooks attached to the boatmen's poles. Opposite Wushan is a small tributary, which brings down salt from brine wells near Ta-Ling, a district city, in boats which Mr. Little regards as exact copies of Venetian gondolas. Wushan is grey and picturesque, its walls following the contour of the hills on which it is built, enclosing fields, orchards, and beautiful trees. A fine temple to the God of Literature in a grove of evergreens on a steep mountain cone 1500 feet in height, and a lofty pagoda on the same peak are striking objects, but the town, though fairly clean, has no look of prosperity, and so far was disappointing.

Toiling up the "Kitten" and "Get-down-from-horse" rapids, we reached the Feng Hsiang, or "Bellows," or "Wind-Box" gorge, the last and one of the grandest of the great gorges, where the Great River is narrowed in places to 150 yards, by vertical walls of rock from 1500 to 2000 feet in height. There are both rapids and dangerous whirlpools, the presence of red lifeboats, as usual, denoting risk. My boat was dragged up inch by inch against a tremendous current, *clawed* up in places where there was no foothold for trackers, and so terrible was the straining of these poor fellows on the rough and jagged rocks that I welcomed the opening out of the stupendous chasm, and our entrance upon a beautiful mountainous country, through which the Yangtze rolls through a valley covered, even in February, with all manner of crops in their freshest green. Just at the mouth, creating two channels—one 100 feet and the other 200 feet in width—lies a black, polished, square mass of rock known as the "Goose-tail" rock; it was fully forty feet above the water when I went up, but when I came down in June it was only just visible. When it is quite covered, the authorities at the city, five miles above, do not allow any junks to descend till it reappears. A remarkable rock ladder connected with early Chinese military history, a grand white limestone peak which curves majestically over the gorge, a fine temple on a cliff with gardens and court-yards—and then the almost painful drafts on the capacity for admiring and wondering which the previous eleven days had made came to an end.

The scenery above the Wind-Box gorge, though less grand, is very varied, the valley and the lateral valleys for ever narrowing and broadening; the distant mountains forest-covered or snow-slashed; the spurs crowned with grand temples, below which picturesque villages cluster, and whitewashed, black-beamed, several-gabled, many-roofed, orange-embowered farmhouses; and every slope and level is cultivated to perfection, the bright yellow of the rape-seed blossom adding a charm to greenery which was never monotonous.

After ascending some troublesome but minor rapids, much bothered all the time by a big cargo boat with seventy trackers of its own, which kept close behind us, always trying to pass its rope over the top of our mast, a quarrel being the inevitable consequence, we arrived in sight of what looked like a smoky manufacturing town, the first time I saw such a sight in China. Really the appearance was produced more by great jets and ebullitions of steam than by smoke, for the "manufacturers" were burning a local coal, much resembling anthracite. At low water there are great sand-banks below the city of Kuei Fu, or Kuei-chow Fu, where a number of salt boilers establish themselves for the winter months, who dig great brine pits in the sand and evaporate the product with coal. The process is rude, and the salt is a bad colour, but the product of this and many other similar wells is one of the chief exports of SZE CHUAN, and a great source of revenue.*

A great bank of boulders, a strong *chipa*, a highly cultivated region, the pleasant valley slopes of which rolled up into hills, pleasant farms, a general sunny smile, a grey-walled city of much picturesqueness, a great fleet of junks moored below it, a mat town to supply their needs, and we were at the city of Kuei-chow Fu.

Ever since leaving Ichang we had been goading the *lao-pan* to hurry, so that we might reach Wan by the Chinese New Year, which was quite possible, but he and all his trackers were determined that we should spend it at Kuei Fu, a favourite place with junkmen, so we had the bad luck of being detained there four days till noisy and gluttonous celebrations of the great festival were past. Not that we were honestly detained, or that the *lao-pan* claimed this holiday, but he resorted to mean Oriental dodges to keep us. We arrived on February 10th, the New Year fell on the 13th, so one day the boat required serious repair, another stores must be laid in, the third the *lao-pan* moved a few hundred yards and then said he must go to some village for a new tow-rope, and another day must be devoted to paying debts! Fortunately it was brilliant weather, though so cold that I had to sit wrapped in blankets with my feet in the bed. But then at home people do not usually sit in what is practically the open air with the temperature at 39°!

Kuei Fu is a large city, with a very fine wall and noble gate towers, and imposing roofs of *yamens* and temples are seen above the battlements. At that time it was very hostile to foreigners, and I made no attempt to enter its stately gates, but walked in the beautiful surroundings among large farm-houses, all *en fête* for the season, with many wolfish dogs, aggressive and cowardly, and crops of wheat and barley already showing the ear stalks, and root crops with much juicy leafage, a farming paradise. Good paths bordered with the yellow fumitory, already in blossom, intersected the country, and

---

* These pits are reported as producing 132 lbs. of salt daily each. Captain Gill learned at Kuei Fu that SZE CHUAN salt brings in a revenue of about £2,000,000 sterling annually, but this seems incredible, as it would make the annual salt production of the province about 237,946 tons.

owing to the recent dry weather, there was an agreeable aspect of cleanliness everywhere. I photographed a suburban temple with a porcelain front, where the priests, as is their wont, were quite polite, but on the way back we were "rushed" by a crowd of men and boys howling and shouting, and using the term *yang-kwei-tze*, "foreign devil," very freely. No Protestant missionaries, and I was told no Roman either, have yet effected a lodgment in this city. Two Chinese telegraph clerks, both Christians, and speaking good English, paid us a visit, and told us that feeling had become so very much more hostile since the "disturbances" that there would certainly be a serious riot if we went into the town.

Outside the walls little is to be seen except the salt boileries on the sand-banks; the manufacture of briquettes; the loading of junks for the low country with big lumps of anthracite coal, which sells for 9s. 6d. a ton at Kuei Fu, and is much used by the blacksmiths; the ceaseless procession of water-carriers, each making the long steep trudge from the river to the city with two buckets for half a farthing; and the aqueduct, a great work of former days, about three miles long, which brings a supply of pure water down a stone channel from a strong spring which spouts from a hole in the rock at a height of 1500 feet or thereabouts. This good gift is not *pro bono publico;* the magistrate who constructed the work was ambitious only to have a private water supply. The paved path leading to the source passes over a steep hill which for more than a mile is a vast city of the dead, occupied by graves some of which are handsome stone structures closed by inscribed slabs of stone, standing on carefully-kept grass platforms, as in Korea, while the majority are circular grassed mounds held together by rubble.

Kuei Fu or Kwei Hwan (*i.e.* "The Barrier of Kueichow") is a decaying city, bolstered up into an appearance of grandeur by its position and its stately wall and gate towers. There all goods going up or down the Yangtze paid *likin*, a transit tax of about 5 per cent. on their value. As (according to Mr. Little) over 10,000 junks go up and down in the year, and each one is delayed for examination three or four days, a large extra-mural population made a living by supplying their needs. Some years ago the Kuei Fu Likin Office was the most valuable in

China next to that of Canton, and the likin duties were the great source of SZE CHUAN revenue. The grand houses, with fine pleasure grounds, of which many can be seen from a height above the wall, testify to the fortunes made by officials in the days when they had the right to levy 5 per cent. on a trade worth possibly £2,000,000 sterling.

But we have " changed all that" by securing the opening of the treaty port of Chungking with the transit pass and chartered junk systems, to which all foreign imports can be carried on payment of duty to the Imperial Maritime Customs at Shanghai. Thus these rich dues go to Peking, and the "Four Streams Province" is the sufferer, and Kuei Fu really can only exact legal dues from junks carrying local merchandise and from salt junks. The reader will at once perceive the reason for the strong provincial hostility which is roused by the opening of new treaty ports, for each one, to a greater or less extent, enriches the Imperial Government at the expense of the provinces, and deprives a great number of officials of their "legitimate" perquisites or "squeezes," in favour, as the people think, of highly salaried foreign customs employés.

On two days, owing to the crowds on the shore, I did not leave the boat. In the bright sunshine, "light without heat," the view was always delightful, as it changed from hour to hour, and disappeared at sunset in a blaze of colour—distant snow peaks burning red after the lower ranges had passed into ashy grey. The picturesque grey city, the magnificent opening of the Feng Hsiang, or "Wind-Box" gorge, the hill slopes in the vividness of their spring greens and yellows, the rapid, with its exciting risks and the life on the water, made a picture of which one could never weary.

Yet five days of crouching and shivering in a six-foot square room, really a *stall*, with three sides only and no window, taxed both patience and resources, especially as the virago and the boat baby were more aggravating than usual, and the trackers ignored the existence of passengers. The *lao-pan* gave himself up to the opium pipe, and was consequently obliterated. Be-dien, my servant, whose temper and pride were unslumbering, made himself unpleasant all round. It would require some very old-fashioned Anglo-Saxon words to describe the smell of the cooking of the New Year viands. Yet somehow I did not feel the least inclined to grumble, and my slender resources held out till the end.

I had Baber's incomparable papers on Far Western China to study and enjoy, a journal to "write up," much mending and even making to accomplish, and, above all, there were photographic negatives to develop and print, and prints to tone, and the difficulties enhanced the zest of these processes and made me think, with a feeling of complacent superiority, of the amateurs who need "dark rooms," sinks, water "laid on," tables, and other luxuries. Night supplied me with a dark room; the majestic Yangtze was "laid on"; a box served for a table: all else can be dispensed with.

I lined my "stall" with muslin curtains and newspapers, and finding that the light of the opium lamps still came in through the chinks, I tacked up my blankets and slept in my clothes and fur coat. With "water, water everywhere," water was the great difficulty. The Yangtze holds any amount of fine mud in suspension, which for drinking purposes is usually precipitated with alum, and unless filtered, deposits a fine, even veil on the negative. I had only a pocket filter, which produced about three quarts of water a day, of which Be-dien invariably abstracted some for making tea, leaving me with only enough for a final wash, not always quite effectual, as the critic will see from some of the illustrations.

I found that the most successful method of washing out "hypo" was to lean over the gunwale and hold the negative in the wash of the Great River, rapid even at the mooring place, and give it some final washes in the filtered water. This chilly arrangement was only possible when the trackers were ashore or smoking opium at the stern. Printing was a great difficulty, and I only overcame it by hanging the printing-frames over the side. When all these rough arrangements were successful, each print was a joy and a triumph, nor was there disgrace in failure.

The day before the New Year was thoroughly unquiet. The population of the boat was excited by wine and pork money, and was fearfully noisy, shouting, yelling, quarrelling, stamping overhead, stamping along the passage outside my cambric curtain, stamping over the roof, sawing, hammering, and pounding rice. A

AUTHOR'S TRACKERS AT DINNER.

mandarin's boat tied up close to my window had engaged a "sing-song" boat, and I had all the noise from both, and many glimpses of the mandarin, a good-looking young man, in fur-lined brocaded silk. Like all others that I have seen of the higher official class, he looked immeasurably removed from the common people. The assumed passionlessness of his face expressed nothing but aloofness and scorn. One of the servants died in his boat after a few hours' illness, during which the beating of drums and gongs, and the letting off of crackers to frighten away the demon which was causing the trouble, were incessant and tremendous. We sailed in company, and shortly after leaving Kuei Fu one of the mandarin's trackers, in a very minor rapid, was pulled into the river and drowned.

I had an opportunity of taking an instantaneous photograph of my trackers at dinner. Their meals, which consist of inferior rice mixed with cabbage or other vegetables fried in oil, with a bit of fish or pork occasionally added, are worth watching. Each man takes a rough glazed earthenware bowl and fills it from the great pot on the fire. All squat round the well, and balancing their bowls on the tips of the fingers of the left hand close under the chin, the mouths are opened as wide as possible, and the food is shovelled in with the chopsticks as rapidly as though they were eating for a wager. When the mouth is apparently full they pack its contents into the cheeks with the chopsticks and begin again, packing any solid lumps into the cheeks neatly at once. When mastication and swallowing took place I never quite made out, but in an incredibly short time both bowls and cheeks were empty, and the eaters were smoking their pipes with an aspect of content. The boats, unless sailing, tie up for meals. The Chinese never, if they can help it, drink unboiled water, which saves them from many diseases, and these men drank the water in which the rice was cooked.

On three such meals the poor fellows haul with all their strength for twelve hours daily, never shirking their work. They are rough, truly, but as the voyage went on their honest work, pluck, endurance, hardihood, sobriety, and good-nature won my sympathy and in some sort my admiration. They might be better clothed and fed if they were not opium smokers, but then where would be their nightly Elysium ?

CHAPTER XV.

NEW YEAR'S DAY AT KUEI-CHOW FU

NEW YEAR'S DAY arrived at last, as cold and brilliant as if it were not belated by six weeks. I took a beautiful walk among prosperous farms where the people were all in gala dress. The houses were decked with flags and streamers, and even the buff dogs had knots of colour round their necks. From above the wall the grey city could be seen brilliantly decorated, and sounds of jubilation came up from it. The suburbs and the mat town on the river bank were gay and noisy, and much money was spent on crackers and explosives generally. The junks were decorated, and the "sing-song" boats blossomed into a blaze of colour. Everyone except my trackers appeared in new clothes, and threw off the old ones with rejoicing.

This was my second New Year in China, and I had seen its approach as far back as Ichang, where, as everywhere, tables appeared in the streets a month beforehand, and all sorts of tempting articles were displayed upon them in a tempting manner. This is the time when things can be had cheap, and many articles of *bric-à-brac* and embroidered dresses are for sale which are not obtainable at any other time. For in order to pay debts, a sacred obligation worthily honoured in the observance, many families are obliged to part with possessions long cherished. The crowds in the streets in gala dresses are enormous; children are gaily dressed, their quaint heads are decorated with flowers, and they receive presents of toys and *bon-bons*. The toy-shops drive a roaring trade.

Red paper appears everywhere in long strips pasted on the lintels and doorposts of houses, emblazoned with the characters for happiness and longevity, and with formal sentences suitable for the festive occasion, many of which are written on tables in the streets which are provided with ink-brushes and ink-stones.

Every shop is brilliant with these red papers pasted or suspended, and with *kin hwa,* or "golden flowers," much made in Shao Hsing, being artificial flowers and leaves often of great size, of yellow tinsel on wires, making a goodly show. The " sing-song " boats were profusely decorated with these, and they are much used for the New Year offerings in temples, and for the annual re-decoration of the household tablets. Thousands of vegetable wax candles, with paper wicks, varying in size from the thickness

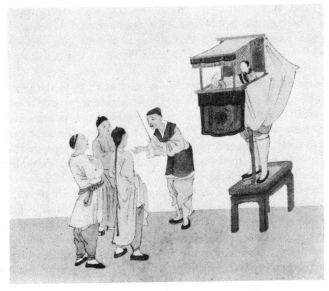

A CHINESE PUNCHINELLO.

of a man's leg to that of his finger, coloured vermilion, and painted with humorous and mythical pictures, and many other things used for offerings in the temples, and ribbons and streamers of all descriptions made the streets, even the mat streets outside Kuei Fu, gay.

For the three previous days unlimited scrubbing of clothes, persons, doors, chairs, shutters, and all woodwork went on ; and though boats were not as universally turned out and cleaned as at Canton, where I spent a previous New Year, a good many of the smaller craft were beached and cleansed inside and out. Even the trackers scrubbed their faces, and appeared a paler yellow.

Towards the evening of that day, between the din of gongs and the constant explosion at every door of strings of fireworks intended to expel evil spirits and prevent others from entering, the noise became exciting. This idea of expelling evil spirits and preventing their entrance at the incoming of the year is the same as is carried out in Korea by the burning in a potsherd at the house door of the hair of all the inmates, which, when cut off or falling out, is preserved for this purpose. The Chinese, like the Koreans, believe themselves surrounded by legions of demons, mainly malignant, who must either be frightened or propitiated.

Religion plays a most conspicuous part in visits to the temples, and offerings. At all the farms near Kuei Fu, trees, fences, barns, and farming implements, as well as houses, had prayers pasted upon them. The junkmen, though not nearly to the same extent as in Kwantung, pasted paper prayers on oars, sweeps, mast, and rudder, and hung them over the boats' sterns; and every house was purified by a religious ceremonial. New Year's Day is kept as the birthday of the entire population, and a child born on the previous day enters his second year upon it. In the houses of well-to-do people such birthdays are great occasions; and abbots, monks, and priests assemble to do them honour, with much noise and many prayers, some read and others chanted from memory, after which the written prayers are burned and libations are poured out. It is the family and social ceremonies connected with idolatry and demonism at this season which are a special difficulty in the way of Christians.

Among other religious duties, some persons, both men and women, burdened with the weight of the sins of the year, employ priests to intercede for them with the unseen powers, and fast, and give away much to the poor. The temples outside Kuei Fu were thronged for the days preceding the New Year with men and women, old and young; and in the midst of clouds of incense rich and poor prostrated themselves before the gods, burning gold and silver tinsel paper, while gongs, bells, drums, and cymbals kept up a ceaseless din.

In the midst of the general winding up of all affairs, spiritual and temporal, and starting on the New Year clear, the great matter of debt is not forgotten. The paying of debts and settling of accounts is a highly praiseworthy custom, and one which we might introduce among ourselves with advantage. Although only a custom, it has all the force of law. If it can be avoided by any sacrifice, no debt is carried over New Year's Day without either an actual settlement or an arrangement regarded as satisfactory by the creditor. To do otherwise would be to secure a blasted reputation. If men owe more than they can pay, custom compels them at this season to put all they have into the hands of their creditors and close their business concerns; and one among the causes of suicide is when men have not enough to pay their debts with. Interest on loans rises, the pawnbrokers' warehouses are choke-full, and most kinds of commodities fall in value, while second-hand clothing and many other personal possessions are to be bought cheap. The future to a Chinese often consists of little more than his funeral and the New Year! People dread the difficulties, expense, and delays of resorting to law for the recovery of debts; and all are agreed on maintaining this wholesome custom, which has a great tendency to weed out from among traders the shifty and dishonest. I have heard that one method of compelling an unwilling debtor to pay his debts is to remove the door from his house or shop, so as to allow of the ingress of evil and malignant demons. This last resort is said never to fail!

All the ceremonies which are to welcome the New Year, with the garnishing of the house with red paper, tinsel flowers, streamers, and the pictures, ornamenting of the ancestral shrine, and the general "redding up," occupy much of the previous night; and the stillness of the first hours of the great day reminds one of an old-fashioned Scotch Sunday.

Towards noon the streets begin to fill, as in America, with men with card-cases paying visits. All are well dressed, even to the coolies, for those who have not grand clothes hire them. Inside Kuei Fu sedan chairs were *en règle*; outside, men made their calls on foot, in many instances cards sufficing, inscribed with a device suggesting the three good wishes of children (*i.e.* sons), wealth or rank, and longevity. Men meeting in the streets greeted each other with profound respect, and with the good wish, "May the new joy be yours," which reminded me of the Syrian salutation on the feast of the Epiphany, or with the words, "I respectfully wish you joy." Universal politeness and good behaviour prevailed, and not a tipsy man was to be seen during the day or evening.

Mourners remain within doors, and strips of blue paper mixed with red denote houses into which death has entered during the previous year. Be-dien told me that in the city, where there are many *literati* and rich men, there were houses with all their wood-work covered with gold-sprinkled red paper, and on the lintels five slips expressing the desire of the owner for the "five blessings": riches, health, love of virtue, longevity, and a natural death. Over some shops was a decorated slip, "May rich customers ever enter this door," and in many stately vestibules, in which handsome presentation coffins were reared on end, there were costly scrolls inscribed with aphorisms and other sentences.*

On New Year's Day gods and ancestors receive prostrations, and are presented with gifts in the temples and in the clan or family ancestral halls. It would be a gross breach of etiquette and an unthinkable outrage if inferiors were not to pay their respects to superiors, pupils to salute their teachers, and children to prostrate themselves before their parents.

When evening came, lanterns, transparencies, and fireworks appeared, and very effective coloured fires reddened the broad bosom of the Yangtze. Hilarious sounds proceeding from closed doors showed that, as in Korea at the same hour, sacrifices were being offered to departed parents, and that families were gathered

---

* Dr. WELLS WILLIAMS, on p. 812 of *The Middle Kingdom*, vol. i., says that a literary man would have such a sentence as—

   " May I be so learned as to secrete in my mind three myriads of volumes " ;
   " May I know the affairs of the world for six thousand years."

While a shopkeeper would adorn his door with such mottoes as these—

   " May profits be like the morning sun rising on the clouds " ;
   " May wealth increase like the morning tide which brings the rain " ;
   " Manage your occupation according to truth and loyalty."
   " Hold on to benevolence and rectitude in all your trading."

Dr. Williams adds that the influence of these and countless similar mottoes which are to be seen throughout the land is inestimable, and is usually for good. At all events it is better to have a high ideal than a low one.

at the final feast of the day. My trackers hung coloured lanterns from the matted roof and feasted on pork with wine, but there was no excess, and it was a real pleasure to see them get one good meal with time to enjoy it. Owing to the moderate use of intoxicants, and that chiefly with food, the three holidays of this universal festival pass by without turmoil or disgrace, and the population goes back to trade and work out of debt and not demoralised by its spell of social festivity.

So the most ancient of the world's existing civilisations comports itself on its great holiday, while our civilisation of yesterday, especially in Scotland, what with " first-footing," " treating," and general sociability, is apt to turn the holiday into a pandemonium.

CHAPTER XVI.

KUEI FU TO WAN HSIEN

THE following morning my trackers, having no fumes of liquor to sleep off, were astir early. There was one long and strong rapid, Lao Ma ("Old Horse"), and a minor one, Miao Chitze ("Temple Stairs"), where the water rushes furiously over a succession of steps with a clear but very rapid channel in the centre. Passenger boats turn out their fares there, and it was piteous to see the women with their bound feet hobbling and tumbling among boulders, where I, who am not a very bad climber, was glad to get the help of two men. Of course, the fathers and husbands gave them no assistance. The fierce cataract of Tung Yangtze, remarkable for a vigorous attempt which was made not very many years ago to overcome its difficulties by building a fine stone breakwater, now in decay, and a succession of *chipas* and eddies, intervened between Kuei Fu and Yun-yang Hsien, or "Clouded Sun City," on the bank of a fine gorge, its grey walls extending far up the mountain on the slope of which the city stands, high above the winter level of the river.

These cities on the Yangtze are captivating to the eye, and the touches of colour given by the glazed green and yellow tiles of the curved roofs of their many fine temples relieve the otherwise monotonous grey. The "City of the Clouded Sun" is not lively, and has very little trade, but it is stately and clean, and its temples are well kept and imposing, specially the Temple of Longevity, which has a wall richly decorated in high relief, in which fine bronze tablets are inlaid.

The glory of the city is, however, on the opposite bank—the Temple of Chang-fei, a warrior who died fighting for his country. The whole scene is beautiful, and it was most mortifying that the crowd which gathered round my camera, looking in at the lens and over my shoulder under the focussing cloth and shaking it violently, prevented me from getting a picture of it. Nature and art have combined in a perfect picturesqueness. On the flat vertical surface of a noble cliff rising from the boulder-strewn shore of the Yangtze are four characters—and what can be more decorative than Chinese characters "writ large"?—which are translated "Ethereal bell, one thousand ages." This bell is believed by the people to ring of its own accord in case of a fire in the district.

TEMPLE OF CHANG-FEI.

Above it, and approached by a fine broad flight of 100 stone stairs, is a magnificent temple in perfect repair, and with its gorgeous decorations lately restored. It has three courts, one three-storeyed and two two-storeyed pavilions, their much-curled roofs tiled with glazed tiles of an exquisite green. Corridors, also roofed with green tiles and composed of elaborate and beautiful wooden fretwork with the peony for its motive, connect the courts. On one side of the temple is a deep narrow glen with fine trees and a waterfall, and over this a beautiful stone bridge has been thrown from the temple door. There are some noble specimens of the *Ficus religiosa*. There were large numbers of visitors, and a ferry-boat is continually crossing. A lovelier place for a religious picnic could not be found.*

At Yun-yang we took in a relation of the *lao-pan*, a Romanist, employed by the French priest resident in the city as doctor to a dispensary. According to him, there are 300 Roman Christians in Yun-yang, who are quite free from molestation. There is no Protestant missionary there or in the country we passed through during the previous eighteen days. On the river bank, after Mr. Stevenson had been talking with a number of men about Christianity, an old man said to him, "Teacher, you say what is good, but it is not all true. You say we have never seen God. Then we can't have injured Him, and so don't need His forgiveness."

Above Yun-yang the country opens out, and the verdure and fertility are most charming. The bright red of the soil, the fresh green of the grain crops and sugar-cane, and the brilliant yellow of the rape made a charming picture. Every now and then a noble specimen of the *Ficus religiosa*, with an altar and incense-burner below it, lent the contrast of its dark green foliage, and substantial farm-houses of "Brick Noggin," each in a clump of bamboo, and fine temples in groves of evergreens gave an air of prosperity to the scene. I was not surprised at the encomiums which previous travellers have bestowed on this province.

Rape is universally grown for the oil. The people have neither butter nor grease for cooking, and their diet would be incomplete without abundance of some oily substance. Imported and native kerosene may take its place as an illuminant, but for cooking purposes it will be always grown. In such a fertile and beautiful region the absence of animal life is curious. There is no pasturage, the roads are not made for draught, and the cheerfulness of horses, cattle, and sheep about a farmyard is unknown. Buff dogs, noisy and cowardly, and the hideous water buffalo, which looks like an antediluvian survival and has a singular aversion to foreigners, represent the domestic animals.

We were delayed considerably by head winds, involving much tracking and rowing, and thumped a hole in the boat's bottom for

---

* Although the Temple of Chang-fei stands 200 feet above the river at low water, the one which preceded it was carried away in a great flood in 1870, when the water actually rose to the height of the present roof. The present gorgeous structure cost 10,000 taels.

PAGODA NEAR WAN HSIEN.

the second time, on which she filled so fast that she had to be run ashore with all despatch, and the miserable attempts at repair delayed us for some hours, as no carpenter would work during the New Year holidays. For the next twenty-eight hours it took four men baling night and day to keep the water down.

At a distance of nearly 1300 miles from its mouth the Yangtze is still a noble river, nobler yet when the summer rise covers the grand confusions of its rocky bed. The "Gorge of the Eight Cliffs," a singular freak of nature, with perpendicular cliffs fluted like organ pipes, through which the river has cut a channel, said by the boatmen to be fathomless, about six miles long, through a bed of hard grey sandstone, detained us for a long time, and was bitterly cold and draughty. Above in a recess in the rock are carved three divinities in full canonicals, painted and gilded, called " The Three Water Guardians." It is said that the reason that no boatmen will move in the dark is that these genii only guard the river by day.

Tiresome rapids detained us again, and I climbed a height to look at some queer erections, which are seen at intervals of about three miles, on elevations along the river from Ichang to Chungking, making a goodly show. They are white towers, with a red sun painted on the front of each, and stand five in a row. The boatmen say that they are to mark distances, but, according to better authorities they are *yen-tun*, or "smoke towers," and have served the purpose of giving alarm in unsettled times by fires of dry combustibles within. Apparently they have not been repaired for many years.

On Ash Wednesday, February 19th, in the afternoon, a fine, white, nine-storeyed pagoda on a bank, and another on a high hill, announced the approach to a city. The river was narrowed by an insignificant gorge, then came a broad expanse of still water resembling a mountain lake, and then Wan appeared. That was one of the unforgettable views in China. The "Myriad City," for position and appearance, should rank high among the cities of the world. The burst of its beauty as we came round an abrupt corner into the lake-like basin on which it stands, and were confronted with a stately city piled on cliffs and heights, a wall of rock on one side crowded with refuges and temples, with the broad river disappearing among mountains which were dissolving away in a blue mist, was quite overpowering.

Its situation on a sharp bend of the Yangtze, backed at a distance of thirty miles by a range of mountains—built on cliffs, and in clusters round temple and pagoda-crowned hills, and surrounded by precipitous, truncated peaks of sandstone, from 700 to 1500 feet in height, rising out of woods through which torrents flash in foam, and from amidst garden cultivation, and surmounted by the picturesque, fortified refuges which are a feature of the region—is superb and impressive. Wan is the first of the prosperous cities of SZE CHUAN that I saw. It has doubled its population and trade in twenty years, and its fine streets and handsome shops, stately dwellings within large grounds, thriving industries, noble charities, and the fringe of junks for over two miles along its river shore, indicate a growing prosperity which is characteristic of nearly every city in SZE CHUAN which I afterwards visited.

We tied up in a crowd of large junks lying in three tiers. Hundreds of coolies were loading and unloading them, and the noise was deafening. Leaving the furious babel of the boatmen, who were dissatisfied with their "wine money," I walked the mile up to the China Inland Mission house, partly by a flight of 150 steep stone stairs, and up back streets, and being bareheaded and in Chinese dress, escaped a very great crowd. No European woman had walked up through Wan before, for it and its officials had been notoriously hostile to foreigners, and Dr. Morrison, of the *Times*, had been ill-treated there only six months before. I was much impressed by the good paving and cleanliness, and the substantial stone dwellings *en route*.

Arriving at a fine Chinese gateway, with a porter's lodge and an outer court, along which are servants' quarters and cow stables, we passed into what is a truly beautiful paved inner court, one side a roofed-in open space used as a chapel, the other a lofty and handsome Chinese guest-room, as shown in the illustration, with an open front, and the living-rooms of the family. A third side is the women's guest-room, and on the fourth are various rooms. Projecting upper storeys and balconies, all carving and fretwork, latticed and carved window-frames with paper panes, tall pillars, and irregular tiled roofs, make up a striking *tout ensemble*, in the

GUEST HALL, C.I.M. WAN HSIEN.

midst of which Mr. and Mrs. Thompson and three ladies, all in Chinese dress, stood to welcome me. It was all so trim and handsome that there was a distinct unseemliness in bringing in my shabby travelling equipments, much the worse for two years' hard wear, and I hurried them into retirement as soon as possible.

The house is beautiful inside, the walls, roofs, and pillars of planed, unvarnished wood of a fine grain, all dovetailed or put together with wooden bolts. Downstairs the large fretwork windows, opening on pivots, are above a man's head. All the furniture, with the exception of some presents, is Chinese, and is at once simple and tasteful. Upstairs are a number of low, irregular, quaint rooms. The one allotted to me was a large one, with a great fretwork window into the court, and another with a superb view of the city and down the river. It had access by a steep step-ladder to an open wooden tower with a pagoda roof and seats for use in the hot weather. This overlooks the houses of many neighbours, and is overlooked. From it are to be seen all the refuges on the surrounding hill-tops, the circuit of the city wall, *yamens*, temples, and pagodas, the broad brown fringe of junks, and the gleaming silver of the Great River.

From 9 a.m. till dusk there was a continuous stream of Chinese visitors, the men entering at one door and the women at another, and passing into their guest-rooms, where they were separately received by Mr. Thompson and Miss Ramsay. A Chinese is a dignified and sensitive man, and likes to be master of the situation. He is miserable in a foreign house, with its promiscuous oddities, and has no idea where or on what to sit, what position to take, and to what etiquette he is to conform himself, and has all the discomfort of a fish out of water. In a Chinese guest-room, on the contrary, there is an ordered and rigid stateliness. A few handsome scrolls from the classics or pictures decorate the walls. A handsome carved black wood table stands against the wall opposite the open front, and on both sides of it are ranged heavy black wood chairs, the highest being next the table. Elaborate lamps hang from the roof.

No matter what the position of a Chinese is, whether he be mandarin, merchant, shopkeeper, or writer, he is absolutely certain which chair etiquette entitles him to take, and when tea and pipes are produced he is as serene and comfortable as in his own house.

At that time, though missionaries had been settled at Wan for some years, and had been able to rent this beautiful house, there was not a Christian in the city. The ladies had only lately arrived, as it had been thought not a safe place for them. Even a month before my visit, when a deep well ran dry, a mob assembled outside the mission-house threatening to burn it and to kill all the "foreign devils," for they had tapped the well and had stolen the golden crab which was the "luck" of the city. The mob was eventually compelled to withdraw, but the mandarin, who only left as I was arriving, came to the house with the serious charge that the inmates had killed children in order to get their eyes, and that their bodies were in the tanks at the back !

Mr. Thompson took him to the back, and the tanks were probed with a long pole, but the accusation was not disposed of by the resultlessness of the search, for foreign magic is believed to be equal to anything. The same official concerted the murder of the missionaries with the elders of the city, and Mr. Davies, who was then in Wan, was severely beaten. Compensation, however, was given him, which he bestowed on the local charities. A new chief magistrate had just arrived, with orders to treat the foreigners well, and all was changed. When Mr. Thompson called at the *yamen* the mandarin conducted him to the seat of honour, escorted him to his chair on leaving, and returned the visit with a large retinue the next day. Of course the Chinese everywhere take their cue from the officials.

So it came about that for several days I was able actually to walk about and to photograph with no worse trouble than the curiosity of the people in masculine crowds of a thousand or more. Four months before I was told that this would have been impossible. My camera would have been smashed, my open chair would have produced a riot, and I should have been stoned or severely beaten.

The streams of visitors to the beautiful guest-halls never ceased by daylight. Miss Ramsay often received forty women at a time. All Sze Chuan women have bound feet, and all wear trousers very much *en évidence*, those of the lower class women being wrapped round the ankles and tied, those of the upper class being wide and decorated. They asked hordes of questions about domestic and social matters from their own grotesquely different standpoint, and wanted to hear what the "Jesus religion" was like, and were quite unable to understand how people could pray "unless they had a god in the room." One day Miss Ramsay, who had been for some years in China, explained to her guests various things concerning our Lord's life and teachings, and an upper class woman, who seemed intelligent and interested, explained it in her way to the others. As she left, Miss R. said, "You'll not forget what I have told you," and she said very pleasantly, "Oh, no, I won't; our gods are made of mud, and yours are made of wood!"

The ignorance which many men of the literary class show is wonderful, and it comes out freely in conversations in the guest-hall. A very grand military mandarin asserted not only that Lin and the Black Flags had driven the Japanese out of Formosa, but that the Straits of Formosa had yawned wide in answer to vows and prayers addressed to the gods by Lin, and that the navies of Russia, England, France, and Japan had perished in a common destruction in the vortex! A picture representing this catastrophe was for sale in Wan.*

They think that the Queen of England is tributary to China, that our Minister is in Peking to pay the tribute, and that the presents which the Queen sent to the Empress Dowager on her sixtieth birthday were the special tribute for the occasion.

They also believed that the American commission which had lately been at Chengtu for the purpose of assessing the damage done to the property of Americans in the previous riots was sent to congratulate the new Viceroy on his appointment!

Also many of the *literati* say—and I had heard the same thing in the north—that outside of China there are five kingdoms united under one emperor, Jesus Christ, who rose from a peasant origin, that one is inhabited by dog-faced people,† and that in another,

---

* The volume from which this picture was taken and enlarged was printed in Shanghai.

† This term "dog-faced" apparently does not bear the meaning which we put on it, for the woman in the illustration on page 487 with a head-dress of solid silver and heavy white silk from the mountains of FU KIEN is a member of what the Fu-chow Chinese call "dog-faced" tribes.

where each woman has two husbands, she has a hole in her chest, and that when they travel the husbands put a pole through it and carry her! They also say that the missionaries come and live in distant places like Wan and Paoning in order to find out the secret of China's greatness and the way to destroy it by magic arts. A map of Asia hangs in the guest-hall, and Mr. Thompson overheard some of the guests saying to each other at different times, "Look at these 'foreign devils'" (*yang-kwei-tze*); "they put China small on the map to deceive their god!"

It is impossible to have patience with their ignorance because of their overweening self-conceit. It is passable in Africa, but not in these men with their literary degrees, and their elaborate culture "of sorts," and two thousand years of civilisation behind them.

Wan Hsien has a very large trade. Its shops are full of goods, native and foreign, and the traffic from the interior, as well as by junk, is enormous, but there are no returns, as it is not an open port. The actual city—*i.e.*, the walled city—which contains the *yamens* and other public buildings, is small, steep, and handsome. It has extended itself into large suburbs five miles in extent, of which the true city is the mere nucleus. They straggle along the river, high up on the cliffs above it, and two miles back, where they are arrested by a rocky barrier at a height in which is excavated and scaffolded a celebrated "Temple of the Three Religions," at the top of 1570 fine stairs, a great place of pilgrimage. This back country, in which are few level acres, is exquisitely cultivated, and is crossed in several directions by flagged pathways, carried over ascents and descents by good stairs. These usually lead to lovely villages, built irregularly on torrent sides, among a great variety of useful trees.

The city is divided into two parts by a river-bed, then nearly dry, but when I saw it in summer it contained a very respectable stream, which serves as the public laundry. I have never seen so beautiful a bridge as the lofty, single stone arch, with a house at the highest part, which spans the river-bed, and which seems to spring out of the rock without any visible abutments.

Graceful pagodas and three-storeyed pavilions guard the approaches. The Feng Shui of Wan is considered perfect. Rich temples on heights above the river and the handsome temple called Chung-ku-lo (Drum and Bell Lodge), overlooking the small gorge below, with a large stage, under a fine three-storeyed pavilion, for the performance of the religious dramas, show that "The Three Religions" retain their hold on the people. The wealth of vegetation is wonderful. Not a barren or arid spot is to be seen from the water's edge to the mountain summits which are the limits of vision. The shiny orange foliage, the dark formal cypress, the loquat and pomegranate, the gold of the plumed bamboo, the deep green of sugarcane, the freshness of the advancing grain

BRIDGE AT WAN HSIEN.

crops, and the drapery of clematis and maidenhair on trees and rocks all delight the eyes. But the uniqueness of the neighbourhood of Wan consists in the number of its truncated sandstone hills, each bearing on its flat top a picturesque walled white village and fortification, to be a city of refuge in times of rebellion. These, rising out of a mass of greenery, with a look of inaccessibility about them, are a silent reference to unpleasant historic facts which distinguish Wan from other cities.

It is not alone that junks fringe the shores, but they are very largely built at Wan, for the passage of the rapids, of a convenient material—the tough, formal cypress which grows on the adjacent hills. They must be at once light and strong, and more disposed to bend than to break.   Many of their fittings have a local origin, and many rich junk builders and junk owners live at Wan.

Foreign goods go up the river to Chungking, the westernmost treaty port, from twelve to twenty days higher up the river, and come down again to Wan.   "The Province of the Four Streams" does not produce much cotton ; and cotton yarn from Japan and India comes in large quantities into Wan to be woven there.   In 1898 there were about 1000 handlooms.   The cotton is woven into pieces about thirty feet long and sixteen inches broad, which take a man two days' labour, from daylight till 9 p.m., to weave.   A weaver's wages with food come to about 600 *cash*, at present about 1*s*. 6*d*. per week of six days.   Can Lancashire compete with this in anything but the output?

CHAPTER XVII.

CHINESE CHARITIES *

AS Moslems regard almsgiving as one of the "gates of heaven," and practise it to a very remarkable extent, so the Chinese have placed benevolence foremost on the list of the "Five Constant Virtues." The character which denotes it is said by the learned to be composed of the symbols for *man* and *two*, by which is somewhat obscurely indicated, on the principle of the spark being the result of the contact of flint with steel, that benevolence should result from the contact of two human beings.

That this is so in China is not the impression which the facts of daily life produce, and the popular view taken of Chinese character in this country is that it is cruel, brutal, heartless, and absolutely selfish and unconcerned about human misery. Among supporters of foreign missions this opinion would be found nearly universal; and, indeed, I have heard the non-existence of benevolence in the vast non-Christian empire of China brought forward as an argument in favour of such missions. So saturated is our atmosphere with the belief that the only charitable institutions in China are those founded by Protestant and Catholic missionaries, that nothing surprised me more than to find that the reverse is the case. Among the many intelligent and frivolous questions which have been put to me since I returned, the one, "Have the Chinese any charities?" has not been among them. It has been reserved for missionaries, and specially the late Rev. D. Hill, of Hankow, and the Rev. W. Lawton, of Chinkiang, to bring this most interesting subject under the notice of readers. The Rev. Arthur Smith gives a chapter of his clever and attractive book, *Chinese*

* The charities of China have been several times alluded to, and it seems fitting before leaving Wan Hsien, where they are both numerous and active, to devote a special chapter to them. The sketch is an imperfect and limited one, but it may help to point the way to a field of very interesting inquiry.

Characteristics, to the same subject, and Dr. Wells Williams glances at it very briefly in *The Middle Kingdom ;* but few out of the many lay writers on China have touched upon it. On my first visit in 1878, Dr. Henry, of Canton, pointed out to me asylums or almshouses for the blind, and for aged persons without sons ; and on my recent visits, following this lead, I made such inquiries as were practicable on this subject, and now venture to present my too scanty notes to my readers.

I have already remarked that the facts which lie on the surface of Chinese daily life do not give the impression of strong benevolent instincts. Wounded men are stripped of their uniforms and are left to perish on battlefields, because "wounded men are no use." The ablest Chinese general in the late war wished to buy machine guns without the protective "mantle" at the consequently reduced price, and on being told by the German agent that this would risk a great sacrifice of life coolly replied, "We 've plenty of men." Yet this same man was most generous to the poor, established soup-kitchens in Mukden, his city, every winter, supplied the hospital with ice for the patients, and, even in the hurry of the last evening before he started with his brigade for the fatal field of Phyong-yang, arranged that the hospital should be supplied with ice during his absence.

I have known a number of coolies refuse to get water from a river a few yards off to assuage the burning thirst of an apparently dying man of their number, who had carried a burden by their side for a fortnight, and had shared their hardships, on the ground that he was "no more any good," and several similar instances, and what they do not practise themselves they fail to understand in others. I have been jeered at as a fool for laying a wet cloth on the brow of a man who had served me for some time and fell out on the road seriously ill, and yet more for having him carried in my chair rather than leave him to die on a mountain-side. On another occasion in SZE CHUAN, when I left my chair and walked up a part of the colossal staircase by which the road is carried over the Pass of Shen Kia-chao, my bearers showed the construction they put on my doing so by asking, "Does the foreign woman think us not strong enough to carry her?" Men of the lower class interpret ordinary humanity and consideration as arising from dread of them, and the traveller is daily coming across instances which look very like brutality, and most foreign residents speak of the Chinese as cruel and brutal.

Some writers, especially the author of *Chinese Characteristics*, while admitting the existence of charities on a large scale, detract from the admiration which such works of benevolence would naturally command by pointing out that they are regarded as "practising virtue," and are considered to be a means of "accumulating merit," and in fact that the object generally in view is "not the benefit of the person on whom the 'benevolence' terminates, but the extraction from the benefit conferred of a return benefit for the giver." The Chinese are perhaps the most practical people on earth, and a curious system of moral bookkeeping adopted by many shows this feature of the national character in a very curious light. There are books inculcating the practice of "virtue," and in these a regular debtor and creditor account is opened, in which an individual charges himself with all his bad acts and credits himself with all his good ones, and the balance between the two exhibits his moral position at any given time.

Mr. A. Smith is a very acute observer, and has had lengthened opportunities of observation, and his conclusions as to the motives for benevolence must be received with respect. May it not, however, be hinted that an equally acute observer setting himself to dissect motives for largesse to charities after a residence of some years in England would consider himself warranted in referring a very considerable proportion of our benevolence to motives less worthy than the desire to "accumulate merit"?

The problem of "the poor, and how to deal with them," has received, and is receiving, various solutions in China, and probably there is not a city without one or more organisations for the relief of permanent and special needs. Foundlings, orphans, blind persons, the aged, strangers, drowning persons, the destitute, the dead, and various other classes are objects of organised benevolence. The methods are not our methods, but they are none the less praiseworthy.

The care of the dead is imperative on every Chinese, but poverty steps in, a coffin is an unattainable luxury, and without help a proper interment is impossible. Hence in all cities there are benevolent guilds which supply coffins for those whose relations are too poor to buy them, and bury such in free cemeteries, providing, according to Chinese notions, all the accessories of a respectable funeral, with suitable offerings and the attendance of priests. Human bones which have become exposed from any cause are collected and reburied with suitable dignity, and bodies which have remained for years in coffins above ground waiting for the geomancers to decide on an auspicious day for the funeral, until all the relations are dead and the coffins are falling into decay, are supplied with new ones, and are suitably interred.

A Chinese is all his life thinking of his burial and the ancestral rites. Among a people to whom a creditable interment means so much, the generous way in which these benevolent obsequies are conducted does more than we can understand to remove the bitterness of mourning. The accompanying illustration shows a neat "chapel" with a well-kept cemetery, where bones have been gathered, those of individuals being placed together, so far as indications allow of it, under neat coverings of concrete.

In the great city of Chinkiang there are an orphan asylum and benevolent institute for girls, with five receiving offices, and a boarding-out as well as an asylum system, a benevolent institute with eighty boys above six, who are apprenticed when old enough, with five teachers in charge, and twenty free day schools for about three hundred boys, whose harsh voices, pitched high, may be heard twanging at the wisdom of the Chinese classics.

Among the Chinkiang benevolent plans for adults there is one, well managed, of inestimable advantage to the struggling farmer or merchant—"The Bureau for Advancing Funds." From it a poor man with security can borrow from 1000 to 5000 *cash* ($1 to $5), which must be repaid in one hundred days by payments made every five days. He can borrow again up to a fourth time.

There are two free dispensaries, with nine doctors in charge. They are open without fees every day, treating about 200 patients, who are not required to pay for their medicines. The Life-saving Institution, with a head office and two or three minor offices, has six well-equipped, well-manned boats always on the river near the port, and ten others dodging about above and below. I was in the steamer *Cores de Vries* when she cut down the s.s. *Hoi-how* to the water's edge abreast of Chinkiang, and I can

A CHINESE BURIAL CHARITY.

answer for the trained alacrity with which several of these boats were at once on the spot, remaining by the *Cores de Vries* even after she was run ashore. Their work is not only to save the drowning, but to remove dead bodies from the water, and these are afterwards buried with seemly rites by the Society in a well-kept private cemetery on the hill in which it has interred 175 rescued corpses within the last ten years. There is a free ferry, with thirteen big boats, for crossing the ofttimes stormy and dangerous Yangtze, which saves many lives of those who would otherwise be drowned by ferrying in cheap and unseaworthy craft. This is the richest of the benevolent institutions.

It is interesting to learn how the actual beggars, who trade upon sympathy by their filthiness, deformities, and sores, are treated. A *Beggars' Refuge* and a *Home for the Aged* exist for the same class. The Beggars' Refuge was begun by a former Taotai. Of its ninety inmates about nine are women. It is not to be expected that it should be clean or sweet. I have seen one in another city which receives five hundred. The beggars are required to bring their clothes and wadded quilts with them, but all else is furnished, and in winter outsiders also receive rice there. Most of the inmates, unless disqualified by age or disease, spend their days begging in the streets.

The rich merchants subscribe to keep up a winter " *soup kitchen*," which feeds about a thousand people daily with rice, at a cost of thirty dollars a day, during the three coldest months. Besides this the General Benevolent Institution dispenses medicines during the summer, and rice tickets during the winter, and has charge of the " Invalid Home," and also provides coffins for the dead poor. This society is richly endowed with land, owning 3000 *mow*.* The original 280 *mow* came from the priests on Golden Island.

Widows are not forgotten. Two associations take them in charge : the *Widows' Relief Society* and the *Widows' Home*. The former has only funds sufficient for 300 pensioners, the lists being filled up as deaths occur. The latter is connected with the *Boys' Orphanage*, and provides a home, food, and clothes for 200 widows. After once entering they are not allowed to go out unless offered a respectable home by a friend, or unless a son has grown to man's estate. Any results of the sale of plain

---

* A mow, roughly speaking, is about one-seventh of an acre.

or fancy needlework are returned to the worker. This care of widows marks a great advance in China on the practice in India and some other Eastern countries.

There are several free cemeteries outside the city, and one of recent origin for children, with a wall six feet high surrounding it, and a keeper in charge, in which 2000 children have been buried in the last four years. In Mukden I first became familiar with the custom, the growth of a superstitious belief, not of lack of maternal feeling, of rolling up the bodies of children in matting and " throwing them away," *i.e.*, putting the bundle where the dogs can devour the corpse, as a sort of offering to the " Heavenly Dog," which is supposed to eat the sun at an eclipse. When foreigners began to settle in the Yangtze treaty ports it came to be currently believed that they asserted a claim against the dogs for these bodies, of which they "take out the eyes and the hearts to make medicine." This was too much; hence this well-walled cemetery was provided. This accusation against foreigners, which is a frequent cause of anti-foreign riots, is current everywhere in the Yangtze Valley. I met with it in its worst form so far west as Kuan Hsien, on the Upper Min, and an angry cry of " Another child-eater!" was frequently raised against myself as I passed through the towns of SZE CHUAN. This goodly list does not exhaust the native charities of the first treaty port on the Yangtze.*

I have dwelt in detail on the charities of Chinkiang because they are typical of those of other great cities ; but the variety throughout the country is infinite, and includes many associations merely for the relief of suffering. In Wuhu a *Life-saving Association* was established in 1874, with which have been associated, under the same managing staff, a gratuitous *Coffin Association*, to help the very poor to inter their relatives decently, and a *Free Ferry Association*, with big, well-found boats, to prevent the poor from risking their lives by crossing the Yangtze in small *sampans*. Large and substantial offices indicate the generous support given to the *Lifeboat Association*, with which are united a *Humane Society* for restoring life to persons rescued from the

* I am indebted for most of the foregoing facts to Mr. W. R. Carles, lately H.B.M.'s consul at Chinkiang, and to the very careful investigations made by the Rev. W. W. Lawton for the Christian Literary Association of Chinkiang.

water, and other kindred benevolent associations. This society, which has societies affiliated to it, and apparently under the same rules, at many of the riverine towns, has four lifeboats at Wuhu, about fifty feet long, ten broad, and fourteen tons burden, well manned and handled, able to face any weather, with crews under strict discipline, and ready to sally forth at a signal. They cruise up and down the river aiding junks in distress, rescuing the drowning, and recovering bodies for burial.

If a rescued man is a stranger and destitute, he receives the loan of dry clothing, and shelter for three days ; if he is ill, he has shelter and medical attendance so long as he requires them. Such destitute rescued persons are supplied with twenty cents for each thirty-three miles of their journey home. A recovered corpse is reported by the society to the authorities, who take charge of any property recovered with it until the relations are found. It is decently buried, and the usual ceremonial for the dead is provided at stated seasons.

This society publishes its rules and accounts annually for general information. Its offices were built by donations from merchants. It receives a subscription of fifty taels a month from the inland customs, and its other funds are subscriptions, rentals of donated lands, and contributions of rice. The society has always a good balance in hand. Besides wages, it pays at Wuhu and the different sub-stations to the boatmen a reward of 1000 *cash*, or about a dollar, for every life saved, and from 300 to 500 *cash* for every corpse.

Another charity also provides coffins for destitute persons, and mat - shelters, often sadly needed, for burned - out families, and medical aid for the sick. This is supported chiefly by subscriptions from shopkeepers and gifts of coffin wood.

A few years ago the Taotai, with the leading "gentry" and merchants, established an asylum for foundlings and the children of destitute parents, which has gradually come to include a charity school, an almshouse for aged and invalid poor, and a free hospital.

Kukiang has several similar institutions, including a *Humane and Life-saving Institution*, established by the tea and opium merchants with the funds of their guilds. In Hankow there are more than twenty charities, supported at a cost of about 100,000 dollars annually. At Wan Hsien, above the gorges and the worst rapids, there are very noble charities, some of them carried on by the Scholars' Guild and the head men of the city, and others by private individuals. Among these are soup kitchens and large donations of rice to the poor in the winter, and in the first month (February) allowances of rice and money to about fifty old people, and gifts of 1600 *cash* each to about 100 poor widows. The Scholars' Guild also supports a foundling hospital. I cannot overlook the noble benevolences of Hsing-fuh-sheo, a Wan merchant, not exceptionally wealthy, who, at a cost of over 8000 dollars a year, supports two dispensaries and a drug store, forty free schools, five preachers of the Sacred Edict, and besides, provides clothing and coffins for the dead poor, and wadded garments for the destitute in winter.*

Among many other ways of showing benevolence is the provision of free vaccination to all who will apply for it; drugs and plasters are given by some to all applicants, and books known as "Virtue Books" are given away by others, or are exposed for sale at less than cost price. There are small associations for providing the neat, canopied, stone furnaces which are seen in all cities and many country places, for the burning of paper on which are written characters. Originally no doubt this practice was established to prevent any defilement of the sacred names of Buddha and Confucius, but a sanctity has come to attach to all written paper owing to the great reverence of the Chinese for literature, and paper is no longer collected by the priests, but by men paid by these societies for the purpose, who go round with bamboo tongs and bottle-mouthed baskets, rescuing the characters from desecration. The benevolence is not apparent to me, although the societies which undertake this work bear the name *Mutual Charitable Institutions.*

Among other good works are the charitably aided provincial clubs for the care of those who become destitute at a distance from home, and who without such aid could not return, or who, having died afar from relatives, could not otherwise be taken home for burial. Among temporary charities partly Govern-

---

* For these very interesting facts regarding Wan, I am indebted to my host there, Mr. Thompson, of the China Inland Mission. Statistics are not available.

ment-aided, but very much supported by private liberality, are the vast soup kitchens, very completely organised, which, on occasions of flood or famine, extend their benevolent and often judicious work over the whole afflicted region, and save thousands of lives. Then there are large donations of wadded winter clothing and wadded sleeping quilts made every year to the destitute ; and societies, something in the nature of charitably aided savings banks, for the twin objects of enabling men to marry and to bury their parents creditably.

Much kindness of a kind is shown to the streams of refugees who in bad years swarm all over parts of China in allowing them to camp with their families in barns and sheds, often giving them an evening meal. Enormous gifts are made to beggars, who, in all the large cities, are organised into such powerful guilds that they can coerce rather than plead, and can ensure that a steady stream of charity shall flow in their direction. In the case of both refugees and beggars, a prudent dread of the consequences of refusal is doubtless answerable for much of what poses as charity, and in this the Chinese and the Englishman are probably near of kin.

In concluding this chapter, which brings additional evidence of the strong tendency to organise which exists among the Chinese, I will mention a few of the methods in which individuals carry out benevolent instincts or seek to "accumulate merit." A Buddhist on a river bank pays a fisherman for the whole of the contents of his plunge-net, and returns the silver heap to the water ; another buys a number of caged birds, and lets them fly. Some build sheds over roads, and provide them with seats for weary travellers ; others make a road over a difficult pass, or build a bridge, or provide a free ferry for the poor and their cattle. A few men club together to provide free soup or tea for travellers, and erect a shed, putting in an old widow to keep the water boiling ; or two or three priests, with the avowed object of securing merit, do the same thing at a temple ; others provide seats for wayfarers on a steep hill. Some provide lamps glazed with thin layers of oyster shells fitted into a wooden framework, and either hang them from posts or fit them into recesses in pillars to warn travellers by night of dangerous places on the roads.

I put forward my opinion on the subject of Chinese bene-volence with much diffidence, laying the motive of the accumu-lation of merit on one side. The Chinese obviously fail in acts of unselfishness and of *personal* kindliness and goodwill. Their works of merit are very much on a large scale, for the benefit of human beings in masses, the individual being lost sight of. They involve little personal, wholesome contact between the giver and receiver, out of which love and gratitude may grow, and no personal self-denial, and in these respects place themselves on a par with much of our easy charity by proxy at home.

It was a great surprise to me, as it will be to the more thoughtful among my readers, to find that organised charity on so large a scale exists in China. Among its defects, in addition to the lack, before mentioned, of kindly individual contact, are the neglect to foster independence by painstaking methods, and the system of peculation from which even benevolent funds do not escape, though it must be added that many Chinese gentlemen give much valuable time to securing their honest and efficient management.

I have not been able to learn whether the benevolent instincts of Chinese women find any outlet. I have been asked by one to give some straw plaiting to a poor widow to do, and by another lady to employ an indigent woman in embroidering satin shoes. I have heard of ladies inviting old and poor women to tea once a week, and even oftener; and Mr. A. Smith narrates one such instance.

It must be remarked that in China certain serious consequences may befall a man who performs an act of kindness individually, and that a dread of such a mishap renders men exceedingly reluctant to give aid and to save life under some circumstances. This possibility is apt to make the Chinese wary as to doing kindnesses per-sonally. A missionary tells how a medical missionary living in one of the central provinces was asked by some native gentlemen to restore the sight of a beggar who was totally blind from cataract. The operation was successfully performed, but when the man regained his sight the same gentlemen came to the operator and told him that, as by the cure he had destroyed the beggar's sole means of livelihood, it was then his duty to compen-sate him by taking him into his service!

In conclusion, the Chinese classics teach benevolence : charity is required as a proof of sincere goodness ; the Buddhist religious writings inculcate relief of sick persons and compassion to the poor, and the worship of the Goddess of Mercy, an increasingly popular cult in China, tends in the same humane direction.   It must be remembered also that the divinities worshipped in China are not monsters of cruelty and incarnations of evil, but, on the contrary, that they may be credited with some of the virtues, and among them that of benevolence.

CHAPTER XVIII.

FROM WAN HSIEN TO SAN TSAN-PU

FINDING that it was impossible for any European to accompany me, I decided to venture on the journey of 300 miles to Paoning Fu alone, and to buy my own experience. The land journey developed into one of about 1200 miles, and was accomplished with one serious mishap and one great disappointment. It was interesting throughout, and taught me much of the ways of the people, and the scenery alone would have repaid me for the hardships, which were many. My greatest difficulty consisted in having to disinter all information about the route and the industries and customs of the people, through the medium of two languages, out of the capacities of persons who neither observed nor thought accurately, nor were accustomed to impart what they knew: who were used to telling lies, and to whom I could furnish no reasons for telling the truth, while they might have several for deceiving me on some points. This digging into obtuseness and cunning is the hardest part of a traveller's day. So far as I could make out before or since my journey, no British traveller or missionary has published an account of the country between Wan Hsien, on the Yangtze, and Kuan Hsien, north of the Chengtu Plain, nor can I find among the very valuable consular reports, to which I cannot too often express my debt, one which has done for this region of Central SZE CHUAN what Mr. Litton, of the consular service at Chungking, has lately done so admirably for Northern SZE CHUAN. Consequently on the greater part of my four months' journey I had nothing by which to estimate the value of the facts which I supposed myself to have obtained.*

---

* I must also mention, in extenuation of sundry faults of which I am conscious, that I went to Western China solely for interest and pleasure, and not with any intention of writing a book, and that, instead of having careful and copious notes, I have only journal letters to rely upon.

The longer one travels the fewer preparations one makes, and the smaller is one's kit. I got nothing at Wan except a large sheet doubly oiled with boiled linseed oil, and some additional curry powder, kindly furnished by my kind hosts from boxes of tinned eatables, sauces, arrowroot, and invalid comforts, which had just arrived, and the like of which were annually delivered, carriage free, at the door of every China Inland missionary, however remote, sent by the late Mr. Morton, of Aberdeen, a thoughtful gift, of great value to the recipients. The reader may be amused to learn the singular monotony of my diet. I had a cup of tea made from "tabloids," and a plate of boiled flour, every morning before starting, tea on arriving, and for 146 days, at seven, curried fowl or eggs with rice. I got another Chinese cotton costume and some straw shoes, and for any other needs trusted to supplying them on the way.

My servant had made himself persistently disagreeable from the beginning, and though a superior, fairly educated, and handsome man, he seemed helpless, useless, lazy, unwilling, and objectionable all round. The impression of my hosts and myself was that he wished to annoy me into sending him back from Wan, and Mr. Thompson thought that he would make my journey very difficult and unpleasant; but the choice lay between giving it up on the threshold and taking him, and I chose the latter.

As the guest of a European, all the difficulties of arranging, bargaining, and paying are lifted off one and put upon a teacher or servant who is used to them, and after much chaffering a bargain was concluded by which three chair-bearers and four coolies were to take me and my baggage to Paoning Fu in nineteen days, a halt on Sundays being paid for at the rate of 25,000 *cash*. These men were not dealt with directly, but were engaged by contract with the manager of a transport *hong*, who is responsible for their good conduct and honesty. I may say at once that they behaved admirably; made the journey in two days less than the stipulated time; trudged cheerfully through rain and mud; never shirked their work; and were always sober, cheery, and obliging. I never met with other than the same behaviour on all the occasions when my coolies or boatmen were engaged from a *hong*.

My light, comfortable bamboo chair had a well under the seat which contained my camera, and, including its sixteen pounds weight, carried forty pounds of luggage in addition to myself. It had bamboo poles fourteen feet long, and a footboard suspended by ropes. Rigid laws of etiquette govern the getting out and in. An open chair in SZE CHUAN, being a novelty, is an abomination, and accounts for much of the rudeness which I received. For some time past the provincial authorities have insisted on all travellers, missionaries included, being attended by two or more "*yamen* runners," (*chai-jen*) or soldiers, who are changed at every prefecture, where they deliver up the official letter which they carry. They were never of any use, and except once, whether soldiers or civilians, always ran away at the first symptoms of a disturbance, but neither were they any nuisance, and they were always apparently satisfied with the trifle I gave them.

These *yamen* runners are attached in great numbers to every magistracy, in large cities to the number of 1000 or more. They are "the great unpaid," but manage to pick up a living, lawsuits being their great harvest, and the serving of writs one of their great occupations. They squeeze litigants, and are about as much detested by the people as bailiffs were by the men of Clare and Kerry.

Thus equipped and wearing Chinese dress, which certainly blunts the edge of curiosity and greatly diminishes the intolerable feminine picking and feeling of one's garments when they are of foreign material and make, I left the shelter and refinement of the hospitable mission house for a solitary plunge into the interior, Be-dien on foot, as sullen and disobliging as could be.

Mr. Thompson kindly accompanied me for the first day's journey to see that things worked smoothly, and we left early on a fine February morning, the air as soft and mild as that of an English April, passing through the very good-looking town and into the pretty open country on a good, flagged road, which was carried up and down hill by stone stairs.

During most of the day we met a continuous stream of baggage coolies, each carrying a bamboo over his shoulder with a burden depending from either end, shifted frequently from one shoulder to the other. Those coming in—and the inward traffic did not slacken for some days—carried from 80 to 140 pounds each of opium, tobacco, indigo, or paper ; and those going out were loaded with cotton yarn, piece goods, and salt, all carefully packed in oiled paper made from macerated bamboo, which is very tough and durable. These men, carrying the maximum load mentioned, walk about thirteen miles a day, and chair and luggage coolies about twenty-five. Occasionally I made thirty miles in a day, as my men were carrying only seventy pounds each.

The coolies choose their own place for breakfast and the mid-day halt of one hour. The first day, even with Mr. Thompson to

BAGGAGE COOLIES.

(From a Chinese Drawing.)

make things smooth for me, I wondered if I could endure it, and I never took kindly to it. The halting-place is a shed projecting over the road in a town or village street, black and grimy, with a clay floor, and rough tables and benches, receding into a dim twilight; a rough cooking apparatus and some coarse glazed pottery are the furnishings. On each table a bunch of malodor-ous chopsticks occupies a bamboo receptacle. An earthen bowl with water and a dirty rag are placed outside for the use of travellers, who frequently also rinse their mouths with hot water.

One or more exceptionally dirty men are the waiters. Bowls of rice and rice water or weak tea are produced with praiseworthy rapidity, and the coolies shovel the food into their mouths with the air of famished men, and hold out their bowls for more. My chair that day and always was set down in front of the eating-house. I went inside and had some lunch, but the dirt, discomfort, and general odiousness were so great that I did not inflict the penance on myself a second time.

People intending to be kind sometimes take pork, rice, or fish out of a common bowl and put it into yours, and to ensure cleanliness draw the chopsticks with which they perform the transference through their lips, giving them an energetic suck !

SZE CHUAN is famous for the number and splendour of what are usually called " widows' arches," though they are also erected to pious sons or patriotic mandarins, specially military mandarins. At times the approach to a city is indicated, not only by pagodas, but by passing under several of these, and occasionally even a rambling, squalid village is entered by passing under an exceptionally handsome one, as was the case on my first day's journey. I attempted to photograph it, and the *chai-jen* made the crowd stand to right and left by a series of vigorous pushes, shouting the whole time, " In the name of the mandarin." * But the people had too much curiosity to be anything but mobile.

These arches, or *pai-fangs*, are put up frequently in glorification of widows who have remained faithful to the memory of their husbands, and who have devoted themselves to the comfort and interests of their parents-in-law and to good works. Through various channels the neighbourhood presents the virtues of the meritorious person to the Throne, and the Emperor's consent to the erection is obtained. The whole affair lends some *éclat* to the town or village. Many of these arches are extremely beautiful. Chinese carving in stone has much merit, even in such an intractable material as granite. The depth and sharpness of the cutting and the undercutting are remarkable, and the absolute *realism*. I never saw a bit of sculpture which showed a trace of imagination. The superb friezes which constantly decorate the superstructure of these arches represent in a most masterly

---

* This word, which we apply universally to Chinese officials, is Portuguese. The Chinese designation is *kuan*.

A PAI-FANG

fashion mandarins' processions, mandarins administering justice, rich men's banquets, interiors of rich men's dwellings, and many other scenes of official and stately life, all rendered with photographic accuracy, and with a wonderful power of catching the expressions of the various faces. It is impossible not to admire the skill of the artists, and at the same time to wish for a trace of ideality in their art. In some places a superb arch enriched with marvels of sculpture straddles across a road which is nothing better than a disgraceful quagmire or a stone causeway in which some of the blocks are tilted up on end, while others have disappeared in the mud. The incongruity does not seem to afflict anyone.

But I must return from this digression on bad roads to the road on which I travelled on that and two or three subsequent days, which has the reputation of being one of the finest in China. It was built fifty-four years ago, and is in splendid repair. It was to lead from Wan Hsien to Chengtu Fu, but I failed to learn whether it fulfils its promise. It is never less than six feet wide, paved with transverse stone slabs, carried through the rice-fields on stone causeways, and over the bridges and up and down the innumerable hills by flights of stone stairs on fairly easy gradients, with stone railings and balustrades wherever there is any necessity for them. Streams are crossed by handsome stone bridges, with sharp lofty arches, and the whole is a fine engineering work.

My journey began auspiciously with a dreamily fine day, which developed into a red and gold sunset of crystalline clearness and beauty. The scenery is entrancing. The valleys are deep and narrow, and each is threaded by a mountain torrent. The hills are truncated cones, each one crowned by a highly picturesque fortified village of refuge, and there were glimpses of distant mountain forms painted on the pale sky in deeper blue. Everything suggested peace and plenty. The cultivation is surprising, and its carefulness has extirpated most of the indigenous plants. It is carried up on terraces to the foot of the cliffs which support the refuges; it renders prolific strips on ledges only eighteen inches wide. Except on the road itself, there was not a vacant space on that day's journey on which a man could lie down.

The first crops, on soil which in that climate produces three and four annually, were in the ground: broad beans with a black and purple blossom with a white lip; rape for oil then in blossom grown on a large scale; opium encroaching on the rice lands, barley and wheat; various root crops, and peas in bud, though it was only February 24th. Even the tops of the narrow dykes separating the rice-fields were planted with single rows of beans.

My coolies stopped several times for a drink and smoke, but did twenty - seven miles. Chair travelling is, I think, the easiest method of locomotion by land. My one objection to it is the constant shifting of the short bamboo carrying pole on which the long poles hang, from one shoulder of each bearer to the other. It has to be done simultaneously, involves a stoppage, occurs every hundred yards and under, and always gives the impression that the shoulder which is relieved is in unbearable pain. Chair-bearing is a trade by itself, and bearers have to be brought up to it. It is essential to keep step absolutely, and to be harmonious in all movements. Of my three bearers the strongest went behind. Two were opium smokers, and the third a vegetarian, who abstained from opium, tobacco, and *samshu*, and was on his way to be rich! There was ceaseless traffic, and as we penetrated further into the country, in addition to the goods before mentioned, the loads consisted of baskets of oil, bean cake, and coal and ironstone, showing that the sources of supply of the latter were not far off. About every half-mile the road passes under a roof with food booths on each side. There were many travellers in shabby closed chairs with short poles, hurried along by two men at a shambling trot. There are so many temples that the air is seldom free from the odour of incense. We met two dragon processions, consisting each of 100 men, and the undulating tail of the dragon was fifty feet long.

Towards evening the hills became more mountainous, and were wooded with cypress and pine, and it was very lovely in the gold and violet light. We halted for the night at the large village of San-tsan-pu, where, though I had travelled for seven months in China, I had my first experience of a Chinese inn, and I did not like it, specially as I regarded it as the type of four or five coming months of similar quarters. I am not ashamed to say that a cowardly inclination to abbreviate my journey tempted me the whole evening. The SZE CHUAN inns have a good reputation; but I was not making the regular stages, and at all events they

GRANITE DRAGON PILLAR.

are inferior on that route, the one which gave me such a shock being one of the best. They are worse than the Persian ordinary *caravanserai*, or the Kurdistan *khan*, or even the Korean hostelry. I felt that I had degenerated into a sybarite, and must summon up all my pluck, and many a hearty meal and ten hours' sleep I afterwards came to enjoy in dens which at first seemed foul and hopeless.

In the best inns there is a room known as the mandarin's room, which can be had by paying for it, with a high roof, a boarded floor, a window, and a solemn-looking table and chairs ; but these very rarely came my way. My introduction to the amenities of Chinese travelling was on this wise, and, as Mr. Thompson was with me, I was much better off than usual. I was carried through the open "restaurant," fitted with rough benches and tables, into a roughly paved yard behind it, where, in the midst of abominations, was the inn well. Several rough doors round this yard gave admission into as many rooms without windows, several of which were already full. My chair was set down, and, after extricating myself from it according to the rules of etiquette, I was attempting to see it unpacked, when I was over-borne by a shouting crowd of men and boys, which surged in after me, and I had to retire hastily into my room.

It was long and narrow, and boarded off from others by partitions with remarkably open chinks, to which many pairs of sloping eyes were diligently applied ; but I was able to baffle curiosity by tacking up cambric curtains brought for the purpose. The roof was high at one side and low at the other, and fortu-nately the wall did not come up to within two feet of it, though the air admitted could not by any euphemism be called "fresh." The floor was a damp and irregular one of mud, partly over a cesspool, and with a strong tendency to puddles. On the other side of the outer boarding was the pig-sty, which was well-occupied, judging from the many voices, bass and treble. There were two rough bedsteads, on which were mats covered with old straw, on which coolies lay down wadded quilts, and sleep four or more on a bed. It is needless to say that these beds are literally swarming with vermin of the worst sorts.

The walls were black and slimy with the dirt and damp of many years ; the paper with which the rafters had once been covered was hanging from them in tatters, and when the candle was lit beetles, "slaters," cockroaches, and other abominable things crawled on the walls and dropped from the rafters, one pink, fleshy thing dropping upon, and putting out, the candle!

I had arranged my plan of operations after my Korean experience, but sullen, disobliging, and apparently stupid Be-dien left me very much to carry it out myself. Between two of the bedsteads there was just space enough for my camp bed and chair without touching them. The oiled sheet was spread on the floor, and my "furniture" upon it, and two small oiled sheets were used for covering the beds, and on these my luggage, food, and etceteras were deposited. The tripod of my camera served for a candle stand, and on it I hung my clothes and boots at night, out of the way of rats. With these arrangements I successfully defied the legions of vermin which infest Korean and Chinese inns, and have not a solitary tale to tell of broken rest and general misery. With absolute security from vermin, all else can be cheerfully endured.

A meal of curry, rice, and tea was not despicable, though I was conscious that my equipments and general manner of living were rougher than they had ever been before, and that I had reached "bed-rock," to quote a telling bit of American slang.

The inn, which was very full of travellers, quieted down before eight, when the slighter noises, such as pigs grunting, rats or mice gnawing, crickets chirping, beetles moving in straw, and other insect disturbances, made themselves very audible, and informed me that I was surrounded by a world of busy and predatory life, loving darkness; but while I thought upon it and on the solitary plunge into China which was to be made on the morrow I fell asleep, and never woke till Be-dien came to my door at seven the next morning with the information that there was no fire, and that he could not get me any breakfast! That was the first of five months of nights of solid sleep from 8 p.m. onwards. I only allowed myself half a candle per day, and after my journal letter was written there was no object for sitting up.

CHAPTER XIX.

SZE CHUAN TRAVELLING

THE following day was misty, grey, and grim, and several of its successors were much like it. One of the local names of SZE CHUAN is "The Cloudy Province." Kind, capable Mr. Thompson returned to Wan after giving the coolies various instructions intended for my benefit; and from thenceforth I depended on myself. The great event of the day was the complete change in Be-dien as soon as I was bereft of Europeans. His pride and temper always remained, and were liable to flare up, or die down into a mephitic state of sullenness, but from that morning till I left China he was active and attentive, was never without leave out of hearing of my whistle, was always at hand to help me over slippery and difficult places, showed great pluck, never grumbled, arranged and packed up my things, interpreted carefully, improved daily in English, always contrived to get hot water and food for me, and on the whole made a tolerable travelling servant.

The travelling was without fatigue. I walked when it suited me, and for the rest might have been in an easy-chair in a drawing-room. The chair-bearers were energetic, and their "boss," a great wag, kept them constantly laughing. Their good-nature never failed. One day when, to relieve them, I walked up a long flight of stairs over a pass, they asked, "Does the foreign woman think we are not strong enough to carry her?" The idea of a wish to be kind to them never entered their heads, yet we gradually came to understand each other a little; and I found my cloak put over my shoulders for me, a wooden stool brought for my feet, sundry little comforts attended to, and a growing interest in photography, reaching the extent of pointing out objects at times "to make pictures of"! By the end of the second day they had all shaken into my "ways," and things went very smoothly.

The day's routine was a cup of tea and some flour stirabout at seven; but, though I was always ready and eager to start at eight, it was usually half-past, and often nine, before we got off. The coolies' first breakfast was often late, and there was the haggling about the bill, neither side liking to give in. It was only a shilling for the board and lodging for myself and my servant! This included his supper and breakfast, my rice, and a room to myself, his share of the coolies' room, an iron lamp fixed on the wall, with an oil well and a wick in a spout encrusted with the soot and grime of years, and if I had a charcoal brazier, the charge was a farthing more. My other travelling expenses came to 4s. 6d. a day; 5s. 6d. covered everything, including a fowl for curry every third day.

My bearers trudged along at an even pace, stopping two or three times for a drink and smoke at tea shops where others congregated, until the halt for dinner at a restaurant of more pretensions, outside of which I sat in my chair in the village street, the unwilling centre of a large and very dirty crowd, which had leisure to stand round me for an hour, staring, making remarks, laughing at my peculiarities, pressing closer and closer till there was hardly air to breathe, taking out my hairpins, and passing my gloves round and putting them on their dirty hands, on two occasions abstracting my spoon and slipping it into their sleeves, being in no wise abashed when they were detected. For at first I ate a little cold rice, but wearying of being a spectacle, and being convinced that as a general rule our insular habit is to eat too much, I gave up this moderate lunch, and contented myself with a morsel of chocolate eaten surreptitiously. On the rare occasions when the villagers wearied of their entertainment, even of gloves, which they thought were worn to conceal some desperate skin disease, and dropped off, small black pigs, with upright rows of bristles on their lean, curved spines, timidly took their place with expectations which were not realised, picking about, even under the poles of the chair, for fragments which they did not find, and even nibbling my straw shoes, and ancient and long-legged poultry were as odiously familiar.

When they had fed and smoked, the men shouldered their burdens, and trudged on till about sunset, stopping, as in the morning, for smokes and drinks, I walking and photographing as it suited me. Sometimes we put up at a wayside inn, without even the privacy of a yard ; this was in very small places, where the curiosity was not so overwhelming.

In towns the case was different. The inn yard was often enclosed by planking and a wide door, within which there might be one, two, or three courts, possibly with flowers in pots and a little gaudy paint. Some of these inns accommodate over 200 travellers, with their baggage. Every room is full, and between money-changing, eating, "sing-song," and gambling, and half-naked waiters rushing about with small trays, and numbers of men all shouting together, it is pretty lively. At the extreme end of the establishment is the "*kuan's* room," with one for attendants on each side. The crowd which always gathered during my passage down the street rolled in at the doorway, blocking up the yard, shouting, ofttimes hooting, and fighting each other for a look at the foreigner. Fortunately doors in Chinese inns have strong wooden bolts, and when my baggage and I were once ensconced I was secure from intrusion, unless a few men and boys had run on ahead to take possession of the room before I entered it, or forced themselves in behind Be-dien when he brought my dinner. If it were merely a boarded wall, a row of patient eyes usually watched me for an hour, and with much gratification, for these rooms are dark with the door shut, and my candle revealed my barbarian proceedings.

But worse than this was the slow scraping of holes in the plaster partition, when there was one, between my room and the next, accompanied by the peculiarly irritating sound of whispering, and eventually by the application of a succession of eyes to the hole, more whispering, and some giggling. It was always a temptation to apply the muzzle of a revolver or a syringe to the opening ! Occasionally a big piece of plaster fell into my room and revealed the operators, who were more frequently well-dressed travellers than ignorant coolies. I used to whistle for Be-dien to hang up a curtain over the holes, after which there was peace for a time, and then the scraping and whispering began again, and often on both sides, till, tired and irritated, I used to put out the candle and lie down, frequently awaking in the morning to find myself in my travelling dress still, clutching my interrupted diary. When one arrived tired after being stared at and pressed upon several times in the day, beginning with the early morning, the fearful hubbub in the courtyard, lasting an hour or more, followed by these grating and rasping processes, was exhausting and exasperating.

Also the landlord's wife, and often a bevy of women with her, used to come in and pick over my things, which fortunately were few, and ask questions, beginning with, "What is your honourable age?" "Have you many sons?" When I confessed that I had none they expressed pity, and a contempt which Be-dien did not scruple to translate. "Why have you left your honourable country?" etc. But they soon tired of the trouble of interrogating me and talked to Be-dien, and when I asked what they were saying, I heard such remarks as these: "What ugly eyes she has, and straight eyebrows!" "Yes, but they see into the ground and where the gold is hid." "Has she come for gold?" "What big feet she has!" (Their own were about three inches long.) "Why is her hair like wool?" and so on.

These people had never seen lead pencils or fountain pens, and everywhere these and the foreign writing, and the fact that a woman could write, (for the gazers were more or less illiterate) attracted great attention. A pronged fork, which they thought must "prick the mouth and make it bleed," was in their eyes a barbarism. I wore straw sandals over English tan shoes to avoid slipping, and this they regarded as a confession of foreign inferiority. I was wearing a Chinese woman's dress with a Japanese *kurumaya's* hat, the one perfect travelling hat, and English gloves and shoes, and this *olla podrida* was an annoyance to them. Their questions were very trivial, and their curiosity appeared singularly unintelligent, contrasting, in this respect, with that of the Japanese. It showed prodigious apathy for adults to spend hour after hour in focussing a stolid stare upon a person whose occupations offered no novelty or variety, being limited to eating and writing. The curiosity of the common people, though boorish, was not rude, but that of the class above them, and above all of men of the literary class, was brutal and insulting, and generally tended to excite hostility against the foreigner.

I developed my negatives in my room at night, as it was almost always a perfect "dark room," and the greatest of my annoyances was when a flash of white light showed that my neighbours had successfully worked a hole in the wall, and that my precious negative was hopelessly "fogged."

The indispensable *yamen* runners are changed at every prefecture, and the passports are examined and copied. These runners are a queer lot. For this duty they get their travelling expenses and something over, and the *douceur* which the traveller bestows. A formal official letter is their warrant. But on many occasions I found myself not with the escort I left the prefecture with, which truly was shabby enough, but with a couple of ragged beggars, to whom the letter with its advantages had been sold by the runners, who thus saved themselves a journey. Occasionally these substitutes strutted in front of my chair down a street waving the magistrate's letter, the wind blowing their rags aside, showing the neglected and repulsive sores by which they excite the compassion of the charitable. The only useful purpose which the *yamen* runners served was occasionally when it was growing late to run on ahead and engage "rooms," and always to take the passport to the *yamen*. I write "the passport" because it deserved the definite article from its size, the grandeur of its seals, and the consideration it claimed for me, besides which it allowed of unlimited travel in the eighteen provinces, as well as in Mongolia and Manchuria, and was of such a nature as to produce an immediate change of manner in every official who read it! Besides this I had a correct and prosaic consular passport issued at Hankow, which I only once had occasion to use.

The compulsory *chai-jen* are, I think, a speciality of SZE CHUAN, and the compulsion rose out of unpleasant circumstances. I never learned that they forced the innkeepers to take less than the usual payment; indeed, I think that Chinese innkeepers are far too independent a class to be forced, nor, though they have the reputation of being brutal and truculent, did I see them maltreat anyone, but I much objected to being sold to the beggars and to being deserted on critical occasions. When soldiers were sent, and any trouble was threatened, they usually slipped off their brilliant coat cloaks and disappeared, and in reply to my subsequent remonstrances said, "What are four against two thousand?" a specious way of excusing themselves, for the mandarin's letter is all-powerful even in a beggar's hand.

Money annoyances began early, and never ceased. Before leaving Wan Hsien I bought 10,000 *cash*, brass coins, about the size of a halfpenny, inscribed with Chinese characters, and with a square hole in the middle. By this they are threaded a hundred at a time on a piece of straw twist, and at that time (for the exchange fluctuates daily) the equivalent of two shillings weighed eight pounds! The eighteen shillings in *cash* with which I started weighed seventy-two pounds, and this had to be distributed among the coolies, the boss, or *fu-tou*, being responsible for the whole. But no reliance is to be placed on the *cash* shop. There may be *cash* wanting, small *cash*, spurious *cash ;* consequently every string must be counted, and this operation frequently took more than an hour. A few *cash* in each hundred are claimed for the "string." On nearly every string small *cash* used to be found, and the haggling and the counting occupied one of the best morning hours. This process, in common with everything which has to do with money, is intensely interesting to every Chinese, and the dullest wits are bright on the subject. Some villages would only receive small *cash ;* others rejected it altogether.

The silver was a greater nuisance than the brass. The silver shoes I got in Hankow had been broken up into four pieces each, but even then they were unmanageably big and had to be chopped again, usually by the village blacksmith with his heavy tools, and weighed again to make sure that all had been returned. Then the man to whom you pay over a fragment of your broken *sycee*, for which the Hong Kong and Shanghai Bank was responsible, puts it first into the palm of one hand, then into the other, looks at it askance, and then says the "touch" is bad, it is inferior silver, and so on. This is after you have agreed to pay a certain weight in silver for an article, say half an ounce. Then it appears that not only is the "touch" inferior, but the ounce of that town is a heavier ounce than the ounce of the last, and that your scale is a bad one, and that the silver must be weighed in a "good scale," *i.e.*, the seller's own ; and between the "touch" and the varying weights, and the differing values of taels, and the charges for breaking and weighing and possibly for assaying the *sycee*, the bewildered traveller, who has three things always to think of—the number of *cash* to the tael, the quality of the silver, and the weight of the tael—would gladly compound by paying a much larger percentage

than all this botheration really costs. One of the greatest aggrava-
tions is when the *cash* strings break just as one is starting, and
a thousand *cash* roll over the inn yard and lose themselves in
heaps and holes. Then the innkeeper exerts himself and clears
the yard of the crowd, and a diligent search is instituted. It is
useless to say "Never mind if a few are left behind," for it is a
point of honour with the *fu-tou*, who is responsible for everything,
that not a *cash* shall be missing.

In this chapter I have endeavoured to glance at the most salient
features of SZE CHUAN travel, leaving others to emerge *en route*.

CHAPTER XX.

SAN-TSAN-PU TO LIANG-SHAN HSIEN

THE first two days passed uneventfully. I was set down to be stared at seven times a day, but the village people were inoffensive. We passed through rich and cultivated country, with many noble farmhouses with six or eight irregular roofs, handsome, roofed, entrance gates, deep eaves, and many gables of black beams and white plaster, as in Cheshire. Next pine-clothed hills appeared, and then the grand pass of Shen-kia-chao (2900 feet) lifted us above habitation and cultivation into a solitary mountain region of rock, scrub, torrents, and waterfalls. The road ascends the pass by 1140 steps on the edge of a precipice, which is fenced the whole way by granite uprights two feet high, carrying long granite rails eight inches square. Two chairs can pass along the whole length. The pass is grand and savage. There were brigands on the road, and it was patrolled by soldiers, small bodies of whom I met in their stagey uniforms, armed with lances with long pennons and short bows and arrows. These bows need a strong man's strength to string them, and bow-and-arrow drill is a great military exercise. The price of rice had risen considerably, *cash* was scarce, and as in some parts even of this prosperous province men do little more than keep body and soul together by their labour, even a slight rise means starvation and death, and it is fierce, cruel want which turns men into robbers in China, many of the stouter spirits preferring to prey on their neighbours in this fashion to depending on their charity. At one point on the pass where there were some trees, three criminals were hanging in cages with their feet not quite touching the ground. The *chai-jen* said that they were to be starved to death. Not far off were two human heads which looked as if they had been there for some time, hanging in two cages, with a ghastly look of inquisitive intelligence on their faces.

All had been robbers. Chinese justice is retributive, and takes

PASS OF SHEN-KIA-CHAO.

little account of human life. We met a number of chained prisoners on their way to Wan, all with that peculiarly degraded and brutish look which a lavish growth of unkempt hair on the usually smoothly shaven head of a Chinese invariably produces. It was impossible not to pity these poor fellows, specially as they were most likely driven to their crimes by hunger, remembering as I did, and that vividly, the judgment-seat of the Naam-hoi magistrate at Canton, with a row of shivering prisoners kneeling on pounded glass on the stone floor in front of it, with their foreheads an inch from the ground. At this time China, with its crowds, its poverty, its risks of absolute famine from droughts or floods, its untellable horrors, its filth, its brutality, its venality, its grasping, clutching, and pitiless greed, and its political and religious hopelessness, sat upon me like a nightmare. There are other and better aspects which dawn on the traveller more slowly, and there is even a certain lovableness about the people. I only put down what were my impressions at the time.

From the rugged summit of the Shen-kia-chao pass we dropped down into cultivated land, and at a large village I put up at an inn where I had a mandarin's room, very shabby and ruinous, and with a leaky roof, which compelled me to shift my bed several times in the night, but as it had a window-frame from which all the paper had been torn off, it was airy, and with a bunch of incense sticks I overpowered the evil smells. The next morning there was a great row before I left, about *cash* as usual, accusations of theft being freely bandied about. I was in my chair in the yard when it began, and soon a crowd of men were brandishing their arms (I don't think the Chinese possess fists) in my face, shouting and yelling with a noise and apparent fury not to be imagined by anyone who has not seen an excited Chinese mob. They yelled into my ears and struck my chair with their tools to attract my attention, but I continued to sit facing them, never moving a muscle, as I was quite innocent of the cause of the quarrel, and at last they subsided and let me depart. I doubt much whether this and many similar ebullitions would have occurred if I had had a European man with me.

It was a pleasant region through which we passed in the grey mist, of small rice-fields step above step in every little valley, the broadest steps at the bottom, of large, handsome farmhouses, large stone tombs in the hillsides, fine temples, wayside shrines, and *pai-lows* or *pai-fangs*. These erections are finer and more numerous in SZE CHUAN than I have seen them elsewhere in China. Some villages on that day's journey were approached under six stone portals, remarkable for their dignity and artistic

WAYSIDE SHRINE.

perfection. Von Richthofen remarks upon some of the SZE CHUAN *pai-fangs* as being "masterpieces of Chinese art." I learned that some of them commemorate, as in Korea, the administrative virtues of local officials, but the genuine value of the tribute is dubious.

I have no hard and fast theory regarding these portals. They would be an interesting subject for investigation. It is quite possible that the Chinese *pai-fang* is an accretion on such primitive structures as the triliths of Stonehenge, the *coran* of India—still, according to Fergusson, used in its ancient timber form at Hindu marriages—the *torii* of Japan, still mostly of wood, and the slighter but nearly similar structure which marks the entrance to royal property in Korea. It is probable that the simpler forms in China are the most ancient, and that superb decoration of many examples belongs to the later centuries. I cannot see any reason for connecting the *pai-fang* with the introduction of Buddhism into China. The *torii* in Japan, the simplest existing form of the structure, is connected with Shinto, which existed centuries before Buddhism travelled to Japan from Korea.

I always objected to halt at a city, but arriving at that of Liang-shan Hsien late on the afternoon of the third day from Wan, it was necessary to change the *chai-jen* and get my passport copied. An imposing city it is, on a height, approached by a steep flight of stairs with a sharp turn under a deep picturesque gateway in a fine wall, about which are many picturesque and fantastic buildings. The gateway is almost a tunnel, and admits into a street fully a mile and a half long, and not more than ten feet wide, with shops, inns, brokers, temples with highly decorated fronts, and Government buildings "of sorts" along its whole length.

I had scarcely time to take it in when men began to pour into the roadway from every quarter, hooting, and some ran ahead—always a bad sign. I proposed to walk, but the chairmen said it was not safe. The open chair, however, was equally an abomination. The crowd became dense and noisy; there was much hooting and yelling. I recognised many cries of *Yang kwei-tze!* (foreign devil) and "*Child-eater!*" swelling into a roar; the narrow street became almost impassable; my chair was struck repeatedly with sticks; mud and unsavoury missiles were thrown with excellent aim; a well-dressed man, bolder or more cowardly than the rest, hit me a smart whack across my chest, which left a weal; others from behind hit me across the shoulders; the howling was infernal: it was an angry Chinese mob.* There

* I was told afterwards that a foreign missionary in an open chair had passed through not long before, and being annoyed at the curiosity and crowding of the people, had gone with a complaint to the *yamen*, and it was supposed by some of my friends that they were avenging this on me.

was nothing for it but to sit up stolidly, and not to appear hurt, frightened, or annoyed, though I was all three.

Unluckily the bearers were shoved to one side, and stumbling over some wicker oil casks (empty, however), knocked them over, when there was a scrimmage, in which they were nearly knocked down. One runner dived into an inn doorway, which the innkeeper closed in a fury, saying he would not admit a foreigner; but he shut the door on the chair, and I got out on the inside, the bearers and porters squeezing in after me, one chair-pole being broken in the crush. I was hurried to the top of a large inn yard and shoved into a room, or rather a dark shed. The innkeeper tried, I was told, to shut and bar the street-door, but it was burst open, and the whole of the planking torn down. The mob surged in 1500 or 2000 strong, led by some *literati*, as I could see through the chinks.

There was then a riot in earnest; the men had armed themselves with pieces of the doorway, and were hammering at the door and wooden front of my room, surging against the door to break it down, howling and yelling. *Yang-kwei-tze!* had been abandoned as too mild, and the yells, as I learned afterwards, were such as "Beat her!" "Kill her!" "Burn her!" The last they tried to carry into effect. My den had a second wooden wall to another street, and the mob on that side succeeded in breaking a splinter out, through which they inserted some lighted matches, which fell on some straw and lighted it. It was damp, and I easily trod it out, and dragged a board over the hole. The place was all but pitch-dark, and was full of casks, boards, and chunks of wood. The door was secured by strong wooden bars. I sat down on something in front of the door with my revolver, intending to fire at the men's legs if they got in, tried the bars every now and then, looked through the chinks, felt the position serious —darkness, no possibility of escaping, nothing of humanity to appeal to, no help, and a mob as pitiless as fiends. Indeed, the phrase, "hell let loose," applied to the howls and their inspiration.

They brought joists up wherewith to break in the door, and at every rush—and the rushes were made with a fiendish yell—I expected it to give way. At last the upper bar yielded, and the upper part of the door caved in a little. They doubled their efforts, and the door in another minute would have fallen in, when the joists were thrown down, and in the midst of a sudden silence there was the rush, like a swirl of autumn leaves, of many feet, and in a few minutes the yard was clear, and soldiers, who remained for the night, took up positions there. One of my men, after the riot had lasted for an hour, had run to the *yamen* with the news that the people were "murdering a foreigner," and the mandarin sent soldiers with orders for the tumult to cease, which he might have sent two hours before, as it can hardly be supposed that he did not know of it.

The innkeeper, on seeing my special passport, was uneasy and apologetic, but his inn was crowded, he had no better room to give me, and I was too tired and shaken to seek another. I was half inclined to return to Wan, but, in fact, though there was much clamour and hooting in several places, I was only actually attacked once again, and am very glad that I persevered with my journey.

Knowing that my safety was assured, I examined what seemed as if it might have been a death-trap, and found it was a lumber-room, black and ruinous, with a garret above, of the floor of which little remained but the joists. My floor was in big holes, with heaps and much rubbish of wood and plaster, and became sloppy in the night from leakage from the roof. There was just clear space enough for my camp bed. It was very cold and draughty, and after my candle was lighted rows of sloping eyes were perseveringly applied to the chinks on the street side, and two pairs to those on the other side. I should like to have done their owners some harmless mischief!

The host's wife came in to see me, and speaking apologetically of the riot, she said, "If a foreign woman went to your country, you'd kill her, wouldn't you?" I have since quite understood what I have heard: that several foreign ladies have become "queer" and even insane as the result of frights received in riots, and that the wife of one British consul actually died as the result. Consul-General Jamieson truly says that no one who has heard the howling of an angry Chinese mob can ever forget it.

The next morning opened in blessed quiet. There was hardly the usual crowd in the inn yard. Carpenters were busy repairing

the demolished doorway. A new pole had been attached to
my chair by the innkeeper. There were many soldiers in the
street, through which I was carried in the rain without my hat.
Not a remark was made. Hardly a head was turned. It was
so perfectly quiet and orderly that after a time the *fu-tou*
suggested that I might put on my hat ! The events of the day
before would have appeared a hideous dream but that my
shoulders were very sore and aching, and that two of the coolies
who had been beaten for serving a foreigner bore some ugly traces
of it. My nerves were somewhat shaken, and for some weeks
I never entered the low-browed gate of a city without more or
less apprehension.

Liang-shan is an ancient and striking city. In the long, narrow
main street, the houses turn deep-eaved gables, with great horned
projections, to the roadway. There are many fine temples with
their fronts profusely and elaborately decorated with dragons,
divinities, and arabesques in coloured porcelain relief, or in deeply
and admirably carved grey plaster, the effect of the latter closely
resembling stone. The city manufactures paper from the
Brousonetia papyrifera, both fine and coarse, printed cottons,
figured silks, and large quantities of the imitation houses, horses,
men, furniture, trunks, etc., which are burned to an extravagant
extent at burials.

CHAPTER XXI.

LIANG-SHAN HSIEN TO HSIA-SHAN-PO

IT was a relief to get out into the open country, though for some time I felt shaken by the two hours' tension of the day before. The drizzle in which I started soon developed into heavy rain, which lasted for nine hours, turning every rivulet into a tawny torrent. It was a very interesting journey even in the downpour. Liang-shan is on the western slope of one among a cluster of ranges, the steep eastern side of which I climbed the day before, and after passing through the town the road dips down into a rolling plain, extending widely in every direction, at that time a great inundated swamp of rice-fields of every size and shape, threaded by a narrow stone road, and abounding in small islands, frequently walled round, on which the large farmhouses stand, screened by bamboo and cypress groves, or temples, oft-times red, with magnificent trees and priests' dwellings surrounding them.

A background of tall pines, cypresses, and bamboo threw into striking relief a temple of unusual appearance, with a fine canopy roof of glazed green tiles, the front rising from the water, the rest of the "island" enclosed by a wall of imperial red. I reached it by wading a hundred yards in very chilly water, and found a plain, square, open building of red sandstone, surrounded by a broad, stone platform. In the centre are two fine palms, in stone vases, and a severe *pai-fang*, on the north platform a plain stone altar, and a tablet with an incised inscription, and behind this a wall with incised inscriptions divided by pilasters; all is severely handsome and absolutely plain. It is a temple of Confucius, and the simplicity of the few which I was able to enter contrasts boldly with the crowded and grotesque monstrosities of the Buddhist and Taoist temples. Truly the "Great Teacher" was one of the greatest of men, for he has cast into a mould of iron for two thousand years the thought, social order, literature, government, and education of 400,000,000 of our race.

Passing Sar-pu, a village composed almost entirely of fine temples, and through Chin-tai, where the temples are of great size, and the carved stone front of one of them of great beauty, under many highly decorated *pai-fangs*, and past some Chinese Chatsworths and Eatons, and large "brick noggin" farmhouses, we re-entered hills and afterwards mountains, crossing the beautiful pass of Fuh-ri-gan by a fine stone staircase of over 5000 broad, easy steps, with a handsome kerbstone, all in perfect repair! These stairs begin at the bridge and inn of Shan-rang-sar, more Tyrolese than Chinese in aspect. Indeed, every day I dropped some preconceived ideas of what Chinese scenery and buildings must be like, and I hope that my readers will drop theirs, if they are of willow plate origin, before they have finished this volume.

I had now entered on the fringe of one of the richest coal regions in the world, seams of coal, practically inexhaustible, apparently underlying the whole surface of Central SZE CHUAN. Limestone mountains and cliffs, and caverned limestone with an infinite variety of ferns, had suggested the probable neighbourhood of coal, and in these mountains it is to be encountered everywhere. It crops out even in the redundant vegetation by the roadside, and near the mountain hamlets the children, with small baskets, hack it daily with rough knives, for cooking purposes. It appears in lumps along the beds of streams, in the sides of the tanks in which bamboo is macerated for paper, and in the mountain-sides, where small collieries, with most primitive " workings," exist.

My attention was several times attracted by sheds among the trees, and by men and boys crawling out of holes in the cliff side with baskets, the black contents of which they deposited in these. Also, occasionally scrambling up to a black orifice in the limestone, I came upon a "gallery," four feet high, down which Lilliputian wagons, holding about one hundredweight each, descend from "workings" within along a tramway only twelve inches wide. From some holes boys crept out with small creels, holding not more than twenty-five pounds, roped on their backs, and little room to spare above them. All these "workings" between Liang-shan and

A CHINESE CHATSWORTH.

Wen-kia-cha, sixty *li*,* were at a considerable height above the torrent, which dashed down what was frequently only a ravine, and all that could be seen were small borings just large enough to admit a man crawling, or, in some cases, the small trollies before mentioned.

In that mountain region, in which I gathered from many symptoms that the people are specially superstitious, the coal seams are only worked on a level, not downwards, for fear of grazing the Dragon's back and making him shake the earth, but they cannot say whether it is a universal dragon, the curves of whose tremendous spine are omnipresent, or a provincial or a local dragon! On the plain from which I had ascended fuel is scarce and dear, and strings of coolies, each carrying two hundredweight, supply it with coal from these mountains. Lump coal, burning with but little smoke or ash, is worth 2s. 6d. per ton at the "pit's mouth," and is retailed at from 4s. to 5s. per ton, according to distance, in the low country. Later I saw many collieries worked with some skill and with a very large "output."

Though it rained heavily all day, the atmosphere was fairly clear. That pass of Fuh-ri-gan is as beautiful as the finest parts of Japan, which it much resembles—lonely, romantic, shut in by high-peaked, fantastic mountains, forest-clothed to their summits, and cleft by deep ravines, with tumbling torrents, fern and lycopodium-fringed. In the forest there were six varieties of coniferæ, oaks, chestnuts, walnuts, the *Cunninghames Sinensis* (?), a tree of great beauty and much utility, the fine evergreen *Hoangho* (*Ficus infectoria*), the *Xylosma japonica*, with laurel-like leafage, and many others, including a leafless tree which was a mass of pink blossoms. Of evergreen shrubs and trailers I counted thirty-seven near the roadside!

But the speciality of these passes is the bamboo. There are high hills forested to their summits with different varieties, a singular and beautiful sight, with an infinite variety of colour. There are the golden-plumed bamboo, with its golden stems and the golden light under its golden plumes, the plumed dark green and the plumed light green, full-plumed things of perfect beauty,

* I cannot give the local distances in English miles, because, though the Chinese *li* is 1818 English feet, the *li* of the mountain and the plain, and even of the good and bad road, differ in length.

as tall as forest trees of average height. There is also a feathery bamboo with branches pointing upwards, a creation of exquisite grace, light and delicate, with its stem as straight as an arrow, and attaining a height of fully seventy feet, all forming a dense but not an entangled mass. At one point, 1400 straight, broad "altar stairs, slope through darkness up to God," a majestic sight, for from either side the great green and golden plumed bamboos droop gracefully to meet each other, and the staircase mounts upward in a golden twilight. Altogether that pass is a glory of trees, ferns, and trailers, mostly sub-tropical, and is noisy with the clash of torrents, though silent as to bird life. During the whole day the only birds I saw were some blue jays.

But not sub-tropical was the raw, damp, penetrating wind, which blew half a gale at the top of the pass, and pretty miserable was the inn in the fertile, green, malarious hole to which we made an abrupt descent of 1500 feet. My stout "regulation" waterproof, which had withstood the storm and stress of many Asiatic journeys, had given way; the waterproof covers of most of the baggage, torn by rough usage, let the water through; and my cushions were soaked. I had only six inches to spare on either side of my stretcher in the absolutely dark and noxious hole in which I slept. The candle-wicks were wet, spluttered, and went out, and I had to eat in the darkness rendered visible by the inn lamp.

But in such country places the people are quiet and harmless, and I sat for a long time in the open public space, where the black rafters dripped black slime. The attempt at a fire was in the centre of the clay floor, over which a big black pot hung from the roof. My drowned coolies huddled up in their wadded quilts, and I in a blanket, and two wretched, ragged, hatless, shoeless, half-clad *chai-jen*, were all trying to light the end of a green sapling with some damp straw. It was truly deplorable, squalor without picturesqueness, and failing to get warm, I went shivering to bed.

The following morning was dry and fair, with a little feeble sunshine. Crossing the Sai-pei-tu Pass, at a height of 1720 feet, on which, as on the Fuh-ri-gan, there were several collieries, all respectful to the dragon's back, we passed through very interesting country all day, at times fascinating from its novelty.

BRIDGE AND INN OF SHAN-RANG-SAR.

Cities of refuge crowded on nearly inaccessible rocks can be seen miles away, one a special marvel, built anywhere and everywhere on an isolated rock, resembling Mont St. Michel, another with a striking temple of enormous size for its centre, with monastic buildings, fortifications, "brick noggin" houses, clinging as they can to the rock, piled one on another round it, the whole surrounded by an embattled wall following the contour of the rock. They are second in picturesqueness only to the lama-serais of Tibet.

As the country became more open, besides these fortified refuges on rocky heights, which suggest possible peril, while the frequency with which solitary houses occur tells of complete security, there are great solitary temples with porcelain fronts in rich colouring, mandarins and landowners' houses rivalling some of our renowned English homes in size and stateliness, distilleries, paper and flour mills; and every town and large village has its special industry—silk weaving, straw plaiting, hat making, dressing hides, iron or brass work, pottery and china, chair-making and bamboo furniture generally, indigo dyeing, carving and gilding idols, making the red paper enormously used for religious and festive purposes, and the imitation gold and silver coins and "shoes" burned as offerings to ancestors, etc.

The weather became so grim that of the large mansions, splendid from a distance, I was only able to get a very poor photograph of one. The mandarin proprietor with many attendants came out to the high-road, and asked me to "take" his family. I said I could not, for I could not finish the portraits in such weather in less than three or four days; and then he asked me to be his guest for those days, and he would give me a large room. I did not wish to pose as an itinerant photographer, and had grave doubts as to what my reception might really be in the women's quarters, and I dreaded the stifling curiosity succeeded by the stagnation of dulness, so I excused myself.

The stone bridges on the road are very fine, with piers terminating in bold carvings, frequently of dragons, but occasionally comically realistic, such as a man carrying an oil basket, a man yawning, a dog with his head between his legs, a woman combing a girl's hair, and the like. Three and four arches with a bold spring are frequent; the parapets are decorated; and though the road may be only six feet wide, on the roadways of some of the bridges three carriages can drive abreast. There are other and older bridges in which the piers are heavy uprights of stone supporting stone flags occasionally twenty-five and even thirty feet long. The new, arched bridges, of which the province may well be proud, are sometimes built by subscription, but are often the public-spirited gift of a local magnate, whose name and good deed are recorded in stone. The wooden bridges, which I found always in good repair, are like those of Switzerland, and, like them, have substantial roofs frequently double and occasionally treble-tiered, often covered with glazed ridge and furrow tiles. Some of these roofs are lined with highly polished carnation-red lacquer, in which the names of the donors, with complimentary sentences, are deeply incised in gold. In some bridges the row of pillars supporting the roof is also lacquered and polished. There are several bridges which I crossed in SZE CHUAN of from eight to twelve lofty stone arches each, which for stability, beauty, span, height, and spring of the arches might compare, and scarcely unfavourably, with some of our finest English structures. In China I never once had, as in Persia, Korea, and Kashmir, to ford a stream because the bridge was either ruinous or too shaky to venture upon.

The industries of the towns and villages produce a large amount of traffic on the roads. Strings of coolies going at a dog trot, carrying paper, salt, tobacco, dyed cottons, hats, and rush piths for lamps, passed us incessantly, but no beasts of burden, and only one saddle pony, which tripped rapidly down one of the longest flights of stairs with ease and agility. The woods are silent; the call of the handsome pheasant to his dowdy mate was the only bird note I heard. There is a great paucity of such animals as make our farmyards cheerful. I did not see horses or mules anywhere between Wan Hsien and Paoning Fu, or sheep. Fowls, geese, and ducks there were in abundance, a few cats, and many old dogs, the young ones having been mostly eaten early in the month.

The water buffalo ploughs, harrows the rice swamps, turns the grain and oil mills, and does many other useful turns. I never saw him used as a beast of burden. It is hard to become reconciled to the appearance of the great " water ox," with his mostly hairless,

A PORCELAIN TEMPLE.

blackish-grey skin, in places with a pinkish hue, and his flat head, carried level with his uncouth, unwieldy body, his flat nose and curved flat horns, looking altogether like a survival from antediluvian days. Buffaloes are uncertain in their tempers, though usually very docile, and, like their owners, are liable to frenzies of fury when frightened.

On this route it was amusing to see very small children leading them out to feed on the grass which grows on the edges of the

THE WATER BUFFALO.

rice dykes, the children clambering on their backs and sitting there while they fed because there was no other dry land to sit on. They are extremely sensitive to the bites of insects, and, for this and other reasons, spend much of their leisure time lying in muddy pools which are dug for their benefit. A group of their grotesque, flat heads appearing above the water is truly comical. They are credited with a great aversion to what the Chinese call the "odour" of Europeans, and I have seen a herd of them "go for" a foreigner in such an unmistakably vindictive fashion that he took to his heels. The buffalo cow gives a small quantity of very rich milk with a peculiar flavour. The beef obtainable in SZE CHUAN is mostly buffalo, and is often the flesh of an animal which has rendered man many years of service.

On that day's journey the heralds of the short and glorious procession of the flowers appeared: plum, peach, and cherry blossom; violets grew in shady places; a clematis lighted up the margins of woods with pendent clusters of bright yellow bloom; pink and white fumitories made the roadside hedges gay; and there were a few others.

The dampness was incredible, and as I had then made nearly two degrees north from Wan Hsien, the temperature had fallen, and the mercury hung at about 44°. I never knew so damp an atmosphere even in Japan. Ferns, mosses, trailers, and all the beauteous vegetation which revels in damp abounded. The leafage of the root crops was lush and succulent. There is no winter, and though only the last of February, the opium crop, which over much of the day's journey was the principal crop, with maize sown between the rows, was eight inches high, and its lower leaves, which are used as food by the people and taste like spinach, were served to me that night for the first time as a vegetable. Travelling all day in such a damp, chilly atmosphere in wet clothes was a little trying. It is impossible to dry anything in the small, poor country inns.

We passed through the town of Yun-i, with a street half a mile long, in which every house is given up to the making or staining of red and yellow paper, which is enormously used, especially at the New Year, which was just over. Everyone nearly was more or less smeared with these brilliant colours, and the stream outside the town was as red as blood. Hundreds of coolies were travelling both north and south with bales of this paper.

I had various qualms as I passed through the low, dark gateway, specially when I saw men running ahead to collect a crowd, calling in at the shops and houses "A foreigner!" or "A foreign devil!" but though the crowd completely filled the street and was noisy, it was neither hostile nor a mob. One cause of the trouble at Liang-shan was that the *chai-jen,* instead of keeping with me, went off to the *yamen.* After that I insisted that one of them, when we reached a town or large village, should walk in front of my chair. At Yun-i a runner went before me striding fiercely, a ragged, scrofulous, shoeless, hatless, wretched little fellow, but as

ORDINARY COVERED BRIDGE

he carried the mandarin's letter, when the people crowded and progress was impeded, he waved his arms and pushed them right and left, shouting the Chinese equivalent of "In the *kuan's* name."

One great feature of that day's journey was coal. Coal cropped up everywhere, and any cutting revealed a seam of coal. Over a hundredweight—100 catties—sold for forty *cash* (about five farthings), picked lumps burning with a clear flame. Miners earn twenty *cash* per 100 catties, and can get 600 in a day. There is iron in the neighbourhood. From one hill I saw a considerable smoke, and the *chai-jen* said it proceeded from large smelting works, but I only give this as hearsay. I observed that many articles which I had elsewhere seen made of wood are in this region made of iron, and that iron is liberally used on household and agricultural implements. In the peasants' houses coal is burned in a hole in the middle of the floor, and the smoke finds its way out anywhere, as it used to do in Highland hovels.

After a very varied day's journey the damp cold became so paralysing, and the mist so thick, that I halted earlier than usual at the small mountain hamlet of Hsai-shan-po, where the wayside inn was new, indeed not finished, and consisted only of a central shed with a fire of bituminous coal burning with heavy smoke in a hole in the middle of the floor, and a room on either side, one occupied by the host, a "decent man," and his well-behaved family. The partitions are lath and plaster, the walls beginning a foot from the ground and ending two feet from the roof, allowing the entrance of some light, much draught, many hens, a few young pigs, and great clouds of smoke.

CHAPTER XXII.

HSAI-SHAN-PO TO SIAO-KIAO

IT was partly to get Sunday's rest in peace and quietness that I put up at this mountain hamlet. I could see to read and write without opening the door, and could move round my bed, and the smells were not so awful as usual. The central shed was full all day, and occasionally the women who came sent a polite request that I would exhibit myself to them, to which I always cheerfully responded.

The "enormous size" of my feet, though my shoes are only threes, interested them greatly. I was much surprised to find that in SZE CHUAN, except among the Manchu or Tartar women and those of a degraded class, foot-binding is universal, and that the shoe of even the poorest and most hard-worked peasant woman does not exceed four inches in length. Though in walking these "golden lilies" look like hoofs, and the women hobble on their heels, I have seen them walk thirty *li* in a day, and some have told me that they can walk sixty easily! Two women came to Hsia-shan-po from a village twenty-seven mountain *li* away, merely out of curiosity to see me, and returned the same afternoon. The hobble looks as if it must be very painful, and is a sort of waddle also.

So great an authority as Dr. Wells Williams writes, "The practice . . . is more an inconvenient than a dangerous custom," but I have never seen a hospital in China without some case or cases not only of extreme danger to the foot or great toe, but of ulcers or gangrene, involving absolute loss by amputation. It is fashion, of course. Hitherto a Chinese woman with "big feet" is either denationalised or vile; a girl with unbound feet would have no chance of marriage, and a bridegroom finding that his bride had large feet when he expected small ones, would be abundantly justified by public opinion in returning her at once to her parents.* It is essentially a native Chinese custom of extreme antiquity, and it is remarkable that the Manchu conquerors, who successfully imposed the "pigtail" and narrow sleeves on the conquered, have totally failed even to modify this barbarous custom.

There is no definite age for beginning to bind the feet, but rich people's girls usually have it done between four and five years, and poor people's either at betrothal or between seven and nine years, according to local custom. The process is very much more painful at the latter age, and the treatment of the big toe is different. In the case of the younger child, four of the toes are doubled under the foot, the big toe is laid on the top, and the deformity is then tightly bandaged. In both cases in adult life, when the process is complete, there is a deep cleft across the sole of the foot between the heel and toes, which are forced close together. If skilfully bound, this cleft ought to be deep and narrow enough to hold a Mexican dollar. The foot-binding process is too well known to need any description.

I saw the initial stage both at Canton and Hsia-shan-po. In the last case the girl was nearly ten, and was just betrothed to an elderly rich man. She suffered agonies, the toes were violently bent under the foot and bandaged in that position, and from the sounds I think that some of the tendons were ruptured. Yet both she and a small child at Canton consented willingly in order to get "rich husbands." The lot of the women of the lower class is rough and severe, and it is not surprising that girls long to escape from it by making rich marriages, even though the escape be by such a path of pain. Then again the weak feminine nature desires to secure the admiration which in poetry, prose, and common speech is bestowed on the "golden lilies."

A woman has to bandage her feet every day of her life, or the "beauty" of the shape is lost, and the whole process of deforming them is carried out by carefully regulated bandaging. The Chinese women greatly object to show their uncovered feet.

* I was present at a "drawing-room meeting" in Shanghai when Mrs. Archibald Little, of Chungking, took the humane initiative of establishing an "Anti-Footbinding Society," which has now many branches, and is undoubtedly commending its aims to many men of the intelligent classes. The mission schools for girls are in general absolutely against the crippling process, and the wives of many of the younger Christians have "big feet."

I have only twice seen them. They are very painful objects and the leg, the development of the muscles of the calf having been checked, tapers from the knee to the foot, and there are folds of superfluous skin. The bandages are not covered by stockings. The shoes worn are very soft, and where possible are of embroidered silk, with soles of stitched leather. The women make their own, and the peasant women sit outside their houses in the evenings stitching or embroidering them.

As a set-off against the miseries of foot-binding is the extreme comfort of a Chinese woman's dress in all classes, no corsets or waist-bands, or constraints of any kind, and possibly the full development of the figure which it allows mitigates or obviates the evils which we should think would result from altering its position on the lower limbs. So comfortable is Chinese costume, and such freedom does it give, that since I wore it in Manchuria and on this journey, I have not been able to take kindly to European dress.

But in SZE CHUAN it varies from women's dress, either Manchu or Chinese, as I had previously seen it worn. All Chinese women wear trousers, but they show very little, often not at all, below the neat petticoat, with its plain back and front and full kilted sides. But in SZE CHUAN (and it may be elsewhere) the feminine skirt is discarded, and the trousers, either of a sailor cut, or full and tightly swathed round what should be ankles, are worn with only the ordinary loose, wide-sleeved garment fastening at the side, reaching only to the knees above them. It is a hideous dress. The petticoat is only worn by outcasts, and this has compelled some of the missionary ladies, who wear Chinese dress, to adopt the wide trousers. I never became reconciled to them. The loose upper garment and half jacket, half, sleeved cloak, is most convenient, as for changes of seasons only easily carried changes of underclothing are needed.

After the disturbance at Liang-shan I took my revolver, which I had previously carried in the well of my chair, "into common wear," putting it into a very pacific looking cotton bag, and attached it to my belt under this capacious garment, hoping devoutly that its six ball cartridges might always repose peacefully in their chambers. It is most unwise to let fire-arms be seen in Chinese travelling.

From Hsia-shan-po onwards the country is less romantic. We had previously left the main road, and encountered Chinese roads at their worst, narrow dykes passing through flooded rice-fields, or through farms where the farmers gradually nibble the road away, or convey it tortuously through their own farmyards, or in a few cases absorb it altogether. The mud for days was deep. It was impossible to walk unless equipped with an arrangement which attached three spikes to the heel of the boot or sandal. The width of the road was usually twelve inches, enough for single file, but when two strings of men carrying chairs or burdens met, the difficulties were great, as there was always the risk of slipping off the road into two feet of chilly water and slime. So when my chair-bearers saw another chair in the distance they yelled as loud as they could, expecting the other chair to give place, and edge off where the strip of *terra firma* happened to widen a little.

On one occasion, however, we met a portly man in a closed chair, travelling with only two bearers, and, in spite of yells, he came straight on till our poles were nearly touching. The clamour was tremendous, my seven men and his two all shouting and screaming at once, as if in a perfect fury, while he sat in supercilious calm, I achieving the calm, but not the superciliousness. In the midst of the *fracas* his chair and its bearers went over into the water. The noise was indescribable, and my bearers, whom I cannot acquit of having had something to do with the disaster, went off at a run with yells and peals of laughter, leaving the traveller floundering in the mire, not breathing, but roaring execrations.

There are roads "of sorts" to every village and hamlet. The one I was travelling on was called by courtesy a main road. There was nothing "main" about it but the bridges, which were always in good repair, and four or five times its width. Had it been reduced to its present dimensions by successful nibblings, or were the bridges built in a glowing prophetic instinct, I wonder? The magistrate of the district is nominally responsible for keeping the roads in order, but responsibility is an elastic term in China. As in Korea, he has the power to order men out to work at repairs, but he rarely does so unless he gets notice of a forthcoming visit of a high official, for the people hate work without pay, and he avoids this method of becoming unpopular.

Nothing could be worse than the road which I travelled for some days. To walk was to slide, wade, slip, and fall in the deep mud; to "ride" gave me the unpleasing spectacle of my coolies doing the same, exposing me to sundry abrupt changes of position, and the difficulty of passing chairs and laden porters on the road made progress slow and tiresome. Yet much produce was on the move, giving the impression that traffic would increase largely if there were better means of communication. One of the many needs of China is good roads. There are many rivers in SZE CHUAN, but its physical configuration usually prevents the linking of these by canals, as in the level eastern provinces, and these infamous roads hamper trade very considerably.

Raw, cold, drizzling hours succeeded Hsia-shan-po. The country is less peopled, and the dwellings decidedly poorer; the corries with their large farmhouses disappeared, and there was even a stretch of gravelly, desolate scenery. Wherever the land is unfitted for rice culture the population becomes thin, as the price of this staff of life is so much enhanced by land carriage as to render it unattainable.

I crossed the pretty pass of Kyin-pan-si, and ferried the Kiu Ho, a clear, bright stream. There is very much opium grown in that region, and some sugarcane, as well as all the usual cereals and root crops. "Small *cash*" appeared, and continued for three days the currency of the region, increasing the exasperation of all transactions. The Kiu Ho is navigable for fair-sized junks considerably above the point at which I crossed it, and there was much traffic in coal at Kiu Hsien, a prefectural city finely situated on the cliffs and hills above it.

Incredible filth, indescribable odours, which ought to receive a strong Anglo-Saxon name, grime, forlornness, bustle, business, and discordant noises characterise Chinese cities, and the din of Kiu Hsien was deafening. I was carried from the river up a fine, new, broad flight of stone stairs, at the top of which a great crowd was in readiness to receive me, but the *chai-jen*, whose rags hardly covered them, and who turned out to be beggars to whom the right of escorting me had been sold, cleared the way, and turning aside at the deep, dark city gate, along a narrow street running under the wall, I was landed among the crowds and horrors of the yard of a Chinese city inn by no means of the first class. However, I got a room, which, though small, dirty, and tumbling to pieces, had an opening upon the roof of a lean-to, used for the malodorous purpose of drying vegetables, overhanging the river, and as I had both air and light I felt in Elysium.

While I was eating my curry, as usual from a piece of mill-board on my lap, with a Jaeger sheet pinned round my shoulders —for it was very cold—two *yamen* officials, in rich brocaded silks and satins, entered, and asked to see my passport, which they copied, using my camp bed for a table. Be-dien was much offended, for it is outrageous, according to Chinese etiquette, for men to enter a woman's room. They asked me why my passport gave me "rank," and made me "equal to the consuls," and how a woman could "belong to the *literati*," to which questions, as at that time I was ignorant of the contents of the document, I could give no intelligent replies.

They told me that Kiu Hsien has 100 schools (in China numbers are always round), and is the centre of a large trade in opium, tobacco, packing paper, and straw hats.

Rooms in Chinese inns usually have good bolts, but this had none, and after dismissing Be-dien it cost me much time and labour to barricade the door. There was an instance of super-stition on the day's journey. I got out of the chair the wrong way, and the bearers were scared. They said it would cause them to die within a year, and they offered incense sticks at the next shrine to avert the calamity. In the morning I was in the family room at the inn when the morning devotions were performed to some gilded strips of paper inscribed with characters. The householder put before them some lighted incense sticks, and bowed three times.

The circumstances of the next day's journey were decidedly unfavourable. We had ten hours of an infamous road in a torrent of rain with a very cold wind. I could scarcely ease the bearers at all, for my leather shoes slipped so badly on the mud, that, even with a stout stick and Be-dien's help, I could not keep on my feet. The road, which was a dyke between flooded rice-fields, never reached two feet in width. It had once been flagged, but some of the stones had disappeared alto-gether, some were tilted up, and others were tilted down, and it was truly horrible. The Chinese hate rain, and, above all, getting their feet wet, and I admired the jolly, manly way in which my poor fellows in their two thin cotton garments trudged through the driving rain and slippery slush till they had done twenty-two miles. When they reached at dusk, quite exhausted, the wretched village of Ching-sze-yao, there was no inn, and it was only after I had sat in the rain in the village roadway for an hour that the *chai-jen* induced a man to take us into a deplorable place.

Shelter it was not. The roof dripped from fifty points, and the walls, having shrunk from the joists, let in the cold wind all round. There was no fire but the fire-pots used for cooking, for the use of which there was much squabbling, and no light, except from a clay saucer of oil, over the rim of which some rush pith projected. I was wet to the knees, my canvas bed was soaked, and all else, from the spoiling of waterproof bags and covers by the hot sun of the two previous summers, but when I saw the coolies lying on damp straw in their undried garments, each with a fire-pot between his knees, and not a quilt to cover him, I felt very Mark Tapleyish, specially when the house-*frau* brought me a fire-pot with which to warm my hands. The poverty and discomfort of this house typified the condition in which thousands of the Chinese peasantry live. They were good-natured people, not over-curious, and the children, who were eaten up by skin diseases, were gentle and docile.

The next day, March 4th, was one of clear, grey twilight, without either wind or rain. In the last fifty miles the country had changed very considerably, and for the worse. The passes over the mountain ranges had brought us into the " Red Basin " of Richthofen, which is estimated as embracing about two-thirds of the province in extent, and, perhaps, eight or nine tenths of its wealth and population. It is supposed to have an area of about 100,000 square miles, and a population of from 40,000,000 to 54,000,000. The soil everywhere is of a deep, bright, rich, red colour, and contrasts with the charm of the varied greenery which, in the absence of winter, the " Red Basin " produces during the whole year.

Probably no part of China supports so large a population to the acre, and it is increasing so fast that thousands of men by unremitting toil only keep themselves and their families a little above starvation point, coolie labour being so redundant as to depress wages to the lowest level. The soil is most carefully cultivated, the soft, red rock being easily crumbled down by the peasants' simple implements, and the whole surface is treated by the methods which we term "garden cultivation," which in that beneficent climate, and with the Chinese habit of carefully preserving the refuse of towns and villages and spreading it on the land, so that the whole, both from plant and animal life, is returned to the soil, two, three, and sometimes even four crops are produced within the year !

Within a few days' journey lie the depopulated but fertile valleys of YUNNAN, a noble field for SZE CHUAN emigration ; but it has not occurred to the Government to bear the considerable expense of deporting a few millions of the toilers of the "Red Basin" to the good lands calling for population, supplying them with seed, and supporting them for six months ! The move would tax the resources of a better-organised administration.

SZE CHUAN is a rich and superb province of boundless resources, and I believe, from what I saw and heard, that the trading and farming classes are very well off, and are able to afford many luxuries, but I certainly saw several overcrowded regions of the "Red Basin," where the condition of the people deeply moved my sympathy and pity, for a docile, cheerful, industrious, harmless population, free, as rural poverty is apt to be, from crime and gross vice, is giving the utmost of its strength for a wage which never permits to man, wife, or child the comfortable sensation of satiety, and which when rice rises in price changes the habitual short commons into starvation.

There were no more grand porcelain-fronted temples, large country mansions, and rich farmhouses, and instead of parallel ranges cleft by fine passes in the grey limestone, there is a singular formation, red sandstone hills and hummocks all more or less naturally terraced, as are also the sides of the many pear-shaped dells which lie among them ; red cliffs, one above another, from fifteen to thirty feet high, supporting narrow strips of red soil about two feet deep ; circular hills, also of some height, diminishing into truncated cones, with natural circular terraces, more or less aided by art, running regularly round them, and usually a single tree, tops what one is tempted to call the "erection." There is a fatiguing conventionality about that part of the Red Basin.

One may, indeed, regard the whole of this vast basin as a mass of low terraced hills and valleys of no width, destitute of any plains but the great Chengtu plain, free from floods owing to its configuration, and drained by fine navigable rivers, with many navigable ramifications, while coal, both hard and soft, is believed to underlie the whole. Salt, petroleum, and iron abound, and copper, silver, gold, and lead are found on the western border, as well as enormous quantities of nitrate of soda and sulphur.

This great depression may be regarded as a sort of winter garden, over much of which the mercury rarely falls below 45°, and a canopy of clouds hanging over it all the winter keeps in the moist heat.* It is said that winter sunshine is so rare in Chungking that the dogs bark at the sun when they see it. For all the rich productions of this Red Basin, which have kept the balance of trade for years in favour of SZE CHUAN, there is, let me repeat, but the one outlet : the Yangtze.

* See Mr. Bourne's Report on the Trade of Central and Southern China, Foreign Office, May, 1898.

CHAPTER XXIII.

SIAO-KIAO TO HSIEH-TIEN-TZE

THE whole country is an undulating sea of green, patterned with red—in truth, rather monotonous for five days of journeying. The mud was abominable all the time, but with straw shoes and grippers I managed to do a good deal of walking. On several days my well-paid chair-men travelled "like gentlemen," for labour is so abundant and cheap that they found plenty of coolies to carry my chair for forty *cash* for four miles (about a penny), and even for less! Every house has its opium field, its bamboo and palm groves, fruit trees and cedars, while the *Rhus vernicifera*, or varnish tree, the *Aleurites cordata*, or oil tree, and the *Cupressus funebris*, which it is impossible to avoid calling "the Noah's ark tree," abound. The cultivation, except the ploughing for rice, is entirely by hand, and is so careful that it is easy to see that most of the indigenous plants have become extinct. Violas, fumitories, and the *anemone Japonica*, all of which grow profusely, but solely along the margins of the roads, were all that then or later I saw in the Red Basin; in fact, husbandry has made a clean sweep of "weeds."

The farmhouses in that region are of mud, with thatched roofs, and look poor. Straw plaiting and the making of the very large straw hats which the coolies wear in summer are the great industries. Bad, nay infamous, roads and small *cash* for three days showed their power of crippling trade. Small villages were numerous, but on a journey of 185 *li* the picturesque little town of King-mien-sze, on the rocky, picturesque, non-navigable King-Ho, which I ferried, was the only approach to a centre of population.

When I reached the small town of Siao-kiao I found it greatly crowded with traders, and the innkeepers so unwilling to receive a foreigner that I had to urge my treaty rights, and then was only grudgingly accommodated. There was a very ugly rush, and then a riot, which lasted an hour and a half, at the very beginning of which my *chai-jen* ran away. My door was broken down with much noise and yells of "Foreign devil!" "Horse-racer!" "Child-eater!" but an official arriving in the nick of time, prevented further damage. He ought to have appeared an hour and a half before. These rows are repulsive and unbearably fatiguing after a day's journey, and always delayed my dinner unconscionably, which, as it was practically my only meal in the day, was trying. The entry in my diary for that evening was, "Wretched evening; riotous crowd; everything anxious and odious; noises; too cold to sleep." My lamp sputtered and went out, and my matches were too damp to strike. It is objectionable to be in the dark, you know not where, with walls absolutely precarious, and in the midst of the coarse shouts of rough men to hear a feeble accompaniment of rats eating one's few things. I object strongly to a mixed crowd blocking up my doorway or breaking in my door, for every one of the crowd knows better; even the most ignorant coolie knows well that to intrude into a woman's room or in any way violate the privacy which is hers by immemorial usage and rigid etiquette is an outrage for which there is no forgiveness, judging from a Chinese standpoint.

The mannerless, brutal, coarse, insolent, conceited, cowardly roughs of the Chinese towns, ignorant beyond all description, live in a state of filth which is indescribable and incredible, in an inconceivable beastliness of dirt, among odours which no existing words can describe, and actually call Japanese "*barbarian* dwarfs"! I wondered daily more at the goodness of people who are missionaries to the Chinese in the interior cities, not at their coming out the first time, but at their *coming back, knowing what they come to*. The village people are quite different, and doubtless have attractive qualities; and it must be admitted that Christianity does produce an external refinement among those who receive it, which is very noticeable. Having relieved my hoarded disgusts by these remarks, I will proceed with my narrative.

The days, though cold and very wet, were a great rest. There was not even the guiding a horse and preventing him from fighting, to distract the thoughts from dwelling on any topic I chose to concentrate them upon. My possessions, except my camera and plates, had been spoilt long ago, so there was nothing to be anxious about; and a few rolls more or less in the red mud did not matter, for my clothes were thickly plastered days before. I could not fare worse than I had done, so I was not anxious about the night's halt; so during the day I revelled in freedom, leisure, and solitude; but when night came, and I sat shivering in some fœtid hole, not fit for a decent beast, with only a bamboo railing between it and the pigsty, I often thought Chinese travelling an utter abomination! *

Even the most monotonous part of the route had many interests and some novelties. It is a marvel how the intense homogeneity of China, its apparent inflexibility, and its actual grooviness, are incessantly disturbed by local custom. The race, it is true, is always the same, and the general features of the costume; every Chinese not a convict has a shaven head and a long queue, and every woman hobbles on deformed feet; but when it comes to environments they differ from day to day, and sometimes from hour to hour. Here in SZE CHUAN house architecture varies almost from day to day; each river has its own form of boat; in one district all loads are slung from the bamboo over the shoulder; in another they are carried in wicker creels fitted on wooden pack-saddles on human backs. In one prefecture the purse is a skin bag attached to the waist; in another it is a stout wooden cylinder tapering at both ends carried across the back, and so with many other things. Food varies with the locality, and crops with the soil. One district rejects large *cash*, and others small, while some use a mixture. Headgear varies greatly. Blue turbans are much worn. The shape of the straw hat indicates the district from which the wearer comes, and local fashion tyrannises even over baggage coolies. I wanted to give to each of mine one of the noble straw hats made near Kiao, but they "could not" wear them in Wan Hsien and its neighbourhood, any more than a fashionable English girl "could" wear a last season's hat.

---

* I must repeat that there are very good inns in SZE CHUAN in the cities, *i.e.* good for China, and at the regular stages, but, besides that I was avoiding cities because of the rough element which they contain, I was travelling less than the usual distance daily, and had to put up with the Chinese equivalent of the "hedge alehouse" accommodation, which the ordinary travelling Chinese would have disdained.

In bridges the varieties are endless, and in *pai fangs* and temple fronts. This ceaseless diversity in unity is very attractive in Chinese travelling, but it has its drawbacks, for on many occasions when, owing to weather or hurry or some other tyranny, I did not photograph some striking peculiarity I never met with it again. It also exposes the veracity of travellers to suspicion. One may describe some peculiarity which is universal in one region, such as the graceful circular or pointed arches of its bridges, while another, whose sole idea of a Chinese bridge is stone uprights carrying flat stone slabs such as the huge lumbering structure "which, with its wearisome but needful length, bestrides" the Min at Foo-chow, accuses him of having drawn upon his imagination for his facts.

For three days of cold, grim, drizzly, or incredibly damp weather, in which natural terraces gave way to artificial, and hills to rolls, and roads occasionally disappeared altogether, and the dull green of the sugarcane at times overspread the country, and the scarcity of rice lands now and then involved a corresponding scarcity of people, we travelled so awful a road that it mattered little when it was altogether lost. It had long since degenerated into the slimy top of a rice dyke a few inches wide, with a flagstone tipping up now and then to show what it once claimed to be. The bad weather put a stop to traffic. The only chair we met in three days came to grief close to us. The bearers fell, the chair was smashed into matchwood, and its occupant, a somewhat pompous-looking merchant, was deposited in three feet of slush alive with frogs, a disaster which afforded my men cause for unbounded hilarity for the rest of the day.

The road is so narrow because the farmers grudge every inch taken from their fields. As one is carried along, the chair hangs over the flooded rice land on either side, and when anyone is seen in the distance he is warned by a series of simultaneous yells to turn off on an intersecting dyke. On one of these days nearly eleven hours of hard travel only produced a result of eighteen miles! My men, though always wet to the skin and often falling as well as slipping, never flagged or grumbled, and trudged along joking and laughing, splendid "raw material"!

The people were not hostile in this country region, and the rain repressed the curiosity which I found specially irksome during the hour I spent twice daily sitting in a village street while my men breakfasted and dined. I became daily more convinced that the mandarins have it in their power to repress any overt expression of anti-foreign feeling. At Kiao, when I left the inn yard where the riot occurred the evening before, though it was crowded, the people were perfectly orderly, and though the long, narrow street was lined with men standing three and four deep on each side, just leaving room for the chair to pass, no one spoke or moved.

That same day the *chai-jen* were changed at the neat little city of Ying-san Hsien, in the centre of a region where the chief industries are making bamboo baskets, and straw plait for hats, and I sat for an hour near the *yamen* entrance, considering the extraordinary amount of business which custom imposes on a Chinese mandarin.

We have a habit, partly warrantable—for the official class in China is the worst of "the classes"—of speaking of "the mandarins" as we might speak of "the wolves" or "the vultures," a rough classification which, like similar methods, is by no means trustworthy. Mandarins are good and bad. The system under which they hold office has a strong tendency to make them bad. Nevertheless there are some good, just, honest men among them, who do the best they can for their districts during their terms of office, earn the esteem and gratitude of the people, and leave office as poor as they entered it. With regard to the bad, their opportunities for squeezing and oppressing are not so enormous as is often supposed, being limited by what I am inclined to call *the right of rebellion*. When an appeal to law comes to involve wholesale bribery, and taxation becomes grinding, then a local rebellion on a small or large scale occurs, the offending mandarin is driven out, the Throne quietly appoints a successor, and peace prevails once more.

A system in which official salaries are not a "living wage" opens the door to large peculation, but withal China is not a heavily taxed country, and the people are anything but helpless in official hands. In spite of all the monstrous corruption which exists, general security and good order prevail, and China has been increasing in wealth and population for nearly two centuries.

What we call mandarins (*kuans*) are all the magistrates subordinate through the intendants of circuits (*Taotai*) to the

Tsung-tuh of a province or provinces, the Governor-General, whom we call a Viceroy. They are prefects or head magistrates of departments, and magistrates for the subdivisions of departments. Under these, but not known as *kuans*, are mandarins' secretaries, often very powerful persons, clerks, registrars, and an army of subordinates, for whom their superiors are responsible. The Chinese call the last "rats under the altar," and fear them greatly. Indeed, it is said that the dread of getting into their clutches has a more deterrent effect on evil-doers than any prospect of punishment. Every mandarin, down to the smallest magistrate, has office secretaries for investigating cases, recording evidence, keeping accounts, filing papers, writing and transmitting despatches, and other formal functions.

Theoretically the relation between magistrate and people is strictly paternal. Some degree of what we call corruption is inseparable from Oriental officialism, and when kept within moderate bounds does not disturb the filial feeling. The whole of a mandarin's time is nominally at the service of the people of his district. Of some, perhaps of a goodly number throughout China, this devotion to local interests may be literally true. Access to his tribunal may ensure a fair trial, and probably in a majority of cases little injustice is done when a case once comes before him.

A gong was hung up at the *yamen* gate, where I have so long kept my readers shivering in the damp east wind. I am told that such a one hangs up at every similar gate, and that on hearing it the magistrate is bound to come out and attend to the complaint. But in practice a man has to bribe his way from the gate to the judgment-seat, and from the gatekeeper to the private secretary, and would be likely to be beaten if he touched the gong. Though the mandarin may be willing to decide justly, the underlings through whom alone approach to the judicial chair is possible do not share his scruples. A man who can afford to grease copiously the palms of runners, clerks, and secretaries, men unpaid or underpaid, is sure to see his petition on the top of the pile on the magistrate's table, while the poorer litigant finds his delayed *sine die*.

It is chiefly on the underpaid and hard-worked magistracy of China that the existence of government depends. No men in

A GROUP OF *KUANS* (MANDARINS).

mercantile positions work so hard as these officials, and if they are conscientious, all the worse for them. Their duties are most multifarious, and are both defined and undefined, executive, fiscal, judicial, and at times even military. They are responsible, not only for the taxes of their districts, but for their order and quietness, depending for much on subordinates whom they cannot trust, and during war, rebellion, and the floods and famines which occur with painful frequency are compelled to an almost sleepless vigilance, lest anything should go wrong, and they should be reported to the Throne. It is said truly that on the Hsien or Fu magistrate the work of at least six men devolves. He is at once tax commissioner, civil and criminal judge, coroner, treasurer, sheriff, and much besides, and he is supposed to have an exhaustive knowledge of everything within his bounds. And withal he must so dexterously regulate his squeezes as that it shall be possible for him to exist, for on his salary, attenuated as it is by forfeitures, he cannot.

Into the midst of this amount of responsibility, multifarious duties, and overwork, comes the foreigner with his treaty rights, a new and difficult element to deal with, and who may be an arrogant, bullying, and ignorant person. I am not apologising for the crimes of mandarins. I have suffered much from the violence of Chinese mobs, permitted, as I believe, if not instigated, by officialism. But I have on several occasions declined to make a formal complaint and hamper a magistrate because of my sympathy with his difficulties. On the one side there are orders from Peking sent down through the Viceroy that foreigners travelling are to be protected, and that their rights under the treaties are to be secured to them; on the other there is the anti-foreign feeling which has been inflamed for years past by agitators, certain of the secret societies, and what are known as the "Hunan Tracts," and which may be provoked into an explosion by any unintentional indiscretion of a foreigner, or, as in my case, by such an outrage on custom as travelling in an open chair! The riot occurs; the foreigner suffers in his person or goods; he lodges a complaint, is backed up by his consul; and the mandarin, who may have been miles away from the scene of the occurrence, is held responsible, and is possibly degraded. The large number of European and American missionaries who have become residents in SZE CHUAN during the last twelve years have also increased the evil considerably. So far as I saw and learned, these men and women, with a very few exceptions, are slaves to the scrupulosity of their observance of Chinese custom and etiquette so far as they know them, and to their anxiety to avoid giving offence in the country in which they live.

But, to begin with, they are foreigners, "foreign devils"; their eyes, their complexions, their ways of sitting and carrying their hands are repulsive, and the belief, sometimes piteous, that they are "child-eaters," and use the eyes and hearts of children in medicine, is now spread universally. Then they have come, if not, as many believe, as spies and political agents, to teach a foreign and Western religion, which is to subvert Chinese nationality, to wreck the venerated social order introduced by Confucius, to destroy the reverence and purity of domestic life and the loyalty to ancestors, and to introduce abominable customs.

This is, I think, a faithful view of missionary aims from a Chinese standpoint, and, bearing in mind the extreme ignorance and intense conservatism of the Chinese, it is not wonderful that there should be continual small disturbances, or that these should have culminated in the great anti-missionary riots in SZE CHUAN in 1895, in which a large number of the missionaries had to fly, and many more owed their lives to the protection given them by the mandarins in their *yamens*.

I would not hold the mandarins responsible for the whole of these outbreaks, though they are and must be held so, but the difficulties of their position are much complicated by the presence within their jurisdictions of aliens whose aims are obnoxious to the majority of the people, and who are slowly creating, under the protection of treaties, societies with views at variance with established custom.

Yet so great is the potency of a word from headquarters that I believe the SZE CHUAN mandarins are now doing their best to protect the missionaries, and wherever I went, and very specially at Paoning Fu, I heard of efficient protection given, even where the means at the magistrates' disposal were very limited, and of consideration and friendliness shown, far in excess of any claims which could be made, and which went to the extreme verge of a prudent regard for official position.

LADY'S SEDAN CHAIR (CHINESE PROPRIETY).

Some of my readers and friends will consider that in the above remarks I have played in another than the Vatican sense the part of "devil's advocate." So be it. I intended, as a matter of honesty and fair play, to "give the devil his due." I am fully aware of the manifold iniquities of the mandarins, and regard the official system as the greatest curse of China, if for no other reason than that it makes it nearly impossible for an official to walk on a straight path. But I wished to note briefly a few extenuating circumstances, and to protest against that rough-and-ready and very misleading system of classification which lumps all mandarins together as an irredeemably bad lot. The system is infamous, but a traveller who has spent some years in travelling in Turkey, Persia, Kashmir, and Korea, is astonished to find that the Chinese are very far from being an oppressed people, and that even under this system they enjoy light taxation in spite of squeezes, security for the gains of labour, and a considerable amount of rational liberty. It is when a Chinese, either through his own fault or that of another, becomes a litigant that his misfortunes begin.

In the hour I spent at the entrance of the *yamen* of Ying-san Hsien 407 people came and went—men of all sorts, many in chairs, but most on foot, and nearly all well dressed. All carried papers, and some big *dossiers*. Within, secretaries, clerks, and writers crossed and recrossed the courtyard rapidly and ceaselessly, and *chai-jen*, or messengers, bearing papers, were continually despatched. Much business, and that of all kinds, was undoubtedly transacted. There was nothing of the lazy loafing of a horde of dirty officials which distinguishes a Korean *yamen*. I was quite unmolested. Successive coolie crowds stood for a time regarding me with an apathetic stare, said nothing, and moved silently away. At last a very splendid person in brocaded silks and satins came out and handed me my passport, and we were able to proceed.

One among my reasons for not making the regular stages was that in town inns a woman-traveller must shut herself up rigidly in her room from arrival until departure unless she desires to provoke a row, while in the small villages and hamlets, where I was frequently the only guest, when the coolies had had their supper I was able to spend an hour in the "house place" with the family, and at a very small expense become friendly with them, and the village headman and one or two more often dropped in, and, under the influence of tea and tobacco and the sight of some of the nearest local photographs, became quite conversational. Be-dien, whose knowledge of English was very fair, improved daily, and was, I think, painstaking; at all events, I made him so!

On such evenings I heard a good deal about mandarins, taxes, industries, prices, carriage of goods, foreigners, missionaries, and other things, all purely local. Occasionally the consensus of opinion about a mandarin was that he was a very bad man, took bribes, exacted more than the "legitimate squeeze" in tax-collecting, decided cases always in favour of the rich, etc. Such must have been very bad cases on which all had reason to be agreed, or the men, owing to the strong distrust and suspicion of each other which prevail, would not have dared to speak out before each other. This is an element which must always be taken into consideration in judging of the probabilities of the accuracy of any statement which is made. On the whole, however, there were not many complaints uttered, and these were usually of the delays of law. Some mandarins were spoken of with something akin to enthusiasm. One had built a bridge, another had made a good road, a third had restored a temple, a fourth was "very charitable to the poor," and in the last scarcity had diminished the luxury of his own table by a half that he might feed the poor, and so on.

Anything like an enlightened idea on a subject not local was not to be hoped for. Few of these headmen had heard of the war, or of the peace of Shimonoseki, and those who had, believed that the "barbarian rebels" had been driven into the sea or into fiery holes in the ground. The immense indemnity paid to the Roman Catholics for their losses in "the riots" touched them more closely, and I heard a good deal said regarding the Roman missions which I will not repeat, and I will also "keep dark" the various criticisms, some of them most trenchant and amusing, which were made on our own missionaries, only wishing that

> "The giftie were gi'ed us
> To see ourselves as others see us."

The attempt to hammer out facts on these evenings was fatiguing and often disheartening, as, for instance, to decide which of six varying statements on one matter had the greatest aspect of probability, and was worth stowing away in my memory, but the interest of mixing in any fashion with the people far outweighed the discomfort of peasant accommodation, even when it was pretty bad. One night Be-dien, after surveying the inside of a very poor hovel, came out looking rueful, and said, " You won't like your room to-night, Mrs. Bishop ; *it's the pigs' room !*" and truly seven pigs occupied a depression railed off in one corner of it.

The second day after leaving Kiao we had heavy rain all day, and the road, which was a barely legible track, mostly on slippery mud hills, was so infamous that, as the bearers were constantly slipping and even falling, I had to do a good deal of being hauled and lifted along ; walking it was not, for my feet slipped from under me at nearly every step. We passed through one vacant, forlorn city of refuge, and spent most of the day in a desolate, treeless, sparsely inhabited, red region, slithering along the side of a high, bleak, mountain ridge, the summit of which (an altitude of 2140 feet) we gained at dark to find a small and most miserable hamlet astride on the top of it. The houses were all shut, and the pouring rain kept everyone indoors. No wonder! The slush was over my ankles, and very cold.

A broad gleam fell across the road, and we made our way to it, as wet as it was possible to be, and took, rather than asked, shelter in a big shed with a loft or platform at one side, fitfully lighted as well as filled with smoke by some branches which were being burned in a great clay furnace, apparently used for the making of iron pots. Several men were shovelling coal into the same, and there was a prospect of warmth. This shed was the front of the mouth and workings of a coal-pit. I was guided into some workings which appeared disused, where there were some pigs, a sunk water-trough in the sloppy clay floor, and an excavation two feet six inches wide by six feet long, into which my stretcher, six feet six inches long, was backed, and projected six inches outside! After a hot supper, I rolled myself, in my wet clothes, in a dry rug, and slept soundly till the torrent of rain slacked off at eight the following morning, when we got on the road again.

CHAPTER XXIV.

HSIEH-TIEN-TZE TO PAONING FU

THE weather continued grim, cold, and damp, with a penetrating east wind. I felt the cold more than on any
previous journey, even when for weeks at a time the mercury
had registered 20° below zero, and on this occasion it never fell
below 40° above, and on some of the "coldest" days was as high
as 45°. Men who had them were wearing their handsome furs
up to March 12th.

After leaving the coal-pit and the bleak hillside, we descended
to a region where the natural terrace formation of the hills was
extensively aided by art, and the country looked as if it were
covered with Roman camps.

At the risk of wearying my readers, I must again remark on the
singularity of the formation of this large portion of the Red
Basin, which is continued in its most exaggerated form at least
as far south as Shien Ching, on the Kialing, fully 270 *li* south
of Paoning. Looking down from any height, it is seen that the
red sandstone has been decomposed into hundreds of small hills,
from 200 to 300 feet high, with their sides worn into natural
and very regular terraces, of which I have counted twenty-three
one above another, while the actual hilltop is weathered into a
most deceptive resemblance to a fort or ruined castle.

Much of SZE CHUAN is remarkable for the scarcity of villages,
but, on the other hand, it is dotted over both with large farmhouses,
where the farmer and his dependants live in patriarchal style,
surrounded by a roofed wall with a heavy gateway, and with large
cottages, the walls of which, with their heavy black timbers and
whitewashed walls, have a most distinct resemblance to the old
Cheshire architecture, while the roofs, with a nearly even slope
from the ridge-pole to the extremity of the deep eaves which form
broad verandahs, have more kinship with that of the Swiss

châlet than with the typical Chinese roof, curving upwards at the corners.

If the tradition be true which declares that in the early days of this dynasty people were sent in chains to colonise this fair province, it may be, as Mr. Baber suggests, that they had not the family and clan ties which lead men to herd together in the communities which are also a necessary element of safety in many circumstances. It was not till the Taiping outbreak that these scattered settlers, who had lived and multiplied for nearly two centuries under conditions of security, found it necessary to combine for mutual protection. It then occurred to them that the numerous precipitous, rocky hills of the region, if walled round near the top, would be impregnable refuges, and they subscribed money and labour, and carried out their idea, sprinkling the country with picturesque *chai-tzu*, or redoubts, to which they ascended in times of dread. It did not occur to them to build permanent dwellings and remain at these altitudes.

In the purely agricultural parts of the province, where there are no local industries requiring concentration of population, such villages as are to be met with elsewhere, in which tenants, labourers, innkeepers, and proprietors, with shopkeepers and artisans, live in communities, are rarely met with. Out of the system of scattered dwellings and minute hamlets, trading arrangements for supplying the wants of the agricultural population have grown up, the like of which I have not seen elsewhere. These are the markets (*ch'ang*).

In travelling along the roads one comes quite unexpectedly upon a long, narrow street with closed shop fronts, boarded-up restaurants, and deserted houses, and possibly a forlorn family with its dog and pig the only inhabitants. The first thought is that the population has been exterminated by a pestilence, but on inquiry the brief and simple explanation is given, " It's not market day."

A few miles further, and the roads are thronged with country people in their best, carrying agricultural productions and full and empty baskets. The whole country is on the move to another long, narrow street closely resembling the first, but that the shop fronts are open, and full of Chinese and foreign goods; the tea-shops are crammed; every house is full of goods and people; from

2000 to 5000 or 6000 are assembled ; blacksmiths, joiners, barbers, tinkers, traders of all kinds, are busy ; the shouting and the din of bargaining are tremendous, and between the goods and the buyers and sellers locomotion is slow and critical. Drug stores, in which "remedies for foreign smoke" are sold, occur everywhere.

The shops in these streets are frequently owned by the neighbouring farmers, who let them to traders for the market days, which are fixed for the convenience of the district, and fall on the third or fifth or even seventh day, as the need may be. The gateway at each end of the street is often very highly decorated. Theatrical entertainments frequent these markets, and if the actors are well known and popular, 4000 or 5000 people assemble for the play alone. The markets are the great gatherings for all purposes. If anything of public opinion of a local character exists, it is manufactured there. There official notifications are made, and bargains regarding the sale or rent of land are concluded. Family festivals even are often held there, and after marriage negotiations on the part of heads of families have been concluded the preliminaries are drawn up and ratified at the market. There the cottons of Lancashire undergo a searching criticism, and are weighed, handled, held up to the light by men who cannot be deceived as to the value of cotton, and are often found wanting. Into the vortex of the market is attracted all the news and gossip of the district. It is much like a fair, but I never saw any rowdyism or drunkenness on the road afterwards, and I never met with any really rough treatment in a market, though the crowding and curiosity made me always glad when it was not "market day."

On the afternoon of March 7th there was some hazy sunshine, and the effect was magical. The route lay partly along the Shanrang Ho, an affluent of the Ku-kiang, itself navigable up to, and for sixty *li* above Sing-king-pa Hsien, so report said. Considerable fleets of colliers lay at different points, vessels carrying from ten to twenty-five tons, flat-bottomed. They were loading, in one case, from a coal-yard of half an acre at least in extent, fenced strongly and carefully with bamboo, in which the coal was piled in big, oblong blocks weighing two hundredweight each, to a height of seven feet, each block being carried from the pit by two men. The colliers are built in compartments, and very strongly, as there are severe rapids both above and below Sing-king-pa Hsien.

A SZE CHUAN FARMHOUSE.

After ferrying this river, along with a number of Buddhist priests, we gradually attained high ground, and secured the granary of a new inn for my room. Being new, the place was clean and dry, and promised well for the next day's halt, and most of the unpacking was done, when the trim, young hostess requested us to "move on." She said her father-in-law was away, and he would be angry with her for receiving a foreigner. I did not care to assert "treaty rights" against the obvious anxiety of so prepossessing a young woman, and we repacked, and slithered along six more *li* of bad roads till we came to a lone farming cottage on the top of a windy ridge, with a most extensive view, where I was very glad to remain for the next day, as I had had rather a severe week. From Sing-king-pa Hsien my *chai-jen* were two young soldiers in the most brilliant of stagey uniforms, and I think that they must have been the reason of my exclusion from the previous inn. Among the many curious proofs of superstitious beliefs one occurred many times on the last days of the journey : a small arch made of bamboo stuck into the slush of a rice-field. This is done in cases of the illness of the owner, and it is believed that the offering will restore him.

On this windy ridge of King-kiang-sze I slept in the granary, which I should have considered extreme luxury, as it was not dark when the door was shut, had it not been that it was only just built, and the mud on the walls was quite wet. The granary was detached from the house, open, as fortunately many Chinese rooms are, for two feet below the roof, and in several other directions, being in fact so draughty that no candle would keep alight in it.

I stayed in bed all the next morning owing to severe chills, the consequence of living in wet clothes, but had to get up in the afternoon to gratify the curiosity of fully thirty women, who had hobbled in from the adjacent hamlets, some of them twenty *li* away, to see "the foreign woman." I feared that they would be greatly disappointed to see me in Chinese dress, but I found that they did not know that foreigners wore any other ! My hair, "big feet," shoes, and gloves were all a great amusement to them, and, above all, my light camp bed, which they were sure would not bear any weight, so they sat down on it back to back to the number of twelve !

Of course they asked many questions, among others did we in our country make away with baby girls? I could not anywhere learn that infanticide prevails in any part of SZE CHUAN in which I travelled, and when I told these women of the extent to which it is practised in some parts of KWANTUNG, the remark was, "Couldn't they sell them for a good price?" Undoubtedly many SZE CHUAN girls are sold to traders from Kansuh. These mothers mostly had large families. The children are not weaned till they are three, and often not till they are four and even five, years old. Of "bringing up by hand" they know nothing—condensed milk has not reached that primitive region. If a mother dies at the birth of her babe, the mothers of the hamlet take the joint responsibility of supplying the orphan with maternal nourishment. They asked me if I had many sons, and when I confessed that I had none, they expressed great sympathy, because there would be no one at my death to perform the ancestral rites. It is quite customary, on hearing of the absence of sons, for women to pump up tears as a conventional requirement, and this propriety was not neglected on this occasion. It occurred to them that I could not have a daughter-in-law, which in their thinking was a great deprivation, not on sentimental, but on purely practical grounds, the daughter-in-law being equivalent to the mother-in-law's slave.

Few of them had been to Paoning Fu, only two days' journey off, and none to Wan Hsien. The markets of the neighbourhood were the boundaries of their horizon, and the festivals of the divinities of their hamlets their gaieties. I like the Chinese women better than any Oriental women that I know. They have plenty of good stuff in them, and backbone. When they are Christianised they are thorough Christians. They have much kindness of heart; they are very modest; they are faithful wives, and after their fashion good mothers. I gave my visitors tea and sweetmeats all round, and they departed, having taught me far more than they learned from me.

During the afternoon men with large shields slung across their backs, and carrying red staves, appeared, and there was at once a considerable fuss and a demand for my passport, the big seals of which made a salutary impression upon them. These officials were "census men," and were engaged in numbering the houses. The taking of a census has not been a popular matter from time

A SZE CHUAN MARKET-PLACE.

immemorial, and in the East an idea of increased taxation is always associated with it.

Like many Chinese systems, the census system is admirable in theory, but frauds, lapses, and neglect render it inefficient. Every city and village is divided into "tithings," or groups, of ten families each, and on every doorpost hangs, or ought to hang, a tablet, *mun-pai*, inscribed with the names of all the inmates of both sexes. If the head of a family omits to make an entry, or fails to register correctly the males of his household who are liable to public service, he may receive from eighty to a hundred blows. If the system were carried out, suspicious strangers could be easily caught, and local responsibility for any crime fixed without any trouble, but a householder finds it convenient to escape filling up the schedule by bribing the "shield men" with *cash* equivalent to twopence-halfpenny.

The next day, for a considerable distance, every house had blossomed into a brand-new *mun-pai*, which indicated the arrival of a new magistrate determined to enforce the law. The talk of the inn was that it heralded additional taxation.

The next day's journey to Heh-shui-tang was through varied and pretty country, much more populous, and with abounding water communication supplied by the Chia-ling, often in that region called the Paoning river, and its branches. The main traffic down the river is coal and salt. There are very many salt wells at a good height on the river bank. The brine is drawn by being pumped once a day, and that only when the river is low, and is evaporated by coal fires, the heavy yellow smoke giving the aspect of manufacturing industry. Salt is a Government monopoly. The Government buys all the salt which is produced, at a rate fixed by itself, and sends it all over the country for sale, making an enormous profit. It is said that the salt produced in SZE CHUAN brings in to the Government a revenue of £2,000,000 sterling! In some places the borings for salt extend to depths of nearly 3000 feet, as the result of the continuous operations of ten or twelve years, two feet a day being very satisfactory progress. "Fire wells" are often found near salt wells, and the "fire" is used for evaporating the salt. The product of the wells seen on that day's journey is small, but fifty boats of about twelve tons were loading with it.

At the pleasant and thriving little town of Nan-pu, which produces a very white salt, the mandarin was polite, and sent four gaily uniformed soldiers with me, who, however, shortly turned themselves into rather shabby civilians, showing, as on several other occasions, that the love of mufti is not confined to English officers. The mandarin's secretary asked if I would like to see anything in Nan-pu. I could think of nothing in the little, quiet, trading town, but for the sake of politeness I said I should like to see a school.

My men were at their midday meal, but bearers were provided, and I was soon deposited in the courtyard of an unpretending building, followed by a great crowd, which was kept from pressing on me by the mandarin's "lictors." The schoolroom contained several tables, some heavy benches, a teacher's chair, a number of "ink-stones," and thirty-three boys, from the ages of seven up to fourteen, who were all learning to read and write.

Near the roof a Confucian tablet, surrounded by inscribed strips of red paper, stood in a niche, and on one side of the schoolroom there was a life-size figure of the God of Literature, with a wooden box half full of ashes in front, in which some incense sticks were smouldering. The teacher was a kindly-looking old man in conventional goggles. He had probably repeatedly failed to pass his literary examinations, and being unfit for manual labour, had become a pedagogue. He held something very like "taws" in his hand, but his pupils had no unwholesome awe of him.

The boys were writing when I went in, *i.e.* tracing printed ideographs placed below thin paper with brushes filled with Chinese ink, which they rubbed on the ink-stones as required. The teacher went round, pointing out faults, and showing them how to hold their pens.

After this they studied, as everywhere in the East, aloud, shouting their lessons at the top of very inharmonious voices, an audible assurance relied upon to convince the teacher that they were giving full attention to their tasks. As soon as any boy had mastered his lesson, he came up to the master and stood with his back towards him while he recited, so that the master might be sure that he was not glancing at the book which he held in his own hand. Mispronunciations were corrected. What I saw constitutes education in such a school, together with formal instruction in proprieties: bowing before the tablet of Confucius on entering the room, saluting the teacher, etc. Such a school may be called a primary school, and the larger proportion of scholars never go any farther. In villages and small towns the parents pay from three to six dollars a year to the teacher, to which are added small presents of food at stated intervals. The hours are long—from sunrise till ten and from eleven till five.

PEDAGOGUE AND PUPILS.
(*From a Chinese Drawing.*)

Evening schools are occasionally opened for those who are occupied in the day. A pedagogue must be a man of good repute, "grave, learned, and patient," and well acquainted with the Chinese classics.

The monotonous reading and writing lessons and the tedium of memorising unmeaning sounds are continued for about two years, and when the pupils have become familiar with a few thousand forms and sounds, then the actual work of teaching begins; and the pedagogue, with the help of a commentary, explains the meaning of the words one by one, taking due care that they are all understood.

This system, as pursued in the humble school at Nan-pu, is the basis of that vast fabric of education which has made China for two thousand years what she is, and has produced among the Chinese a greater veneration for letters than exists in any country on earth, letters and literary degrees, absolutely apart from the accidents of birth or wealth, being the only ladder by which a man, be he the son of prince or peasant, can attain official employment, honours, and emoluments, China being in fact the most truly democratic country in the world.

It is easy to laugh at an education which for boys of all ranks consists solely in the knowledge of the ancient Chinese classics, and there is no doubt that it stunts individuality, belittles genius, fosters conceit, and produces incredible grooviness. But, on the other hand, there is no education, unless it might be one strictly Biblical, which furnishes the memory with so much wisdom for common life, and so many noble moral maxims. Whatever of righteousness, virtuous domestic life, filial virtue, charity, propriety—and just dealing exists among the Chinese, and they do exist—is owed to the permeation of the whole race by the teaching of the classics.*

The six school books (classics in themselves) which are introductory to the study of the classics are, *The Trimetrical Classic*, arranged in 178 double lines, the first of which contains the much-disputed doctrine, "Men at their birth are by nature radically good." It inculcates filial and fraternal duties, and much besides, as the following extract shows: "Mutual affection of father and son; concord of man and wife; the older brother's kindness, the younger one's respect; order between seniors and juniors; friendship among associates; on the prince's part regard, on the minister's true loyalty; these ten moral duties are for ever binding among men." This classic concludes with a number of fascinating incidents and motives for learning taken from the lives of ancient sages and statesmen.

---

* These are all attainable in scholarly translations, and, along with chapter ix. of Dr. Wells Williams' invaluable volumes, *The Middle Kingdom*, should be read by everyone who takes more than a merely superficial or commercial interest in China.

If a boy never goes farther than this, his memory is stored with excellent examples and principles.

The second book is the *Century of Surnames*. The third is unique in the world, the *Millenary, or Thousand Character Classic*, which consists of exactly 1000 characters, no two of which are alike in meaning or form. It treats of many important subjects, and, like the *Trimetrical Classic*, abounds in praises of virtue and exhortations to rectitude. Its text is absolutely familiar to all the people, and a Christian preacher who shows himself acquainted with it is sure of an interested audience.

The fourth school classic is called *Odes for Children*, and contains thirty-four stanzas of four lines each, chiefly in praise of literary life, such as this :—

> " It is of the utmost importance to educate children ;
> Do not say that your families are poor,
> For those who can handle well the pencil (pen),
> Go where they will, need never ask for favours."

In all the school classics many examples are given of intelligent youths entering on life without advantages, who by application, virtuous conduct, and industry, have raised themselves to the highest offices in the empire.

The fifth school classic is the *Canons of Filial Duty*, a book of 1903 characters only, purporting to be a report of a conversation between the *Great Teacher* (Confucius) and Tsang Tsan, a disciple. Whether it is actually what the Chinese believe it to be or not, its influence has been and is enormous, extending unweakened through a period of many centuries, and laying by its principles and maxims the foundations of the social order which prevails, not only in China, but in Japan and Korea. This paramount teaching begins with the sentence, "Filial duty is the root of virtue, and the stem from which instruction in the moral principle springs." It contains an axiom which has great weight : "With the same love that they" (scholars) "serve their fathers, they should serve their mothers." Many books have been written to illustrate these *Canons*, one a toy book, *The Twenty-four Filials*, containing twenty-four quaint and delightful stories of filial devotion. This is a most popular collection of tales, and the examples embroidered on satin, or painted on silk, or coarsely daubed on paper, are to be seen everywhere.*

* A translation of these is given in the *Chinese Repository* (vol. vi., p. 131).

The sixth and last is the *Siao Hioh,* or *Juvenile Instructor,* a book whose influence is estimated as enormous. It has had fifty commentators, one of whom writes of it, "We confide in the *Siao Hioh* as we do in the gods, and revere it as we do our parents." It is in two books, divided into twenty chapters and 385 short sections. The first book treats of the elementary principles of education, of the duties we owe to ourselves in regard to demeanour, dress, food, and study, and of the duties which we owe to our kindred, rulers, and fellow-men, and it gives illustrative examples of the good results of obeying these maxims, taken from ancient history as far down as B.C. 249!

The second book seems somewhat of a commentary on the first, or an elaboration of it. It gives a collection of virtuous and wise sayings of great men who lived after B C. 200, and these are followed by a number of examples of conduct in distinguished persons, showing the effect of good principles and the advantage of following the teachings of the first book. The most elaborate rules of etiquette are laid down with a view of promoting mutual reverence, and the Chinese of to-day receives his guests at his outer door and conducts them, with the most careful attention to elaborate rules of precedence, through courts, and up flights of steps to his guest-hall, he and they moving their feet and accepting or declining attention in slavish accordance with the rules of this ancient classic.

The Chinese of to-day, in thought, action, and etiquette, are the product of these school books. I see no possibility of spontaneity so long as education is *solely* on these lines. In reading the translations of these classics, in spite of a certain insistence upon trifles, and perhaps of exaggeration of unimportant points, I have been enormously impressed by their admirable moral teaching as a whole. Virtue is inculcated by precept and example on every page, and with the solemn sanctions of antiquity. Deficiencies there are, but there is not a single thing in this curriculum which a man ought not to be the better for learning, or one thing which it would be desirable for him to forget. If he is unable to go farther, he is possessed of what may be called the kernel of the best literature of his country, and his national feeling is fostered by the fact that the noble truths and examples impressed on his mind are not of foreign origin, but have originated within the frontiers of the Middle Kingdom. The missionaries show at once their appreciation of the *Chinese classics*, as well as a judicious desire to conserve Chinese nationality and keep the pathway to official employment open, by giving great prominence to this classical teaching in their schools.

"Villages had their schools, and districts their academies," says the *Book of Rites* (B.C. 1200), and I looked with reverence on the dirty, cobwebby walls of the little private school at Nan-pu as their historical successor.

I asked the teacher how many of his thirty-three pupils were likely to go on with their education and compete at the examinations, and he replied, "Three," holding up three fingers, on one of which was a carefully-tended nail an inch and a half long, that there might be no mistake. The parents of the pupils were poor, and would not be able to keep them at school for more than three years at the outside, while shopkeepers, farmers, and country gentlemen would not keep them there more than five years unless they meant to go on to the literary examinations. In the case of these well-to-do persons, several families living in the same street hire a well-qualified teacher at a stipulated salary to teach their boys, and the instruction is given in light, well-aired rooms. In such a school as I spent an hour in, the teacher provides and furnishes the room according to the number and position of his pupils. On a boy entering a school he receives his *shu-ming*, or " book name," by which he is known during his future life.

If I have conveyed what I wish to convey, clearly, it will be evident that Chinese education in the primary schools is limited to the teaching of virtue, duty, and etiquette. There is no provision for developing the intellectual powers, nor has general learning any place. There is a complete want of symmetry in the mental training, but if it fails to form broad and well-balanced minds, it must be admitted that the exaggeration is in the best direction in which distortion could occur.

That night I felt profound regret at concluding the first stage of my journey, and the soft, dreamy sunshine of the next day increased it. The country is soft in its features, and very pretty and prosperous-looking, abounding in industries, and consequently in villages and small towns, and produces everything that is good for food. The road adheres pretty closely to the valley of the

Chia-ling, which we ferried twice. Its water is translucent, and of an exquisitely beautiful peacock green. It is one of the great arteries of commerce of the Yangtze Valley, and though, like the Yangtze, obstructed by rapids and given to the production of great sand-banks, specially below Paoning Fu, it and its affluents afford invaluable means of communication.

This river, uniting with the Yangtze at Chungking after receiving such fine tributaries as the Ku, the Fu, and the Pai-shui, is navigable for boats of 5000 catties up to the flourishing little town of Pai-shui-Chiang, actually over the border of KANSUH, and over 500 miles by water from Chungking. These big boats trade chiefly with Nan-pu, which produces salt, taking salt up and bringing coal down. There are smaller boats carrying 2000 catties, of which I saw many, which go right down to Chungking, carrying KANSUH tobacco, sheepskins, furs, and medicines. Mr. Litton, of H.B.M.'s Consular Service, saw seventy boats at one time moored off the city of Kuang Yuen, near the frontier of KANSUH.

The country is much affected by the great sand-banks formed by the river, which become bound together by the fibrous roots of a sword-grass, and alter the channel, forming, after a few years of deposit, fine arable land. The road I travelled from Heh-shui-tang, after skirting the Chia-ling at a great height for many miles, under cliffs abounding in recessed temples, in which groups of divinities carved in the rock receive hourly worship from wayfarers, enters Paoning Fu by a pontoon bridge about 130 yards long.

After the treelessness of much of the region I had traversed, and the comparatively poor soil and inferior dwellings, the view of Paoning and its surroundings was most charming in the soft afternoon sunshine. Built on rich alluvium, surrounded on three sides by a bend of the river, with temple roofs and gate towers rising out of dense greenery and a pink mist of peach blossom, with fair and fertile country rolling up to mountains in the north, dissolving in a blue haze, and with the peacock-green water of the Chia-ling for a foreground, the first view of this important city was truly attractive.

In the distance appeared two Chinese gentlemen, one stout, the other tall and slender, whose walk as they approached gave me a suspicion that they were foreigners, and they proved to be Bishop Cassels, our youngest and one of our latest consecrated bishops, and his coadjutor, Mr. Williams, formerly vicar of St. Stephen's, Leeds, who had come to welcome me. We ferried the Chia-ling, and passing through attractive suburbs, either green lanes with hedges, trees, and vegetable gardens, or narrow flagged roads, very clean, bounded by roofed walls and handsome gateways of private houses, we reached the China Inland Mission buildings, consisting of a neat church, very humble Chinese houses for the married and bachelor missionaries, guest-rooms, and servants' quarters, all cheerful, but greatly lacking privacy. This was a pleasant halt after a journey of 300 miles without a really untoward incident, except the riot at Liang-shan.

RECESSED DIVINITIES, CHIA-LING RIVER.

CHAPTER XXV.

PAONING FU AND SIN-TIEN-TZE

PAONING FU, where I spent a week, is, in spring at least, a very attractive city. There is a pleasant sleepiness about it. Trade is neither so active or so self-asserting as usual. There is obviously a leisured class with time to enjoy itself. Large fortunes are not made ; 45,000 taels is looked upon as wealth, and there are no millionaires to overshadow the small traders. Junks of eighteen tons and over can ascend to Paoning during much of the year. There is a considerable coal trade on the Tung river, and the city being in the centre of an important silk region, there is a degree of activity about the silk trade. There are such small industries as dyeing cottons, making wine and vinegar, and the export of pigs' bristles and hides, but nothing is pursued very energetically. Among the population of about 20,000 there are a small number of Mohammedans, and wherever they exist beef and milk are attainable luxuries. In Paoning they cure and spice an excellent salt beef, which I found an agreeable variation from fowls on my further journey.

Officially, Paoning Fu is an important city, having a *Taotai*, a prefect, and a hsien, and many of its beautiful "suburban villas" are the residences of retired and expectant mandarins. Its suburbs are quite charming, and its suburban roads are densely shaded by large mulberry trees and the *Aleurites cordata*. Farther outside, are several fine temples in large grounds, and the public library. Paoning proper, with the *yamen* and other official residences, streets of shops, and private dwellings with large wooded gardens, is surrounded by a wall twenty feet high, in good repair, with a flagged walk, ten feet broad, on the top of it. From this the aspect of the city was idealised by a coloured mist of pink and white—peach, plum, apricot, and cherry blossom, flecked with crimson from the double flowers of hardy, decorative peach trees. There are four fine but dilapidated gateways.

TEMPLE OF GOD OF LITERATURE, PAONING FU.

One of the gates was securely shut, and all persons who desired to enter or leave the city on that side were compelled to make a long *détour*. This closing of the north gate against the God of Rain is by a ceremonial act of the mandarin. Rain was in excess, and this was a significant hint to the rain god. Elsewhere I had seen the south gates of cities closed in drought against the God of Fire, who can only enter a city from that quarter. Fires are much dreaded during drought, when the timbers of houses are baked into a condition of perilous inflammability.

Outside the walls of Paoning Fu, which supply a delightful walk, are fine clean turf banks, and a turfed trench or moat, and fine trees; and the river front on the west side is truly grand, a terrace twenty-five feet broad being supported by a noble stone wall in twenty-five tiers, with broad stone staircases descending from the terrace to the river, short green turf, clean white sand, and clear green water below.

The finest of the suburban temples is dedicated to Went-zu, the God of Pestilence. I visited this with Mr. Williams. It was not possible to get any point of view on the level, for a photograph, and the chair-bearers suggested my taking one from the stage of an open temple theatre opposite, and brought a ladder to help me up with. In going back, a man of the literary class attacked Mr. Williams for this, and the next day the servants of the missionary ladies begged them not to go outside their house, for nothing was talked of in the streets and tea-houses but this "outrage," and the probable indignation of the gods, and the people were saying they would "kill all the foreigners." Mr. Williams said that he had never heard such cries of "foreign devil," and "foreign dog," as at that time, and that it is observed that these cries and the hatred which prompts them increase the longer foreigners remain in a city.

Paoning, so far as its population goes, is unfriendly to foreigners, and the mission houses were wrecked a year previously, and the missionaries, some of whom were married women with young children, escaped to the *yamen*, where they received shelter and protection for some time, the mandarins then and since having shown much friendliness and desire for their safety. It is a complex situation on both sides.

Paoning is a great centre of China Inland Mission work. The

directors of this body, which is undenominational, endeavour so far as is possible to group the missionaries of each ecclesiastical body together, and in this part of SZE CHUAN they all belong to the Church of England. Outside of the "sphere of interest" of the C.I.M. the Church Missionary Society has several mission stations, chiefly to the north and west of Paoning, and altogether in that region there are about sixty Anglican missionaries, several of them being university men, working on much the same lines.

Dr. Cassels, who was one of the pioneers, and formerly well known as an athlete at Cambridge, had recently been consecrated bishop, and came from the splendours of his consecration in Westminster Abbey to take up the old, simple, hardworking life, to wear a queue and Chinese dress, and be simply the "chief pastor." The native Christians gave him a cordial reception on his return, and presented him with the hat of a Master of Arts and high boots, which make a very seemly addition to the English episcopal dress, giving it the propriety which is necessary in Chinese eyes, and in mine the picturesque aspect of one of the marauding prelates of the Middle Ages, the good bishop having a burly, athletic physique! Since his return, several of the lay missionaries have been ordained deacons.

The church, or cathedral, of which an illustration is given, was built almost entirely with Chinese money and gifts. It is Chinese in style, the chancel windows are "glazed" with coloured paper to simulate stained glass, and it is seated for two hundred. The persons represented as standing outside are Bishop Cassels, Mr. Williams, and the Chinese churchwarden. There are both churchwardens and sidesmen.

I witnessed a Chinese service at which nineteen persons of both sexes who had been confirmed on the previous Sunday received the Holy Communion. At matins, which followed, the church was crammed, and crowds stood outside, where they could both see and hear, this publicity contrasting with the Roman practice. The understanding that all should be silent during worship was adhered to. A Christian, formerly a Mohammedan of some means, and another, who had been a Taoist, read the lessons. The Bible, an Oriental book both in imagery and thought, is enjoyed and understood by Orientals, but I doubt much if it will be possible or even desirable to perpetuate the Prayer Book

THE RIGHT REV. BISHOP CASSELS, D.D., PAONING FU.

CHINESE PROTESTANT EPISCOPAL CHURCH.
PAONING FU.

as it stands. It is so absolutely and intensely Western in its style, conceptions, metaphysic, and language of adoration, and, I think, is partly unintelligible as a manual of devotion. It contains any number of words which not only (as is to be expected) have no equivalents in the Eastern languages, but the ideas they express are unthinkable by the Eastern mind. Already many Eastern Christians are claiming an "Oriental Christ, not a Christ disguised in Western garb"—it may be that they will claim too a form of worship which shall be Oriental both in thought and expression, instead of one which represents to them in their most sacred moments an exotic creed.

The China Inland Mission has some very humble Chinese houses built round two compounds, in which two married couples, three bachelors, and, in the bishop's house, two ladies were living, and at some distance off there is a ladies' house, then occupied by five ladies. There are several guest-halls for Chinese visitors, class and school-rooms, porters' and servants' rooms. The furniture is all Chinese, and the whitewashed walls are decorated with Chinese scrolls chiefly.

I never saw houses so destitute of privacy, or with such ceaseless coming and going. Life there simply means work, and work spells happiness apparently, for the workers were all cheerful, and even jolly. Studying Chinese, preaching, teaching, advising. helping, guiding, arranging, receiving, sending forth, doctoring, nursing, and befriending make the mission compounds absolute hives of industry. It was a great drawback that medical help was nearly 300 miles off, and that the one trained nurse in the two missions was not ubiquitous. Much needless suffering and risk to life were the results. Happily in one of the beautiful suburbs, a noble Chinese mansion, a palace in size and solidity, was for sale for an old song, the half of which was purchased, and after undergoing alterations was opened a few months after my visit with a mandarin's procession and great ceremony as the "Henrietta Bird Memorial Hospital"—the men's department under Dr. Pruen, a physician of ten years' Chinese experience, and the women's under Miss Gowers, who also had considerable experience. The other half and a separate courtyard adjoining have been bought for a dwelling for the bishop, where he may carry on his work with fewer interruptions.

The ladies of this mission lead what I should think very hard lives, owing to their painful deference to Chinese etiquette, and their great desire to avoid doing anything which can give offence. As for instance, they never walk out without an elderly Chinese woman with them, or are carried except in closed chairs.

I left this hive of industry, and devoted lives, and glowing hospitalities with Mr. and Mrs. Williams and their children for a few days at Sin-tien-tze, where the China Inland Mission has obtained a large farmhouse for a sanitarium and centre of country work at a height of 2870 feet. Paoning is only 1520. This, in lat. 31° 55', was my farthest point north on my SZE CHUAN journey.

Shortly after leaving Paoning the road mounts the northern hills, and keeps along a high barren ridge, or *liang-tsu*, for 130 *li*, the air becoming more bracing and delicious every hour. I have observed that in Western China an altitude of 3000 feet is equivalent, in the dryness and bracing qualities of the air, to 7000 feet in Japan.

We stayed for a night in a large, rambling inn in a market-place when it was not market day, and were quiet. Long flights of stairs conduct travellers to the top of the ridge, which is often less than ten feet broad, and falls down in natural rock-supported terraces to the valleys below. At the close of the second day's journey the cultivation nearly ceased, the hills were bare and rocky, the road a mere straggle ; and where two or three ridges meet, on turning a corner round a pine-clothed knoll, we came upon a large, lonely house with a dead, blank wall round it, and were heartily welcomed by its inmates, three ladies, who for some time past have conducted a mission to the scattered houses and hamlets of the neighbourhood with remarkable success.

A great gateway gives admission successively into two courts with their surrounding rooms. The common " sitting-room," or, to use an Americanism, " living-room," is extremely tasteful and pretty—pre-eminently a " lady's room," furnished with bamboo tables, chairs, a lounge, and foot-stools, and a folding screen covered with blue cotton, on which Christmas cards are prettily arranged. Blue cotton table-cloths, embroidered in white silk, covered the tables. The floor was matted. Chinese red scrolls

C.I.M. SANITARIUM, SIN-TIEN-TZE.

hung on the whitewashed walls ; there were books and flowering plants ; and the room combined daintiness with solid comfort. Doors, with elaborate fretwork filled in with tissue paper, take the place of windows. The woodwork of all the rooms is varnished.

I expressed admiration and some wonderment that "at such a distance" (possibly from civilisation) such pretty furniture could be procured. It may be that my hostess thought she read in my remark some hint at "missionary luxury," for she very kindly offered to enlighten me as to the cost of furnishing in Western China. The substantial and good-looking chairs cost fourpence each, the lounge two-and-sixpence, and the rest in proportion ; the whole coming to a trifle under nineteen shillings, and all was produced in the neighbourhood, material and labour costing almost nothing. During my five days' visit the weather became bitterly cold, and snow fell for the greater part of two days, but did not lie. No efforts brought the temperature of my room up to 40°, which was low for the 21st March, in lat. 31° 55′.

CHAPTER XXVI.

SIN-TIEN-TZE TO TZE-TUNG HSIEN.

ON this second long journey, involving a distance of three hundred and thirty miles, I was persuaded into a slightly more luxurious style of travelling, *i.e.*, I took an additional man, well acquainted with the province and its ways, who went on first, towards evening, cleaned out a room, and had hot water ready for tea. I got new oiled sheeting and an apron for the chair, and with some unleavened bread, curry for three days, a supply of Paoning smoked beef and some chocolate for lunch, I felt myself in luxury. Yet, with eight men, my expenses were only seven shillings per day.

At Sin-tien-tze I had to quit my companions, who are as full of brightness, intelligence, and culture as they are of goodness. Mr. Williams walked with me through thawing snow the first eight miles to the great market-place of Shang-wa-li-tze, where, not being market day, the only living creature was a deformed cat. I had excellent cooking, and we made long journeys, accomplishing thirty miles on some days. The snow soon disappeared, and though the roads were slimy, straw shoes, grippers, and the cold, keen air enabled me to walk a good deal, which was very pleasant.

At the first midday halt there was considerable confusion, for a young married woman had committed suicide with opium, and was lying apparently dead. In great fear of something—I know not what—the villagers appealed to me for remedies, which I succeeded in forcing down her throat, and also put plasters of hot vinegar and cayenne pepper behind her ears. I was proceeding to put them on the soles of her feet, but there were no soles, only a crumple of deformed toes, a cleft, and a heel. Then I tried for the calves of the legs, but there were no calves, only a bone, a few muscles, and a great bag of crinkled skin. I was more fortunate

in finding that she had a back to her neck! I was told that it was
a quarrel with her mother-in-law which had driven her to suicide.
I had a bad quarter of an hour before she became conscious, for,
had she died, the opium would have been acquitted, and the
blame would have been laid on the foreigner. When she came
sufficiently to herself to be herself, she was demented with rage,

ENTRANCE TO A MARKET-PLACE.

and tore and scratched everybody near her. I did not think that
her husband was interested in her recovery.

An idea, though possibly only a local one, is, that when a person
commits suicide by opium, the spirit is refused entrance at the
gate of Hades, because it has not completed its natural term of
life, and it seeks, by inducing another to do the same, to transfer
its crime to that person.

The relations showed me the courtesy of offering me food, which I reluctantly ate out of coarse, unglazed basins: a strip or two of fat pork, some bean curd floating in grey sauce, some black beans, tasting like rotten cheese, some small onions, pickled dark brown, some rice, mixed with chopped cabbage, and some chopped capsicum.

I had previously eaten bean curd, and old eggs which are an expensive delicacy, and formed part of a Chinese dinner given to me at the English Legation at Seoul. At the next village I saw the process of preparation. Ducks' eggs alone are used, and they must be quite fresh. They are steeped in a solution of lime, with the addition of salt. The lime penetrates the shell and turns the white into a dark, bottle-green jelly, while the yolk becomes hard and nearly black. After this the egg is wrapped up in clay, which is dried by gentle heat. It will then keep a year or more. Such eggs are very good, indeed they are one of the few Chinese delicacies which I can eat with equanimity. The variety of food eaten by all classes in China is amazing. It would require four or five pages to put down what I have myself seen in the eating-houses and food shops on this journey.

After leaving Sin-tien-tze, I entered a richer and more prosperous region, with a very productive soil, much mineral wealth, and important industries both in towns and villages; and the food shops reflected the prosperity. There was fresh pork everywhere. Every village seemed to have killed a pig that morning. In most places bread made of wheaten flour was to be got in the form of dumplings, leavened, but steamed, not baked. These make good toast. Bean curd is everywhere also, and is universally liked. It is pure white, as if made with milk, and resembles in insipidity unflavoured *blanc mange*, made with Carrageen moss. There is scarcely a hamlet in which it is not sold. The beans are ground between two mill-stones, the upper one having a hole in the centre. Into this the beans are poured along with water, and the thick white cream which results from the grinding is caught in a trough below. Plenty of gypsum and some salt are added, the cream is boiled, the froth is thrown away, and the residue, after undergoing considerable squeezing in a cloth, is poured into flat, deep trays to set; when cold it is cut up into bricks. Every traveller

in China, Japan, and Korea makes acquaintance with this preparation. Beans are enormously used, fresh, and made into
patties, and preserved in equal parts of brine and syrup, when
they taste like hazel nuts.

Patties, or pies, are universal, and the itinerant pieman
frequents all markets and places where men congregate. Vegetable patties of beans, chopped cucumbers, vegetable eggs, and
sweet potato are much liked, and so are patties of pork, and salt
fish, and frog, but the last are somewhat of a luxury. Then there
are cakes of wheaten flour containing chopped and fried onion,
or a spoonful of treacle, and cakes of ground millet, with sugar-
candy or scorched millet on the top, and the same pieman often
sells bags of popcorn, melon seeds, and pieces of sugarcane.

Water-melon seeds ought rather to be classed with amusements
than with food. As in Persia, they are enormously used; it is
difficult to write consumed. They descend to the poorest class,
but chiefly on holidays. Their use implies leisure and sociability.
I never saw a man eating them alone, except on a journey.
They are a national custom. Where our men would enjoy themselves drinking wine or spirits, the Chinese play with melon seeds.
Eating them seems a masculine amusement, and the higher a
Chinese is in rank the more melon seeds he consumes. One dare
not speculate on what the consumption of the Son of Heaven
must be. Doubtless they serve the useful purpose of helping
to supply the system with fatty matter.

In some parts of SZE CHUAN water-melons appear to be grown
entirely for their seeds. I have seen the cooling, delicious pulp
thrown on the road, while the seeds are carefully preserved, and,
as in Tibet the proprietors of apricot orchards allowed me to eat as
many apricots as I liked, provided that I returned them the stones,
so I have been allowed to eat melons, if I returned the seeds.
Huc writes that on the rivers "huge junks may be seen loaded
entirely" with these "deplorable futilities." I do not pretend
to such a remarkable vision, but at good inns I have seen parties
of six or eight well-dressed merchants, with carefully-tended,
pointed finger-nails an inch long, spending three or four hours
in cracking melon seeds, plate after plate rapidly disappearing.
Piles of shells of melon seeds some inches high often greeted
me in inn rooms. Every wayside restaurant sells them. Groups

of children sit apathetically in village streets eating them. They are served before, with, and after every meal, with tea and wine, and at all social gatherings. Men crack and eat them while they are bargaining or discussing business, or are travelling in sedan chairs. And the dexterity and rapidity with which they extract the small kernel from the tough shell is worthy of squirrels and apes. This consumption of melon seeds is a feature of the whole empire, and I really believe is, as a pleasure, second only to " foreign smoke."

Our ideas as to Chinese food are, on the whole, considerably astray. It is true that the rich spend much in pampering their appetites, that the foolish extravagance of providing meats, fruits, and vegetables, out of season at "dinner parties" prevails among them as among us, and that such delicacies as canine cutlets and hams, cat fricassees, bird's-nest soup—a luxury so costly that it makes its appearance on foreign tables—stewed *holothuria*, and fricassee of snails, worms, or snakes are to be seen at ceremonious feasts. I have been myself in dog and cat restaurants in Canton, but they are only frequented by the extravagant.

I think in addition to the enormous variety in Chinese articles of diet, multiplied a hundredfold by culinary art, the food is wholesome and well cooked, and that the cooking is cleanly, steaming being a very favourite method. Cleanly cooking and wholesome and excellent meals are often produced in dark and unsavoury surroundings, and those foreigners who travel much in the interior learn to find Chinese food palatable. My chief objection to it is the amount of vegetable oil used, and the prevalent flavour of garlic. The bulb well applied is an excellent condiment, but it is startling to meet with it in unexpected places, and everywhere.

Rice, wheat, Italian millet, and maize are the grains chiefly eaten, but rice is the staff of life, and is regarded as absolutely indispensable. But it is not eaten by itself, even by the poorest, but mixed with fried cabbage, or with such dainty relishes as rotten beans, or putrid mustard, or soy, or Chili sauce. Among common expressions, to "take a meal" is "to eat rice," and the salutation equivalent to "How do you do?" is literally "Have you eaten rice?" *

* Dr. WELLS WILLIAMS, *Middle Kingdom.*

The Chinese list of culinary vegetables about quadruples ours, and with the exception of rice they are the great result of garden cultivation and heavy manuring, some of the root crops receiving individually at stated intervals a supply of liquid manure. Cucumbers, melons, and radishes weighing a pound each, are produced in enormous quantities. More than twenty sorts of peas and beans are cultivated—one monstrous bean being eaten with its soft squashy pod. Leaves are important articles of diet, beginning with the opium leaf. There are pig weed (*Chenopodium*), sow thistle (*Sonchus*), ginger, radishes, mustard, clover, shepherd's purse, succory, sweet basil, lettuce, celery, dandelion, spinach, purslane, artemisia, amaranthus, tacca, and numberless others which have no English names. In addition to carrots, turnips, parsnips, Jerusalem artichokes, sweet potatoes, enormously used, and "Irish potatoes" increasingly grown, they have aquatic edible roots, among others the big root of the *Nelumbium*, water-caltrops, and water-chestnuts.

Onions, garlic, leeks, scallions, and chives are consumed both by rich and poor, and it is seldom possible to be out of their odour. Cabbage, broccoli, kale, colewort and cress are eaten enormously, both fresh and preserved, as well as musk and water-melons, pumpkins, squashes, gourds, tomatoes, and brinjals, besides many eccentric pods, of the names of which I have not a notion. One of the most delicious of all Chinese vegetables is the young shoot of the bamboo, which looks like huge asparagus, and is eaten boiled. The Chinese consume enormous quantities of pickled cabbage and onions, as well as candied roots and fruits, and others preserved in syrup. Even the common potato is dignified by this treatment.

In the absence of butter and oily foods, the use of much oil in cooking is a physical necessity, but the European palate would require a long education before it could enjoy the strong flavours of some of the vegetable oils, such as castor oil, sesamum, and ground nut. Lard and pork fat are used also.

Very little land in the Yangtze Valley is used for the rearing of animals for food. Pork is the principal meat used, and I suppose that every family possesses a pig. Beef is rarely obtainable, except where there are Mohammedans. I never saw mutton west of Ichang, or, indeed, sheep till I reached the mountains.

Pork, fowls, geese, and ducks really represent animal food over much of SZE CHUAN. If young cats and dogs are bred for the table they are fed on rice. Locusts, grasshoppers, silkworms and grubs are eaten, being fried till they are crisp. In some cities human milk is sold for the diet of aged persons, great faith being placed in its nutritive qualities.

Undoubtedly much of the grain, especially millet, which is grown between Sin-tien-tze and Mien-chuh is used for the distillation of spirits. There are no vines in SZE CHUAN, so what we call wine is unknown. There are water-white spirits distilled from both millet and barley, and a sort of beer like the Japanese *sake* made from rice, from which spirits can be distilled. I never saw a drunken man in fifteen months of Chinese travelling, or heard mirth of which strong drink was the inspiration. Men take spirits in very small quantities, and almost invariably with their food. They never drink anything cold, which safeguards them from the worst results of the abominably contaminated water. They drink plain hot water, the water in which rice has been boiled, tea, and decoctions of various leaves.

I have dwelt so long upon food, because for two hours of every day I had nothing to do but study it and inferior cooking as well, for several months, and saw infinite varieties of food in the different parts of the province at different seasons during my long journey. On the whole, except in times of scarcity, the Chinese is a fairly well-fed person.

The journey of March 23 was along the top of a ridge over rocky ground, and along limestone terraces incapable of cultivation. There were no villages, and few houses, but we passed through two market-places of large size. The country, as seen from the ridge, is all low, undulating ranges, sprouting up now and then into conical protuberances, till suddenly, from an altitude of 2300 feet, there is a view of a narrow valley and an extraordinary bend of the Chia-ling. Then comes an abrupt and difficult descent of 800 feet, on ledges of rock and steep flights of broken stairs, and at its foot the small town of Mao-erh-tiao, with a very fine temple lately restored. Boats of twenty tons, salt laden, were lying in the clear, blue-green water along the bank. It was a delightful day's journey, the sky very blue, the air dry and as keen as a knife, and I reached a fairly good inn where the curiosity

AUTHOR'S ARRIVAL AT A CHINESE INN.

was not overpowering. The coolies were, if possible, cheerier and better than those from whom I had reluctantly parted, and as they were not opium-smokers they were able to feed themselves well, and thought nothing of travelling thirty miles a day at a good pace.

Other halcyon days followed, of keen air, light without heat, and country which, if not actually pretty, led one continually to believe that it was about to become so. The plumed bamboo and orange and pommeloe groves had vanished, and on the high altitudes which the road pursues, which are very barren and rocky, there was almost no cultivation, and on one day's journey of twenty-three miles we only met four people, and passed eight houses and a small market-place.

Whenever the elevation was lower, as at times where the road runs along the edges of limestone cliffs, there are deep valleys well wooded and cultivated, but the upland soil is very poor and bears scanty crops. What is called a road is only a narrow foot-path, winding along the edges of wheat-fields, through rocky clefts or ferny defiles, so narrow that the chair continually bumped both sides, or under cedars or other big trees, over the tops of which trailing red and white roses have grown, sending down streamers, then in the pink flush of their spring leafage, over the road. This beautiful climber, which grows with prodigious rapidity, also flourishes in Korea.

There were pretty little bits, sweet, restful, rural scenes, great breezy sweeps, and freedom; no calling of "Foreign devil" and "Foreign dog." The people were quite disposed to be friendly. On arriving one afternoon at a specially lofty hamlet, having learnt much caution as to the use of my camera, I asked if I might "make a picture" of a mill worked by a blindfolded buffalo-cow, as we had not any such mills in my country, and they were quite willing, and stopped the cow at the exact place I indicated. They were friendly enough to take me to another mill, at which two women grind, turning the upper stone by means of poles working in holes. The Chinese use a great deal of wheat flour; it can be purchased at all markets and large villages, and I never used any other. It is not a good colour, and owing to some defect in the millstones one is apt to be surprised by grits. After seeing the mills I showed the people a number of my photographs taken *en route*, to show them that I was not doing anything evil or hurtful, but they said, though quite good-naturedly, that it was "foreign magic."

At the same hamlet I got a room in a new inn which, though on the road-level on one side, was two storeys above a winding stream and some undulating agricultural country on the other. On that side it actually had a window and a view. The boards were new, and though the chinks were wide and the air which

AN OX MILL.

entered was keen, I congratulated myself heartily on such un-usually pleasant surroundings. This was premature. When the bustle of unpacking was over, noises all too familiar made me look through the chinks of the floor, and I saw that I was over a pigsty the size of my room, inhabited by nine large, black sows.

It was the only night of my journey on which I had no sleep, and my servant, who had the next room to mine, said that he did not sleep after eleven, for the groaning, grunting, routing, and quarrelling were incessant. I had shared a room with pigs twice on the journey, but they were quiet by comparison.

Looking through my floor at daylight, I saw that eighteen young pigs had been added to the family. This sleepless night was a bad preparation for an early start, and a long and very cold day's journey.

The road leaves Tien-kia-miao, a remarkably clean and attractive village, by a level bridge on twelve stone piers, and

A HAND MILL.

soon rises again to barren altitudes, looking down on well-cultivated valleys wooded with cedars. Along every rocky path men were crowding with their wares to a neighbouring market, bamboo hats and baskets, sugarcane, fowls, and straw shoes being the principal wares. It was some time since I had seen any foreign cottons exposed for sale in these markets.

The soil of the region I had traversed for a fortnight, except in the basin of Paoning, is poor and unfitted for rice, and the people are chiefly hardworking peasant farmers and coolies. Without having any mission from associated or dissociated Chambers of Commerce, my interest in the subject led me to make continual inquiries into the local trade and the requirements of the people, and something as to the latter was to be learned in conversation with the women.

Apart from the general question of weight and make, the general verdict was that the widths of our cottons are wrong, and that widths above fifteen inches cut to waste in making Chinese clothing. Another complaint was that our goods, put up as they are in wrappers intended to impose on "semi-civilised" people, constantly make a display of colours which in China are "unlucky." Another was that the printed cottons, besides offending in this respect, are coarse in pattern, colouring, and style, more fitted for outside barbarians than for the refined tastes of a civilised people! If these, which may appear minor matters, were attended to, there is probably an opening for both our white and printed cottons among the *middle and upper classes of Western China*. But I am not a convert to the roseate views which many people take of the enormous potentialities for our trade in SZE CHUAN if the means of communication are improved by steam on the Yangtze and other methods. It is not that our cottons are too dear, but that the great majority of the people don't want them at any price. That is, that the strong, heavy, native cottons woven by hand, wear four times as long, and even when they are reduced to rags serve several useful purposes. A coolie will not buy a material which will only last a year, when, for the same price or less, he can get one which will last three, or even four years.

Coolies dispense with all clothing but cotton drawers in summer, and these must be strong to resist hard wear; and they say that our cottons are too cold for winter. This is obvious, for a yard of Chinese home-spun cotton cloth, fifteen inches wide, weighs over twice as much as a yard of British calico over thirty inches wide, and resists the wear and tear of hard manual labour and the ofttimes profuse perspiration of the labourer. More than two millions sterling worth of raw cotton and Sha-shih heavy home-spun cottons are supposed to be imported into SZE CHUAN annually, just because the wear requires, and must continue to

THE TA-LU.

require, the heavy make. Later, in Sin-tu Hsien, a prosperous town of 15,000 inhabitants, twelve miles north of Cheng-tu, I saw some Japanese cotton goods, fifteen inches wide, made on looms, which the alert cotton-spinners of Osaka had adapted for the Korean market, and which were of an equally heavy make with the Sha-shih goods, and scarcely to be distinguished from home-spun cloth. The shopkeeper highly approved of these goods, and said that if he could get them there would be a large demand for them. Possibly British "workhouse sheeting" of the same width might meet with similar approbation.

At the hamlet of Lu-fang, where I was stopped by an official with a card from the district mandarin, who kept me waiting an hour while he copied my passport on a stone and provided fresh runners, the by-road by which I had journeyed for some days joined the Ta-lu, the great Imperial road from Pekin to Cheng-tu. I travelled along this westwards to Mien-chow. A thousand years ago it must have been a noble work. It is nominally sixteen feet wide, the actual flagged roadway measuring eight feet. The bridges are built solidly of stone. The ascents and descents are made by stone stairs. More than a millennium ago an emperor planted cedars at measured distances on both sides, the beautiful red-stemmed, weeping cedar of the province. Many of these have attained great size, several which I measured being from fourteen to sixteen feet in circumference five feet from the ground, and they actually darken the road.

The first ascent from Lu-fang under this solemn shade is truly grand, nearly equalling the cryptomeria avenues which lead up to the shrines of Nik-ko, Japan. Each tree bears the Imperial seal, and the district magistrates count them annually. Many have fallen, many have hollow trunks, and there are great breaks without any at all. Still, where they do exist, the effect is magnificent. This road, like much else in China, is badly out of repair, many of its great flagstones having disappeared altogether. There was a great deal of traffic on it, and not a few saddle horses and mules were tripping easily up and down its stone staircases It was quite cheerful to be once more on a travelled highway abounding in large villages and towns, with good inns and much prosperity.

These were days of delightful travelling without any drawbacks. The weather was beautiful, the air sharp, and the people well-behaved. There was no fatigue or annoyance, the accommodation was fair, and there was literally nothing to complain of; the travelling was fit for a Sybarite. The soil is rich, and enormous quantities of opium were grown; indeed, in some long valleys there was no other crop. Wu-lien, where I slept one night, is the cleanest and prettiest little Chinese town that I saw—prettily situated, with a widish main street, good inns, fair shops, and singular cleanliness, and the people were very mannerly. It has a level stone bridge, supported on twelve stone piers decorated with finely-carved dragons' heads.

On the road from Wu-lien to the large town of Tze-tung Hsien there is some very pretty country, rich in agricultural wealth, and growing much opium, which unfortunately in good years pays better than any other crop, and is easy of transit. Wheat, which was only two or three inches above the ground on the high ridges, was bursting into ear in the valleys, and peas and beans were in their fragrant beauty. There was much pink and white mistiness of peach and plum, and yellow fluffiness of mimosa, and the people were astir and alert, performing spring pilgrimages to popular shrines, men and women in separate companies.

There are two very fine and ancient temples of brown cedar to the gods of Literature and War in a cedar wood on the road, with most picturesque hilly surroundings, a lovely spot, and the tides of pilgrimage set strongly towards them. The God of War there as elsewhere is very attractive to women, as may be seen any day in his great temple in the native city of Shanghai. Perpetual incense burns on these altars, and the priests claim the round-numbered antiquity of two thousand years for the temples.

There were very many companies of from ten to thirty well-dressed women on the road, some of whom had hobbled on their crippled-looking feet for fifteen miles, and were going back the same day; and many large bands of men, each led by a man with a gong, carrying a small table with incense sticks burning on it, the procession followed by another coolie loaded with red candles, large and small, with thick paper wicks, incense sticks, and red perforated paper for the God of War. His temple was crowded, and dense clouds of incense rolled from the open front into the atmosphere of heavenly blue. The God of Literature is chiefly worshipped by the *literati*, and there were only a few sedan chairs with their occupants and attendants at his splendid shrine.

The Ta-lu failed to keep up its reputation. Its great flags were tilted up or down, in mud-holes, or had disappeared; its noble avenue was spasmodic and often non-existent for miles, leading to the prophecy that it would disappear altogether, as it did. But the vanished grandeur was made up for by the extraordinary traffic—baggage coolies, chair-bearers, sedan chairs, passengers on foot and on horseback, varied at times by marriage and funeral processions, or batches of criminals tied together by their queues, being led to justice. Of the numbers of weight-carrying coolies, divested of the upper garment, on the road, there were very few free from hard tumours or callosities on both shoulders, and many of them have deep, cracked wounds in their heels. A man carries a load five miles before he earns a bowl of rice.

At intervals there were small huts, each sporting a military flag, and with halberds or lances with silk pennons leaning up against them. Sometimes these were in a village, but occasionally the flag, which is very showy, having a pennon end, and seen afar off, was only supported by a heap of stones on the roadside. There were no soldiers in uniform, but possibly the two or three peasants lying by every flag were men in mufti. Sometimes boys were carrying firearms of an ancient type, bows and arrows, or heavy swords. The people said that the flags were to frighten the rebels, and that the men were watching for them, but the region seemed in a state of profound peace.

The peasants' coffins on the road were those of the poorest class, and were carried at a run, merely wrapped up in blue cotton. A mandarin's coffin on its way to Mien-chow was draped with blue kilted silk, tasselled at the four corners, and was carried by twenty men in red tasselled hats, slung on a heavy beam, with a boldly carved dragon, an emblem of official position, at both ends. The coffin was surmounted (as were those of the peasants) by a tethered live cock. A cheap coffin costs from five to ten dollars, and from that up to two thousand. There is much trade done on the Chia-ling in coffin wood and coffins. I saw many junks loaded with both.

At one place in China, where there was no inn, I slept in a room with a coffin which had been unburied for five years, because the geomancers had not decided on a lucky site or date for the interment, and for the whole time incense had been burned before it morning and evening. Of course if there is a family burial-place the services of the geomancer are seldom required except for the date of burial.

The coffin of the mandarin on the Ta-lu was not on its way to interment, therefore the usual procession was dispensed with, but nearer Tze-tung Hsien we met a large funeral for which we had to leave the road.* On this occasion the corpse of a well-to-do merchant, unburied for a year, was being borne to the grave.

In order to prevent any disagreeable consequences from interment being delayed for months or years, the coffin-boards are three or four inches thick, the body is covered with quicklime or is laid on a bed of lime or cotton, and afterwards the edges of the lid are closed with cement, and if the body is to remain in a dwelling-house, the whole is made air-tight by being covered with Ning-po varnish. A coffin is sometimes retained in a house by a defaulting tenant to prevent an ejectment for rent, and it is occasionally attached by creditors, in order to compel the relations to raise money to release it. So strong is the feeling in China regarding suitable burial, that a son if he has no other means will sell himself into slavery to provide the expenses, and burial clubs and charitable societies for providing the destitute with seemly funerals are numerous.

On this occasion a band of music came first, then the monstrous coffin on a bier carried by at least forty men in red coats and scarves, covered by a canopy embroidered in gold thread, on which was tethered a living fowl. Behind came the ancestral tablet in a sedan chair, the sacrifice, and some red tablets, on which were inscribed in gold the offices held by the deceased, followed by the male mourners dressed in white. The eldest son, apparently sinking with grief, though it was a year old, was

* Funeral ceremonies and superstitions are given in detail in *The Middle Kingdom*, vol. ii., p. 244.

supported by two men. Women and children followed, wailing at intervals. A man preceded the whole, strewing paper money on the ground to buy the good-will of such malignant or predatory spirits as might be loafing around.

One man was loaded with crackers, another carried the libations which were to be poured out, and the rear of the procession, which was ten minutes in passing, was brought up by a great concourse of friends and neighbours, and a great number of bamboo and paper models, admirably executed, and many of them life size, of horses with handsome saddles and trappings, mules carrying burdens, sedan chairs, houses, rich clothing, beds, tables, chairs, and all that the spirit can be supposed to want in the shadowy world to which it has gone. These, with a quantity of tinsel money, are burned at the grave, the tablet and sacrifice are carried back, the former to be placed in the ancestral hall, the latter to be feasted on or given to the poor. The ceremonies of the interment, as my readers are aware, only initiate the long years of ceremonial with which the dead are honoured in China.

CHAPTER XXVII.

TZE-TUNG HSIEN TO KUAN HSIEN

AN hour after leaving the great temples of Ta-miao, with their throngs of pilgrims and the remarkable friendliness of the people, we came upon the walls, gates, and towers of Tze-tung Hsien, the approach to which is denoted by a graceful eleven-storeyed pagoda on a neighbouring hill. I had not been through a large walled city since the riot at Liang-shan, and I had to brace myself up for entering this one, which has a reputed population of 27,000 people. The inhabitants were very orderly however, and though the streets were greatly crowded, the people looked pleasant. The Liang-shan riot is known to all the mandarins, and obviously they have no wish for a repetition of it, and I adhere to my belief that they are in most, if not in all cases, able to prevent attacks on foreigners.

Tze-tung Hsien is a clean and prosperous looking city, with wide streets lined by good shops, in which the goods are more displayed than is usual. It is surrounded with well-cultivated country, and good country houses, and trades in vegetable oils, cottons, and raw and spun silk, some of the strong, coarse "oak silk" being brought in for manufacture. Oil is made from the seeds of the *aleurites cordata*, rape seed, pea nuts, and opium seed. Opium oil bears the highest price. The town has a stirring aspect, and its walls and gateways are in good repair. Outside, the Fou River is crossed by a noble stone bridge of nine arches with fine stone balustrades, carrying a flagged roadway eighteen feet broad. The centre arch is thirty feet high. It is the finest bridge that I had then seen in China. A grand temple outside the walls, and an elaborately carved triple-storeyed *pai-fang*, complete the attractions of this thriving city.

On the western route from Tze-tung Hsien the country becomes increasingly fertile, and the road more dilapidated. The cedars

WOMAN REELING SILK.

have disappeared, and the pavement is only four feet in width. The traffic in oil, cotton, and tobacco was great, and crowds of pilgrims, very respectable looking, with gongs, incense tables, and offerings, were trudging to the Ta-miao temples. They said that they were making offerings to the God of War for having driven the "barbarian rebels" into the sea! There were funerals, too, and a train of twelve led horses, each carrying a red flag, with on it a mandarin's name and official titles. These were heavily laden with luggage, and in front there was the mandarin's coffin, with a live cock upon it, carried by forty men.

The prevalent impression left by this great road is that of toil and poverty. Rice had risen considerably in the previous three weeks, which meant to many millions that they would never get a full meal. The region I had entered is one of the most crowded parts of the Red Basin and of China, and I often asked myself, "Why are there so many Chinese?" They seem to come into the world just to bury their fathers. That night again I slept in a room with a huge coffin, which had been waiting interment for some years, and incense was regularly burned before it.

On March 28th I reached Mien-chow, a city of about 60,000 souls, the largest that I had yet seen in SZE CHUAN. The journey from Paoning Fu had been most propitious in all respects, and the fine weather had come at last. I entered the city by a bridge of boats over the Fou, a great tributary of the Chia-ling. Mien-chow has a curious geographical situation. The Fou basin, in which it stands, though north of Chengtu and nearer the water parting, is on a lower level than the basin of the Min, from which it is divided by a low ridge. So Mien-chow is actually 250 feet below Chengtu, its altitude being 1350 feet.

It is a well-built and clean town, with a fine wall, and a river front well protected by a handsome bund of cobbles and concrete, with eight slanting faces. The Fou is navigable, and when the water is high, boats can descend to Chungking in six or seven days. There is an enormous wheelbarrow traffic from Mien-chow to the capital, principally of sugar and tobacco. The busy and crowded streets are lined with shops, in which every conceivable article in iron is displayed, from surgical instruments, to spades, plough-shares, and articles in wrought iron. There are fully half a mile of such shops. The great trade of Mien-chow, however, is in silk, and much cotton is woven in its neighbourhood. The shops display German and Japanese knick-knacks, foreign yarns, and printed cottons, besides Kansuh furs, brocades, silks, temple furniture, and drugs. The shops, with their varied, and in many cases costly, contents show that the neighbourhood has great purchasing power.

The passage through the thronged streets took nearly an hour, but all was quiet. I was not allowed to go to an inn, but was most kindly received at the Church Mission House, a dark and not agreeably situated house in a crowded Chinese quarter, inhabited by the two ladies who, after four years of patience and difficulties, have effected a permanent lodgment in what is well known as a hostile city. They spent the first two years at an inn, and so little were they thought of, that the mandarin, when urged to take some action against them, replied, "What does it matter? they are only women!"

During this time all their attempts to rent a house failed, because the officials threatened to beat and imprison anyone letting a house to a foreigner; but a fortnight before my visit a man ruined by opium smoking let them have for ten years the place into which they had just moved, close to the great temple of Confucius. Access to it is through an area inhabited by Chinese—a forlorn, dirty yard—and through an inner yard full of Chinese, who seemed to be always gambling or smoking opium, a third yard being the newly-acquired property, from which some of the Chinese had not yet cleared out. The two last courts are rented by the Church Missionary Society, and have subsequently been improved and made habitable, and "The Emily Clayton Memorial," a dispensary with a surgical ward under Dr. Squibb, a qualified English doctor, has been opened in the outer of the two compounds.

It was interesting to see what missionaries in China have to undergo in the initial stage of residence in a Chinese city. The house was utterly out of repair—dirty, broken—half the paper torn off the windows, and the eaves so deep and low that daylight could scarcely enter. There was an open guest-hall in the middle used constantly for classes and services; endless parties of Chinese passed in and out all day long, poking holes in the remaining windows, opening every door that was not locked,

THE REV. J. HEYWOOD HORSBURGH, M.A.,
IN TRAVELLING DRESS.

taking everything they could lay hands on ; and the noise was only stilled from four to six a.m.—men shouting, babies screaming, dogs barking, squibs and crackers going off, temple bells, gongs, and drums beating—no rest, quiet, or privacy.

There were two services in the guest-hall on Sunday, conducted by Mr. Heywood Horsburgh, the superintendent of the Mission, and several classes for women also, but all in a distracting babel—men playing cards outside the throng, men and women sitting for a few minutes, some laughing scornfully, others talking in loud tones, some lighting their pipes, and a very few really interested. This is not the work which many who go out as missionaries on a wave of enthusiasm expect, but this is what these good people undergo day after day and month after month.

The place where the two ladies spent two years, consisted of a guest-room at an inn in one of the most crowded of the city streets, a living-room through it, a kitchen through that, and for a sleeping-room, a loft above the living-room, reached by a ladder, just under the unlined tiles. There was no light in any room, except from a paper window, into the semi-dark passage. The floors were mud ; wood, water, charcoal, and all things had to be carried in and out through the living-room ; no privacy was possible; the temperature hung at about 100° for weeks in summer; there were the ceaseless visits of crowds of ill-bred Chinese women, staying for hours at a time ; and without and in the inn, seldom pausing, there was the unimaginable din of a big Chinese city. Under these circumstances their love and patience had won twelve women to be Christians.

Mr. and Mrs. Cormack, of the China Inland Mission, and a thirteen months' baby, arrived before I left, he very ill of malarial fever. They were swept out of Chengtu in the riots, losing all their possessions, and with this infant had been moving for seven months, having lastly been driven out of Kansuh by the Mohammedan rebellion. During the whole seven months they had never been in one place more than twelve days. It is a grave question whether married men and married women ought to be placed in regions of precarious security. Mr. Heywood Horsburgh's house at Kuan Hsien had just been attacked and bored into by a number of burglars, and between the terror caused by this, and the hostile cries in the streets, which they understood too well, his delicate, sensitive young daughters, one of them twelve years old, had become so thoroughly nervous that the only possible cure was to take them home. I saw several ladies in Western China who, after escaping from mobs with their young children, were affected in the same way.

Mr. and Mrs. Horsburgh and I left Mien-chow on March 31st, a grey, dull day, but clear. We left the Ta-lu and travelled by infamous roads, often only a few inches wide, frequently on the top of rice dykes. Great mountains, snow-crested, spurs of the Tibetan ranges, loomed through the clouds to the north-west, while we journeyed through the eastern portion of the great Chengtu plain, the rich, well-watered soil green with barley and opium, and beautiful with miles of rape, largely grown for oil, rolling in canary yellow waves before a pleasant breeze. Large farmhouses had reappeared, farming hamlets, and big temples, all surrounded by fine trees. There are frequent water-mills of a very peculiar construction, said by experts to be the oldest form in the world, the wheel being placed horizontally just above the lower level of the water.

Before we left the Ta-lu, the great highway to the capital, the wheelbarrow traffic was enormous. These "machines," with a big wooden wheel placed so near the centre of gravity as to throw the weight of the load as little as possible on the driver's shoulders, carry goods on platforms on either side and behind the wheel, which is solid. One man can propel five hundredweight. Heavy loads have one man to propel and another to drag them. They move in long files, their not altogether unmelodious creak being heard afar off, and the stone road is deeply grooved by their incessant passage.

After two pleasant days' journey we reached Mien-chuh Hsien, a town of 50,000 people, according to the statement of the magistrate's secretary. It is not a handsome town, but it has a beautiful modern bridge over a branch of the Fou, of six stone arches, a fine roof, iron balustrades, and a central roofed tower. It is a busy and prosperous city, with many fine temples and grand mountain views. The production of paper, especially coloured paper, is its speciality, but it also manufactures largely wood and horn combs, indigo, and fine wheaten flour. Much salt is made in the neighbourhood, and in the hills thirty *li* off there are coal

WATER MILL, CHENGTU PLAIN

BRIDGE AT MIEN-CHUH.

mines, producing coal which burns with a clear white flame, and little ash. There, as elsewhere, the missionaries have introduced English articles of utility, which have "caught on" among the Chinese.

A cordial welcome awaited us at the Church Missionary Society's house. The initial stage, as I saw it at Mien-chow, was passed, and we were received into as trim a little home as one could see anywhere, or wish to see. Turning from the street, where the people did not molest even by curiosity, down a narrow alley and through a door, down a passage on one side of which is the guest-hall, we entered a small and very bright compound, cheery with pots of primulas and chrysanthemums, with five small cottage rooms round it, with paper windows, but light, cheerful, and homelike, with simple daintinesses, and a bright coal fire in a quaint corner fire-place. The place is just a few Chinese cottages, formerly used as a gambling den. Mr. and Mrs. Phillips, who have transmogrified it chiefly by their own handiwork, had only lately been able to rent it owing to the opposition of the mandarins, who can bring many threats and much pressure to bear on persons who would otherwise be willing to lease property to foreigners.

The anti-Christian element everywhere seems a feeble one in the opposition. It is to foreigners, simply as such, that the objection is made, as "child-eaters" pre-eminently; and in Mien-chuh the people said that the missionaries wanted the houses for hellish purposes, and that they would dig under them and make a way to England, and that foreign soldiers would come by it and take their lands, and that they wanted lock-up rooms in which to hide the golden cocks which they dug out of the mountains by night!

I left Mien-chuh with Mrs. Horsburgh on a somewhat unlucky journey, still travelling over the Chengtu plain in a westerly direction. The time of year for theatricals, which are a great passion with the Chinese, had begun. There is a large temple outside Mien-chuh, with the usual adjunct of a stage, richly decorated, with a massive canopy roof, for the "religious drama." But on this day, being the festival of the god to whom the temple is dedicated, this was supplemented by temporary theatres and booths covering fully half an acre of the temple grounds, and the great court was crammed with a closely-wedged mass of Chinese, and the adjacent grounds and the road were such a crush of people that our chairs could hardly get through. There must have been from twelve to fifteen thousand present.

These plays are got up by the priests, who send the neophytes round with a subscription paper, afterwards pasting the names of the donors, inscribed on red sheets, on the walls of the temple. The priests let the purlieus for the occasion for the sale of refreshments, and also for gambling tables and other evil purposes, and usually make a profit out of what is professedly a religious celebration. When the subscription list has been filled up, the priests engage the best talent that their funds will allow of.

Theatrical companies in China retain their original strolling character, and there are few permanent theatres, the erection of the great sheds, in which several thousand can be accommodated, being a separate branch of the carpenter's trade. A play usually lasts for three days, and the periods for sleeping and eating are wonderfully minimised. Business is suspended in the neighbourhood, and the people act as if the drama were the only thing worth living for. It is not etiquette for women of the upper classes to frequent the theatre, and private theatrical performances are given in rich men's houses, but women of the lower classes, generally carrying babies, attend in large numbers and usually sit in the galleries. Lads perform the female parts, with grotesque success, transforming their feet into excellent representations of "golden lilies," and hobbling and tottering to perfection.

I have only been present at two Chinese plays. They interest me greatly, and it is on the stage alone that the gorgeous costumes of brocaded and embroidered silk of former dynasties are to be seen. The scenery is simple and imperfect. The orchestra fills up all pauses vigorously, and strikes a crashing noise at intervals during the play to add energy or fury to the performance. Ghosts or demons appear from a trap-door in the stage. The scenes are not divided by a curtain, and the play proceeds on its lengthened course with only intervals for sleep and eating. The imperfect scenery makes it necessary for the actor to state what part he is performing, and what the person he represents has been doing while off the stage. There are comic actors who have only to appear on the boards to convulse an audience with laughter, and tragic actors who are equally successful in making men (or women) weep. There is no applause in a Chinese theatre. Admiration is expressed by a loud and prolonged sigh, as if indicating that the tension had been too great, or by an utterance between a sigh and a groan. A crowd absorbed with theatricals is usually peaceable, and the police are always at hand, but in country places a play is apt to assemble the roughs of the neighbourhood, as I learned the next day to my cost.

Chinese theatricals are very clever, for without anything which can be called scenery, and without a curtain, and with my own complete ignorance of the language, the actors by their admirable acting presented to my mind very distinct stories, in the one case of political intrigue, and in the other of military patriotism and self-sacrifice. The morals of the Chinese stage, so far as the sentiments of the plays are concerned, are said by severe critics to be good; the acting was quite unobjectionable when I was present, but I have understood that it is not invariably so. The earnestness of attention, and the delight on a sea of yellow faces at one of these theatrical representations are most interesting.

As we journeyed westwards, the plain became more and more luxuriant, and the aspect of wealth and comfort more pronounced. The great farmhouses are enclosed by high walls, and are shaded by cedars or cypresses, bamboo groves and fruit trees, the latter in early April in all the beauty of blossom. Groves of superb timber failed to conceal the gold and colour of grand temples. There were water-mills, canalised streams with many branches, —from which everywhere peasants, with fans and umbrellas, were pumping water by the contrivance shown in the illustration on next page—and rivers with broad winter beds, two of them spanned by very fine roofed bridges, rafters and supports lacquered red, and decorated with tablets in black and red lacquer, bearing the names incised in gold of the public-spirited men who had restored them.

In the afternoon an incident occurred which goes to show that the Chinese need a gospel of civilisation as well as of salvation. The road had left the rich and populous part of the plain, and had reached a broad and completely dry river-bed, full of round water-worn stones, crossed by a long covered bridge leading into the small town of Lo-kia-chan, at which, at the top of the sloping shingle bed of the river, a theatrical performance was proceeding before a crowd of some six thousand people. Mrs. Horsburgh proposed that we should not cross the bridge into the town, but should continue along the river bank opposite to it and cross the bed lower down. My idea usually is, and was then, to take "the bull by the horns," but I deferred to her long experience, and she went on at some distance in front in a closed chair and in scrupulously accurate Chinese dress, I following in my open chair and in my *olla podrida* costume — Chinese dress, European shoes, and a Japanese hat.

TREADMILL FIELD-PUMP.

The crowd caught sight of my open chair, which, being a novelty, was an abomination, and fully two thousand men rushed down one shingle bank and up the other, brandishing sticks and porters' poles, yelling, hooting, crying "Foreign devil," and "Child-eater," telling the bearers to put the chair down. In the distance I saw my runners proving their right to their name. When I afterwards remonstrated with them, they replied, "What could two men do against two thousand?" but a resource of power lay in the magistrate's letter. Then there were stones thrown, ammunition being handy. Some hit the chair and bearers, and one knocked off my hat. The yells of "Foreign devil," and "Foreign dog," were tremendous. Volleys of stones hailed on the chair, and a big one hit me a severe blow at the back of my ear, knocking me forwards and stunning me.

Be-dien said that I was insensible for "some time," during which a "reason talker" harangued the crowd, saying it had done enough, and if it killed me, though I was only a woman, foreign soldiers would come and burn their houses and destroy their crops, and worse. This sapient reasoning had its effect. When I recovered my senses, the chair was set down in the midst of the crowd, which was still hooting and shouting, but no further violence was offered, and as the bearers carried me on, the crowd gradually thinned. I had a violent pain in my head, and the symptoms of concussion of the brain, and felt a mortifying inclination to cry. The cowards, as usual, attacked from behind.

After three very painful hours, in which I should have been glad to lie down by the roadside, we reached the great, walled, district city of Peng Hsien, with wide, clean streets, fine shops, temples, and guildhalls, a flagged roadway curved in the centre, and stone sidewalks, and what is regarded as a great curiosity, a lofty pagoda riven in twain, each half standing up perfect. The city, the population of which is officially stated at 28,000, manufactures brass and iron goods, iron being mined in the neighbourhood, and coal not far off.

Here, again, there was a display of rowdyism. "The city ran together," and for half a mile I was the subject of insult, though not of actual violence. The street was nearly impassable from the crowds beating on my chair with sticks, hooting, yelling "Foreign devil," "Foreign dog," "Child-eater," and worse, yelling into my ear, kicking the chair, and spitting. We were carried into a very fine inn, which ran very far back, its courtyards ending in a guest-hall, with oranges and lilies in pots in the middle, and a mandarin's room of much pretension beyond.

A masculine crowd filling the courts surged in after us, keeping up a frightful clamour. The innkeeper put me into the mandarin's room, and begged me not to show myself; and Be-dien went to the *yamen* to make a complaint regarding the outrage at Lo-kia-chan. As soon as he left, the crowd began to hoot and yell and thump the door. I got up and barricaded it with the heaviest furniture I could drag. Then they got a spade, or wedge, and began to force it open. I deplored my helpless condition—faint, giddy, and with a cracking headache, and an unmannerly crowd of men ready to burst in. The bolt and barricade were on the verge of yielding, when the mandarin's secretary and another official arrived, and at once produced order.

They interviewed Mrs. Horsburgh, who was really able to tell very little, and then I was unearthed, and gave my evidence with a bandaged head and a sense of unutterable confusion in my brain. The mandarin sent an apology for the rudeness in Peng Hsien, but partly excused the people, as they, he said, had never seen an open chair or a foreign hat before. The secretary said that they had sent to arrest the ringleaders of the disturbance at Lo-kia-chan, which I did not believe, but was glad of his courtesy. It was difficult for him to understand that I could be so severely hurt when there was no effusion of blood. Soldiers were posted in the courtyard for the night, and in the morning, besides runners, there were four soldiers at my door, who marched, two before and two behind my chair for the day's journey to Kuan Hsien. I had a very bad night, and felt very ill the next day, with everything wavering before my eyes. I suffered much for a long time from this blow and the brain disturbance which followed, but I will dismiss the unpleasant subject from these pages by saying that I did not get over the effects for a year, and that it was my last experience of violence in China.

Perfect quiet prevailed in the crowded street of Peng Hsien. The Chengtu plain grew richer and richer, the plumed bamboo and the cedars and *cupressus funebris* round the great farmhouses grander, and towards afternoon snow-peaks, atmospherically up-lifted to a colossal height, appeared above the clouds in the north, with craggy and wooded spurs below them, descending abruptly to the magnificent plain. Everywhere living waters in their musical rush echoed the name of the great man who before the Christian era turned the vast plain into a paradise. There was a covered bridge over a wide rushing river; a dirty, narrow suburban street, a narrow alley, and then a cheerful compound, in which a brown-spotted *dendrobium* was blooming profusely, shared by three Scotch missionaries of the China Inland Mission, and six of the Church Missionary Society, women predominating.

WOODEN BRIDGE, KUAN HSIEN.

At the back of the house the clear, sparkling Min, just released from its long imprisonment in the mountains, sweeps past with a windy rush, and the mountain views are magnificent, specially where the early sun tinges the snow-peaks with pink. Why should I not go on, I asked myself, and see Tibetans, yaks, and aboriginal tribes, rope bridges, and colossal mountains, and break away from the narrow highways and the crowds, and curiosity, and oppressive grooviness of China proper?

CHAPTER XXVIII.

KUAN HSIEN AND CHENGTU

KUAN HSIEN (2347 feet, Gill) is one of the best-placed cities in China, at the north-west corner of the Chengtu plain, immediately below the mountains which wall it in on the north, and, indeed, scrambling over their spurs just at the fine gorge of the Couching Dragon, from whence the liberated Min bursts in strength to gladden the whole plain. The Mien-chuh road has not a fine entrance into the city—the Chengtu road, which I travelled three times, approaches Kuan under six fine *pai-fangs*, elaborately, and, indeed, beautifully decorated with carvings in high relief in a soft grey sandstone.

Apart from its situation, it is an unattractive town, with narrow, dirty streets, small lifeless-looking shops, and a tendency to produce on all occasions a dirty crowd, which hangs on to a foreigner, and which on my arrival greeted me with—"Here's another child-eater." It has an outpost air, as if there were little beyond, and this is partly true. It has a possible population of 22,000. It is not a rich city, and its suburbs do not abound in rich men's houses. But it is distinguished, first for being the starting point of the oldest and, perhaps, the most important engineering works in China; and secondly, as being a great emporium of the trade with Northern Tibet, which is at its height during the winter, when as many as five hundred Tibetans, with their yaks, are encamped outside its walls. The Tibetans exchange wool, furs, hides, musk, hartshorn, rhubarb, and many other drugs for tea, brass ware, and small quantities of silk and cotton. Tibetan drugs are famous all over China. The Tibetans, as I learned from personal observation in Western Tibet, are enormous tea drinkers. The tea churn is always in requisition, and Tibet takes annually from China 22,000,000 pounds. The wool, which helps largely to pay for the tea, and which is so abominably dirty that fifteen per cent. of it has to be washed away, comes from pasturages from 9000 to 12,000 feet in altitude.

Musk is a most lucrative import. The small deer (*cervus moschus*), of which it is a secretion, is said to roam in large herds over the plains surrounding the Koko Nor. A single deer only produces a third of an ounce, and it sells for eighteen times its weight in silver at Chung-king, and is largely smuggled. Chengtu reeks with its intensely pungent odour. Rhubarb, the best quality of which grows not lower than 9000 feet, is also a very valuable import, and other drugs are estimated at £95,000 annually, and are quintupled in value before they reach the central and eastern provinces. Aconite, a root largely used for poisoning in Western Tibet, is imported into China as a medicine, singular to say, criminal poisoning being very little known. Deer horns in the velvet, for medicinal uses, are also largely imported.

Much of the trade is done at Matang, in the mountains, a savage hamlet which I afterwards visited, in the month of August; and very much more comes down from Sung-pan ting, about 570 *li* to the north of Kuan, where it is chiefly in the hands of Mohammedan merchants, who act as go-betweens. Wool brought from Sung-pan to Chung-king has to pass six *likin* barriers; so I understood from Mr. Grainger, of the China Inland Mission at Kuan Hsien, to whom I am much indebted for carefully gathered information on this and other local points of interest.

The glory of Kuan is the temple in honour of Li Ping, a prefect in the aboriginal kingdom of Shu, the ancient SZE CHUAN, the great engineer, and his son, whose work has redeemed the noble plain of Chengtu from drought and flood for two thousand years. Just above Kuan Hsien there is a romantic gorge with lofty grey cliffs, down which one branch of the Min, a cold, crystal stream, rushes wildly; but still, rafts and boats, carrying lime and coal from above, make the passage, often to their own destruction. On the right bank, high on the cliff, is a picturesque temple in a romantic situation, with a beautiful roof of glazed, green tiles, erected in honour of Li Ping or his son, whose name has been so completely lost out of history that he is known only as "The Second Gentleman."

Above this perilous gorge the Min is about two hundred yards wide, with more or less mountainous banks heavily wooded, and at the point where the Tibetan road crosses it, on a very fine bamboo suspension bridge about 200 paces long, the grandest temple in China stands, on a wooded height finely terraced, and adorned with stately lines of cryptomeria and other exotic trees, one teak-tree in a courtyard being eighteen feet in circumference. These noble shrines, with their fine courtyards and the exquisitely beautiful pavilions and minarets which climb the cliff behind the temple, and are lost among the cryptomerias of the summit, are the most beautiful group of buildings that I saw in the far East, combining the grace and decorative witchery of the shrines of the Japanese Shoguns at Nikko, with a grandeur and stateliness of their own.

This noble temple is scrupulously clean and in perfect repair. Magnificent objects of art, as well as tanks surrounded with exotic ferns, decorate its courtyards; living waters descend from the hill through the mouths of serpents carved in stone; noble flights of stone stairs lead to the grand entrance and from terrace to terrace; thirty Taoist priests keep lamps and incense ever burning before the shrines; an Imperial envoy from Peking visits the temple every year with gifts; and tens of thousands of pilgrims, from every part of the plain and beyond, bring their offerings and homage to these altars.

The temple left on my memory an impression of beauty and majesty, which nature and art have combined to produce. Outside, glorious trees in whose dense leafage the lesser architectural beauties lose themselves, gurgling waters, flowering shrubs with heavy odours floating on the damp, still air, elaborately carved pinnacles and figures on the roofs, even the screens in front of the doors decorated with elaborate tracery; while the beauty of the interior is past description: columns of highly polished black lacquer, a roof, a perfect marvel of carving and lacquer, all available space occupied with honorary tablets, the gift of past viceroys, while the shrines are literally ablaze with gorgeously coloured lacquer and painting, and the banners presented by the emperors wave in front. The galleries facing the effigies of the great engineer and his son are carved most delicately with lacquered fretwork; and on pillars, galleries, and everywhere, where space admits of

ROOF OF ERH-WANG TEMPLE.

its decorative use, is Li Ping's motto incised or inscribed in gold, " *Shen tao t'an ti tso yen* "—" Dig the bed deep, keep the banks low."

Although there is a shrine to Li Ping in this splendid " Erh-Wang " temple, it was possibly erected in honour of " The Second Gentleman," the temple to the father being (believed by Mr. Grainger) the more recent erection above the gorge of the Couching Dragon. Every Chinese Emperor, from the Tsin dynasty, 246 B.C., downwards, has conferred the posthumous title of *Wang*, or Prince, upon Li Ping and his son. A stone tablet in one of the temples records the story, which I learn from Mr. Grainger, who has translated the inscription.

The Chengtu plain, which these deservedly honoured engineers may be said to have created, is the richest plain in China, and possibly in the world. It may be about 100 miles by seventy or eighty, with an area of about 2500 square miles. It produces three and even four crops a year. Its chief products are rice, silk, opium, tobacco, sugar, sweet potatoes, indigo, the paper mulberry, rape and other oils, maize, and cotton, along with roots and fruits of all kinds, both musk and water-melons being produced in fabulous quantities. From any height the plain looks like a forest of fruit trees, while clumps of cypress, cedar, and bamboo denote the whereabouts of the great temples and fine farmhouses with which it is studded.

It has an estimated population of 4,000,000, and is sprinkled with cities, and flourishing marts, and large villages, Chengtu, the capital, having at least 400,000 people. Along the main roads the population may be said to constitute a prolonged village. The abundance of water power produces any number of flour and oil mills, the plain is intersected in all directions with roads which are thronged with traffic, and boats can reach the Yangtze from Kuan Hsien, Chengtu, and Chiang Kou.

Oranges reappear in splendid groves, mixed up with the vivid foliage of the persimmon ; mulberry trees are allowed to grow to their full height and amplitude ; spinning and weaving are going on everywhere ; the soil, absolutely destitute of weeds, looks as if it were cultivated with trowels and rakes, "tilled," as Emerson felicitously said of England, "with a pencil instead of a plough." There are frequent small temples, or rather shrines, to the God of the Soil, of solid masonry, the image being enclosed by open fretwork, in front of which the incense sticks smoulder ceaselessly, the long-drawn creak of the wheelbarrow is never silent during the daylight hours, agricultural energy and activity

OIL BASKETS AND WOODEN PURSE.

prevail, and the plain is a singular and, perhaps, unrivalled picture of rustic peace and security.

This population of four millions depends not only for its prosperity, but for its existence, on the irrigation works of Li Ping and "The Second Gentleman," carried out long before the Christian era. Without these, as has been truly said, "the east and west of the plain would be a marsh, and the north a waterless desert," and this great area with its boundless fertility and wealth,

BARROW TRAFFIC, CHENGTU PLAIN

and its immunity from drought and flood for two thousand years, is the monument to the engineering genius of these two men, whose motto, "*Dig the bed deep, keep the banks low*," had it been applied universally to rivers of insubordinate habits, would have saved the world from much desolation and loss.

With a faithfulness rare in China, Li Ping's motto has been carried out for twenty-one centuries. The stone-bunded dykes are kept low and in repair, and in March the bed of the artificial Min, created by Li Ping, by cutting a gorge a hundred feet deep through the hard rock of the cliff above Kuan Hsien, and which has been closed by a barrier since the previous November, with its subsidiary channels, is carefully dug out, till the workmen reach two iron cylinders, sunk in the bed of the stream, which mark its proper level. The silt of the year, which is from five to six feet thick, is then removed. The whole plain contributes to this expensive work, and a high official, the *Shui Li Fu*, or " Prefect of the Waterways," is responsible for it.

In late March, or early April, there is a grand ceremony, sometimes attended by the Viceroy, when the winter dam is cut, and the strong torrent of the Min, seized upon by human skill, is divided and subdivided, twisted, curbed by dams and stone revetments, and is sent into innumerable canals and streams, till, aided by a fall of twelve feet to the mile, there is not a field which has not a continual supply, or an acre of the Chengtu plain in which the musical gurgle of the bright waters of the Tibetan uplands is not heard—waters so abundant that though drought may exist all round, this vast oasis remains a paradise of fertility and beauty.

At Kuan Hsien, where I spent some little time recovering from the assault at Lo-kia-chan, and in projecting a further journey, the feeling of the people towards foreigners was definitely hostile. It had been originally opened to Christian teaching by a lady, who, after living alone there for a considerable time (but that was before " the riots," the modern landmark in SZE CHUAN history), left for England during my visit, much regretted ; but since the riots " the Jesus religion " had made very slow progress. Slanders against the missionaries were circulated and believed, and the special one that they stole and ate infants, or used their eyes and hearts for medicines, was disagreeably current in Kuan Hsien.

The foreign ladies, four of whom had been hidden for eleven weeks of the hottest part of the previous summer, during the disturbances, in a room without a window, were very nervous, as was natural, starting when shouting was heard, not knowing what it might mean, and even those men who were hampered by wives and young families, at times looked anxious. No one who has heard the howling of a Chinese mob can forget it—it seems to come up direct from the bottomless pit! One of these young wives, during the disturbances, escaped through a window with her three infants to a ledge above the river while her husband kept the mob at bay.

So when I left for Sin-tu Hsien and Chengtu I escorted a lady, whose nerves had received such a shock in the riots that she was afraid to travel alone. My escort was of little value, for the people of the villages were lavish of their infamous epithets, pulled away the blinds of her chair, pulled out her hairpins and terrified her, while I was ignored.

It was a very long day, and when we reached Sing-fang Hsien, a busy town, long after dark, we had a pilgrimage from inn to inn, finding them all full, and the people hooted us all along the street till we found refuge in a hostel by no means "first-class." The heat had set in fiercely, and the mercury was 83° in the shade. The following day, after a short journey in intense heat over the glorious and busy plain, we reached the house of Mr. Callum of the Church Missionary Society, at Sin-tu Hsien, a thriving town of about 15,000 people, with a pleasant promenade on its walls, and a very fine temple just outside them. The industry of this town, as of Kuan Hsien, is chiefly the making of straw sandals.

The third day's journey with Mr. and Mrs. Callum was still over the glorious plain, which became yet richer and more densely populated as we neared Chengtu, the restaurants, always crowded with coolies and travellers, almost lining the road, and the wheelbarrows making a nearly ceaseless procession.

If one could disabuse oneself of the belief that opium is the curse of China and is likely to sap the persistent vitality of the race, there could have been nothing but unstinted admiration for the wonderful beauty of the crop in blossom, as I saw it in its glory on that sunny April day on the Chengtu plain, which in some places seemed to have no *raison d'être* but its growth. The

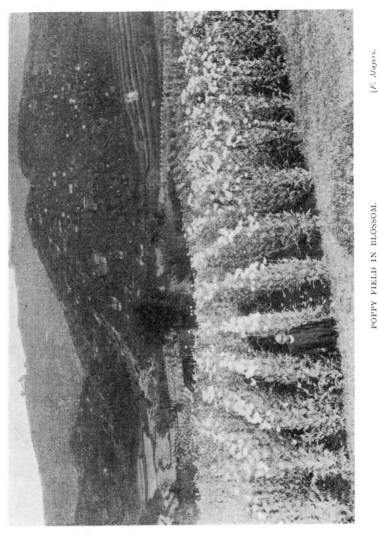

POPPY FIELD IN BLOSSOM.

[*F. Mayers.*]

season had been without a drawback, and every leaf and flower had attained to its full maturity of loveliness.   The blossoms were white—white fringed with rose-pink, white with white fringes, ruby-red, carmine, dark purple, pale mauve, and rose-pink. Waves of colour on slope and plain rolled before the breeze. Houses were almost submerged by the coloured billows.   Far and near, along roads and streams, round stately temples and prosperous farmhouses, rippled and surged these millions of corollas, in all the glory of their brief and passionate existence—

THE WHITE OPIUM POPPY.

the April pulse of Nature throbbing through them most vigorously, —the poppy truly in the ascendant.

There is a remarkably fine stone bridge on that route to Chengtu, with dragons surmounting each pier, and very emphatic abutments.   I had heard very much of Chengtu as being among the finest cities, "a second Peking," etc.   On entering it by the west gate, and the gates are very imposing, green glades lead into the Tartar quarter, a region of large, walled gardens, well wooded, and good-sized houses, frequently much decayed.   In a street of shops several of the signs are written in Manchu.   In this quarter it was refreshing to see the tall, healthy-looking women with "big feet," long outer garments, and roses in their hair, as in Manchuria, standing at their doorways talking to their friends, both male and female, with something of the ease and freedom of Englishwomen.

It was some distance along wide cleanly streets and through charming "residential suburbs," as I must call them, though they are within the walls, to the "palatial residence" in which the members of the China Inland Mission have been quartered by the Viceroy at a low rent since the absolutely complete destruction of the mission premises in the riots, a destruction which was also complete in the case of the houses and hospitals of the various other missions, even the bricks of which the buildings were constructed being carried away. This house, in which I was most hospitably received, had been assigned by the Government to the American Commission which came from Peking to assess the losses incurred by their "nationals," and there was glass in the windows and matting on the floors, and dainty muslin blinds and curtains everywhere.

There is a large Romish mission, and American and Canadian missions besides the China Inland Mission, the Protestant missionaries living and working in much harmony, though in some respects, chiefly externals, on differing lines. Things had never settled down comfortably since the riots, and the official class at least was much embittered by the enormous damages claimed and obtained by the Roman mission. Stories of child-eating were current, and I am sure that the people believe that it is practised by the missionaries, for in going through Chengtu on later occasions I observed that when we foreigners entered one of the poorer streets many of the people picked up their infants and hurried with them into the houses; also there were children with red crosses on green patches stitched on the back of their clothing, this precaution being taken in the belief that foreigners respect the cross too much to do any harm to children wearing the emblem.

I see little or no resemblance to Peking in Chengtu. Without emphasising the other essential points of difference, Chengtu is neat and clean, and a comparison of its odours with those of Peking is impossible, for those of musk overpower all else! Indeed, along with the tea, silk, opium, and cotton, which it

THE AUTHOR IN MANCHU DRESS

imports from the rest of the province, its great trade is in the numerous wild products of Tibet—rhubarb, drugs, furs, and above all, musk.

It is a very prepossessing city; and its noble wall in admirable repair, the successor of one ·built in the third century B.C., is about fourteen miles in circuit, sixty-six feet broad at the base, forty at the top, and thirty-five feet high, while what may be regarded as a somewhat formidable "earthwork"—an inner embankment almost the width of the wall—supports it along almost its whole circuit. This structure, the top of which is a superb promenade, is faced with hard and very fine brick, and has eight bastions, which are pierced by four fine gates, rigorously guarded, for the purpose of exacting the native customs and *likin*, which are very hard on foreign imports.

A stream, banked by stone revetments, runs through Chengtu from east to west, frequently bridged, and in one place spanned by three stone bridges, each of a single arch, close together. There are many moats and broad pieces of water, and the main river, about a hundred yards wide, is crossed by many bridges, one of them roofed, and lined on both sides by the stalls of hucksters; but the great stone bridge, half a mile long, with "a richly painted roof supported on marble pillars," described by Marco Polo, has ceased to exist! Canals and streams abound, and are crowded with shipping of small size, chiefly plying to Chung-king and the ports west of it, cargo and passage junks, and *wupans* with hooped bamboo roofs, in one of which I afterwards made the downward passage, and *sampans*. The waters were very low, and the craft much jammed together.

The city has wide, well-paved streets, crossing each other at right angles, and the handsome shops make far more display than is usual in China, the jewellers' shops specially, with their fine work in filigree silver, and even rich silk brocades are seen gleaming in the shadow in the handsome silk shops, as well as *pongees*, both of local manufacture, and costly furs, and the snowy Tibetan lambskin can be seen from the streets exposed for sale. Within, respectable, richly-dressed shopkeepers await customers, and serve them with due dignity, but make no attempt to ensnare them. Farther back, in the obscurity, is the representation on a large scale, frequently taking up the whole end of the shop, of *Dzai-zen-pusa*, the God of Wealth, the Japanese *Daikoku*, and the British Mammon, with an altar and incense before him. To him, as the "luck of the shop," the merchant, his apprentices, and all his employees must offer worship morning and evening, and no cult is so universal.

Chengtu has many scent shops, and most articles of Chinese manufacture are exposed at the shop fronts, but there was a very small display of foreign goods.

The strange, wild figures of the trading Tibetans in the streets, the splendour of the trains of officials and *literati*, who ride horses almost concealed by expensive trappings, or are carried at a rapid run in carved and gilded sedans, with poles bent up high in the middle, so as to raise the magnate above the heads of the plebeian herd, and the air of prosperous business which pervades the streets, are all noteworthy. It is a city which owes absolutely nothing to European influence. The commercial arrangements by which its business arrangements are run, its posts, banks, and systems of transferring money are all solely Chinese. There, without difficulty, I cashed the draft I brought from a Chinese merchant at Hankow. Chengtu owes nothing to Europe, except a grudge for the excessive indemnity she has had to pay for indulging in the luxury of riots.

The Viceroy, or Governor-General, is a very important official, and lives in great state, with a large military force at his disposal, as befits a man who represents Imperial power in a province as large as France and more populous, and who coerces or administers all Tibetan countries, and the wild borderland which I afterwards visited, which is neither Chinese nor Tibetan—and even the decennial tribute mission from distant Nepaul is allowed or forbidden to go on to Peking much at the Viceroy's pleasure. A request was made to this great man for a letter which would further my journey, and it was promised by a fixed time, but I never got it.

The crowded, busy streets of Chengtu fringe off into truly charming intra-mural suburbs, green and quiet, where deep gateways admit into beautiful gardens bright with flowers and shady with orange and other fruit trees. There are tanks full of water-plants brightened by the gleam of goldfish; the cool drip of falling water is heard; trellis-work, green with creepers or bright with the blossoms of scarlet-runners, shades the pathway ; the scent of tea-roses floats on the sunny air ; and all these groups of pleasant residences tell of affluent ease and the security in which it is enjoyed.

The view from the city wall of the plain, with its beauty and fertility, with suggestions of snow peaks far away, is very striking. Some of the temples are very fine, specially the Wen-shu-yuan (literary college), situated near the north gate.*

This grand building, dating at the latest from the thirteenth century (A.D.), has been rebuilt by several dynasties, and has gone on increasing in wealth and magnificence till its priests and monks are justly proud of its splendours, of which the severe heat, even in the green shades of its grandly timbered surroundings, on the day of my visit prevented me from seeing more than a half. They may be proud of its exquisite cleanliness, too. By the time I reached Chengtu I had come to think that Chinese temples are much maligned on this score, but certainly the Wen-shu-yuan and the " Prince's Temple " above Kuan Hsien excel them all in this virtue, which is said to approach so closely to godliness. All the more remarkable is it here, because the temple is a "theological college" as well as a monastery, a large number of students for the priesthood bringing up the number of the inmates to one hundred and fifty.

All the interstices between the smooth and well-laid flag-stones of the courtyards are kept clean and free from grass ; stone-work, wood-work, gilding, paint and lacquer are all in perfect repair, and the fine roof is kept from the injuries caused by sparrows by a man who walks about the court with a cross-bow. The refectory opening from the court, with twenty-five tables set with tea, vegetables, and rice bowls for six each, for the vegetarian community, is as clean as all the rest ; the wooden tables, chopsticks, and bowls all having that attractive look of well-scrubbed wood which we associate with an old-fashioned English farmhouse.

It is not possible to say whether the course of study and devotion prescribed for both priests and students produces equal

* A detailed description of this building is given by Captain Gill in *The River of Golden Sand*, vol. ii., p. 13. Chengtu has been often visited, and two or three times described by English travellers, so that I consider myself exonerated from giving more than mere notes of my impressions of it.

purity of soul. In the Chapel of Meditations, resembling those which I saw in the monasteries of Western Tibet, both orders must spend some hours of every day in front of the Buddhist images, striving by all means known to them to reach a state of holy ecstasy, in which they are blind to all impressions from the seen. It may be possible that the prolonged watching of the curling and ascending clouds of incense produces a condition approaching hypnotism.

Severe guest-rooms, furnished according to the most rigid Chinese etiquette, chapels, some filled with costly gifts and curiosities, or with tablets to munificent donors, resplendent in gold on black lacquer, libraries of the religious classics, and picture galleries containing portraits of the deceased abbots, vestries for vestments, and dormitories occupy this fine pile of buildings. In the entrance portico, the idol photographed as an illustration recalled me to the fact that China is a stronghold of idolatry. On the other side the divinity looks like a douce, respectable English squire of the days of George III.

DIVINITY IN WEN-SHU-YUAN TEMPLE, CHENGTU.

CHAPTER XXIX.

KUAN HSIEN TO SIN-WEN-PING

BEFORE I left Kuan for Chengtu I had decided on extending my journey up the Siao Ho, a western branch of the Min, on which the mountain town of Li-fan Ting is situated, into the mountainous borderland which lies between China proper and Tibet, the country of some of the reputed aboriginal tribes which concurrent rumour said were under the rule of a woman. At Kuan and Chengtu no information could be got regarding the country west of Li-fan, except that Tibetans trading to Kuan said that "everything could be got at Somo," which appeared to be the residence of the ruler. As there was little use in undertaking such a journey without a more efficient interpreter than Be-dien, Mr. Horsburgh kindly suggested that Mr. Kay, a lay member of the Church Missionary Society, who has a considerable knowledge of colloquial Chinese, should accompany me. I had a hazy intention if things went well of attempting to get down to Ta-lien-lu by the Chin-chuan and Tatu river, returning to the Yangtze by Ya-chow and Chia-ling Fu, but the season was late for this.

When I went to Chengtu I left my travelling arrangements to be made in my absence, simply indicating what they were to be, and that they were to be in writing. A favourite axiom of mine is the late General Gordon's saying, "I am my own best servant," and as a general rule I attend to the smallest details of a journey in advance myself, down to every strap, buckle, and horseshoe. On this occasion the suffering following the blow on my head and my journey to the capital had induced me to trust to others, who, however kind, were without travelling experience; and on returning I found that the travelling arrangement was the exact opposite of the one I had indicated, and that, instead of the coolies having been engaged from a hong with a written agreement, a servant had been allowed to make up a family party on indefinite lines!

Two days of hot, heavy rain delayed the start, and gave ample opportunity for the exercise of those innumerable acts of thoughtful kindness which these small, isolated communities delight in showing to strangers, and which can never be forgotten. There were two disagreeables. Be-dien had been in a shocking sulky fit for two days, and would not answer anyone who spoke to him; and instead of the promised letter from the Viceroy came an indignant note from Mr. Vale, of Chengtu, saying that at the last moment it had been refused.

On the third day the rain became a quiet downpour, tailing off at midday into a misty drizzle which continued; and as further waiting was undesirable, I started, in my three-bearer chair, with five porters, two *chai-jen*, Mr. Kay, his servant, and Be-dien. As my European clothing had fallen to pieces, I was dressed as a Chinese and wore straw shoes. My baggage was all waterproof, and instead of oblong Japanese baskets and bundles protected by oiled paper, I had two deep, square bamboo baskets as better fitted for the mountains, and no loose packages but my camera. Unfortunately, as preventing accurate observations, a year before I had sent home the instruments lent to me by the Royal Geographical Society; a pony had rolled on my hypsometer, and an aneroid barometer kindly lent to me was not reliable, and I had no means of ascertaining the amount of its unreliability before I left China.

The beautiful gorge outside the city, and the grand Prince's Temple were drowned in mist, out of which heavy odours of gardenia drifted. All the vegetation, under the genial influences of heat and moisture, was in full beauty, and there, as everywhere, vigorous plants of the Japanese anemone bordered the road. The climbing roses were in blossom, and, weighted with moisture, hung almost down to our heads. Rocks were matted over with the *hymenophyllum Wilsonianum*, as thick as the fleece of a sheep, and the hare's-foot fern began to make its appearance along with the familiar *polypodium vulgare*.

We left Kuan by the west gate, near a very fine temple, to which the picturesque mass of lacquered pillars and roofs in the illustration is only the outer entrance. Passing above the divided

ENTRANCE TO GROUNDS OF CITY TEMPLE, KUAN HSIEN.

waters of the Min, and Li Ping's simple contrivances for preserving the banks, which consist far more frequently of long
cylindrical baskets of bamboo network containing stones as big
as a man's head than stone revetments, we crossed the Min by
a very fine bamboo suspension bridge, which scarcely vibrated
more under our tread than did the old Menai bridge under a
carriage.

These bamboo bridges are a feature of the Upper Min, and are
remarkably graceful, specially when thrown across at a considerable height. In the better class there is a covered bridge-house
at each side and stone piers. Six bamboo ropes each as thick as
a man's arm are stretched very tightly across the river by strong
windlasses firmly bedded, which are used for re-tightening the
ropes as they "give." These ropes are kept apart by battens
of wood laced vertically in and out. The plank roadway is laid
across the lower of the ropes, and follows their curve, which owing
to the use of the windlasses for tightening up is not great. These
bridges are renewed always once, and sometimes twice, a year,
an operation taking two days and under. Owing to the extreme
width of the river at the Kuan bridge, there are three or four
spans with stone piers. Usually these suspension bridges are
carried right across. The roadway is sometimes trying to the
nerves, for planks tip up, or tip down, or disappear altogether,
or show remarkable vivacity when the foot is placed upon them,
and many a gaping hiatus, trying to any but the steadiest head,
reveals the foam and fury below.

The road follows the river at a height and dives into the
mountains, which are at first of sandstone, with curious strata
running up at right angles to the valley, and then of limestone.
The valley is populous, smoky, and trafficky. Lime-kilns abound,
and a considerable population is employed in working the coal
seams, which occur chiefly in the sandstone; while hundreds of
coolies, carrying both coal and lime, were moving towards Kuan,
and many more were loading vessels and rafts, which, if they
escape the risks of the gorge below, can reach Lu-chow on
the Yangtze.

At the end of nine miles, turning by a short cut up a romantic
tributary of the Min, through a gorge of entrancing beauty,
where forest trees and flowering shrubs were linked by an

entanglement of flowering trailers, crossing a river by a covered bridge, we arrived at Fu-ki, where there was a quiet, pleasant inn, one of several of the same character on this route, where, instead of evil odours, the scent of syringa from the hill behind entered my room. It was very quiet and peaceful. There was no crowding or boring holes in the plaster, the river hummed monotonously below, the mercury was under 60°, and altogether it was a delightful change from the crowding, curiosity, noise, and blazing heat of the Chengtu plain.

Again the next day we started in a steady downpour, which ceased at the top of the very pretty temple-crowned pass, over four thousand feet in altitude, of Niang-tze-ling, after which it was fine and cool. The road drops down from the pass to the deep canyon of the Min, which bifurcates at Weichou, and the river and mountain scenery become increasingly stupendous, reminding me greatly of the road from Kashmir to Tibet after it reaches the Indus. Two fine bamboo suspension bridges near the foot of the pass, others higher up, and a number of rope bridges of Tibetan pattern give both easy and difficult access to the other side. There was a decided Tibetan influence in the air, which I welcomed cordially. Red lamas passed us on pilgrimage to Omi Shan, and numbers of muleteers in sheepskins and rough woollen garb, their animals laden with Tibetan drugs, and, better than these, some "hairy cows" (yaks), which had not yet lost the free air of their mountain pastures, and executed many rampageous freaks on the narrow bridle path. Lamas and muleteers were all frank and friendly, asked where we were going, how long we had been on the road, enlightened us on their own movements, and cheerily wished us a good journey. Most of the mules had one or more prayer-flags standing up on their loads, for the Tibetans are one of the most externally religious peoples on earth.

The Min* from the pass of Niang-tze-ling assumes the character which it retains more or less to the source of the Siao Ho or lesser branch. It is a fine, peacock-green river; then, though

---

* The fall of the Min between its bifurcation at Weichou and Kuan Hsien, taking the altitudes of these two towns as the basis of the calculation and the Chinese *li* at its average length, is twenty-seven feet to the mile, but from Weichou to Li-fan Ting it is no less than forty-five feet to the mile.

at low water, of considerable volume, booming, crashing, and foaming through canyons and gorges in a series of cataracts, hemmed in by cliffs and mountains so precipitous as rarely to leave level ground enough for a barley patch.

The bridle track, a very good one on the whole, though there are some shelving rock slithers, has been cut, not blasted, in the rock, at times on steep declivities and at times on precipices, and follows the up and down left bank of the Min ascents and descents at a height with great fidelity. It is not broad enough for a loaded mule to pass a chair, and the sight of a caravan in the distance always caused much agitation and yelling, the Tibetan muleteers invariably drawing off on the first margin they could find, and greeting us with courtesies and good wishes as we passed them. I envied them the altitudes and freedom to which they would return from the cramping grooviness of China.

Now and then the road is scaffolded, or steps are cut in the rock, or it passes under an arch of rock, or a bridge carries it across a lateral chasm down which a crystal torrent dashes, after turning two, three, or four rude mills placed in dizzy positions one above another. It is so severe that we only did thirteen miles in nine hours, and I saw plainly what I had suspected from the first, that one of the scratch team of bearers was not up to his work.

The whole of the first fortnight's journey was along the deep, wild gorge of the greater or lesser Min. It differs widely from ordinary Chinese travelling, and has a strong resemblance to the wild gorges of the Yangtze. The mountains rise from the river to a height of over 3000 feet. Ghastly snow-cones look over them, their slopes, always steep, often break up into cliffs 400 or 500 feet high; the river has often not a yard of margin, and hurries along, crashing and booming, a thing of purposeless power and fury, which has never been tamed of mankind, its sea-green colouring a thing of beauty, and its crests and stretches of foam white as the snows which give it birth.

These mountain sides, as far as Weichou, are completely covered with greenery, dwarf ashes, oaks, chestnuts and beeches, big enough for use by the charcoal-burners. Coarse grasses, thistles, yellow roses, a very pretty yellow cistus, bryony, brambles, yellow jasmines and flowering creepers in abundance, all dwarf, with the barberry in blossom, covered the stony, broken hillsides. Three species of warm-scented artemisia and fuzzy brown balls of uncurling fronds of ferns were expanding in the crevices of the rocks, and the rocks themselves were often tinged rose-pink with the early leaves and delicate clasping fingers of Veitch's *Ampelopsis.*

It was a clear escape from the crowds of China. The traffic on the road was mostly Tibetan. There is little room for crops ; an occasional patch among the rocks near the river, and small fields, then growing rape, and later starved barley, terraced great heights,

DOUBLE ROOFED BRIDGE.

where the mountain slope is less steep than usual. Small as the population is, it does not grow enough for its wants, so many of the men hunt the deer and wild boars on the mountains and sell the carcases in Kuan in the winter, and others trap the fur-bearing animals, which appear to be an inferior sable and marten.

There are a few hamlets on the road, which subsist chiefly by supplying the needs of travellers, but the restaurant was usually hidden away, and made no display on the "street." Rice is scarce and not always attainable, and wherever we halted, instead of the appetising displays of ready-cooked viands which tempt the coolie appetite, there was rarely even a fire, and it was always an hour before anything was cooked. The inns, though much better than any I had been accustomed to, and often built of new boards, do not provide any fire in the mornings unless by special arrangement, and till this was understood I started without tea. Their stock of food was soon exhausted, even at the larger villages where we halted for the night, and the descent upon them of twelve hungry persons was manifestly unwelcome. Some of the hamlets are built at great heights, and are accessible by rugged paths and steps cut in the rock. The people are hardy, rough, and fairly friendly. The Chinese are, to my thinking, men of plains and rivers and slimy paths—a rice-eating people, associating with the water buffalo. Here they are abruptly metamorphosed into hardy mountaineers, hunters, maize and millet fed. Even the women, though still binding the feet, are independent in their air and movements, and perform feats in crossing rivers. The country is a cross between China and Tibet. However, there are no temples, and few shrines or other signs of religion.

Fully one-third of the population is on the west side of the Min, cut off from the high road with its business and gaieties by a furious torrent, and in most cases too poor to construct bamboo suspension bridges. Their strong nerves enable them to get over the difficulty. I know of no sight in China which fascinated me so much as their rope bridges, which we met with on the second day, and which occur sometimes at frequent intervals, as far as Weichou, from which point I saw no more of them.

The mountaineers stretch a plaited bamboo cable at a great height across the gorge, tighten it as well as they can, and secure each end round a round stone or a convenient rock. Sometimes a shed is built over the terminus and a shrine close by. Every mountaineer provides himself with two semi-cylinders of hard wood, often hinged, about a foot long. With perfect *sang-froid* he places these on the cable, and binds them together with a rope. As if it were the most natural thing in the world, he proceeds to suspend himself from the cylinder by ropes passed under his knees, his waist, and the back of his neck; some dispensing with the last.

He is then hanging under the rope, and, gripping it fast by the slide, he gives the solid earth a shove and casts off. No matter how tightly a long rope is strained, it must still "sag" considerably in the middle, and down the passenger rushes at tremendous speed, head foremost, down hill across the chasm, with an impetus which sends him a little way up the other slope. Then, letting go the cylinder, he puts his hands on the rope above his head, and hauls himself up hand over hand, slowly and laboriously. When he reaches land he detaches the cylinder, packs it and the

TIBETAN ROPE BRIDGE.

rope into his basket, shoulders his burden—and both men and women continually carry small sacks or bundles of wood across— bows at the shrine, and goes his way.

I saw a woman cross carrying a load on each side. It took her ten minutes to ascend from the middle of the rope, which must have been ninety feet above the torrent, to land. Her face was purple with the effort, and her hands must have been pretty sore, for she spit upon them several times during the crossing. Even children are trusted to these arrangements, which need considerably more nerve than the *Jhulas* of the Himalayas. In some places to minimise the difficulty there are two rope bridges, each descending from a high to a low level.

It is only occasionally at the mouth of one of the grand lateral gorges which open on the valley that there are any trees, and then they are very fine, specially walnuts and the exotic Zelkowa, and the *Salisburia adiantifolia*, with a few sturdy conifers, and the villages are surrounded by peaches, apricots, and the Japanese *loquat* (*Eriobotrya Japonica*).

It was a delightful day's journey to Sin-wen-ping, and the keen mountain air and the novelty and freedom were full of zest. Solitary grandeur, the deafening din of the Min, the green crystal affluents which descend upon it down glorious gorges, the precipices rising a thousand feet from the water, the abrupt turns where progress seems blocked, and each mountain barrier is grander and loftier than the last, and then the majesty of the day's journey culminates at a mountain village with a fine suspension bridge, beyond which the road looks only a thread along the side of a precipice.

When the bearers reached Sin-wen-ping they said they would go no farther, for there was a " big wind " farther on, which would blow the chair into the river, and the porters said they could not carry the loads against it. Then it came out that Be-dien had left behind the lanterns which I bought a few days before; so the men carried their point of making a day of thirteen miles. Again I urged that the agreement with them should be put in writing; but it was not done, and I found later that it was on quite different lines from those I had laid down. I saw grave difficulties ahead, and should have been glad to ride and be rid of the men, but I had left my saddle in Korea.

It was very cold in the inn, only half my room being roofed, and the mercury, which was 83° on the Chengtu Plain, was only 40°. It was invigorating and delicious. The people, too, were very friendly, and did not manifest their curiosity rudely. A runner arrived from the capital with a big official envelope addressed to me, containing letters with the Viceroy's seal; but as they were addressed to the mandarins of Pi Hsien where I did not halt, and Kuan Hsien which I had left, and made no reference to the regions beyond, they did not promise to be useful. On the *yamen* at Chengtu refusing the promised letters, Mr. Vale telegraphed to H.B.M.'s Consul at Chung-king, and this was the result.   The letters stated to the mandarins that at Liang-shan and Peng Hsien the mob had attempted by violence to break in my door, and that I had been attacked with stones, all within the Viceroyalty, and the Viceroy directed the *kuans* to take efficient measures for my protection.

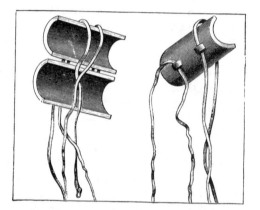

HAND SLIDES FOR TIBETAN ROPE BRIDGE.

CHAPTER XXX.

SIN-WEN-PING TO LI-FAN TING

AFTER leaving that quiet place, where the temperature was only 52° at 7.30 a.m., we plunged at once into a wild part of the gorge, very thinly peopled and desolate, on which grim snow-peaks looked down from the head of every lateral cleft. The traffic on the road was altogether Tibetan, partly accounted for by the junction of the road to Mou-Kung Ting, a thousand *li* away, with the Sung-pan Ting road, which we were following. There were large caravans of very big, powerful mules, loaded either with wool or with medicinal roots, and with a merry inclination to lunge at us with hoofs or teeth as we passed them ; the rough, uncouth muleteers always cheerful and friendly as they exchanged with us their national salutation *zho*.

One man at least in each caravan—every man having charge of four mules—can shoe his own beasts, and I had the luck, in consequence of a mule kicking off his shoe as we passed him, to see that the method is the same as in Western Tibet. They tie the fore and hind legs of the animal together, cast him, put a pole through the lashings, the ends of which are held by two men, and cold shoe him, paring the hoof only very slightly, using very long nails with tacket heads.

The Mou-Kung Ting road is one of the great routes of Tibetan traffic, of which we saw much less after passing the junction.

The gorge is very narrow, so narrow that at times the road is scaffolded over the water, or is carried by rough steps cut in the face of the precipices. We ascended 800 feet during the day. The traces of spring diminished, the hills were brown and bare, the apricots were hardly in blossom, the few trees were leafless, the people still wore their wadded clothes, and it was pleasant to walk a good deal. Yet here and there were thick carpets of a sky-blue dwarf iris, a fragile thing, looking misplaced among its rough surroundings, and patches of a blue bugloss, and dwarf shubberies of a barberry in blossom.

Things had changed. Thatched roofs had given place to thin slabs of stone, or rough boards held down by big stones. All ornament had disappeared. China seemed left behind at such a great distance, that every Chinese I saw looked as if he must be like myself, a foreigner. The men were hardy mountaineers, and carried their loads on pack saddles, striding like men, rather than at a dog trot, on the swinging bamboo. Even the women can

HUMAN PACK SADDLE FOR TIMBER.

shoulder packs and dangle from rope bridges, and the children have an air of freedom.

A short day's journey ended at the hamlet of Shuo-chiao, where the gorge opens out, and for a brief period the Min is vulgarised into various branches clattering and boiling among beds of Brobdingnagian shingle. It is a wild place, among high mountains, a single village street, a fine suspension bridge, a mill or two on the shingle, and goats on the ledgy slopes. The inn at the end of the street, where I spent two nights, was new, and hung over a branch of the river. My room, having no ceiling, was lofty. The boards were clean, and there were no bad smells. The noise of the river was tremendous. Besides the roar of the water, there was a sound of paving stones being thumped on paving stones, and a perpetual clatter of shingle. I had to shout as loud as I could to make my servant hear. But it was very restful. I was entirely ignored. No one intruded into my room, and when I took a walk unattended no one followed me.

Food was scarce, and an inroad of twelve travellers involved much arrangement. Shuo-chiao is not a usual halting-place, and the stocks were low. The people fell back on making macaroni, and sandwiches with chopped garlic between layers of steamed paste. Macaroni is made of a very close dough of barley meal, very much kneaded, and rolled out on a clean table over and over again till it attains the desired toughness and thinness, when the operator cuts it into long and narrow strips, which are hung over a string to dry. When wanted these strips are boiled, and are eaten with chopped capsicum or onion.

The following day's journey to Weichou was novel and interesting. The sky was grey and threatened rain, and the snow-peaks loomed grimly through flurries of dark clouds. We ascended to a height of over 4300 feet into a barren region, where winter lingered. The few villages have characteristics of their own; each consists of a long, clean, paved, narrow street, the houses built of stone, the walls with more or less of an inward slope, as if under Tibetan influence—all dwellings two-storeyed, the upper storey of dark wood, with carved, overhanging balconies with supporting beams also carved, and with very deep eaves with long and elaborately carved wooden pendants. Such villages are usually by torrent sides, with fruit trees, cedars, and poplars clustering about them, and are approached by picturesque bridges. The street terminates at either end with a decorative gateway, often with a small tower and wind bells.

In many places where the Min has a narrow bank, there are ruined villages with only ruinous walls standing; and in each house there are one, two, or three graves. On one larger open space there are great numbers of graves, said to be those of soldiers who died fighting; and the whole of the slaughter and destruction is attributed by the villagers to the Taiping rebellion. This is plausible, but doubtful.

In crevices there were minute fronds of the silver fern, which grows profusely all along the canyon ; but nature was still asleep. Limestone and grey sandstone predominate, and the curiously marked strata are occasionally vertical. Basalt, however, appears in some of the lateral ravines, and pink granite ; and the torrents which tumble over the latter are exquisite in their sparkle and purity. A traveller who, except on one day's journey from Wan, has not tasted unboiled water for more than two years, would wish to be thirsty to drink of these icy and living waters.

At Wen-chuan Hsien, a small prefectural town packed among high mountains, with a very poor but clean street, a picturesque entrance, and a fine Confucian Temple, I sat in the grey street while the *yamen* officials copied my passport at a table, and an old man, who seemed influential, kept the dirty and too often leprous crowd of men and boys from pressing on me too closely. Nothing is ever done privately in the East, and several men leant over the scribes, reading the imposing-looking document, when one exclaimed, with an air of consternation, "She is given rank !" Others exclaimed incredulously, "A woman can't have rank !" But the scribes settled the point in my favour ; and then there was a discussion as to how I had got rank—if it were literary rank, or if I were the wife of a great mandarin in my own country—a suggestion combated on the ground that I wore poor cotton clothing, and had no jewels. Wen-chuan is the most hopelessly dull official town that I saw in China.

The night before, at Shuo-chiao, I was told that after passing Wen-chuan we should see the villages of the " Barbarians," on the heights ; and I heard a tale with which travellers bound for the aboriginal tribes have been plied from Marco Polo down to Captain Gill. The innkeeper said that these people would offer hospitality, but it was dangerous to eat with them, for they believed that if they poisoned a rich man his wealth would come to them without violence, and that they would think that I was rich (in spite of my poor cotton clothing), and would put poison in my food, and that in about three months I should die of a disease akin to dysentery ! He also said that these tribes are ruled by a very great queen, who will not let any stranger enter her territory—obviously the same woman of whom I had heard rumours at intervals for some months previously.

At last, and for fifteen *li* before reaching Weichou, the objects of interest became novel and plentiful, startling in their novelty. Singular dwellings made their appearance, crowning hilltops or poised on ledges—isolated or in clusters. The earlier specimens have high, dead, stone walls, flat roofs, and an upper storey covering a third of the roof, but without a front wall. Before long such houses aggregated themselves into villages on great heights, and without any apparent means of access, though that they were inhabited was obvious from the patches of cultivation about them. Among them appear tall towers, sometimes to the number of seven; they are picturesque and fantastic beyond all imagination. Of course these are the dwellings of the Man-tze (Barbarians), supposed by most ethnologists to be the aborigines of Western China; and it was not a little disappointing, on turning the glass upon them, to see nothing but Chinese with their queues and blue cotton, and hobbling women loafing round such extraordinary habitations. I use the word *loafing* advisedly. It is usually quite inapplicable to a Chinese, and among these mountains, as elsewhere, he has plenty of grit, but population is scanty, and competition has ceased to be keen, so he has leisure for a lounging study of the welfare of his crops and his pigs.

So, among villages crowning rocky mountain-tops or clinging to scarcely accessible mountain-sides, some of them very Tibetan, others with definite characteristics of their own, the road finds itself at the small prefectural town of Weichou, at the junction of the Ta Ho and the Siao Ho (the Great and Little rivers), in a superb situation, much embellished by the unconscious art of the builder, with *yamens* on rocky heights, and the grey city wall following the steep contours of the hills which surround the town. The north road on the left bank of the Ta Ho leads to Sung-pan Ting, and the west road, mostly along the right bank of the Siao Ho, to Li-fan Ting and beyond. Weichou is the town called by Captain Gill on his map Hsin-Pu-Kuan.

At this point mules for the farther journey should have been engaged.

It is a good sixty-five *li* from Weichou to Li-fan Ting, and we left at 6 a.m. My expectations were high, but they were more than fulfilled. From Weichou to Somo there is only one dull bit of about three miles. As far as Li-fan Ting the scenery is

colossal and savage, Tibetan in its character, resembling somewhat the wild gorges of the Shayok; and, beyond Tsa-ku-lao,
the westernmost official post of China in that direction, the
grandeur and beauty exceed anything I have ever seen—Switzerland, Kashmir, and Tibet in one.

Outside Weichou there are two suspension bridges, over which
I had to walk. They were "on their last legs," and were taken
down when I came back. They vibrated, the wind swayed them
unpleasantly, and as the loose planks were only laid at intervals,
and some had disappeared, and the swinging structures hung like
inverted arches over boiling surges, the crossing was not agreeable,
and it is as little so when on this road the chair turns a corner of
the narrow path on the edge of a precipice 500 or 600 feet in
depth, and hangs for an appreciable interval over the abyss
below.

The day was the most brilliant for three months, and the
journey from first to last was magnificent, but the wind, which I
found such a merciless foe in Central Asia, rose at the same hour,
9 a.m., and blew half a gale till near sunset, reaching its maximum
of force at 2 p.m., making photography impossible, several times
nearly overturning the chair and its bearers, and filling eyes, nose,
and mouth not only with gritty dust, but with irritating alkalis.
This is the daily routine in these mountain valleys. On crossing
the bridges we entered at once the gorge of the Siao Ho, or Li-fan
River, in which we remained for twelve hours—a river flashing in
cataracts, eddying in rapids, with never a quiet reach—a deep,
clear, olive-green stream, its grand course accompanied by a deep
undertone of a heavy booming in its caverned depths. Its career
is through a rift among mountains, seven, eight, and nine thousand
feet in height, broken up by stupendous chasms and precipices,
and into red-brown, but seldom grey, peaks—the higher like
needles, the lower crested by villages, to all appearance inaccessible; the mass riven asunder, laterally, in many places in so
remarkable a manner as to show on one side the rock corresponding to the cleavage on the other, so that if the sides could be
brought together they would be an exact fit.

Occasionally the mountains and precipices recede sufficiently from
the river to give scanty space for villages at their feet, with poplars
and scanty crops of bearded wheat on sandy soil, and at the lateral

BAMBOO SUSPENSION BRIDGE, WEICHOU.

openings alluvial fans occur, bearing fair crops of wheat and maize, as well as pear and apricot trees, just providing a scanty subsistence for a scanty population. Limestone, grey and red sandstone, and a very hard conglomerate are the predominant formations, but a granite with a pink tinge makes an occasional innovation, and the pot-holes in the river, where it was possible to investigate them, were found to be fashioned of grey granite. One remarkable feature of the region is the enormous quantity of nitrate of soda. Its efflorescence in places whitens the mountains as if with snow, and so checks vegetation as to reduce it to coarse plants of strong constitutions, with tough fibres and woolly leaves. Sulphur abounds also, and fragments of an iron ore, which I afterwards learned is brown hematite. There are nitre works at Weichou, and sulphur is supplied in small quantities for making powder, but the cost of land carriage is great, and it is chiefly used locally for tipping matches.

The road is a great work of modern origin, and must have cost a large sum. It is in excellent repair. It is cut, not blasted, for much of the way out of solid rock. In places it is necessary to carry it out over the river on a wooden framework, supported on timbers driven into the river-bed, or to " scaffold " it by carrying it out on stakes driven horizontally into the rock. In one place a fine gallery, decorated with stone tablets to the man who presented the road to his district, has been cut through the rock, and wherever steps are necessary, they have been carefully made. At this distance of 2000 miles from the coast, and half that from the capital, it is somewhat surprising to find so marked a sign of civilisation as an excellent road in thorough repair.

I cannot attempt to convey to the reader any idea of the glories and surprises of that long day's journey. It was a perfect extravagance of grandeur of form and beauty of colouring, and the sky approached that of Central Asia in the brilliancy of its bright pure blue. Every outline was sharp, but the gorges were filled with a deep blue or purple atmosphere ; the sunlight was intense. There was no dawn of spring on the bare rock faces of the mountains, no gloom of pine in any rift—grandeur and vastness are the characteristics of the scenery—peaks and precipices are piled on each other, and through the rare openings there were gleamings far away of sunlit cones of unsullied snow.

There are villages on hilltops, on rocky peaks, reached by stairs cut in the rock, on ledges of precipices, into which the back rooms are excavated without obvious means of access, and villages where the houses are three, four, five, and even seven storeys high, clinging to steep mountain-sides, or hanging on to cliffs above tempestuous streams. These villages are on heights five, seven, and even nine thousand feet above the sea—barley and bearded wheat ripening in July at eleven thousand—and from one to three thousand feet above the Siao Ho. All are built of stone, all look more or less like fortifications, all have flat roofs, and most have brown wood rooms or galleries, much decorated with rude fretwork, supported on carved beams projecting from their upper storeys.

Most of these villages possess mysterious-looking square stone towers, sloping very gently inwards from base to summit. These are from forty to ninety feet high. The bases of some of them are thirty feet square; the sides are pierced by narrow openings, wider, however, than loopholes. The doors are fifteen feet and upwards from the ground, and I did not see any with any present means of access. Some have lost many feet of their height, I suppose from age and weather, but many are perfect, and have projections near the roofs, which on a small scale are like the projecting rooms of the modern villages. Three and four in a single village is not an uncommon number, and occasionally there are as many as seven. At a distance they give the romantic villages in the ravines the prosaic aspect of smelting works, but they add a singular dignity and picturesqueness to those on the heights. They are built without mortar of blocks of undressed stone, " well and truly laid," in spite of the difficulty of the inward slope, and the stones are of sufficient size to suggest an inquiry as to how they were elevated to their present positions. Those towers which are still perfect are roofed, which may account for their preservation. There are great numbers of them between Weichou and Li-fan Ting, after which they occur but rarely till the head-waters of the Chin-shuan are reached.

As the Man-tze say that " their fathers and their fathers' fathers never remember a time when they were free," so they cannot remember any legends regarding the use of these towers, except that in " old times" fires were lighted on their roofs to recall absent villagers to the defence of their homes against an approaching enemy. Some think that they were granaries, but the so-called thinking of people in their stage of mental development is of little value.

Perhaps mine, in the absence of a greater array of facts, is not worth much more! It appears certain, from a consensus of testimony, that these buildings have two and three floors, reached by steps, *i.e.* notched timbers, like those which at this day lead up to Man-tze roofs. Very large, rough, earthen jars, which might have

ANCIENT TOWERS AT KANPO.

contained water, were shown to me as having been found in one of them. It is quite possible that at a late date the roofs were used for beacon fires, but from certain indications in a few cases I am inclined to believe that easily-removable approaches of stone and earth led up to the doors, by which stores could be taken up and cattle driven in, the final entrance, after the removal of these slopes, being made by means of notched timbers, easily drawn up into the building ; and that the towers were refuges, in which the cattle were below and the people above, food for man and beast being stored in the same building. This theory accounts for the number of towers often found in the same village. It is quite possible that the chief or headman and each of the richer villagers possessed such a refuge. The style of building is far beyond the capacities of a "barbarous" people.

Along the lower waters of the Siao Ho, all the Man-tze villages which have not been more or less destroyed—with the exception of a few which have been deserted, and are ready for occupation to-morrow, with the lands belonging to them, have been taken possession of by the Chinese, and evidently with much slaughter, for the number of graves is very great. Even the villages on the heights above that part of the river have not escaped Chinese absorption.

At one time, and that not long ago, the aboriginal population must have been large, both to the south and west of Weichou, but not a Man-tze was to be seen within forty *li* of it. Many a blackened ruin of a once happy Man-tze hamlet stirs the travellers' wrath, and it is hardly less aggravating to find Chinese families comfortably living in the picturesque dwellings of the slaughtered or expatriated aborigines. There were many tales told of the treachery of the "Barbarians," and of the necessity of extirpating them—such tales as are to be heard in America, Australia, and every land in which the stronger race has ousted the weaker one. When at Li-fan Ting my farther progress was vehemently opposed, I had some reason to think that the officials feared that when I was once fairly among the Man-tze I should hear other versions of these stories.

About forty *li* from Weichou, where the lateral clefts in the precipices are dark and savage, and rocky peaks crowned with fantastic lama-serais rise abruptly from rocky spurs, the villages on the heights become more numerous, and the presence for the first time of Man-tze inhabitants (who are rigid lamaistic Buddhists like the Tibetans) is denoted by long flags inscribed with Sanskrit characters on tall poles fluttering gaily in the strong east wind which blows down the canyon all day long. Occasionally a wooden bridge on the cantilever principle, like the Sanga bridges in India, of which many specimens are seen between the Zoji-la and Leh in Ladak, crosses the furious torrent. Most of the Man-tze villages are on the left bank of the Siao Ho, and by the destruction of these bridges, which are much out of repair, they could be rendered impregnable.

These villages are indescribable. The cattle and fodder are kept below, and the windows and loopholes only begin from fifteen to twenty feet from the ground. Brown projecting rooms and balconies at a great height, the gay flutter of red and white prayer-flags, notched timbers giving access to roof above roof, fuel-stacks on roofs, towers suggesting peril and defence, and not seldom a headman's house above, as large as a feudal castle, which it much resembles; while high above that, looking like an outgrowth of the rock, and only attained by flights of steep rock steps, crowning the peak which dominates every village, are almost invariably the piled-up temples, towers, and buildings of a lama-serai, with their colour and gloom, the flutter of their prayer-flags, and the sound of the incessant wild music of horns, drums, and gongs. An air of mystery pervades the whole, for with all this cheerful flutter of flags and the sound of music and the signs of industry it was very rarely that any inhabitants were to be seen, just the glint of a woman's red petticoat now and then, or the red frock of a lama in relief against the grey rock.

These tribes are not Tibetan, though they are down on most maps as " Tibetan tribes," but in the extraordinary picturesqueness of their lama-serais and villages they reminded me vividly of the Shayok, and the fantastic monasteries of Deskyid and Hundar in the Tibetan Nubra Valley.

It is a temptation to linger on that day's journey. I did actually linger on it, for one of my bearers, as I expected, was quite unequal to his work, and I had to walk a good deal and allow of many halts for rest. The halting-places were magnificent, but food was scarce and dear, as every cattie of rice must be brought up from the low country. Although we ascended on that day 988 feet, the climate became perceptibly milder, and from what I observed later, it appears quite possible that in temperature each degree west is equal to a degree south. Grain crops, poplar, apricot, and pear trees were in their first vivid green, the silver fern was in its beauty, the golden fern was well advanced, the bugloss was in bloom, and in places where the canyon opened a little there were narrow lawns of the finest turf, on which the Tibetan traders camp in the season, on which red roses with coarse, woolly calices were already in blossom. There was no traffic, and even an unloaded pedestrian, unless he were a red lama telling his beads, or twirling his prayer cylinder, was a rarity.

In the late afternoon, at an abrupt and superb turn of the river, we crossed a cantilever bridge high above the torrent, on the other side of which is a fine village of extraordinary Man-tze houses, clinging to ledges of a conical peak crowned by a small temple and a very large and fantastic lama-serai. A tower, ninety feet high, very ancient, and in good repair, gives dignity to the picturesqueness of Ta-fan. The road attains the village by a steep, winding stairway of steps cut in the rock, and passes through a gateway into cool shadow created by high, massive, stone houses on either side. So massive are they, and so high are the windows above the ground, that they suggest memories of villages in the Engadine.

I rested in a large house in which, as in the others, a Chinese was living with his family. These aborigines had grand ideas of habitations. I entered into a guest hall panelled with brown wood, with two rooms on each side and a large room behind. A gallery of brown wood, with rooms opening from it, runs round the hall at a height of about eight feet from the floor. It was very cool and clean, and I sat in a Chinese easy-chair, glad to be out of the bluster. My host, who was the head-man, was a very courteous Chinese, and offered me wheaten cakes, honey, and tea. He said that all the houses in the canyon were built by "Tibetans," though Chinese live in the lower villages; that if a Chinese builds a new house he builds it after the same fashion, for that nothing but Tibetan building—specially the inward slope of the very thick walls—can stand the tremendous winds. The village subsists less by agriculture, for which there is not sufficient irrigation, than by the Tibetan traffic in the trading season.

The headman asked me why I was travelling to be murdered by the "Barbarians," and evidently attached no value to my statement that it was to see the country. I wished then and elsewhere that I had been able to say that it was in order to write a book, for that would have given me "rank," and would have been an intelligible explanation.

After leaving this village the mountains closed in again upon the pass, their forms growing in wild majesty ; there were glimpses

KAN-CHI.

of snow-peaks with pines on their skirts, and where the shadow was bluest and deepest, and the peaks are loftiest and sharpest, on a small patch of partially level ground, separated from a very high and bare mountain, with precipices which Captain Gill estimates at 3000 feet in height, by the roaring river, stands the wild mountain town of Li-fan Ting, the residence of a small magistrate, though only possessing a population of five hundred.

Before we actually reached it waves of sunset gold rolled down the pass, distant snow-cones blushed red, every peak took on purple or amethyst—there was a carnival of colour. The wind fell to a dead calm, there was a touch of frost in the dry air, when suddenly the whole glory of mountain and chasm died out, and the colour vanished, leaving only the distant snow-peaks burning red against a sky of tender green.

This small, grey city, on whose expansion Nature places her veto, looks the final outpost of Chinese civilisation—the end of all things. A well-built, narrow, crenelated wall runs between Li-fan Ting and the river, hems it in, and then in a most fantastic way climbs the crests of two mountain spurs, which wall in a ravine behind the town, bare and rocky as all else is, looking like great flights of uncannily steep stairs, following the steep and irregular contour of the ground.

A clear blue torrent, tumbling down at the back, thunders through the town, and is utilised for many Lilliputian water-mills, mostly with horizontal wheels, as on the plain. These mills are round, and look like small Martello towers, and only a man below the average height can stand upright in them. Poplars, willows, pear, and apricot trees contrast pleasantly with the bare mountain-sides, and soften the grey outlines of the small mountain town. Above Li-fan, and 2200 feet higher, is a Man-tze village, in which the people have made Chinese intermarriages, and have assimilated themselves to their conquerors.

Li-fan has one long, narrow, grey street of two-storeyed houses, the upper storey with its balcony being of brown wood. It is very clean, but cleanliness is not much of a merit—indeed, it is a necessity of that altitude and in a dry atmosphere. It has no industry or trade of its own, and subsists almost entirely on the through trade from Tibet at certain seasons. It has a remarkable *yamen*, which, lacking space for lateral expansion, has developed skywards; a temple on a rock, brilliantly coloured; and a fine temple in the narrow street, rich in effective wood-carving, and possessing a huge bas-relief of the Dragon. The rarefied air is singularly dry, and so it continues until the Pass of Peh-teo-shan, 70 *li* to the westward, marks a decided change to humidity. On the nights of April 22nd and 23rd there were three and four degrees of frost.

In this quaint town on the first day of the tenth month of each year, the mandarin, with all the pomp which Li-fan can muster, fires the biggest gun in the town at the opposite mountain to preserve "the luck of the place." It is believed, at least by the people, that if this ceremony were not performed there would be tumults, followed by plague, pestilence, and famine, and that the town would be given up to bad luck. To save the luck some of the lamas make pilgrimages to an image cut in the rock at the base of the Snow Dragon, a grand mountain to the south of Li-fan.

The inn, where unwillingly I spent two days, is not bad, and was quite free from smells. My room was at its extreme end, close to a crashing, booming torrent, to the mountain, and to the red temple, which, like the *yamen*, has developed skywards. It had two large holes in the floor, and two windows under the roof, from which all the paper was torn, so that the tremendous wind by day found easy entrance.

As soon as we arrived the usual official visit was paid, and with much politeness of manner obstacles were thrown in the way of my further progress. Two *chai-jen* were placed at my door, one of them sleeping across the threshold. Much consideration for the safety and comfort of a lady was expressed—a novelty in China. There were neither roads nor inns, it was said; the people were savages, the tribes were fighting, it was dangerous to proceed. The next morning the prospect for departure was badly clouded over. The veneer of politeness had disappeared, and the official manner had become dictatorial. Senior officials from the *yamen* mounted guard, and a sentry was stationed at the inn gate. I was a prisoner in all but the name. *Chai-jen* could not be provided, they said. The mandarin was absent, and no arrangements could be made till the Viceroy of SZE CHUAN had been communicated with. Going beyond Li-fan was a thing unheard of.

ROCK TEMPLE, LI-FAN TING.

All other foreigners had turned back,* they could not be respon-sible for me any farther. They bullied and threatened my men, and forbade the townspeople to give me supplies or porters.

The other difficulties, which I had foreseen from the first, came to a head. Owing to the want of a contract I was in the power of the chair-bearers. One of them was nearly in-capable of carrying me, and not having recovered from the severe blow at Lo-kia-chan I was not capable of much walking. The only man in Li-fan who could carry a chair was engaged in that man's place in the morning, but was "ill" at night. The authorities had forbidden him to go, and had taken the precaution of laying the same prohibition on the mules, though if I could have dispensed with the men I was prepared to make the journey on a pack-saddle. Finally and fatally, Mr. Kay, who was very much in the power of the servant who had got the team together, when the men said that all must go or none would go, engaged them all for the whole journey, and under the circumstances we were then absolutely in their power so far as going forwards was concerned. Such a tribe of rice-eating men, carrying their loads from the shoulder, would, under any circumstances, have been unsuited to the journey. But what was done could not be undone, and there was "no use in crying over spilt milk."

The *chai-jen* smoked their opium pipes across my door, but retained wits enough to pounce on me if I stirred, and even obtruded their unwelcome presence when I climbed on the roof to photograph. On the second evening the officials made a last effort to induce me to wait till they sent a runner to the capital and back.

The last morning I woke everybody at 4.30, and was ready to leave at 5.30 ; but it was not to be. The officials were already there frightening the coolies with stories, intimidating them, and threatening to have them beaten for disobedience, and there was a violent altercation between them and Mr. Kay, in which some very strong language was used on both sides, which did not mend matters. When I came out they tried to shut me into my room ; but I managed to get into my chair. They told the bearers not to carry me. I told them to move on. The

---

* I could not hear of any but Captain Gill, and three Russians a few months before, and all had reasons of their own for doing so.

officials then tried to shut us in by closing parts of the outer door of the inn ; but Mr. Kay opened them, and held them open till the frightened porters and my bearers had passed through. It was but fifty yards to the city gate.   I feared they would close it, but they contented themselves with following us there, crying out, " We wash our hands of you ! " and hurling at us the epithet " Foreign dogs ! " as a parting missile, throwing down the gauntlet by sending us off without *chai-jen,* telling the brazen lie that the road I proposed to take was not in China !

From this point there was the pleasurable excitement which attends a plunge into the unknown, for I had not been able to learn that missionary zeal, or geographical research, or commercial ambition had penetrated the regions beyond, or that any English traveller has given any description of it, and I only regret that my lack of scientific equipment should make my account of it meagre, and in some respects unsatisfactory.

CHAPTER XXXI.

LI-FAN TING TO TSA-KU-LAO

THE sixty *li* from Li-fan Ting to Tsa-ku-lao (spelled by Mr. von Rosthorn of the Imperial Customs in a letter to me Tsaku-nao) have much the same characteristics as those of the day before. The scenery is magnificent, and even more fantastic. Nitrate of soda, sulphur, and iron-ore abound. Sandstone has disappeared, giving place to limestone, conglomerate, schistaceous rock, grey and pink granite, basalt, and mica. The Siao Ho, still a full-watered and vigorous stream, occasionally narrowed to forty feet, plunges over pink granite ledges in a series of cataracts as the canyon opens out, and there are smooth, green lawns, with much wealth of dwarf, crimson roses, and much gloom, in many graves and dismal remains of Man-tze houses partially destroyed. Some of the pot-holes in the river are remarkable for their size, and still contain the smoothly-rounded stones by the action of which they have been formed. Pine woods appeared on hill crests and on the northern slopes of mountains.

Many Man-tze villages, now deserted, are ready for occupation, and others in romantic situations, now occupied by Chinese, are very striking architecturally, each with a Man-tze feudal castle piled on a rock above it. These villages were always built at the mouths of gorges where lateral torrents joining the Siao Ho formed alluvial fans with arable soil enough to support small populations. The picturesque stone houses, more like fortifications than dwellings, straggling up these gorges, perched on ledges of rock, harmonised most artistically with the wildness of the landscape, but it was impossible to photograph them owing to the tremendous wind.

Four hours after leaving Li-fan we halted at the large village of Wei-gua, with a very large lama-serai, said to contain two hundred lamas, cresting the rock above it, and a fine castle in a dominant position. The illustration gives the lower and un-picturesque fragment of the village grouped round the remains of a large square tower. There we were overtaken by two *chai-jen*, the Li-fan officials having thought better of it, and an hour later by a third on horseback! This tardy courtesy roused my suspicions, and Mr. Kay and his servant went on ahead to obtain accommodation and make inquiries at Tsa-ku-lao, little thinking that the astute Li-fan officials had sent on a messenger in the morning to the local magistrate ordering that accommodation and transport should be refused! To this hour I am unaware of "the reason why."

After Mr. Kay went on, and the horseman arrived, I endeavoured to circumvent the *chai-jen*, for I had seen them, with much mystery, slip a letter into his hand, after which he tried to get in front of me. I jumped out of the chair, and set up my tripod on the narrow road, which he could not pass, and after a long attempt at photography, baffled by the wind, told him and the others to keep behind, and not to leave me. The horseman kept trying to get in front, but as the path is very narrow and mostly on the edge of a precipice, I managed to dodge him the whole way by holding a large umbrella first on one side, and then on the other!

A few miles from Tsa-ku-lao the *chai-jen* managed to pass me, and began to run towards a short cut, impassable for a chair. I sent Be-dien to stop them, and to my surprise he out-ran them, collared them, and held them till I came up, when I again ordered them behind the chair. Mr. Kay met me, saying that neither inn nor house would give us shelter, and that he had found that it would not do to make any inquiries about the farther route. However, we were received by a very good inn, where the people were very civil, and where I had an excellent room, with a large window looking on a mountain across a clean grassed space.

Soon after I got in difficulties began. Two officials arrived, and politely told many lies. They said that there were no places to sleep in on the road, that the snow on the passes was forty feet deep, and crevassed, that the tribes were fighting each other, that they were robbers and would rob us of everything, and repeated the Li-fan lie that the route is not in China, and

VILLAGE OF WEI-GUA.

that they could give us no protection. I produced a Chinese official map, and showed them that it lay far within the limits of the jurisdiction of the Viceroy of SZE CHUAN, and, being fairly roused, and determined to proceed at least to Somo, I produced my passport, telling them that it had been granted on an application made by the English Tsung-li *yamen* at the request of the Grand Secretary (the Premier), and that they could see for themselves that it gave me rank, and enjoined on all mandarins not only not to put any obstructions in my way, but that, whether by land or water, every aid was to be given.

I further said that if this obstruction were persisted in, I should write a formal statement of the case to the British Consul at Chungking, to be officially forwarded by him to the highest quarter, and that they knew what that would mean. On the top of all, I produced the Viceroy's letter to the *kuans* of Pi Hsien and Kuan Hsien. They were quite quenched, and said they would repeat this to the mandarin, and I should have his decision in an hour, and they bowed themselves out, taking my passport with them.

They returned in half an hour, saying that the mandarin would send soldiers with us to the limits of his jurisdiction, but that then we should be among the "Barbarians." This seemed like a victory, yet I felt by no means sure that we should not be prevented from hiring mules, and be delayed into returning. The next day a last effort was made to hinder my westward progress, with a vehemence which was almost piteous, entreaties being resorted to when threats failed, but all collapsed on a special clause in my passport being again pointed out to these secretaries.

Tsa-ku-lao, the outpost of Chinese officialism, is gloriously situated at an altitude of about 6210 feet,* where the mountains swing apart, and at an abrupt bend of the river there are branching valleys and unencumbered heights. There are poplars and willows about the little town of 400 people, and a great Man-tze tower

---

* A pony had rolled on my hypsometer, and I spent much of the day at Li-fan in constructing another with the aid of a tinsmith. It was but a rude construction, but as it made the height of Li-fan come to within ten feet of that given by Captain Gill, I venture to present the altitudes of Tsa-ku-lao and a few other places as approximations to the truth.

looks through them like an English church tower. One long, clean, narrow, and highly picturesque street, lined with shops vending gaily-coloured articles of Chinese manufacture, cuts the town in twain. Above it, where the houses are piled on ledges of rock in most artistic disorder, is a very large lama-serai, with a very quaint pagoda temple on a height above it. The houses in the street are two and three storeys high, with carved projecting upper rooms, and peaked roofs with deep eaves, from which depend carved wooden drops.

At the western exit the road drops abruptly down through the picturesque gateway seen in the illustration by 500 feet of steep stone steps to a bridge, which connects the trading with the official town. In the latter the *yamen* is an interesting-looking building in pure Tibetan style, with a Man-tze tower sixty feet high adjoining it. The population of Tsa-ku-lao is a mixed one, and many of the children show an agreeable departure from the Chinese physiognomy. The red woollen habits and peaked hats of the red lamas, the varied costumes of the tribesmen who were in the town for purposes of trade, and the thirteen differing styles of hats, the most interesting being made of a species of lichen, were a very pleasant variety.

An agreeable variety it was, too, that the curiosity of the people for the first time in a journey of two years was tempered by politeness, for each batch of would-be sightseers, always women, sent in advance to know if I would receive them, and they always left after visits of conventional length, remarking that I must be tired !

We spent two nights there, because the coolies heard such tales of the road that they engaged mules to carry their loads, the bamboo over the shoulder with its dependent burdens being unsuited to the exigencies of mountain climbing, and the mules were away on the mountain. During that day, in which I visited the quaint official town, and photographed the gateway amidst a crowd of red and yellow lamas, tribesmen, and Chinese, who fell back when they were asked to do so, I received about fifty visitors, so that their supposition that I was tired was not far wrong. Of this number three, obviously of the Tsa-ku-lao "upper ten," had been in Kuan Hsien, a few had been in Wei-chou, but none had been in Matang or Somo, and they said that

STREET OF TSA-KU-LAO.

there were very high mountains to cross, and that the snow was very deep. No woman could get to Somo they thought. They had never seen a foreign woman, and Russia was the only foreign country that they knew by name.

Fine, strong, comely, healthy-looking women they were, with pleasant faces and manners, and minds narrowed to the interests of Tsa-ku-lao. Some of their children were really pretty. The court of the inn was always full of red and yellow lamas, mule-teers in picturesque jackets and leggings, and hats like *sombreros*, Tibetans in sheep - skins, and tribesmen whose physiognomies showed a complete departure from the Mongolian type. It was altogether exciting, and the keen air was bracing and stimulating. The picturesqueness of the little outpost town in the brilliant sunshine and under the clear blue sky was fascinating, and the friendliness and politeness of the people created a new atmosphere which it was pleasant to breathe. The sun went down in glory and colour, there was a perfect blaze of stars in the purple sky, and the mercury fell to the freezing-point. The " Beyond " beckoned, and though I knew that the travelling arrangements must break down from their inherent unsuitability, I fell asleep prepared to follow.

CHAPTER XXXII.

THE "BEYOND"

THE scanty hoar frost lay on the ground at five the next morning, and the sun rose, as he had set, in glory, flooding the canyons with a deluge of amber light. There was a considerable delay before starting, and to the last I feared the wiles of Chinese officialism: but it turned out to be only the usual difficulty of the first start with animals—weighing and adjusting loads and the like. There were three strong, whole-backed, pleasant-faced red mules, and the muleteer was equally pleasant, a Man-tze lama, quite a young man, who proffered hospitality for the next few days among his friends, inns having ceased. The thought of "poisoned feasts" never crossed my mind!

The greater part of the bizarre population of the quaint mountain town escorted us to the gateway. Superb weather favoured our departure. The heat of the sun melted the snows towards midday, adding volume to the thunderous roll of the Siao Ho, above which, after descending to the water's edge, the bridle-track is carried over spurs and abutments of limestone. There is a decided change in the scenery. The river, no longer closely hemmed in by the walls of a tremendous cleft, is broader and stiller; there are shingle banks and stretches of cultivated land, and it cuts its way through the ranges instead of following their clefts. A marked feature of this stretch of the Siao Ho is the extraordinarily abrupt bends which it makes, and that at most of these a sugar-loaf peak, forest-clothed below, and naked rock above, rises sheer from the river-bed, possibly to a height of from 2000 to 3000 feet. Great openings allow of inspiring views of high, conical, snow-clothed peaks, heavily timbered below the snow; one group, called by the Chinese "The Throne of Snow," consisting of a great central peak, with nine others of irregular altitudes surrounding it.

A SUGAR-LOAF MOUNTAIN, SIAO HO.

Climbing the Peh-teo-shan spur by a long series of rocky, broken zigzags, cut on its side through a hazel wood, and reaching an altitude of about 9270 feet in advance of my men, I felt the joy of a "born traveller" as I watched the mules with their picturesque Man-tze muleteer, the eleven men no longer staggering under burdens, but jumping, laughing, and singing, some of them with leaves of an artemisia stuffed into their nostrils to prevent the bleeding from the nose which had troubled them since leaving Weichou, the two soldiers in their rags, and myself the worst ragamuffin of all. There were many such Elysian moments in this grand "Beyond."

The summit is thick with poles, some of them bearing flags inscribed in Tibetan characters in honour of the Spirit of the Pass, and there is a large cairn, to which my men added their quota of stones. Fifteen or sixteen hundred feet below, the river looks like a green silk cord interwoven with silver. There is a sharp bend and a widening, from which rise two conical peaks, forest-clothed and craggy. Lateral gorges run up from the river, walled in by high, frowning, forest-covered mountains, breaking into grey, bare peaks, and crags gleaming in the sunshine. To the north-west the canyon broadens. Mountains rise above mountains, forest-covered, except where their bare ribs and buttresses stand harshly out above the greenery, and above them great, sunlit, white clouds were massed, emphasising the blue gloom of pines; and far higher, raised by an atmospheric effect to an altitude which no mountains of this earth attain to, in the full sunshine of a glorious day, were three illuminated snow-peaks, whose height from the green and silver river, judged by the eye alone, might have been 30,000 feet! They might have been "the mountains of the land which is very far off," for the lighted clouds below separated them from all other earthly things, and their dazzling summits are unprofaned by the foot of man.

The descent to the river is long and steep, the sun was hot; the aridity and sparse vegetation of most of the road up to the pass are exchanged for comparative humidity and a wealth of small trees and flowers; the river broadens considerably, breaks up into several channels with shingle beds and tamarisk, till it and the canyon narrow together at a point where a wooden cantilever bridge is thrown across at a considerable height from two natural piers of rock.

There, a very dirty Chinese village faces a Man-tze village of towers and lofty stone houses. After a halt, during which I sat on a stone in the broiling sunshine, much vexed by dust and the aggressiveness of both children and pigs, we crossed the bridge and shortly entered Paradise. There the hideous black pig was left behind! The river divides, each branch having its

REVOLVING PRAYER CYLINDERS.

own glorious gorge apparently closed by snow-peaks. There are small fair lawns, on which nature has clumped maples and ilex; great forest trees coming down to the water, wreathed with roses and clematis; and a showy, detached temple—the only one in the region—the household or lama-serai house of worship from thenceforth taking the place of the public temple. At its entrance are two large prayer-wheels.

Close beside it the road passes under an arch, on each side of which are six prayer-cylinders, which revolve on being brushed by the hand; and near it is a much-decorated "prayer-wheel," in a house of its own, bestriding a stream, worked by water power, the lama in attendance receiving so much for each revolution. This cylinder is twelve feet high, with a diameter of four feet, and is said to contain 100,000 repetitions of the well-known Buddhist mantra "*Om mani padme hun*." Beyond, there was a man engaged in making idols after the fashion described by Isaiah the prophet, a bridge of uncertain equipoise over one branch of the river, and a little farther on the main branch of the Siao Ho, descending from the north-west, is joined by streams of nearly equal volume from the south and north, coming down through canyons full of superb vegetation, above which rise, mostly in groups, peaks of unsullied snow.

The vegetation above this meeting of the waters, and with few breaks for many a day's journey, is tropical in its luxuriance. The canyon is very narrow. On the left the mountains descend to the torrent in a series of precipices. On the right a space, averaging twenty yards in width, gives room for the bridle-path and for a perfect glory of vegetation. From this rise forest-clothed precipices and peaks as on the other side. Between them thunders the small river, narrower, but much fuller in volume than below, green with a greenness I have never seen before or since, and white with foam like unto driven snow, booming downwards with a fall of over sixty feet to the mile, its brilliant waters hasting to lose themselves 2000 miles away in the turbid Yellow Sea.

Mosses and ferns soften the outlines of boulders and drape the trunks of fallen trees. Tree-stems are nearly hidden by ferns and orchids, only one of the latter, a purple and brown spotted *dendrobium*, being in blossom. A free-flowering, four-leaved white clematis, arching the road with its snowy clusters, looped the trees together, and a white daphne filled the air with its heavy fragrance. Large white peonies gleamed in shady places. White and yellow jasmine and yellow roses entwined the trunks of trees, and the flowering shrubs, mostly evergreens, were innumerable. Ivies and varieties of the *ampelopsis* lent their familiar grace. Spring is fantastic there, and in freaks of colouring mimics the glories of autumn. Maples flaunt in crimson and purple, in pale green outlined in rose-red ; the early fronds of the abundant hare's-foot fern crimson the ground ; there were scarlet, auburn, and "old gold" trees ; and as to greens, there were the dark greens and blue-greens of seven varieties of pines, the shining dark greens of ilex, holly, and yew, the dull, dark greens of cedar and juniper, the shining light greens of birch and beech and many another deciduous tree, and the almost translucent pea-green of the feathery maple—red, purple, and green, alike admitting the vivid sunshine as through stained glass.

The ground, concealed by mosses in every shade of green, gold, and auburn, by a crimson-cupped lichen, and the crimson of the young hare's-foot fern, was starred with white and blue anemones, white and blue violets, yellow violas, primulas and lilies, white and yellow arabis, and patches of dwarf blue irises, while our own lily of the valley looked out modestly from under the shrubs, and I recognised lovingly among the beautiful exotic ferns our own oak and beech—our *filix mas* and *Osmunda Regalis*, at no disadvantage among their foreign associates.

So exquisitely beautiful were the details that it was hard to look up and take in the broader features of the unrivalled witchery of the scene, where the foliage of the maple lighted up the gloom of holly and ilex with its spring pinks and reds, where a species of poplar rivalled it in lemon-yellow, where the delicate foliage of the golden-barked birch was copper-red, and every shade approaching green was represented, from the glaucous blue of the balsam pine, and the dark blue-green of its coniferous brethren, to the pale *aqua marine* of deciduous trees in clumps among the pine woods below the snow.

For, piled above the forest-clothed cliffs and precipices which wall in the river, and blocking up every lateral opening, were countless peaks or splintered ranges, cleaving the blue sky with an absolute purity of whiteness. High up, in extraordinary situations of dubious access, are Man-tze villages, much like fortifications, their suggestion of human interests and flutter of prayer-flags giving life to the scene. The river sympathetically adapts itself to its changed surroundings. Its colouring is a vividly transparent green, to which it would be an injustice to liken an emerald. Over it drooped, from the contorted stems of trees covered with ferns, orchids, and trailers, long sprays of red and white climbing roses, and within the cool toss of its spray, film ferns and the beautiful *trichomanes radicans* flourished in boundless profusion, almost transparent under the trickling sunshine. The

BRIDLE TRACK BY THE SIAO-HO.

river descends in falls and cataracts, in sheets and glints of foam, under bending trees, and trails of clematis and roses, pausing now and then in deep green pools in whose mirrors roses, clematis, and snow-peaks meet; but, its thunder-music, echoing from gorge and precipice, pauses never.

For hours we passed through this fairyland of beauty and fragant and aromatic odours, which it is a luxury to recall; then the odorous air grew damp, the peaks flushed, the shadows on the road deepened, the canyon "swung open to the light," through the great gates of the west the sunset glory rolled in waves of red and gold, and on a low hill bearing the name of Chuang-fang, and a few traces of cultivation, there was a lonely Man-tze dwelling.

The host, as a relation of our intelligent and courteous young lama, made us very welcome, but his wife, a very handsome woman, on coming in from the hill with a load of wood, looked astonished to find a foreign woman and twelve men in possession of her house. That dwelling, typical of the poorer class of Man-tze houses, has two roofs, each reached by a deeply-notched tree-trunk, exactly like those used by the Ainu of Yezo. It has an entrance-chamber common to men, mules, and fowls, an inner room or kitchen, scarcely lighted, with a fire and "cooking range" on a raised hearth in the centre, from which the stinging wood smoke finds various outlets in the absence of a chimney. In the better houses, a hole in the roof into which a hollow log is cemented offers a more conventional exit. The fire is the place of family gathering and eating, and man, wife, and children eat together. These people possess the term "hearth-side." The woman, though not young, was really beautiful, after a European type, and had very fine teeth, but her rich complexion was somewhat dulled by dirt; for these people, like the Tibetans, wash only "once a year"—*i.e.*, very rarely.

With much politeness I was escorted by her up the notched timbers to a first and then to a second roof, which, being the threshing-floor, was swept very clean. At one end there was a high frame for drying maize upon, and at the other a roof sup-ported on four posts, but with an open front, which is the granary. This space was divided by a great grain tray and my curtains, I occupying one end, and the servants, soldiers, and some of the coolies the other. The sharp frosty air was elixir, and the red-gold of sunset and the rose-pink of sunrise on the snows which enclose the valley made a night in the open air very delightful.

It was too windy for a candle, and my food, prepared in the smoke below, was eaten by the light of a nearly full moon in the delicious temperature of 30°. To be away from crowds, rowdy-ism, unmannerly curiosity, rice-fields, stenches—from slavery to custom, enforced by brutality, and from many a hateful thing—to be out of China proper, to be among mountains whose myriad snow-peaks glitter above the blue gloom of pine-filled depths, to breathe the rarer air of 8000 feet, to be free, and in a new uplifted

VIEW FROM CHUANG FANG.

world of semi-independent tribes, and fairly embarked on a journey, with Chinese officialism apparently successfully defied, and last, but not least, the complete disappearance of rheumatism from which I had suffered long and badly, made up an aggregate of good things. Anything might happen afterwards, but for that one day I had breathed the air of freedom, and had obtained memories of beauty such as would be a lifelong possession.

Sleep came in the middle of these pleasant thoughts, and I did not wake till sunrise, with its waves of rosy light rolling up the glen, began to take the chill off the frosty air. There was additional snow on the mountains, and the higher pine woods were hoary.

These hospitable people do not receive payment for their hospitality, nor do they use money—silver being only appreciated for its use in jewellery, and copper not at all. The roof, or the guest-room, if there be one, is at the disposal of any reputable wayfarer; but he must bring his own food, for they have none to sell. Fortunately, I had needles, scissors, and reels of silk with me, which there and elsewhere made the hearts of many women glad.

The scenery the following day was, if possible, more glorious than before, and the intense blue and singular *glitter* of the sky. The road still pursues the right bank of the river, the canyon is slightly wider, and for most of the way seven snow-peaks are an apparent barrier. In the forests near the road there were nine species of pines and firs, and eight of maples, besides cedars, yew, juniper, elm, holly, oak, poplar, alder, ilex, plane, birch, pear, etc. A white honeysuckle added its exquisite fragrance to the aggregate of sweet odours. The woods were full of white peonies, sky-blue larkspur and aconite abounded, and yellow roses revelled in the sunshine on the smooth lawns by the river on which the Tibetan traders camp in the season. My coolies, having no loads to carry, were much excited about the peonies. The roots are an expensive drug in China, and the men said they could get a dollar each for them, so there was a great raid upon them.

After crossing and recrossing the Siao Ho on wooden cantilever bridges, we reached Ku-erh-kio, a purely Man-tze village, piled on an abrupt height where a lateral gorge with a tributary stream debouches on the river. This was the last point to which I was attended by Chinese officialism, and the first where there was a representative of the *Tu-tze* of Somo, the territory on which I then entered. There the soldiers from Tsa-ku-lao, jolly young fellows, delivered the mandarin's letter to the *T'ou-jen*, or headman, and returned.

A Man-tze official escort was at once provided, consisting not of armed and stalwart tribesmen, but of two handsome laughing girls, full of fun, who plied the distaff as they enlivened our way to Chu-ti. Nor was this fascinating escort a sham. Before starting each of the girls put on an extra petticoat. If molestation had been seriously threatened, after protesting and calling on all present to witness the deed, they would have taken off the additional garments, laying them solemnly (if such laughing maidens could be solemn) on the ground, there to remain till the outrage had been either atoned for or forgiven, the nearest man in authority being bound to punish the offender. Mr. Baker mentions a nearly similar custom among the Lolos of Yunnan. *En route* we passed several Man-tze villages, and at each the people came out and

CASTLE AT CHU-TI.

brought us wooden cups of cold water, indulging in much fun with my men, as several of them could speak Chinese. Nearly all the women were handsome. They were loaded with silver and coral ornaments, plied the distaff as they joked, and were free, not to say bold, in their manners.

Chu-ti consists of two Chinese houses, a bridge, and a large Man-tze house, with some cultivation round it, on the left bank.

There we were hospitably received by our muleteer's elder brother, though when he saw the army of coolies he said he did not keep an inn, and begged that nothing might be stolen. I was at once provided with a clean room on the roof, "the best guest-room," with a window-frame, in which was fixed a prayer-cylinder revolved by the wind, which whirred monotonously by day and night. Many of the people from a village on a height, which is only accessible by a series of ladders, spent the evening on the roof with much frolic and merriment. Of the foreigner they have

HEADMAN'S HOUSE, CHU-TI.

no notion, and as I was clothed in brown wool they thought I was a Man-tze of another tribe. Some of the women were beautiful, and even in middle life they retain their good looks and fine complexions.

This stone dwelling, arranged, as are all the better class of houses, apparently for defence, has three floors, reached by steep, wide step ladders inside. Cattle, mules, fodder, and agricultural implements occupy the first, the family the second, and on two sides of its flat roof, which is protected by a parapet two feet high, are the family temple and guest-rooms. This flat roof, which is also the threshing-floor, is the general gathering-place, the wrestling-ground, and the place where the women weave their woollen stuffs on their portable looms. On the roofs of the temple and guest-rooms, which are partially covered for use as granaries, the men play cards, chess, and a game resembling *Go*. On all roofs, even of the poorest class, there is at the eastern corner a small

ALTAR OF INCENSE ON MAN-TZE ROOF.

clay furnace with a chimney, called "the altar of incense." In this at sunrise, the householder, man or woman, looking eastwards, burns a bundle of the green twigs and foliage of the yew, of which two species are accessible. This may possibly be a relic of a nature-worship anterior to Buddhism. All well-to-do persons have a temple on the roof, as in Tibet, with images of the Buddhist triad against the wall, an altar with the usual emblems and offerings, a drum, gong, horn, and cymbals, and as many of the insignia of Buddhism as their means allow them to obtain. The householder can act as priest, and every man or woman can present his or her invocations and offerings, and in Man-tze homes there is scarcely an hour from sunrise to sunset in which the dull beat of the drum and "*Om mani padme hun*," reiterated in a high-pitched monotone, are not heard.

Snow-peaks above, and snow-peaks below, reddened gloriously at sunset and sunrise, the view from the roof was absolutely entrancing, and the first half of the next day's march was even lovelier than before. At one of the finest parts some tribesmen were building a bridge, and from it some muleteers, chiefly girls, with much laughter, were driving some unladen mules through a very rough ford. Many of the men crossed, and asked for help in building their bridge, which I would willingly have given them, but that my silver was far behind on the mules. They became very obstreperous, and one put his arm across the road to prevent my chair from passing. We got on, however, for a few *li*, and waited there for the mules. *Chai-jen* had ceased at Chu-ti.

On the same morning the bearer who had always been unfit for his work, and who denied himself food in order to get opium, for he was an immoderate smoker, collapsed and fell by the roadside with a fluttering pulse and a temperature of 104°. I put him in my chair and walked as long as I could, and then he had to lie down, and I paid a man to stay with him. An hour passed, and no mules; and I was so afraid that the men at the bridge had robbed the muleteer, for they were a rough lot, that Mr. Kay went back. Another hour passed, and then the mules came all right, and the sick man, moaning and breathless, supported along by Mr. Kay, who is both strong and kind.

Higher up the canyon opens out into a valley of divided streams and shingle beds, either absolutely bare, or covered with the *Hippophæ rhamnoides* and a species of tamarisk. The receding mountain-sides are gashed by summer torrents, and the vegetation is scanty. There was a broad camping-ground among trees, and the coolies made fires and cooked their rice, a number of Somo women from a village on a height—nearly all of them handsome, in the Meg Merrilees style—looking timidly on.

The sick coolie was laid under a tree, and I put a wet pocket-handkerchief on his burning brow. Then latent Chinese brutality came out, showing that on these men the popular cult of Kwan-yin, who is really a lovable creation, had no influence. There were five baggage coolies carrying nothing, and when I proposed that they should divide one mule's load among them and let him ride, they refused. He had been working, sleeping, and eating

SICK UNTO DEATH.

with them for twelve days, yet when I asked if they were going to leave him there to die, they laughed and said, "Let him die; he's of no use." Though the water he craved for was only a few yards off they did not care to give him any. When appealed to again they said, "No matter; Mr. Kay can look after him.' And so he did, for when I had walked till I was exhausted that he might be carried, Mr. Kay nearly carried him for the remaining distance, and slept without his wadded gown in the keen frosty air, that he might have it. The others laughed at his sufferings, at me for bathing his head, and, above all, at my walking to let him ride.

After we crossed to the right bank of the dwindling river a great number of Man-tze men and women met us, and escorted us up steep stony slopes to the large village of Mia-ko, with its many-storeyed houses, a feudal castle, and a lama-serai like an ugly factory, with 150 monks. We were received in the house

LAMA-SERAI AND HEADMAN'S HOUSE, MIA-KO.

of the *T'ou-jen*, the father of our muleteer, who has a patriarchal household of married sons and daughters with their children, and farms on a large scale.

The great treeless hillsides are well suited for agriculture, and though the altitude of Mia-ko is nearly 10,000 feet, wheat ripens in July. At that height, the Dover's powder with which I dosed the coolie failed to produce its usual effect, nor was any other sudorific more successful. In the dry, rarefied air my umbrella split to pieces, shoes and other things cracked, screws fell out of my camera (one of Ross's best), my air-cushion collapsed, a horn cup went to pieces spontaneously, and celluloid films became electric, and emitted sparks when they were separated!

The soil of the mountain-sides is sandy, and potatoes, which have only lately been introduced, do well. There are many large villages scattered over these slopes, and the people have great flocks of brown goats and sheep, the latter a flop-eared, hornless, long-woolled breed, with fat tails weighing from three to six pounds. They also breed herds of *dzo*, a very valuable hybrid between the yak and cow, and capable of carrying 80 lbs. more than either the horse or mule. The male is used for ploughing, and the female gives more milk than any other of the bovine race. Of it they make butter, which, as in Tibet, appears to become more valuable with years, and which is largely used, along with salt and soda, in the preparation of tea, which is churned in a wooden churn till it is as thick as chocolate. From the hair of the *dzo* and yak the Man-tze make a heavy felt, used for cloaks in cold and wet weather, and for boots. As far as the divide, snow only lies for a few days at a time, and judging from description, the frost is never severe.

Man-tze cultivation is rough and untidy as compared with Chinese. Indigenous flowers muster strong among the crops, and irrigation is not understood. Drought is the great enemy of agriculture, and the crops in this great valley were in urgent need of rain.

In the late afternoon of our arrival Mia-ko was deserted, and a long procession of men and women, each carrying a heavy burden on the back, wound slowly up the hill to a point where it was reinforced by a similarly burdened company from our village, and the united force was met by a large body of lamas, including our muleteer, in their sacred vestments, chanting Sanskrit prayers. The burdens under which the people bent were the Buddhist scriptures, which, when complete, weigh 90 lbs., and to carry this sacred load is regarded as an acceptable act of merit. Before the prolonged service ceased there was "a sound of abundance of rain," the wind rose, the rain fell in torrents, and the soil of disintegrated granite imbibed it as if it never could be satisfied.

Mia-ko is a noisy and cheerful village, and after Tibetan fashion, very religious. There is a low building on the hillside containing a number of revolving prayer-cylinders, ranged round it at a convenient height. Round this in the early morning the villagers go in procession turning the cylinders. With brief intervals all day long in my host's family temple one or another repeated prayers in a monotone. On the roofs are tall poles, each surmounted by a trident, or a ball and crescent, or bearing narrow, white prayer-flags of their own length. Groups of poles with similar flags are erected in memory of the dead, whose ashes often rest below in small cinerary urns. It is "merit" to make clay medallions, with which portions of these ashes are frequently mixed, and to stamp them with Sakyamuni's image, or to finger the clay deftly into models of *chod-tens*.

We had any number of these jovial, laughing, frolicking people on the roof at night, men and women on terms of equality. They drink *chang*, a turbid barley beer, as the Tibetans do. We were detained for some days at Mia-ko. The mules were lost on the hills, and stories were current of two mighty robbers, who were making a part of the road dangerous, and were keeping the country in alarm, and who successfully evaded capture, though a reward of sixty taels (£9) was offered for them dead or alive. The *T'ou-jen* was averse to our taking that route without an escort of ten spearmen, who had to be hunted up in the adjacent villages, and this took time. Into the midst of this detention dropped down a Chinese mounted officer, "a captain of a thousand," with baggage and a mounted servant, and orders to keep me in view, whether to help or hinder I knew not, but strongly suspected the latter. Both carried swords and revolvers. This was most unwelcome, and the delicious sense of freedom in which I had been revelling vanished.

The food question caused me uneasiness, though I was always assured that "everything was to be got at Somo." The people would not sell us so much as an egg, and the detention made such a serious inroad on our supplies that I reduced myself to tea, and damper baked in the ashes and pullable into long strings.

After the first curiosity, which was never vivid, was over the people pursued their usual avocations on the roof, reciting prayers, weaving, and making clothes in the day, and wrestling, fencing, and making a general frolic in the evening. Mia-ko is a very well-to-do village, and both sexes were loaded with silver jewellery.

The Siao Ho makes a preposterous turn above it, and we took a short cut over the pass of Shi-Tze-Ping (10,917 ft.), rejoining the river twenty *li* later. Heavy snow fell on the mountains during the previous night, whitening many of the lower hills, turning their shaggy pines into grey beards, and lying heavily on the superb coniferæ of the pass, where red and white rhododendrons and a large pink azalea were blooming profusely. At that elevation the mercury was 26° at 6 a.m., and as a strong north-east wind was blowing the cold was intense. At noon one thousand feet lower the mercury stood at 72°.

From the summit there is a distant view of a long, snowy range, with a blunt and wavy outline, on which five peaks, evidently of great altitude, are superimposed. Hitherto the mountains, at least near the river, though dazzling white, had not reached the majesty of eternal snow, but on this range the guide said "it was always as it was then," that the peaks were known as "the Snowy Mountains," that the highest was called Tang-pa (sacred), and that the Great Gold River (Chin-shuan) rose among them. It was a pass of that range that we afterwards crossed, and it is probably identical with that mass of peaks and ranges marked on the Chinese maps as "Snowy Mountains," running on the whole in a south-western direction between 29° and 32° N. lat. and 101° to 103° E. long. It is only possible to make a rough guess at the altitude of those peaks. In May Captain Gill found the snow line three degrees to the eastward of this point at an altitude of 13,000 feet, and estimates the limit of perpetual snow as at least 14,000 or 15,000 feet, which, allowing for the steady rise in temperature of every degree west in that latitude, would give a snow line of 15,000 or 16,000 feet above the sea level. Taking the snow line in the middle of May as a rough basis for calculation, I should estimate the height of the timber line at nearly 13,000 feet, and the height of Tang-pa as 5000 feet above that.

A steep descent of three hours through an entrancing forest brought us back to the Small River, there a full-watered, clear, green torrent, about forty yards wide, compressed within a narrow canyon, tumbling among gigantic boulders in glorious cataracts, forest trees of larger size than had been seen before bending over it, festooned with climbing roses and white and sulphur-yellow clematis, while all lovely things which revel in moisture and warmth—ferns, mosses, selaginellas, and the exquisite *Trichomanes radicans*—flourished along the margin of its turbulent waters. It was grander and far more beautiful than ever, and absolutely solitary.

One feature of the vegetation west of Mia-ko is a pea-green trailer (possibly *Lycopodium Sieboldi*) with pendants eight and ten feet long, which takes possession of coniferous trees, dooming them to a slow death, but replacing their dark needles by a tint which in masses is very attractive. These trailers are used by the Man-tze for hats, much worn by lamas. Some of the red trunks of the conifers, branchless for fifty feet and more, measure from nineteen to twenty-one feet in circumference six feet from the ground, hollies seven feet, yew eleven, twelve, and even thirteen feet, and an umbrageous and very beautiful species of poplar from seventeen to twenty feet. Occasionally the canyon widens for a short distance, and there are smooth lawns, on which nature has planted artistically clumps of pines and birches, the latter, instead of white, with " old gold " bark, which they shed in spring. Almost the only flowers at that altitude were a dandelion, with a stalk an inch long, and a lovely, short-stalked, mauve primula, which in places carpeted the ground. Some of the canyon walls, rising forest-covered tier above tier, cannot be less than 3000 feet in height, and at that season their luxurious covering embraced every tint of yellow, red, and green.

After fully forty *li* the canyon broadens into a luxuriant valley, apparently closed at its western end by one of the great Tsu-ku-shan ranges, and the yak and *dzo* fed in large numbers on the rich pasturages which confer prosperity on the Man-tze hamlet of Hang-Kia. This should have been the halting-place, and though there was apparently no accommodation the Chinese officer intended it to be so. High words were exchanged between him and Mr. Kay, who went back to hurry up the mules, while I sat in the roadway watching the snow which was then obviously falling on the pass, while it was raining below. To make a long story short, owing to unpropitious circumstances not worth narrating, and a loss of heads and tempers, my better judgment was overborne, and against it, and in spite of my showing that Matang could not be reached anyhow in less than eight hours, the order to start on this most foolhardy venture was given, and we left Hong-Kia at 3.15, the coolies and I not having fed since eleven, and reached the foot of the pass at 6.30. A few *li* higher this branch of the Min rises as a vigorous spring under a rock.

We ascended to a considerable height by a number of well-engineered zigzags, meeting Man-tze travellers armed with lances and short swords, and journeying in companies from dread of the notorious banditti. Some of my men had armed themselves with lances. As darkness came on the coolies were scared, and begged me to have the mule bells taken off. They started at every rock, and asked me to have my revolver ready! Their noses had been bleeding at intervals for some days, and at the altitude we had attained the hemorrhage in some cases was profuse, and was accompanied by vertigo, vomiting, and some bleeding from the mouth, and the baggage coolie who had most unwillingly taken the sick bearer's place was at best a malcontent. When we got into mist, and broken shale, and snow, after stumbling and falling one after the other, they set the chair down, very reasonably I thought, and no arguments of Mr. Kay's addressed either to mind or body induced them to carry it another step.

It was then 8.30 and very dark. A snowstorm came on, dense and blinding, with a strong wind. I was dragged rather than helped along, by two men who themselves frequently fell, for we were on a steep slope, and the snow was drifting heavily. The guide constantly disappeared in the darkness. Be-dien, who was helping me, staggered and eventually fell, nearly fainting—he said for want of food, but it was "Pass Poison," and he was revived by brandy. The men were groaning and falling in all directions, calling on their gods and making expensive vows, which were paid afterwards by burning cheap incense sticks, fear of the bandits having given way to fear for their lives—yet they had to be prevented from lying down in the snow to die.

Several times I sank in drifts up to my throat, my soaked clothes froze on me, the snow deepened, whirled, drifted, stung like pin points. But the awfulness of that lonely mountain-side cannot be conveyed in words: the ghastly light which came on, the swirling, blinding snow-clouds, the benumbing cold, the moans all round, for with others, as with myself, every breath was a moan, and the certainty that if the wind continued to rise we should

ELEPHANTIASIS.

all perish, for we were on the windward slope of the mountain. After three hours of this work, the moon, nearly at her full, rose, and revealed dimly through the driving snow-mist, the round, ghastly crest of the pass, which we reached and crossed soon after midnight, when the snow ceased. I have fought through severe blizzards in the Zagros and Kurdistan mountains, but on a good horse and by daylight, and not weakened by a blow. On the whole this was my worst experience of the kind.

An hour's descent in deep snow on the edge of a precipice, from below which came up the boom of tumbling water, brought us to a forest of the straightest and tallest pines I ever saw, glorious in the moonlight, and vocal with the crash of waters. Then I became aware that Mr. Kay, who is very absent, and the guide had disappeared. The coolies declined to carry me, and wanted to leave me there, and it was only after half an hour's altercation between them and my servant, during which my wet clothing froze hard, that they took up the chair. The forest tracks were baffling, and the true track was soon lost in the snow, not to be recovered till at 2 a.m. we emerged on great, grassy slopes, and an hour later, my party, exhausted, shivering, starving, drenched to the skin, and all alike in frozen clothes, found a wretched shelter in the one room of a Chinese hovel with a sloping floor on the bleak, boulder-strewn hillside on which the forlorn village of Matang huddles at an altitude of over 9000 feet.

The Pass of Tsu-ku-shan, which we had crossed, is the great water-parting of that region, the waters on the east seeking the Min, and those on the west the Chin-shuan or Ta-kin Ho, both meeting in the Yangtze at Sui-fu, this glorious region being geographically in the Yangtze Valley. When I recrossed the pass, a very easy one, one hundred and twenty-four snow-peaks were visible from its summit. Its approximate altitude is 11,717 feet. It is a long, bare, unimpressive mountain wall.

The hovel allowed of my pitching my camp-bed behind a cambric screen, but there was no room for the wretched coolies to lie down, so they sat round a big, log fire, cooked their food, talked, and thawed and dried their frozen clothes. I thawed mine by rolling myself up in a blanket, but unlike them was unable to eat, or even drink tea for many hours, and lay there much stupefied until noon the next day, when we moved to what posed as an inn, a wooden stable ninety feet long, with stalls seven feet high for human beings on both sides, in one of which I was thankful to find solitude, a fire-bowl, and necessary rest for some days.

The inn-keeper and his wife, Kansuh Mohammedans, were kind. They gave me an egg, and took me to sit by their big, log fire in their horrible kitchen, on the ground that we were worshippers of the same God. The fire was welcome, for there were heavy snowstorms, and on one day the mercury fell to 29°. Whether in storm or sunshine Matang, "out of the season," is a ghastly place, a forlorn, unpicturesque village of low, stone cabins, with rough, timber roofs kept down by stones. It is bisected by a torrent of the same name, a feeder of the Chin-shuan, rising on the pass above. There is a very good cantilever bridge. Its population of 170 includes a number of Chinese who have married Man-tze women. Snow lies there for six weeks.

In July and August the scene changes, and Matang becomes a great international market. The inn is crammed with men and horses. Yaks and Tibetan tents cover the grassy slopes, Chinese dig on the mountains for medicinal roots, which are also brought from Tibet in incredible quantities, and are bought up chiefly by Mussulman traders, broken silver, the only currency accepted, passes freely from hand to hand, goods are bartered, and for two months the Chinese and Tibetan traders do a very large trade in cattle, horses, wool, hides, sheep, musk, rhubarb, hartshorn, and much besides.

Some of the Matang Man-tze women were extremely beautiful, after the Madonna type. I twice secured a giggling group in front of my camera, but I no sooner put my head under the focussing cloth than there was a stampede, and partly in fun and partly in fear the laughing beauties fled like hares, so the reader must take their good looks on trust.

Outside a hole near the roof, which served for a window, a genuine Tibetan dog was chained, as big as a small bear, with rusty brown wool, four inches long, and a superb face. His voice was more like a roar than a bark, and his growl was portentous. These dogs are very savage, and his owner said that he could kill a man by tearing open his throat, which is their method of attack. I got his owner, on whom he fawned foolishly, to measure him, and from the root of his bushy tail to his nose he measured four

CHINESE OFFICER AND SPEARMEN, MIA-KO.

feet three inches. He kept a malignant watch on me, and I could not move in my room without provoking his fierce, resonant growl. These dogs shed their fur in the summer.

After a detention, owing to snowstorms and difficulties of transport, which made a further serious inroad on the stores, we left Matang early in May, accompanied by the Chinese officer, who had wisely remained in the Hang-Kia valley, and ten stalwart spearmen from Mia-ko. I started on foot, accompanied by this escort, leaving the others to follow at their leisure; some of the baggage being on *yaks*, which having been as usual lost on the mountain, caused considerable delay. When our force was mustered it numbered twenty-five men. Two of the wild-looking tribesmen rode big yaks, monstrous in their winter coats; all were armed with lances, and short, broad-bladed swords, and a few carried long and much-decorated matchlock guns. Of course we saw nothing of the bandits, and when we had passed their beat the spearmen quietly disappeared, apparently ignorant of their right to *baksheesh*. The ghastly, grinning head of a third bandit hung in a cage in the village.

The road, which is a singularly good one, crosses the Matang river by a good bridge, near its junction with a vigorous stream descending from the north-west, and then follows their united course in a southerly direction for forty *li* to their union with the Rong-kia.

The scenery on that day's journey is the loveliest of all. This Matang river whose birth we had seen on that awful night on the pass, raging in cataracts, and great drifts of sunlit foam, and slowing at times into deep green eddies, makes the most abrupt and extraordinary turns, each one giving a new and glorious view. The canyon reminds me of some of the finest parts of the Rocky Mountains, but the abundance of deciduous trees and flowering shrubs, trailers, and plants, and the aquamarine " Fairy Moss," hanging in five-feet streamers from the trees, give it an added beauty. Everything was draped in auburn, gold, and green. The pine forests are vast and magnificent, and through the purple madder of the leafless birches their terra cotta stems gleamed. The dark, ever-green ilex and holly contrasted with the brilliant spring green of the elæagnus, hawthorn and willow; primulas, narcissus, and *scillae* starred the mossy ground, maiden-hair and other ferns flourished on the tree trunks, trailers of a pure white clematis hung over the path, mosses and film ferns draped every harsh angle and every boulder out of sight, and gorgeous butter-flies and dragonflies glanced like "living flashes of light." Every vista at every turn above the dark pine forests is blocked by peaks, then in the dazzling purity of new-fallen snow.

Our course consisted of constant climbing over high steep spurs, which descend on the right bank of the river. There is one

VILLAGE OF RONG-KIA.

fine waterfall. In the afternoon a long and very severe ascent terminated at the top of a spur crowned by a village and a lama-serai above the confluence of four valleys and three streams, the Matang from the north, the Rong-kia from the east, and the Kin-ta from the south. These unite to form a broadish, full-watered river, very green, to which the Man-tze give the name, which I reproduce as Rong-kia, or "Silver Water," but which the Chinese along its banks call the Ta Chin or Ta Kin-Shuan (Great Gold River), which, if they are correct, is the upper portion of the Tatu or Tung River.

CANYON OF THE RONG-KIA.

After an ascent, and a halt at an extraordinary village of square towers, from each of which a single, brown wood room projected at the top, another steep ascent took us to the top of a spur, from which we looked down on the valley of the Rong-kia below its junction with the other streams, there a broad, swift river, free from rapids and cataracts, and bridged in several places.

The first view of it sleeping in the soft sunshine of a May noon was one never to be forgotten. The valley is fully one mile wide, and nine miles long, and snow peaks apparently close its western extremity. All along the "Silver Water" there were wheat fields in the vivid green of spring; above were alpine lawns over which were sprinkled clumps of pine and birch, gradually thickening into forests, which clothed the skirts of mountains, snow-crested, and broken up here and there into pinnacles of naked rock. At short distances all down the valley are villages with towers and lama-serais on heights—villages among the fair meadows by the bright, swift river, with houses mounted on the tops of high towers, which they overhang, their windows from thirty to fifty feet from the ground—and stretching half-way across, a lofty, rocky spur, then violet against a sky of gold, developed into a massive, double-towered castle, the residence of the *Tu-tze* of Somo, the lord of this fair land. In the late afternoon it looked like that enchanted region—

> " Where falls not rain or hail or any snow,
>   Or ever wind blows loudly."

The warm spring sunshine blessed it, the river flashed through it in light, the sunset glory rolled down it in waves of gold, its beauty left nothing to be longed for.

The Chinese officer rode up saying, " There is now no more fright," (who was frightened I know not), and passed on to Somo, saying he was " going to make things smooth for us," but, as I think, carrying orders to the *Tu-tze* from headquarters to bar my further progress. The castle gained rather than lost, as we approached it by a bridge over a lateral stream near a fine specimen of an ancient tower, about eighty feet high. It occupies the greater part of a rocky spur or bluff, rising 390 feet above the river. A few mean houses cluster on ledges outside the castle wall.

The spur is so precipitous on the east side as to look inaccessible, and is climbed with difficulty by anyone carrying a burden. At the foot of the rock there is a covered, open gateway, with revolving prayer-cylinders on both sides. The ascent is by steep zigzags, which we were an hour in climbing. The climb brought us into the centre of a Man-tze crowd, and of a cluster of

SQUARE TOWER, SOMO.

mean and dirty Chinese hovels, huddling against the rocks, in which we were told that the *Tu-tze* "had provided lodgings." This was an insult. The lodging for the whole party was one small, dark, dirty room, filled with stinging wood-smoke from a fire on the floor.

I sat outside in the midst of a crowd which had no rudeness in it, while Mr. Kay, with sanguine impetuosity, went up "to see

DISTANT VIEW OF SOMO.

the *Tu-tze*" and claim fitting accommodation. He found both doors barred in his face, and two savage dogs on guard. Nothing daunted, he climbed a wall and dropped down into the outer court of the castle, and in the lion's den itself obtained a good room for me on the roof of a Man-tze house within the great gate, high and breezy, and looking both up and down the valley.

"Passports and recommendations are no use here," replied the haughty ruler to a request for furtherance, and when a polite message was sent asking at what hour Mr. Kay might have the honour of an audience, the proposal was rudely negatived. The Chinese officer, who was entertained in the castle, had obviously done his work efficiently.

Though Somo was nominally the goal of my journey, and I was more than satisfied to have reached it, I cherished a project of getting down to Ta-tien-lu (Darchendo) from Cho-ko-ki by a route only traversed previously, so far as Europeans are concerned, by Mr. von Rosthorn—involving a journey of twenty-one days. On making careful inquiries, however, I learned that a tribal war had broken out, and that the bridges over the Rong-kia had been destroyed, a fact which Mr. Kay verified by a long day's journey of investigation. This involved two long days' march on foot over a difficult mountain, and I was much prostrated, and also suffering from my heart from the severities of the night on the Tsu-ku-shan pass. In addition, the coolies, the bane of the journey, were breaking down from fever one after another, the stock of rice was nearly exhausted, and an order had been given that supplies and transport southwards were to be refused. I was too weak to make a resolute attempt to overcome these difficulties, which probably, as in the case of other would-be Tibetan travellers, were insurmountable, and every reader who is also a traveller will understand the indescribable reluctance with which I abandoned the Ta-tien-lu project. After it was given up, the *Tu-tze* sent a present of salted goat, flour, honey, and ancient and hairy butter, which enabled me to give my men a good meal.

The days passed quickly in learning as much as I was able to extract from the Man-tze elders regarding their customs. The *Tu-tze* sent several times for my watch, and eventually sent a very big man with his own, a valuable old thing, with many rubies, which had stopped for years, and asked me to repair it! It was a very simple derangement, and I put it right, when he sent again asking if I could mend pianos, as he had one with broken strings! Then he sent for Be-dien, to whom he put many questions, and fascinated him. He told him that he could only protect us for forty *li* farther, when we should reach the territory of the Cho-ko-ki, a hostile tribe. At one time Be-dien came into my room with an avalanche of "savages" behind him, one handsome young woman clinging to his arm, to his great annoyance, for he was a "very proper young man," or posed as such.

Throughout the Man-tze villages the absence of any painfully disfiguring diseases, goitre excepted, had been remarkable. In Somo, however, there was one Chinese with a tumour on his jaw as large as a supplementary head, and another suffering from severe elephantiasis, of which distressing malady an illustration is given on page 427.

CHAPTER XXXIII.

THE MAN-TZE, I-REN, OR SHAN-SHANG-REN

IN this chapter I put together such information as I was able to gather about the people to whom I have introduced my readers. I only give such statements as at least four persons were agreed upon, and confine my remarks to the four tribes of the Somo territory, estimated at 20,000 souls, which are unified under the rule of the *Tu-tze* of Somo.* The designation Man-tze or I-ren, which is simply Chinese for "barbarian," is perforce accepted by these people from their conquerors. When questioned, however, they divided themselves into Somo, Cho-ko-ki, He-shui, and other tribes, and on being pressed further, they declared themselves Shan-shang-ren, or mountain people. They said that they had heard that in ancient times their fathers came from the setting sun, but they knew of no days when they and the Chinese did not live among each other. The tribal spirit is completely extinct among those tribes, who have accepted one ruler; but the Somo people hate the Sifans to the north-east and the Cho-ko-ki men to the south.

The head of one or more tribes is called a *Tu-tze*. He is appointed directly by the Emperor of China, and for life; but a long-established custom has made the office practically hereditary, and in the absence of a son a daughter may be invested with it, as in the case of Somo, where in recent years, and for a considerable time, a woman sustained the dignity of the position. It is only in a case of flagrant misconduct that the Emperor would exercise his right of removing a Man-tze ruler. The *Tu-tze* has absolute authority over his own tribesmen, including the power of life and death. The land is his, and the cultivator pays a tax of thirty per cent. of the produce, out of which the ruler con-

* In this case a *Tu-tze* is a tribal chief, recognised as such by the Chinese Government.

tributes the annual tribute to China. The tribesmen are free to build anywhere without paying ground rent. Chinese under Man-tze rule have to obtain permission to build, are not allowed to make charcoal, and pay ground rent. In the case of the murder of a Chinese, the murderer may be taken into Chinese territory to be tried by a mandarin, but actually he is rarely caught, and the crime is usually compromised by the payment of blood-money by his relations. If a Chinese wishes for a

A MAN-TZE VILLAGE.

Man-tze wife he must pay the *Tu-tze* thirty taels (about £4 10s.) for the privilege.

Under the *Tu-tze*, and appointed by him, are village headmen or *T'ou-jen*, who usually hold office for life, and are frequently succeeded by their sons. They collect taxes, settle disputes, try small cases by tribal law, and meet the *Tu-tze* once a month at his castle to report what has been going on, and to discuss what has to be done, and once a year to choose the tribal representatives who are to carry the tribute to Peking. China has done wisely in fringing her borders with quasi-independent tribes whose autonomy is guaranteed by custom, and whose love of the freedom they enjoy would convert men and women into a respectable guerilla force in case of invasion.

The religion of the Man-tze is Buddhism or Lamaism of the Tibetan type. Except in Western Tibet I have never seen a country in which the externals of religion are so prominent. Nearly all the larger villages have lama-serais on heights above them ; rock Buddhas, and Buddhas in relief on tablets are numerous; poles twenty feet long, with narrow prayer-flags of nearly the same length, flutter from every house-roof; groups of prayer-flags in memory of the dead are planted beside every village ; a temple is prominent on the roof of every well-to-do house ; and prayer-cylinders turned by water-power or hand are common near the roads. Daily offerings are made in all dwellings ; every second son is a lama ; the formula, " *Om mani padme hun*," is everywhere heard ; the presence of lamas is essential for every act in the round of social and agricultural life ; and literature is wholly confined to Buddhist classics. Prayer-wheels revolved by the wind are common in windows ; and when people grow old, and dread such an unfortunate re-birth as a reappearance in the body of a horse, dog, or mule, a prayer-cylinder, revolved by swinging it, is constantly in their hands.

The lamas receive large sums for prayers, and for such ceremonies, in cases of illness, as the reading of the Buddhist scriptures in the house, accompanied by chanting, blowing of great horns, and beating of drums. A death is their chief harvest, for, besides the fees paid to them for the services customary at death and burial, any good clothing which the deceased person has possessed is their perquisite, as well as the silver and coral head-ornaments of the women, which go to help to pay the expense of opening a passage for the soul into the other world. If the family wishes for these it must redeem them from the lamas. According to the wealth of the deceased is the time occupied in this arrangement. It may be three months or longer. In the case of the poor three days is the limit. A re-birth into the Western Heaven is reserved for lamas.

They dispose of bodies after death by rules of their own. In a few very rare cases, where the horoscope of life, death, and the future is favourable, the corpse is buried " earth to earth " without coffin or clothing. Throwing the body into the river, or exposing it on a mountain-side to the fowls of the air, are also practised at their bidding; but cremation, accompanied by the recitation or chanting of the scriptures, is the usual method. Afterwards the ashes are placed in an earthen pot, which is buried, a prayer-flag or flags being erected on the spot. On the days of death and burial, as well as during the interval, there is weeping, but it is not prolonged or repeated, and ancestral worship is not practised. The clothing of a corpse is always removed immediately after death, and it remains naked until it is disposed of by one of these three methods.

Among the noteworthy characteristics of Man-tze life is the position of women. They are not only on an equality with men, but receive considerable attention from them, and they share their interests and amusements everywhere. Men and women are always seen together. A woman can be anything, from a muleteer to a *Tu-tze*. Social intercourse between the sexes is absolutely unfettered. Boys and girls, youths and maidens, mix freely. Love-matches are the rule, and I saw many a handsome young face illuminated by a genuine love-light. The young people choose each other, and either of them may take the initiative. When they have settled the preliminaries, the prospective bridegroom sends a friend to the prospective bride's parents, informing them of his wish to marry their daughter. Consent follows almost as a matter of course, the bridegroom sends a present of a bottle of wine to the bride's father, and the courtship is fully recognised.

Next the lamas are consulted, to ascertain if the horoscopes of the youth and maiden fit. If not, the difficulty may be overcome by prolonged, vicarious chanting of the scriptures, and liberal fees. The lamas also choose an auspicious day for the marriage. The marriage ceremony consists in the bride and groom publicly joining hands, drinking wine from a double-spouted bowl, and accepting each other as husband and wife, after which there is a three days' feast in the bride's home. She and her husband then go to their own house, and there is another three days' feast. There are no contracts of marriages for a limited period, as in Western Tibet. Whether the choice has been for good or ill, it is for life, divorce being permissible only in the case of childlessness, and the contract can only be cancelled by the *Tu-tze*. It would

SOMO CASTLE (BACK VIEW).

not be correct to infer from this that the Man-tze are a moral people. Their standard of morality is low, and the lives of the lamas have no tendency to raise it. Plurality of wives is an appendage of the position of the *Tu-tze*, and is, I think, the practice of rich men, but monogamy is the rule, and polyandry, though said to be the custom of the Sifans to the north, does not exist. No presents, except the bottle of wine previously mentioned, are made by the bridegroom to the bride's father ; but her parents, according to their wealth, endow her with cattle, horses, and fields, the last of which, to use our own phraseology, are "settled upon her." A widow does not wear mourning, and is at liberty to make a second marriage. On the death of her husband, unless she remarries, she assumes complete control over his property, and at her death it is divided among the sons, who frequently, however, agree to live together and keep it intact. If there is trouble concerning property, the *T'ou-jen* usually settles the matter, and if he fails to make an amicable arrangement, it is referred to the *Tu-tze*, whose decision is final.

Good health is the patrimony of these people. There are a few lepers among them, and rheumatism is rather prevalent, but few maladies are known, and measles appears to be the only epidemic which affects children. I did not see one case of skin disease or deformity on the whole journey. They spoke of old age and what they call "exhaustion" as the usual causes of death. Goitre, however, is frightfully prevalent in many of the villages. In some, *seventy-five per cent.* of the people are afflicted by it, and it often begins in childhood. It does not seem to affect either the health or spirits. The people think that it comes from drinking snow-water, but it was specially common in some villages where the sources of the water supply are far below the snow. The lamas virtually prohibit all medicines not supplied by themselves, and it is only those Man-tze who have been corrupted by contact with Chinese civilisation who use any others. They incline to fatalism regarding illness, relying chiefly on amulets, charms, and religious ceremonies. "If a man is very ill he dies," they say, "and when he is not he gets better."

They have a language of their own, but it is written in Tibetan characters, and all notices and inscriptions on tablets and signposts are in the same. In the villages nearest to China proper, many of the people speak Chinese as well as Man-tze, and the *T'ou-jen* in all villages, but further west very few even of the elders understand it, and the *Tu-tze* himself is unable to read the Chinese characters.

The products of the Somo territory, so far as export goes, are *nil.* The magnificent timber is useless, as the rivers, from their abrupt bends and enormous boulders, in addition to their turbulence, do not admit of its being rafted down. So far as I could learn, there are no golden sands to tempt even the Chinese adventurer. Sulphur and nitrate of soda abound. The Man-tze grow wheat, barley, oats, maize, buckwheat, lentils, and a little hemp. In good years they raise enough for their requirements, but more frequently have to barter their cattle and coarse woollen cloth for food. Their transactions consist of barter only, silver being known solely for its use in personal adornment. There is no prospect for Manchester in that quarter. Pieces of red and green cloth for the decoration of boots are brought from Russia through Tibet, and these and the brass buttons on clothing are their only imports. Both sexes dress in woollen materials, spun, woven, and dyed by themselves, and sewn with their own hempen fibre.

Their views are narrow, their ideas conservative, and their knowledge barely elementary. England is not a name to conjure with in their valleys. They know of China and Tibet, and have heard of Russia, but never of Britain. Of the war and the *wojen* they were in complete ignorance. I found them hospitable, friendly, and polite, not extravagant in their curiosity, of easy morals, full of frolic and merriment, singularly affectionate to each other, taking this life easily and enjoying it, and trusting the next to the lamas.

In the regrettable absence of photographs it is difficult to give any idea of their appearance. There are few under-sized men. They were a little taller than my coolies, who were the average height of Chinese. They are deep chested, as becomes mountaineers ; their build is robust, and their muscular limbs betoken strength and agility. Their walk is firm and springy, and in wrestling and putting the stone—favourite amusements—the display of muscle is superb. The tribes vary as to good looks, though not as to physique, especially the women, some of whom have the oval face, regular features, and beauty of the brunette type which we associate with the Madonna, while others are plain, and resemble Neapolitans. The complexion is as dark as that of the natives of Southern Europe, but a trifle redder; the large dark eyes and eyebrows are level, the nose straight, the mouth usually small and thin-lipped, the foreheads high but not broad, and the ears large, and rendered unshapely by the weight of the earrings. The cheek-bones are not in any way remarkable. The characteristic of the Man-tze face is that it is European in feature and expression, and recalls the Latin races. Owing to a sort of timidity, and to the fashion of hair-dressing of both sexes, it was unfortunately impossible to procure any head measurements.

The men shave their heads and wear cloth or fur caps, but some of the elders said that in former days all the hair was gathered above the forehead, and twisted into a horn wrapped up in a cotton cloth, and often " as long as a hand." A similar style is mentioned by Mr. Baber as characteristic of the Lolos of Yunnan. The *coiffure* of the women is most elaborate. The front hair is divided, and plaited into from twenty to thirty plaits not wider than a watchguard, and waxed down each side, considerably reducing the forehead. The back hair, with considerable additions, is divided and brought round the head in two massive coils over a folded blue cloth, which hangs a little over the brow. Strings of large coral beads are twisted round these coils, but at the sides only. The circumstances of a family are indicated by the size and beauty of the coral and silver of the headgear. Jewellery is largely worn by both sexes—earrings, necklets, chains of alternate coral and silver filigree beads, and bracelets set with large turquoise or red coral. The ornaments are often really beautiful and of fine workmanship. When I asked by whom they were made, they invariably replied, " By the Arabs."

The women wear woollen under-garments, short loose jackets with wide sleeves, and skirts reaching a few inches below the knees, as closely pleated as the kilt of a Highlander, sometimes exchanged indoors for a long, loose robe. Dark brown and madder-red predominate in apparel. They wear long leather boots, upon which are stitched up the front and sides decorative strips of scarlet and bright green cloth.

The men wear a gabardine and girdle of native cloth, frequently dark red, over a woollen under-garment; leggings, and decorated leather boots or hempen shoes. The cloth or fur cap is often varied by the SZE CHUAN turban. They have no soap, and never wash. A corpse is designated as the "twice washed." In the rarefied air of the high altitudes which they inhabit, some of the most unpleasant consequences of dirt are not apparent. I must add that every house in which I received hospitality was tolerably clean, and that I was not aware of the presence of vermin.

There is a singular absence of bird-life in the Somo territory. A species of francolin and ringed pheasants were seen, the blue jay, the crow, and the ubiquitous magpie. The men said that there are boars, small bears, and deer in the forests, but that the trade in hartshorn and horns in the velvet for Chinese medicines had driven the latter back, "they knew not where." There are also at least two species of monkeys, both large, and one with thick, long hair. The brown bear, the yellow wolf, the musk deer, the badger, and the otter are also found, but the Man-tze are not scientific in their descriptions.

The *Tu-tze's* rule only extends for forty *li* to the south of Somo. He is proud of his practically independent position, and when my servant interpreter presented my Chinese passport, and a letter from the Viceroy of SZE CHUAN, he said that he did not read Chinese, and that passports and Viceroys' letters were of no use there!

Somo castle, on its eastern side, is a most striking building, built into the rock of the spur on which it stands. It has a number of windows with decorative stone mullions, the lowest over twenty feet from the ground. Its many roofs are planted thick with prayer-flags, and projecting rooms and balconies of brown wood, with lattice-work fronts, hang from its eastern side over the precipice. The castle yard is spacious and singularly clean; the entrance is handsome, and is faced by a huge dragon, boldly and skilfully painted on a plastered stone screen. Poles with crowns from which yaks' tails depend, and the trident, as in Western Tibet, surmount the entrance. The whole is most substantially built of stone, and I looked in vain for any trace of decay or disrepair. The altitude is about 7518 feet.

ENTRANCE AND JUDGMENT-SEAT.
SOMO CASTLE.

CHAPTER XXXIV.

FROM SOMO TO CHENGTU FU

THE refusal to sell food produced uncomfortable consequences. I bestowed my personal stores on the coolies, and being left with only a little chocolate, a few squares of soup, and a pound of flour, was often compelled to still the gnawings of hunger with peppermint lozenges; and what was worse, the men were on half-rations. Just before we left, the *Tu-tze* sent a welcome present of half a bag of flour, and as supplies were not refused on the way down the worst was over. At Matang we were detained two days by a severe snowstorm, which glorified the pine forests on the skirts of the Tsu-ku-shan Pass, which was bare, pale, and uninteresting, and took four hours to cross even in the sunny daylight. From the summit about one hundred and twenty snow-peaks were visible, some rising sharply into a very blue sky, others with snow-clouds swirling round their ghastly crests—all clothed to a considerable altitude with interminable forests of pine, hoary with new-fallen snow, under the bright May sunshine.

Passing through fine herds of yaks and *dzo*, and by villages and detached houses, we sought shelter in vain. The people were all " on the mountain," and every house was locked. After a severe day of twelve hours we were directed off the road, through groves of fine Spanish chestnut trees, to an alp, on which is a small Man-tze house inhabited by one Chinese, where I slept on the roof, next two rows of humming prayer-cylinders, and in the morning had a glorious view of snow-peaks and forests.

It is scarcely credible, but the downward journey was more gloriously beautiful than the upward. The peacock green, transparent Siao Ho, with its snow-white cataracts, thundered through the trees in a yet goodlier volume, between cliffs on which the great, red-stemmed pines are securely moored, flashed past velvet lawns starred with blue and white anemones, and pink and white peonies; past clumps of daphne giving forth hot-house odours in the warm sunshine, under the living scarlet of maples, through the blue gloom of colossal pines, every one of its innumerable bends giving a fresh view. The ice was half an inch thick every

HESHUI HUNTER, AND NOTCHED TIMBERS.

morning on the heights. We lodged in headmen's houses, where at one halt I had a guest-room twenty-four feet long.

At Ku-erh-Kio, where after a journey of eleven hours I sat nearly two hours among dogs, pigs, and fowls, waiting for the people to return from the mountain and give us shelter, I slept for the last time on a roof under the stars, the earliest sight in the morning being glories of light and shade, of forest, cataract, and mountain, and the sparkle of a peak reddening in the sunrise, like unto the Matterhorn, which the people called Ja-ra (king of mountains).*

A thirteen hours' journey thence took us to Tsa-ku-lao. We were benighted and lost the road, and were "set in darkness in slippery places," on lofty precipice ledges, and the coolies were

A HESHUI FAMILY, KU-ERH-KIO.

so exhausted that they fell several times on the five hundred rocky steps by which the quaint border post is reached. Chinese inns, officialism, passport delays, and *chai-jen* had to be endured again from that point. At Li-fan Ting the officials sent presents

* Captain Gill met with a mountain of the same name on his Tibetan journey, so it would appear that Ja-ra is a Tibetan name. I could not unearth any Chinese name for the mountain.

when we arrived, saying that they hoped I would forget their conduct, "and turn the light of my countenance once more upon them to vivify them."

The heat became severe as we descended; the vegetation near the road was limited to grey, dusty tufts of a species of artemisia; the winds were tremendous, and the Man-tze villages at great heights, where the people have neither horses, cattle, nor sheep, and depend solely on the rainfall for their crops, were praying for rain, and below Weichou, finding Sakyamuni deaf to their entreaties, were turning to the forgotten gods of the rivers and the hills.

From an ethnological point of view the Man-tze deserve some attention, as they differ considerably from the Sifan to the north and the Lolos to the south. In religion and many customs they approach closely to the people of Western Tibet, while in appearance they differ most remarkably from both Tibetans and Chinese. Their handsome, oval faces; richly-coloured complexions; thick, straight eyebrows; large, level eyes, sometimes dark grey; broad, upright foreheads; moderate cheek bones; definite, though rather broad noses; thin lips, somewhat pointed chins, and white, regular teeth are far removed from any Mongolian characteristics, and it is impossible not to believe that these tribes are an offshoot of the Aryan race.

During the week's descent from Tsa-ku-lao, the winds were fearful, almost carrying my chair and bearers over a precipice, and the country was scorched, and afflicted with driving dust-storms. The heat had then set in for the summer, the Yangtze was rising, and I was suffering so severely from the effects of the night's "death-struggle" on the Tsu-ku-shan pass, that I was anxious to reach a cooler climate, so only rested a few days among the hospitalities of Kuan, and then crossed the Chengtu plain for the fourth time, doing forty miles in one day with the mercury at 93° in the shade, and arrived at Chengtu among very unpleasant demonstrations of hostility from the military students who were "up" for examination. Four of the examiners had passed me on the road, or rather I respectfully cleared off it to make way for, and contemplate them. Besides four bearers to each chair, a number of soldiers were roped on, and behind them came a train of twenty-six laden mules, and twenty-five laden porters, carrying, I doubt not, much besides personal baggage. I was told that these officials make large investments in SZE CHUAN drugs, on which, as they pay no taxes *en route*, and the unfortunate local officials bear the cost of carriage, they make great profits in Peking. Numbers of attendants are essential to dignity in the East. A mandarin going to pay a visit in his much-decorated chair is usually preceded and accompanied by an irregular procession of lictors with staves or whips, boys carrying red boards bearing the official's name and style, and *chai-jen* in red-tasselled official hats. The lictors push the people to one side, the boys shout, and the bearers yell. When the great man leaves his own *yamen* three small mortars are fired, and if he visits an official, the same noisy process is repeated.

Forced labour for relays of bearers, porters, and horses for the lesser dignitaries, is called for, and on a much-travelled main road this is a heavy burden on the villagers.

A DRAGON BRIDGE.

CHAPTER XXXV.

DOWNWARD BOUND

THE deep blue, glittering skies of the high altitudes were exchanged for the mist and dulness which have conferred upon SZE CHUAN the name of "The Cloudy Province," and with the lower levels came mosquitoes and sandflies, and a day shade temperature from 82° to 93°, very little alleviated during the night. I left the capital in a small flat-bottomed *wupan*, drawing four inches of water, with a mat roof, and without doors at either end. Yet my cambric curtains were never lifted, and when I desired it I enjoyed complete privacy at the expense of partial asphyxiation. At that time, May 20, the water was so low that no bigger boat could make the passage, and numbers of small, trim house-boats were aground.

It was the start for a river journey of over 2000 miles, the first thousand of which were accomplished in this and similar boats. It was a delightful and most propitious journey, and introduced me to many new beauties and interests, and to a most attractive area of prosperity. For the first day the boatmen made more use of their shoulders than of their oars, lifting and shoving the boat, which "drave heavily" over sand and shingle and often bumped like a cart over paving-stones. For the ascent of the river breast-poles are used by men wading. From Chengtu Fu to Sui Fu the Min is called by the Chinese the Fu, from the three Fu cities on its banks. After Be-dien had shopped for three hours, the result being only a small bag of charcoal, we dropped down under a fine stone bridge of several arches to a pretty village with a pagoda, "a sweet place," where we tied up for the night.

We joined the main river, not then more than eighty yards wide, below the An-shun Bridge, an antiquated or ancient structure, and spent a long day in battling with the shallows, and with the peasant farmers, who had thrown many dams of shingle in

VILLAGE ON THE MIN

bamboo cages across the river to keep up the water for their own purposes. They refused to open a passage, though this only involved kicking away the stones between the cages and replacing them, demanded 2000 cash as toll, and seized on my boat, and with shod poles and much vociferation barred my progress several times. Native boats were passing through for thirty cash, and some thirty or forty at each dam were smashing against each other for the first turn. Eventually, when forty men got hold of my little *wupan* and tried to intimidate me, I asked them to show me the paper authorising them to demand this toll, on which they collapsed.

In a number of places there are rows of gigantic water-wheels, four or five together, from thirty to forty-five feet in diameter, by which all the adjacent country is bountifully irrigated. The sleepy hum of these huge wheels, the richness of the cultivation, and the fresh greens of the woodland, in which prosperous-looking villages basked drowsily in the summer sunshine, were all charming. But at times the water was so shallow that the boatmen had to precede my boat to work a channel for her, one of them leading her by the nose, and another pushing her from behind. This dragging, and the quarrels with the peasants about getting through their dams, occupied the first day.

The next day was a rapture. A river locally called the Nan joins the Min at Chiang Ku, about sixteen miles below Chengtu, and after the junction water was abundant. Su-ma-tou, a busy place in lat. 30° 28′ (Baber), is the limit of navigation for large junks. At Peng-shan Hsien the river widens out after the union of all its perplexing subdivisions. Below Meichow, a large and busy place, the country breaks up into picturesque hills of no great height, divided by fertile valleys, through one of which I caught a momentary and only glimpse of the unrivalled majesty of Mount Omi.

Villages embowered in fruit trees, of which the illustration is an average specimen, adorn the banks of the bright river. Young wheat, mustard and beans in blossom, with mulberry trees between the fields, clumps of bamboo, and pines cresting every knoll and hill, made up a lovely picture—a vision of peace, plenty, and prosperity. Indeed, the whole river journey from Chengtu to Chungking consists of a series of beautiful pictures, combined with varied and prosperous industries. It is a lovely part of China, and the white, timbered houses, the vividly red soil, and red sandstone rock, the dark, light, blue, and yellow greens, and the fascination of the smooth, fine lawns, which ofttimes slope down to the sparkling water, have a very special charm. The "Cloudy Province" failed to keep up its character, and if the sky was not very blue, the sunshine was brilliant. The gardenia, often a large shrub, grows profusely on the slopes, and it and the bean gave forth delicious odours. Strings of gardenia blossoms hang up at that season in all houses, every coolie sticks them into his hair, and even the beggars find a place for them among their rags. For a farthing a large basket of them can be bought.

I reached Chia-ling Fu (1070 ft.), where I remained for some days, in eighty hours from Chengtu Fu, including stoppages—the estimated distance being about 130 miles. The approach to this attractive and important city from the north is extremely pretty, indeed beautiful. The country is very hilly, and great, red sandstone bluffs, heavily wooded, with pagodas and temples, and much carving in rock recesses, with scarlet azaleas and gardenia blossoming everywhere, would have riveted my admiration to the left bank had it not been for the overhanging red sandstone cliff and the picturesque houses of the city on the right.

Chia-ling Fu, said to be a city of 50,000 souls, is a place of great importance commercially, as three large rivers—the Min, Ya, and Tatu—there form a junction, and for a brief space the river is like a lake. It is perhaps the greatest centre of sericulture and silk weaving in the province, and is also the eastern boundary of the white wax trade. Its white silks are remarkable for lustre and purity of colour. It is a rich city, and the capital of one of the most fertile and lovely regions on earth. It is besides the starting-point for most of the pilgrims to the temples of Omi-Shan and "The Glory of Buddha." The city wall is of bright red sandstone, which is finished with a few courses of hard grey brick. The south gate was rigidly closed against the Fire God. A handsome, uphill, residential street, green and peaceful, leads to the west gate, and on this the China Inland Mission and Canadian Methodists have their mission houses. In

WEST GATE, CHIA-LING FU.

Mr. Endacott's garden are some specimens of the singular rock-dwellings so fully described by Mr. Baber in his papers on Western China. Chia-ling trades in opium and timber as well as in silk and white wax. Silk and umbrella shops are conspicuous. Every view from every point is beautiful.

On the face of the cliff on the opposite side of the river is a figure in the rock, cut in very high relief, of Maitreya Buddha—truly colossal, being 380 feet in height. The nose is said to be nearly five feet long, and the head from thirty to forty feet high. Grass is allowed to grow on the head, eyebrows, upper lip, and ears, to represent hair. This figure is unfortunately partly concealed by the redundant vegetation which surrounds it. It is an interesting specimen of the religious art of about a thousand years ago.

Leaving the hospitalities of Chia-ling Fu for a boat journey of 345 miles, in a rather old and leaky little *wu-pan*, which, however, did 133 miles in seventeen hours, I halted several times on the way down to visit some of the remarkable rock dwellings in the cliffs which in many places border the river. They are difficult of access, and besides tearing my stout Chinese dress to pieces, I was considerably bruised and scratched. I took ropes, grippers, and three men with me.[*]

At a farmhouse where I landed near the hamlet of Sing-an, there was a sandstone coffer, seven feet long, used as a cistern. The farmer sold me two axe-heads of a hard, green stone, with a dull polish, which he found along with the coffer while digging a buffalo pond. To the finest of the excavated dwellings that I visited, I descended, holding on to trees and rock projections with hands and grippers, having a rope round my waist. There was a rock platform in front of the opening, not now accessible from below. The face of the rock has been smoothed, and eaves which project two feet have been left. The four times recessed doorway is five feet six inches high. At one side of this, as well as in the doorways of the interior, there are the remains of stone pivots on which doors could be hung. Above the doorway is

---

[*] A careful and deeply interesting account of these excavations is given by Mr. Baber in "A Journey of Exploration in Western SZE CHUAN." See *Supplementary Papers*, vol. i., *Royal Geographical Society*.

a frieze as represented in the illustration, eighteen inches in depth, which is repeated over a stone altar against the wall, and again over several recesses, one of which is obviously for a fire, and has a stone shelf above it, and the others were probably beds. Two doorways give access to rooms, one of which is 14 ft. by 12 ft., the other 12 ft. by 12 ft. The former is nine feet high, and has a

FRIEZE IN ROCK DWELLING, MIN RIVER.

rounded roof, below which runs a deep and well-executed frieze carved with arabesques and curious human figures, the faces of which are certainly not Mongolian. In this room are both an altar and a stone tank. The outer room measures 30 ft. by 20 ft. 7 in., and is 7 ft. 4 in. in height. In another of these singular excavations there are settees cut into the rock with a fashionable slope of seat and back, the front being actually rounded for comfort! In a third there is a curious arrangement resembling pigeon-holes for letters, and the frieze resembles one figured in Mr. Baber's paper, and is what is known in heraldry as the "disc-and-label" pattern—a severe but very decorative ornament. In that dwelling there was an arrangement of holes in the doorway, showing that the doors had worked on some description of hinge. Over the lintel of one doorway is the trident symbol. All the dwellings (five) visited by me, had what must have been small sleeping chambers attached to them. The walls of the principal rooms show traces of careful finish, and some have obviously been panelled. There is a stately seemliness about these abodes, which implies that those who constructed and occupied them must have made some advances in civilisation, and have valued privacy.

BOAT ON THE MIN.

The finest of them, so far as is known, both in size and decoration, is a day's journey only from Sui Fu, but the access involves severe climbing, and risks which I did not care to run. These dwellings occur in great numbers, from a point not far above Chia-ling Fu down nearly to Luchow, a distance of fully 220 miles.

The ever broadening and deepening Min, passing through lovely and prosperous country, took me rapidly to Sui Fu (Hsu-chow Fu), a large city with a population, according to the officials, of 150,000. It is well situated on a high, much wooded, rocky promontory between the Min or Fu and the Chin-sha, which there unite to form the great river known by us as the Yangtze, where a temple-crowned point of rock dominates the busy city. On the opposite side of the Min are fantastic mountains with singular rock forms, on one of which is the highly picturesque temple of " The Sleeping Buddha," approached by steps cut in the rock below.

The Chin-sha is only navigable to Ping-shan, a difficult forty miles above Sui Fu. It was rising fast, and its great volume of turbid water contrasted with the clear bright Min, which kept apart from it in disgust for some time. Sui Fu is a very lively place, being the great entrepôt of the large transit trade between SZE CHUAN and Northern YUNNAN, as well as a considerable distributing point.

Above Ping-shan, the Lolo, tribes which the Chinese have failed to subdue in two thousand years, keep the country in a state of chronic insecurity, fatal to trade routes. Besides the transit trade, Sui Fu does a large business in silk, opium, and sugar. The "residential suburbs" are full of good houses in wooded grounds, extending far up the Min, their owners reaching their pleasure boats by handsome flights of stone stairs. The American Baptists and the China Inland Mission do mission work in Sui Fu, and a great deal of valuable medical work. Though "child-eating," as elsewhere, is believed in, the people are not unfriendly, and the mandarin was specially courteous. Before I left he sent round to all the street officers to say that, whether I went through the city in a chair or on foot, there was to be no crowding, following, or staring. He sent four *chai-jen* in official hats to walk in front of me, and go down with me to

Luchow, and two petty officers to see that no one interfered with my camera, on pain of being beaten.

I left Sui Fu on the glorious evening of a blazing day, and once more, after a land journey in SZE CHUAN of nearly 1200 miles, was afloat on the Yangtze—there a deep, broad river, flowing among low, pretty hills, much wooded, and terraced for cultivation.

TOWN ON THE YANGTZE.

SUBURB OF SUI FU.

TSIANG NGAN HSIEN, WITH ENTRANCE TO ROCK DWELLING.

CHAPTER XXXVI.

LUCHOW TO CHUNG-KING FU

ON the brilliant afternoon of the day after leaving Sui Fu, I reached Luchow, an important trading city, with a reputed population of 130,000. It is prettily situated on rising ground at the confluence of the Yangtze and To rivers. The latter drains a considerable area, and by it and its connections cargo boats of about fifteen tons can reach the Great River from Kuan Hsien. Luchow appears to be a quiet, fairly well governed, busy city. One great industry is the making of umbrellas, and it has a large trade in sugar and other SZE CHUAN products. According to its own officials, eighty per cent. of its male population are opium smokers. In good shops, there and elsewhere, opium pipes are supplied gratuitously to customers in back rooms, just as cups of tea are in Japan. The China Inland Mission has both men's and women's work in Luchow, and I was hospitably received in the mission-house. The mercury was 93°, and no one could sleep at night.

The people are not what would be called hostile, yet they curse Mr. James, the missionary, in the streets, and believe that all the five are "child-eaters," and that the comeliness of the ladies is preserved by the use of children's brains! This scandalous accusation is current everywhere in SZE CHUAN. Even at quiet Chia-ling Fu, when two beggar boys were brought into the compound to be photographed, the report spread like wildfire through the city that they had been taken in for the purpose of being fatted for eating! The hostility to foreigners has increased rapidly in many parts of the province. Mr. A. J. Little, writing from SZE CHUAN some years ago, mentions that the phrase "Foreign devil," and other opprobrious epithets applied to foreigners elsewhere, were unknown, and other travellers have mentioned the same thing. Now, a language rich in abominable terms is ransacked for the worst, to hurl at the foreigner.

I left Luchow on May 30th in great heat, and contrary to custom, travelled till nine o'clock, making fast to a snag in a broad reach or bay of shallow water. The mercury stood at 91° at four p.m., and the men suffered from the heat. I have observed that sunstroke is far more to be dreaded in damp than in dry climates. It is common in SZE CHUAN among the Chinese. The boatmen called it *lei-su*, "death from exhaustion." They feared it, and well they might, for their shaven heads were only protected by small towels. The blue turban, much worn in the province, may have originated in an instinct of defence. The Chinese suffer greatly from mosquitoes. I have seen curtains of a heavy, green canvas even in poor men's houses, but men as poor as my boatmen have no protection, and, being compelled by the heat to sleep naked, their bodies are covered with inflamed lumps from mosquito bites. They are very patient. They suffered so much from this cause that in the stifling twilights, when thousands of these pests were abroad, I almost grudged myself the immunity gained by sitting under a mosquito net made by attaching a net roof and curtains to a Chinese umbrella frame.

The men fanned themselves as long as they could keep awake. As the heat increased the use of the fan became universal among men. Coolies fanned themselves at the treadmill pump, bearers as they ran along with chairs, porters with loads, travellers on horseback and on foot, men working and resting, shopkeepers at their doors, mandarins in their chairs and on the judgment-seat, and sentries on guard. Soldiers marching to meet an enemy fan themselves on the march, as I saw in Manchuria during the Japanese war, and the bloody field of Phyong-yang was strewn with the fans of the dead and dying Chinese. Fan-making is one of the great industries of China. Nearly 2,000,000 fans were imported into Chung-king in 1897.

Except for the heat, the downward journey was quite delightful; the country is so fertile and beautiful, and has such an air of prosperity. So long as we were in motion there was a draught, as the boat was quite open, but the still nights were stifling, specially with the curtains down. The boatmen were harmless, good-natured, obliging fellows. They tied up whenever I wanted

PAGODA NEAR LUCHOW.

to land if it were at all possible, and though they were obliged to pass from bow to stern through my "room," they always asked leave to do so if the curtains were down. The lovely country was a very great charm. The variety of scenery, trees, flowers, and cultivated plants was endless, and new industries were constantly becoming prominent. The only matter for regret was that the rush of the fast-rising river carried us all too swiftly past much that was worthy of observation.

A visit to a coal-mine interested me greatly. The mine was in a hillside, three miles from the river, and employed eighty men. The manager said that the output was the equivalent of forty tons daily. The men got sevenpence per day, with rice, broad beans, cucumbers, and tea. Each hewer and carrier (in pairs) must deliver at the pit's mouth daily the equivalent of a ton. The pay with food comes to tenpence per day, and the actual cost in labour of a ton is twentypence. The mine is extremely well ventilated by three revolving fans, which drive the air into it through bamboo tubing. The men work in two shifts of twelve hours per day of twenty-four hours, eating their rice in the mine three times daily. Every tenth day is pay-day and a holiday. Each carrier burns nine ounces of Tung oil daily, and each hewer six, the lamps being attached to the brow by a band round the head. There was a bath for the miners, which in the dim light appeared to be a stone coffer, supplied with hot water. The tunnel by which the workings are reached, and down which the coal is carried in wheeled baskets running on a wooden tramway, is six feet high, and about six hundred feet long. I could do no more than glance at the workings. The coal seam was about four feet thick, the galleries very low, and the hewers lay on their sides and hacked the coal sidewise. It appeared to be a fairly hard bituminous coal, and there is a great demand for it at the town of Peh-Shi, where, after land and river transit, it sells at seven shillings per ton. The manager, an intelligent and fairly polite man, told me that hard coal is also found in the neighbourhood, but is much more expensive to work. This coal-mine appeared well appointed, and the miners well fed and cheery. They seemed to have less consideration for the Dragon's back than those on the Paoning route!

The night after leaving Luchow, while tied up to a snag in

a broad and shallow reach, all in my boat were wakened out of a sound sleep by what might have been the "crack of doom." There was a sound as if all the cannon of the universe had been fired close to the *wu-pan* on either side, accompanied by a hiss in the water, a glare of blue light, a gust which lifted the boat, and stripped off some of the mats of the roof, and then a torrent of rain. By the next morning the Yangtze had risen twelve feet, and our snag had "gone under," forcing us to seek the familiar protection of the shore.

Among many storms, one only, at St. Paul, Minnesota, has fixed itself in my memory. That was in a hotel lighted by gas and full of people. This was out in a lonely place in "darkness which could be felt," among men of another race and speech, in a frail craft. The thunder, not rolling, but bursting like explosions; the ceaselessness and vividness of the forked lightning; the otherwise pitch darkness of the night; the hot and mephitic atmosphere; the occasional terrific gusts of wind, threatening to blow the half-unroofed boat to pieces; the roar of the rain, the loneliness and mystery of our position; the silence from human movement and speech; the hours it all lasted; the surprise after every tremendous explosion to find myself alive, and the fear that some of the men were killed, made that night an awful memory.

During the whole storm no one spoke or moved hand or foot. I felt paralysed, a sensation, as I afterwards found, common to all Europeans who passed through the same experience. The boatmen, who were lying in the water, never stirred. When the explosion gave place to magnificent rolls, and the rain moderated, the men spent an hour in baling the boat. All the matches were afloat and much else, and our food was mostly spoiled. A thousand waterfalls tumbled down the hillsides, the stony or sandy river banks were no more, of a few riverine villages the roofs alone were to be seen, fields in numbers with their growing crops had slid bodily down the slopes, leaving great patches of naked rock behind, and the Yangtze, a broad, turbid, terra-cotta flood, was rioting over the submerged confusions of its rocky bed in swirls and violent eddies.

After hurrying through a less beautiful and much devastated region, landing only at Shih-men, on the left bank, where there

THE AUTHOR'S *WU-PAN*.

is a fine temple with five green-tiled roofs, and much fishing is done, the scenery again changed, and for four hundred miles is a succession of indescribably beautiful pictures, combining hill and valley, rock and woodland, with a greenery and fertility of which no word-painting could give any idea. Towns and villages, piled on knolls, looked out from among fruit trees; and temples and pagodas on heights lent their infinite picturesqueness.

One of the most beautifully situated towns is the unwalled town of Peh-Shih, with a (reputed) population of 11,000. Timbered white houses run steeply up diverging limestone cliffs; every outline is broken by the configuration of the ground; the ornamental and economic trees are superb; the density of their foliage was phenomenal. The centre of the town, which has no room for expansion, is picturesquely crowded with striking temples and guildhalls, much enriched with gold and colour. The great industry of the town is "wine" making. Wine is exported on a large scale in forty-gallon jars, which come down on bamboo rafts from Lu-chien, where they are made, and these afterwards take the wine up the Ya and other turbulent rivers. A fleet of these quaint constructions and a great number of junks lay along the shore, and there was an air of prosperous business about the town.

The roof of my boat had to be refitted with mats, some of which had been blown off in the storm, and I took a long inland walk, and without molestation! The cultivation was marvellous. I have no space to dwell upon the infinite variety of the crops or on the trees of all climates which were flourishing in juxtaposition,* or upon the striking fact that there, 1600 miles up the river, the

---

* Among the trees and plants behind Peh-Shih, which were interesting as growing in one locality, were: the orange, pommeloe, pomegranate, apricot, peach, apple, pear, plum, persimmon (*Diospyros Virginiana*), loquat (*Eriobotrya Japonica*), date-plum (*Diospyros Kaki*), the Chinese date tree (*Rhamnus Theezans*), walnut, Spanish chest-nuts, the *Ficus religiosa*, palms, bamboos, cypresses, pines, the "varnish tree" (*Rhus-vernicifera*), the Tung oil tree (*Aleurites cordata*), mulberry, oak, the *Cudrania triloba*, much used for feeding young silkworms, a hibiscus, plane, the *Sterculia platinifolia*, the *Paulonia Imperialis*, three varieties of soap trees (*Acacia negata, Gymnocladus Sinensis*, and *Gleditschia Sinensis*), the tallow tree, and very many others, my specimens of which were so destroyed by damp as to render subsequent botanical identification impossible. Hemp was considerably grown, and of two economic shrubs, both new to me, there were several patches, the *Boehmeria nivea*, from the fibre of which grass cloth is manufactured, and the *Fatsia papyrifera*, from the pith of which rice paper is made.

social and commercial organisation, and the arrangements for
what the Chinese regard as comfort and convenience, were as
complete as in Che-kiang. A little later it might have occurred
to me that this beautiful and prosperous region is claimed as in
the British "sphere of influence." Carefulness and thrift were
shown by what was to me a novelty. All along the river shore

METHOD OF CARRYING *CASH* AND BABIES

people were fishing from rocks with nets, for straws, twigs, and
bits of wood to use for their cooking fires.

I reached Chung-king, the westernmost of the treaty ports, and
the commercial metropolis of SZE CHUAN early the next morning
(June 1st), after coming slightly to grief in a rapid above it, and
remained there during three grey, steamy, misty days, in which
the mercury was almost steady at 87°. Between Chung-king and
Sui Fu, if not higher, steam navigation at that season appeared

FISHING VILLAGE, UPPER YANGTZE.

perfectly practicable. The junk and raft traffic is very large. Coal and lime are found in abundance near Chung-king, and at Pa-Ko-Shan, five miles below Sui Fu, and also twenty miles above it. Specimens of this coal brought to England have been pronounced to be suitable for steam purposes.*

* The estimated distance to Cheng-tu by the windings of the rivers is :—

Chung-king to Luchow	125 miles.
Luchow to Sui Fu	87 ,,
Sui Fu to Chia-ling Fu	130 ,,
Chia-ling Fu to Cheng-tu Fu . . .	133 ,,
Total	475 miles.

CHAPTER XXXVII.

THE JOURNEY'S END

WHETHER Chung-king (altitude 1050 ft.) is approached from above or below, it is a most striking city. It is surprising to find, 1500 miles inland, a town of from 400,000 to 500,000 people, including 2500 Mohammedans, as the commercial capital of Western China, one of the busiest cities of the empire. Its founders chose a site on which there is no room for expansion, and its warehouses, guildhalls, hongs, shops, and the dwellings of rich and poor, are packed upon a steep sandstone reef or peninsula lying between the Yangtze and its great northern tributary, the Chia-ling, and rising from 100 to 400 feet above the winter level of these rivers. As I descended upon it down a somewhat turbulent rapid, which half filled the boat and drowned a fowl, it reminded me of Quebec, and made me think of the packed condition of Edinburgh when it was yet a walled city.

A noble-looking, grey city it is, with towers, pavilions, and temples rising above its massive, irregular, crenelated grey wall, with broad, steep, and crowded flights of stone stairs, twenty feet broad, leading up from the river to the gates, with an amphitheatre of wooded and richly cultivated hills rising steeply 1600 feet from the water for its background; the fleets of big junks, and craft of all descriptions, which lie crowded along its shores and in every adjacent bay and reach, and the life and movement on land and water, combining to form a noble and most striking spectacle. Nor is Chung-king as a city "alone in its glory," for on the Yangtze, just below its junction with the Chia-ling, which divides it from Chung-king, stands the walled city of Limin-fu, its white houses covering a number of hills and cliffs, and at its feet hundreds of junks. Another city, Kiang-peh, completes the trio. These cities, with their com-

WALL OF CHUNG-KING, WITH GATE TOWERS.

CHUNG-KING SOLDIERS, CUSTOMS GUARD.

mercial organisation owing nothing to Europe, I think more than all others, gave me an idea of what China *is* and *must* be.

Chung-king Fu has often been described in detail, and I will only give a few impressions of it. Passing to the Taiping gate up a flight of stone stairs, always sloppy from the passage of water carriers, and crowded with cotton-laden coolies, I reached the house of the Commissioner of Customs by steep streets cut in the rock. The Customs House, infinitely picturesque, is on a small rock plateau, with only four feet of space between it and the rock behind. The view is ideally picturesque, with the pagoda and gardens of a Guild of Benevolence below the plateau, and the great flood of the Yangtze, then two-thirds of a mile wide, rolling between the city and the fine hills on the further shore. But space is lacking. The Chinese soldiers who guard the Commissioner seemed to block up the little that there is, and trees and trailers there and everywhere in the hot, moist climate of Chung-king, choke up every foot of ground. The mercury stood at 88° during my three days' visit; there was no sunshine for the dogs to bark at, and the moist air was absolutely still. As compared with many or most, the "grounds" of that house are spacious !

Chung-king was opened as a treaty port in 1891, but the China Inland Mission rented a house there in 1877, and were followed by missionaries of other societies, who, however, all had to fly from a severe riot nine years later. Mr. Archibald Little settled there as a merchant eight years before the opening—a rare instance of mercantile pluck with few imitators, and now, besides the foreigners on the Consular and Customs' staffs, there are other "venturers," chiefly "transients," and about thirty missionaries of different societies, with mission chapels, schools, and hospitals. The English and German steamers, which are to be placed on the route from Ichang next year (1900), will doubtless stimulate foreign settlement, and will bring Chung-king within the globe-trotter's sphere. If specially-built gunboats can "patrol" the upper Yangtze, outbreaks of hostility to foreigners will doubtless cease, and the quarrels will be among the foreign nationalities, each anxious to circumvent the others in the matter of concessions.

Below the huge reef on which Chung-king stands, is a town

of mat and bamboo houses outside the wall. As the Yangtze rises some ninety feet in summer above its winter level, and was rising fast when I arrived on June 1st, this town had mostly disappeared, and the highest remnant was being carried away hurriedly on men's backs, each hour of removal giving an added dignity to the grand, grey city, looking down on the grand, yellow-ochre flood. In Chung-king, as in many another city of the upper Yangtze, the harmony between man's work and nature is yet unbroken, and the evil day of foreign inartistic antagonisms, incongruities, and uglinesses has not yet dawned.

This commercial capital has a great present, which we are hoping to improve upon to our advantage.* It is connected by water with nearly every considerable town in the province, and wholesale trade is by boat. Exports bound east must pass it, and also the imports brought up to pay for them. For foreign goods it is the sole wholesale market in SZE CHUAN, and is so for provincial trade to a great extent, and the province, it must be repeated, is as large as France, and vastly more populous. To it the merchants and shopkeepers of the whole population of from 55,000,000 to 70,000,000, which includes Tibetan tribes, Lolos, and a few so-called "dog faces," resort to make their purchases.

Mr. A. J. Little is the only British merchant resident in Chung-king. The Chinese merchants deal directly with Shanghai through their own men. More than half of the buyers sent

---

* Mr. Bourne estimates the imports of cotton and cotton goods as follows :—

Raw cotton	£500,000
Native piece goods, home spun . .	1,000,000
Indian yarn	600,000
Lancashire cottons	300,000
	£2,400,000

And the exports, which are chiefly raw or half-manufactured produce, as follows :—

Opium	£1,800,000
Salt	300,000
Drugs	400,000
Silk	200,000
Miscellaneous articles, insect wax, tobacco, sugar, musk, wool-skins, hides, feathers, bristles, etc.	600,000
	£3,300,000

The returns for 1898, not yet out, are expected to show a very considerable increase.

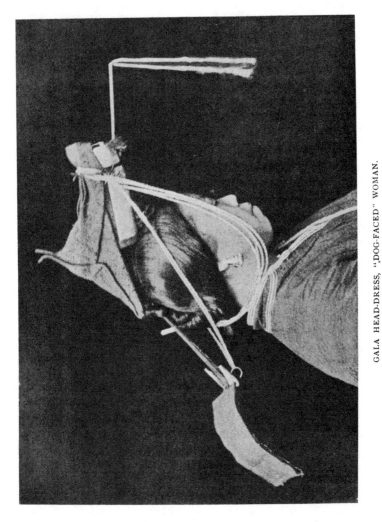

GALA HEAD-DRESS, "DOG-FACED" WOMAN.

(*See also page 117.*)

down have an interest in the business. They deal with the Chinese importers, and pay ready money in Shanghai, but sell to the provincial merchants on long credit, the rate of interest being 14⅔ per cent. per annum on foreign cotton goods. The seller naturally wishes payment to be deferred, and the buyer desires to hasten it, as he receives the same percentage as discount. Exchange between Chung-king and Shanghai is always in favour of Chung-king, and when the Yangtze is in its summer flood, 1000 taels in Shanghai can often be bought in Chung-king for 880.

The intricacies of Chinese business at Chung-king are appalling. Excessive subtlety and ingenuity characterise all the trade rules and customs, and even the " Blackburn Commission," aided by the experience of Mr. Bourne, found it a work of much labour to master their complications! It is scarcely wonderful that the average British merchant, who knows nothing better than *Pidgun*, instead of following in the steps of our bold " Merchant Venturers," sticks at Shanghai.*

At Chung-king, more almost than elsewhere, I was impressed with the completeness of Chinese commercial organisation. It may be too complex, and lacking in initiative, to serve our purposes, but it serves their own, and I heard there, as elsewhere, that the high standard of commercial honour and probity which has been worked out, renders dealings with Chinese merchants very satisfactory.

Eight of the other provinces are represented by guilds in this great trading city, with their handsome guildhalls, and rigid laws of association. There are an abundance of exchange banks (banks selling drafts on distant places), seventeen of which are in the hands of men from SHAN-SI, which has a speciality for banking talent, and there are over twenty large *cash* shops or local banks, which exchange *cash* against silver and *vice versâ*. These banks do not make advances on goods, but lend on personal security at from ten to twelve per cent. per annum, and employ agents who hang about the business quarter, learning the proceedings of customers, so as to gauge their credit. A bank would lend as much as 200,000 taels to a merchant on personal security

---

* Readers are referred to sections 28 to 33 of Mr. Bourne's report on *The Trade of Central and Southern China*, May, 1898. (Eyre and Spottiswoode.)

only. They have very rigorous methods of ensuring the honesty of *employés*.

It was with great regret that I left Chung-king on my last *wu-pan* voyage. There were few, if any, small houseboats on the berth, and the big ones would only go down at an enormous price, because of the difficulty and profitlessness of the return. Foreigners of the two services, as well as merchants, regard a *wu-pan* as we regard a steerage passage, and even my kind host

THE AUTHOR'S LAST *WU-PAN*.

declined to connive at my proceedings, but Mr. Willett, of the China Inland Mission, befriended me; the *wu-pan* was engaged, and I left Chung-king on a sultry June afternoon, with the mercury at 88°, and never regretted my firmness on the subject of a boat, for I was thoroughly comfortable, could create draughts at will, and my boatmen were quiet and most obliging, and were ready to land me at any place where landing was practicable.

The force and volume of the river, which had then risen about forty-five feet above its winter level, were tremendous. Its low-water width at Chung-king, according to Blakiston, is 800 yards, but it was then about two-thirds of a mile wide, a swirling, leaping, yellow flood, laden with the mud with which it enriches the Great Plain. Caught in its torrent, the *wu-pan*, with two men rowing easily, descended at great speed. When we reached rapids, five men pulled frantically with yells which posed as songs, to keep steerage way on her, and we went down like a flash—down smooth hills of water, where rapids had been obliterated; down leaping races, where they had been created; past hideous whirl-pools, where to have been sucked in would have been destruction; past temples, pagodas, and grey cities on heights; past villages gleaming white midst dense greenery; past hill, valley, woodland, garden cultivation, and signs of industry and prosperity; past junks laid up for the summer in quiet reaches, and junks with frantic crews, straining at the sweeps, chanting wildly, bound downwards like ourselves; and still for days the Great River hurried us remorselessly along. There was no time to take in anything. A pagoda or city scarcely appeared before it vanished —a rapid scarcely tossed up its angry crests ahead, before we had left it astern; one fair dissolving view was all too rapidly exchanged for another; and we were tying up among the many hundred junks which fringed the shore of the " Myriad City," which is as beautiful from above as from below, before I realised that we were half-way thither.

But in this delirious whirl there were episodes of rest, when I landed on green and flowery shores above the submerged boulders, or below picturesque cities and temples, and had leisure either to enjoy detail or to loathe it. The latter was my mental attitude when I landed with my *chai-jen* (rather an infliction in a small boat) at the important town of Fu-chow, where a clear stream, about 200 yards broad, and navigable for 200 miles, joins the turbid Yangtze. There are many queer crafts on the branches of the Yangtze. The navigation of some of these rivers is so intricate and dangerous, that the owners of these risky constructions are obliged to consent to provide coffins for their crews in case of disaster, and there are colliers built for *one* down-river voyage, after which they are broken up; but the queerest of all crafts are the *Wai-pi-Ku*—the " twisting stern " junks used for the navigation of the Fu-ling, locally known as the Kung-tan Ho, or "River of the Rapid of Kung." I saw one of these at Wan, and thought it was a junk which had had a severe accident! The sight of forty or fifty large junks at Fu-chow, each one with her high stern twisted a quarter round, so that the stern deck is at right angles to the quarter deck, was absolutely laughable. The stern deck is nearly perpendicular, and is climbed by rungs. These extraordinary boats are without rudders. My boatmen said that none but "twisted stern" junks could twist through the whirlpools and reefs of the river. It was not very wise for me to enter Fu-chow, and as I was followed by an immense and not over polite crowd I did not dare to use my camera on the *Wai-pi-Ku*.

Fu-chow is perhaps the most picturesque city on the Yangtze, built on ledges of rock, tier above tier, at the head of a reach so enclosed by steep hills as to look like a lake. There is a fine pagoda on a height near it, and it abounds in large temples in commanding positions. The deep gateway in the thick wall is scarcely more than eight feet high. The narrow street into which it leads was thronged, and even women were carrying creels, either loaded with coal dust, or small children. I managed to dodge the fast accumulating crowd, and get on the wall, from which the view up the Fu-ling is magnificent. My visit, however, was rather "a fearful joy."

The city appears full of temples, literary monuments, and public buildings, but it has an air of neglect and decay, and it and its suburbs are dirty and malodorous. It is a great junk port, and at times, though not, I think, increasingly, the Fu-ling is used for the transit of goods both to Hankow and Canton. The latter city can be reached by this method with only two portages (?). There are large mat and bamboo suburbs below one part of the wall, but very little of them was left, owing to the rapid rise of the river, which also had led to the removal of many of the mat villages of the trackers. Fu-chow again looked glorious from below. A tremendous whirlpool, in which, sometimes, descending junks are caught to their destruction, is formed in summer near the city. We went uncomfortably near its vortex.

I landed also at Shih-pao-chai ("Stone Precious Castle"), a place of pilgrimage. The south-east side of the rock (not given in the illustration) has a nine-storeyed pavilion, resting on a very

"STONE PRECIOUS CASTLE,"

SHI-PAO-CHAI.

strikingly decorated temple built against it, through which access to the summit is gained. On the flat top there is a temple of three courts. The pavilion building has curved and decorated roofs, and looks like a magnificent eleven-storeyed pagoda. A large village lies at its feet. My films were spotted with damp, and would have failed anyhow, owing to the overpowering curiosity of the people. This rock and its talus are about 300 feet in height.

A glorious sunset and a morning of crystalline purity in a bay above the "Windbox Gorge"; a rapid swirl through the solemnity and grandeur of the gorges which I ascended slowly and toilsomely six months before; the Yeh-tan, fierce and perilous; the Hsin-tan, a mere water-slide, down which my *wu-pan* slipped easily; a lovely walk up the Nan-po glen, and in fifty-six hours from Chung-king, exclusive of stoppages, the boat emerged from the Ichang gorge upon the broad reach of eddying water, on which the pleasant treaty port of Ichang is situated.

After receiving hospitality for a few days at the British Consulate I left Ichang, and found the mirrors, enamel, and gilding of one of the fine river steamers very distasteful after a thousand miles in a *wu-pan*. Hankow, though by no means at its worst, was damp and sultry, with a temperature over 90°, and alive with mosquitoes. Even on the voyage down to Shanghai, which was devoid of any incident,—except that five minutes after leaving Chin-kiang we cut the anchored steamer *Hai-how*, tea-laden for Canton, down to the water's edge—the damp heat was severe, and even the breeze was hot.

It was the end of June when I reached Shanghai, to find it sweltering in a "hot wave," sunless and moist. My journey on the whole had been one of extreme variety and interest, and I was truly thankful for the freedom from any serious accident which I had enjoyed, and for the deep and probably abiding interest in China and the Chinese which it had given me, along with new views of the physical characteristics of the country, and of the resourcefulness and energy of its inhabitants.

CHAPTER XXXVIII.

THE OPIUM POPPY AND ITS USE*

M Y acquaintance with the opium poppy began in the month of February on the journey from Wan Hsien to Paoning Fu. It is a very handsome plant. It is expensive to grow. It has to be attended to eight times, and needs heavy manuring. It is exposed to so many risks before the juice is secured that the growth is much of a speculation, and many Chinese regard it as being as risky as gambling. Besides its cultivation for sale, on a majority of farms it is grown for home use, as tobacco is, for smoking. It is a winter crop, and is succeeded by rice, maize, cotton, beans, etc. Certain crops can be planted between the rows of the poppies. Much oil, bearing a high price, is made from the seed. The lower leaves, which are abundant, are used in some quarters to feed pigs, and also as a vegetable. They were served up to me as such twice, and tasted like spinach. In some places the heavy stalks are dug into the ground ; in others they are used as fuel, and after serving this purpose their ashes provide lye for the indigo dyers. It appears from much concurrent testimony, that in spite of heavy manuring the crop exhausts the ground.

The area devoted to the poppy in SZE CHUAN is enormous, and owing to the high price of the drug and its easy transport its culture is encroaching on the rice and arable lands. The consequences of the extension of its cultivation are serious. It is admitted by the natives of SZE CHUAN that one great reason of the deficient food supply which led to the famine and distress in the eastern part of the province in 1897, was the giving of so much ground to the poppy that there was no longer a margin left on which to feed the population in years of a poor harvest.

* In order to avoid the fragmentariness of references to the Opium Poppy and Protestant Missions, at intervals throughout this volume, I have adopted the more convenient arrangement of giving a chapter on each of these subjects.

I shall not touch on the history of the growth and use of opium in China. The authorities evidently regarded the introduction of both as a grave peril, and they were prohibited under Imperial decrees. I learn on what I regard as very reliable authority, that sixty years ago, when Cantonese brought opium cough pills into KWEICHOW and YUNNAN, and the consumers found themselves unable to give up the medicine, that the authorities were most active in suppressing its use, and even inflicted the punishment of death on many of the refractory in YUNNAN. It was then and later smuggled about the country in coffins!

Now, on many of the SZE CHUAN roads opium houses are as common as gin shops in our London slums. I learned from Chinese sources that in several of the large cities of the province eighty per cent. of the men and forty per cent. of the women are opium smokers; but this must not be understood to mean that they are opium "wrecks," for there is a vast amount of "moderate" opium smoking in China. In my boat on the Yangtze fourteen out of sixteen very poor trackers smoked opium, and among my chair and baggage coolies it was rare to find one who did not smoke, and who did not collapse about the same hour daily with the so-called unbearable craving.

The stern of my boat was a downright opium den at night, with fourteen ragged men curled up on their quilts, with their opium lamps beside them, in the height of sensuous felicity, dreaming such Elysian dreams as never visit the toiling day of a Chinese coolie, and incapable of rousing themselves to meet an emergency until the effect of the pipe passed off. Farther astern still, the *lao-pan* and his shrieking virago of a wife lay in the same blissful case, the toothless, mummied face of the *lao-pan*, expressive in the daytime of nothing but fiendish greed, with its muscles relaxed, and its deep, hard lines smoothed out. Some of these men, whose thin, worn, cotton rags were ill-fitted to meet the cold, sold most of them at Wan, rather than undergo what appeared to be literally the *agonies* of abstinence. On my inland journey I heard incidentally of many men who had sold both wives and children in order to obtain the drug, and at Paoning Fu of a man and his wife who, having previously parted with house, furniture, and all they had, to gratify their craving, at the time of my visit sold their only child, a nice girl of fourteen, educated in the Mission School, to some brutal Kansuh fur traders, who were returning home. It is quite usual when a man desires a house and land which are the property of an opium smoker, for him to wait with true Chinese patience for one, two, or three years, certain that the owner will sooner or later part with it for an old song to satisfy his opium craving when he has sold all else. It is common for the Chinese to say, "If you want to be revenged on your enemy you need not strike him, or go to law with him—you have only to entice him into smoking opium."

The Chinese condemn all but most moderate opium smoking and gambling as twin vices, and not a voice is raised in defence of either of them, even by the smokers themselves. The opium habit is regarded as a disease, for the cure of which many smokers voluntarily place themselves in opium refuges at some expense, and at a great cost of suffering, and in the market towns, thronged with native traders, there is to be seen on many stalls among innumerable native drugs and commodities, a package labelled "Remedy for Foreign Smoke," "foreign smoke" being the usual name for opium in Western China. I was impressed with the existence of a curious sort of conscience, if it can be called such, among the devotees of opium, which leads them to consider themselves as moral criminals. The Chinese generally believe that if a man takes to the opium habit it will be to the impoverishment and ruin of his family, and that it will prevent him from fulfilling one of the first of Confucian obligations, the support of his parents in their old age. The consensus of opinion among smokers and non-smokers, as to the crime of opium smoking and its woeful results, leads me to believe that it brings about the impoverishment and ruin of families to an enormous extent. Chinese said several times to me that the reason the Japanese beat them was that they were more vigorous men, owing to the rigid exclusion of opium from Japan.

In May I saw the crop harvested. Women and children are the chief operators. In the morning longitudinal incisions are made in the seed vessel, the juice exudes, and by the evening is hard enough to be scraped into cups, after which it turns black, and after a few days' exposure is ready for packing. Heavy rain or a strong west wind during this process is very injurious.

Maize, tobacco, and cotton have been previously planted, and make a good appearance as soon as the poppy stalks have been cleared away.

Eight years ago it was rather exceptional for women and children to smoke, but the Chinese estimate that in SZE CHUAN and other opium-producing regions from forty to sixty per cent. are now smokers. Where opium is not grown the habit is chiefly confined to the cities, but it is rapidly spreading.

Its existence is obvious among the lower classes from the exceeding poverty which it entails. Millions of the working classes earn barely enough to provide them with what, even to their limited notions, are the necessaries of life, and the money spent on opium is withdrawn from these. Hence the confirmed opium smoker among the poor is apt to look half starved and ragged. Still I am bound to say that I did not encounter any of those awful specimens of physical wreckage that I saw some years ago in the Malay States from the same cause.

Among the well-to-do and well-nourished classes the evils of opium are doubtless more moral than physical; among the masses both evils are combined. The lower orders of officials and "*yamen* runners," with their unlimited leisure, are generally smokers. Among my official escorts in SZE CHUAN, numbering in all 143 men, all but two were devotees of opium, and I was constantly delayed and inconvenienced by it. My coolies frequently broke down under the craving, and that at times as inconvenient to themselves as to me. In two towns I had to wait two hours to get my passport copied because the writers at the *yamen* were in the blissful haziness produced by the pipe.

So far as I have seen, the passionate craving for the drug, called by the Chinese the "*Yin*," (which appears to be the coming on of severe depression after the stimulant of the pipe has passed off), involves great suffering, and total abstinence, whether voluntary or enforced, produces an anguish which the enfeebled will of the immoderate smoker is powerless to contend with. The craving grows, till at the end of eighteen months from the commencement of the habit, or even less, the smoker, unless he can gratify it, becomes unable to do his work.

He feels disinclined to move, miserable all over, especially at the stomach and between the shoulders, his joints and bones ache badly, he perspires freely, he trembles with a sense of weakness, and if he cannot get the drug, he believes that he will die. I cannot learn how soon a man comes to consider himself a victim of the habit. Those who place themselves in opium refuges with the hope of cure, endure agonies which they describe to be "as if wolves were gnawing at their vitals," and would, if permitted, tear off their skin to relieve the severe internal suffering.

On my SZE CHUAN journey we were benighted on a desolate hillside, and had to spend the night in the entrance to a coal-pit, cold, wet, and badly fed. My coolies had relied on being able to buy opium, and though they were comparatively moderate smokers, they suffered so much that some of them were rolling on the ground in their pain. Dr. Main, of Hangchow, thinks that very few can be cured in opium refuges, which they enter for twenty-one days, for the debility, stomachic disorder, and depression which follow the disuse of the drug are so great, that six months of tonics and good feeding would be necessary to set them on their feet again. On the contrary, the poor wretch, low in purse, depressed, feeble, trembling, leaves the shelter of the refuge to be tempted at once to a smoke by old associates, while in cities like Hangchow and Fuchow from eight hundred to a thousand registered opium shops display their seductions, and he turns aside to the only physical and mental comfort that he knows.

I have little doubt that in the early months of the habit there is a widespread desire to abandon it. Opium refuges, in spite of the fair payment which is asked for, are always crowded. The shops and markets abound in native and foreign remedies for "foreign smoke." The native cures all contain opium, chiefly in the form of ashes, and the foreign, which are white, contain morphia. The attempts at self-cure number tens of thousands, and are very piteous, but in many cases it is merely the exchange of the opium habit for the morphia habit, and at this time morphia lozenges are making great headway in China, as an easy and unsuspected means, specially in travelling, of obtaining the sensations which have become essential to existence. The importation of morphia into China is now enormous—135,283 ounces in 1898 It is sold everywhere, and in the great west, as well as nearer the seaboard, shops are opened which sell a few articles as a blind, for the lucrative sale of the much-prized morphia pill or lozenge. Among the native cures which I have heard of the only one which seems at all efficacious is the so-called "Tea Extract," *Scutellaria vicidula*. The *Jsai li* sect, which makes abstinence from opium one of its tenets, uses this cure invariably, but the ordinary smoker is unwilling to face the severe suffering which it entails.

Smokers, I have learned, may be divided into three classes: first, the upper class, not driven by failure of means or sense of duty to abandon an indulgence which they can well afford, and which they do not enjoy to excess; second, the respectable class of small merchants, innkeepers, shopkeepers, business men, and the like, who find their families pinched and themselves losing caste by reason of their habit; third, the class—which the Chinese estimate to consist of forty per cent. of the whole in the cities, and twenty per cent. in the country—which has drifted beyond hope, and is continually recruited from those above it. In this are found thieves, beggars, actors, the infamous, the lost and submerged, the men who have sold lands, houses, wives, and children, and live for opium only, much as the most degraded of our dipsomaniacs live for spirits.

Besides these, there are many who are not obliged to have recourse to selling and pawning to get along, but who curtail such things as the education of their children, and flowers for their wives' heads, and who, from having eaten meat twice daily, eat it only once, or substitute for it a purely vegetable diet, which must contain much honey and sugar to relieve the heat and dryness of the mouth which the pipe produces. Then there are large numbers of smokers who have barely enough to feed themselves upon, who must eat in order to work, and who have not one *cash* left for opium. These borrow right and left, and part with all they can pledge for anything, borrowing every year from fresh lenders, and paying back a fraction of the old debts till they can borrow no longer, and drop into the submerged class aforesaid. Among these are seen the ragged, mummied wretches, who *kotow* to former acquaintances, and beg from them the ashes of their opium pipes, even drinking these with hot water to satisfy the craving.

Rich smokers smoke what is known as "Canton opium," the import from India, which they compare to a coal fire, and the native drug to a wood one. But the manufacture of the latter is improving rapidly; and as it is increasingly used to mix with the Indian, a generation is growing up in the upper class which knows only the mixed drug, and apparently only the old, rich smokers use pure Indian opium, the consumption of which has fallen off enormously, though in 1898 the value of the Indian import was £4,388,385.

The mysteries of the preparation and the varieties of the product baffle the non-smoker. Both Chinese and Indian opium are now largely prepared with the ashes of the drug already once smoked, much of it flowing, only imperfectly burned, into the receiver of the pipe. In the strongest prepared opium, four ounces of ashes of the first degree are added to every ten of crude opium. Ashes of the second and even the third burning are also used. Many of the poorer classes have to content themselves with a smoke of opium ashes only, and the lowest of all users of the drug have to satisfy themselves with eating or drinking the ashes of the third burning.

There is a class which can afford to buy the pure drug, but which finds that it does not satisfy the craving, but this is merged in a far larger one of old and inveterate rich smokers of one tael's weight per day, who smoke not even the very best prepared Indian drug, for their craving needs far stronger stimulation, but ashes of the first degree. Such men give the prepared extract, weight for weight, value for value, for the ashes, and contract with opium shops to be supplied with all their ashes of the first burning. For the rich, inveterate smoker an ounce of prepared extract is mixed with six ounces of ashes of the first degree. This habit has in Chinese a specific bad name.

Pure opium appears to be seldom sold, as it fails to satisfy the craving of the practised smoker. It is not only that ashes are mixed with the fresh drug, but that they are reboiled, and after being made up with treacle to the proper consistence are resmoked, and their ashes are then eaten by the poorest class.

Morphia, the active principle of opium, not being consumed in the smoke owing to its lack of volatility, the eating of the ashes, which contain seven per cent. and upwards of it, has a very serious effect. The fact that opium is smoked three times makes it impossible to estimate either the quantity consumed or the amount spent on the indulgence, but these are, of course, greatly in excess of that indicated by any possible returns.

Among the adjuncts of opium smoking used by rich smokers is what is called "water tobacco," supposed erroneously to be all washed in the water of the Yellow river. It is retailed in thin cakes of a brick-red colour, and is said to be mixed with arsenic, and that its excessive use, with or without opium, is dangerous to health.* This tobacco is invariably smoked in "water pipes" by the upper classes in SZE CHUAN.

In the chapter on the Hangchow Hospital I have mentioned the impetus given to suicide by the painlessness of death by opium, and will not refer to it again. In this chapter I have only touched upon such mysteries and results of opium smoking as I have seen in my limited experience, or have heard of directly from Chinese through my interpreters, or facts stated in a careful paper, *The Use of Opium*, by Dr. Dudgeon, of Peking. Except for the quotation of a remark of Dr. Main, of Hangchow, on opium refuges, I have not obtained any of my material from missionaries. †

From all that I have seen and heard among the Chinese themselves, I have come to believe that even moderate opium smoking involves enormous risks, and that excessive smoking brings in its train commercial, industrial, and moral ruin and physical deterioration, and this on a scale so large as to threaten the national well-being and the physical future of the race.

The most common reasons which the Chinese give for contracting the habit are pain, love of pleasure, sociability, and the want of occupation. They say that a moderate use of the pipe "advances the transaction of business, stimulates the bargaining instinct, facilitates the striking of bargains, and enables men

* *Report of a Journey to North Sze Chuan*, 1898. By Mr. G. J. L. LITTON, of H.B.M.'s Chinese Consular Service.

† This is not from any distrust of the accuracy of their facts, for no foreigners know the lives and ways of the Chinese so well as they do, but simply because many people think that they are prejudiced.

to talk about secret and important matters which without it they would lack courage to speak of."

It is strangely true that in this industrial nation there are hundreds of thousands of people with little or nothing to do. There are the wives of the wealthy, retired, and expectant mandarins, leisured men of various classes, *literati* waiting for employment, the great army of priests and monks, and the hangers-on of *yamens*, besides which there are Government officials whose duties occupy them only one day in a month. These remarks apply chiefly to urban populations.

Outside of commercial pursuits an overpowering shadow of dulness rests on Chinese as upon much of Oriental life. The lack of an enlightened native press, and of anything deserving the name of contemporary literature; the grooviness of thought and action; the trammels of a rigid etiquette; the absence of athletics, and even of ordinary exercise; the paucity of recreations, other than the play and the restaurants, which are ofttimes associated with opium shops and vicious resorts; and the fact that the learned having committed the classics to memory, by which they have rendered themselves eligible for office, have no farther motive for study—all make the blissful dreams and the oblivion of the opium pipe greatly to be desired.

It is obvious that opium has come to "stay." So lately as 1859, in SZE CHUAN, which now exports opium annually to the value of nearly £2,000,000, the penalty for growing it was death, in spite of which the white poppy fields were seen in conspicuous places along the Great River; and in 1868 an Imperial edict against its cultivation was supplemented by a proclamation to the same effect by the Viceroy of the province, and both have remained dead letters.

At all times the beautiful *Papaver somniferum* has been regarded as the enemy of China. There are no apologists for the use of opium except among foreigners. The smokers themselves are ashamed of their slavery. All alike condemn it, and regard opium as a curse as well as a vice, and from all which came under my own observation in fifteen months, I fully agree with them.

I will conclude this chapter with a few extracts from officials whose knowledge of the evils which are following the constantly increasing use of the drug, cannot be gainsaid. The first quotation is from the British Consul at Tainan, Formosa. Consul Hirst says :—

"As long as China remains a nation of opium-smokers there is not the least reason to fear that she will become a military power of any importance, as the habit saps the energies and vitality of the nation."

The next is from Consul Bourne, who accompanied the "Blackburn Commission" to the west and south of China, in the winter and spring of 1896–97. Mr. Bourne believes that the provinces of YUNNAN and KUEI-CHOW raise opium annually to the amount of about three millions sterling.

"There is no doubt," he writes, "that here (Kuei-chow) the officials tried to stop the cultivation of the poppy, but this must have been very difficult, because an export such as opium, light in weight for its value, is just what these provinces, with their wretched means of communication, want. To-day, without opium, Yunnan and Kuei-chow would have no means of paying for imports. Unfortunately," he says, writing of YUNNAN, "opium has become almost the medium of exchange in this province, as I explained in a former report."

Writing on the deplorable condition of YUNNAN (p. 58), he says :—

"After Yang-kai, poppy fills the whole cultivated area, covering the valley with white and purple (this is in the province of Yunnan), a gorgeous spectacle to the eye, though not agreeable to the mind, for one must attribute chiefly to opium, I think, the extraordinary failure of this province to recover from the devastation of the rebellion.

"The drug is so cheap and handy that the men almost all smoke, and most women, especially among the agriculturists, who tend the poppy and collect and sell the juice—the class that is elsewhere the backbone of China, if, indeed, China can be said to have a backbone. I was assured by an English missionary who has long resided in the province, and in whose judgment I have great confidence, that in eastern and western circuits (Tao) of the province, which embrace more than two-thirds of its area, 80 per cent. of the men and 60 per cent. of the women smoke opium. In the southern circuit the habit is not quite so general. He had no doubt that the vice had a very bad effect on the race. At all events, every traveller must be struck by the great extent to which the fertile valleys—the only land well cultivated—are monopolised by the poppy; by the apathy and laziness of the people; and by the very slow recovery, during twenty-five years, from the losses of the rebellion. Another bad result of opium being so ready at hand is the frequency of suicides, especially among women."

At the close of 1898, a book was published by H. E. Chang Chih-tung, who is described by foreigners long resident in China as having been for many years one of the most influential states-men in the country, and as standing second to no official in the empire for ability, honesty, disinterestedness, and patriotism. He has filled in succession three of the most important Viceroyalties in the empire. He deals with the opium habit as with a huge national evil. Under the heading "The Expulsion of the Poison," he writes thus :—

(1) "Deplorable indeed is the injury done by opium! It is [as] the Deluge of the present day or [an invasion of] some fierce beasts, but the danger [arising from it] is greater than [the danger arising from] those things . . . The injury done by opium is that of a stream of poison flowing on for more than a hundred years, and diffusing itself in twenty-two provinces. The sufferers from this injury amount to untold millions. Its consequences are insidious and seductive, and the limit has not yet been reached. It destroys men's abilities, it weakens the vigour of the soldier, it wastes their wealth,* until it results at length in China being what she is to-day. This destruction affects the ability of civilians and soldiers alike. The injury is worse than any waste of wealth. Men's wills are weakened, their physical strength is reduced. In the manage-ment of business they lack industry, they cannot journey any distance, their expenditure becomes extravagant, their children are few. After a few tens of years it will result in China becoming altogether the laughing-stock of the world."

(2) "Shanghai and Yangchow both have associations for breaking off the opium habit. Their general object may be said to be that each member should control his dependents. As for the opium-smokers, masters will not employ them as servants, teachers will not have them as scholars, generals will not take them as soldiers, farmers will not use them as labourers, merchants will not employ them as assistants, foremen will not have them for workmen."

---

* "This year the value of foreign goods imported amounted to more than eighty million [taels]. The export of Chinese products might be about fifty million [taels] or more. The foreign drug [*i.e.*, opium] was valued at more than thirty million [taels]. Thus there was a leakage. China is not impoverished by commerce, but the im-poverishment comes from the consumption of opium."

The writer concludes by saying :—

"If Confucius and Mencius were to live again, and were to teach the empire . . . they would certainly begin by [teaching men] to break off opium."

How is China to emancipate herself from this rapidly increasing habit, which is threatening to sap the hitherto remarkable energy of the race?

CHAPTER XXXIX.

NOTES ON PROTESTANT MISSIONS IN CHINA

TWO thousand four hundred and fifty-eight Protestant workers (including wives) represent the missionary energies and the many divisions of Christendom. The native Protestant communicants number 80,632.*

The shock which China received through her defeat by Japan has produced, among other results, a disposition to make inquiries regarding the God, faith, and learning of those "Western Barbarians" from whom Japan received the art of war. Although hostility to Christianity as a destructive and socially disintegrating power has been recently evidenced by the anti-Christian riots at Kien-ing and elsewhere, the spirit of inquiry gathers volume, and expresses itself in large gatherings in street-chapels and churches, the thronging to mission schools, and the avidity with which Christian literature is purchased. Those who profess themselves ready to abandon heathenism and connect themselves with Christianity are more than the missionaries can instruct. In MANCHURIA there are six thousand inquirers in connection with the Scotch and Irish missions. In the FU-KIEN province the movement towards Christianity is on so extensive a scale as to attract the serious attention of the provincial authorities, as well as emphatic recognition by our own consuls. In one mission alone of the American Board, in another province, the number of inquirers into the Christian religion is estimated at 12,000.

The growing influence of Christianity, however, cannot be measured either by the numbers of communicants or inquirers. For many years past, large numbers of Christian men and women have been scattered through nearly all the provinces of China,

---

* In *Les Missions Catholiques*, vol. xxiii. (1891), M. Louvets returns the number of Roman Catholic converts in Pechili, Manchuria, Mongolia, and Shantung as 73,620 in 1870, and in 1890, including 2000 in Kansuh, as 155,900.

making their homes among the Chinese, with the avowed object of promulgating what is known as the "*Jesus Religion*." Their methods of propagandism—preaching, conversation, schools, dispensaries, hospitals, and the circulation of Christian literature only differ slightly. Their knowledge of Chinese is necessarily imperfect, and they often make grotesque and even serious blunders. As their methods and mistakes in the language are much alike, so too are their lives. The keenest Chinese critic finds no difference in conduct and the motives which rule it, between the Scotch missionaries in MANCHURIA, the China Inland Mission and Canadian, etc., in SZE CHUAN, the Church Missionary Society in the FU-KIEN Province, and the German and American in KWANTUNG. These 2500 men and women are seen under the "fierce light" of criticism which beats upon them, whether at home or abroad, to lead pure, just, truthful, kind, honest, virtuous, patient lives, restraining temper and suffering long. These lives preach a higher standard of living than is inculcated by the highest Chinese teaching, and by slow degrees produce results which cannot be tabulated. The fame of the foreign teacher's payment of wages agreed upon, without drawbacks, his truthfulness, justice, kind treatment of servants,* control of temper, and accessibility, travels far, and each life so lived is an influence making for righteousness in the neighbourhood, exciting inquiry into the "Jesus Religion" and foreign learning, and exercising a distinct influence on surrounding morality in certain directions.

The direct part of missionary work need scarcely be touched upon. It consists in awakening the conscience to a sense of sin, by the preaching of "righteousness, temperance, and judgment to come." It dwells upon the justice and love of God, on the atonement of Christ, on that Divine Fatherhood before whose infinite compassions there is not a stranger, an alien, a foreigner; on the "one sacrifice for sin once offered"; and teaches that the purpose of the sacrifice, and of law and gospel, is, that men may live "soberly, righteously, and godly in this present world," in preparation for a stainless and endless life. It teaches that the morality of the Great Teacher is but a "shadow of good things to come"—of the higher and perfect morality demanded by the

---

* A servant of my own, not a Christian, gave a quaint reason for liking to serve missionaries—"I never get boots at my head in the foreign teachers' houses."

Divine law, and that the power outside ourselves which "makes for righteousness" and "helps our infirmities," is the power of God; that "God is love," and yearns over His wandering children; that He has "showed man what is good," and that "His only begotten Son," who in some mysterious manner "bore our sins in His own body on the tree," is "He who is alive for evermore," and "ever liveth to make intercession," and that He "hath abolished death, and brought life and immortality to light through His Gospel."

This, in brief, is the teaching of all Protestant missionaries in China, to whatever church they belong, and with one or two exceptions all regard baptism as an obligatory confession of faith, and as the evidence of a complete break with the beliefs and practices of heathenism.

Under such teaching 80,000 Chinese in 1898 were making a public profession of the Christian faith. Many annually lapse; the greater number owing to family influence, and difficulties in the abandonment of the time and custom-honoured social observances connected with idolatry; some because they find the moral restraints of Christianity too hard for them, and others because they hoped for worldly advantages which they failed to obtain. A large number of professing converts are employed by missionaries as servants, gatekeepers, teachers, printers, translators, and writers, of whose sincerity it may not always be possible to judge, as foreign employment is much coveted.

But after putting these and other dubious converts aside, there remains a large body of native Christians, gathered into societies, which after long and careful inquiry I believe to be fully up to the average mark of our churches at home in essential knowledge, and above it in practice, specially in propagandist zeal and liberality—societies of men and women, in which the virtues of purity, honesty, self-denial, and charity are apparent. These converts contribute liberally out of their poverty to Christian objects, specially for the advancement of Christianity in their own country, in some regions contributing 6s. per head per annum. These Christian societies are constantly showing an increasing disposition to help themselves by the building of church edifices, as at Paoning Fu and elsewhere, and by contributing the entire support of not a few of their own pastors.

A large number of these converts are earnest and successful propagandists, and the very large increase in the number of Christians during the last five years is mainly owing to the zeal, earnestness, and devotion of Chinese converts, both men and women, who owe their conversion and instruction, as well as guidance and inspiration, to the foreign teachers.   In Manchuria a few years ago the senior missionary told me that out of between three thousand and four thousand converts he estimated that not more than twenty had received Christianity directly from the European missionaries, and the same proportion holds good with regard to the six thousand inquirers at the present date.   In Che-kiang the present Bishop of Victoria estimated the number of converts through the work of Chinese as 80 per cent. of the whole.

These societies, in the beginning very small, and numbering from ten up to over four hundred members, are gradually crystallising into brotherhoods, with a very strong bond of union and definite aims of their own.   They show in a marked degree the strong Chinese tendency to combination and association, and may be regarded as guilds.   At present among the communicants there is a strong desire to conserve the purity of the churches by a careful exercise of discipline.   Members who fall back into evil ways, as many do, are " suspended," and if incorrigible are sloughed off, and it certainly would not be possible for such abuses as disgraced the church of Corinth to exist in the infant churches of China.

In brief these Christian societies are earnest in propagandism, zealous for purity and discipline, liberal in their contributions, desirous for instruction, docile and teachable, and apparently increasingly anxious to translate Christian doctrine into righteous living.   These bodies in very many places are slowly exercising an influence in favour of righteousness, and are thus among the many influences which are tending to undermine the old superstitions.

If China is to be Christianised, or even largely leavened by Christianity, it must inevitably be by native agency under foreign instruction and guidance.   The foreigner remains a foreigner in his imperfect and often grotesque use of the language, in his inability to comprehend Chinese modes of thinking and acting, and in a hundred other ways, while a well-instructed Chinese teacher knows his countrymen and what will appeal to them, how to make "points," and how to clinch an argument by a popular quotation from their own classics. He knows their weakness and strength, their devious ways and crooked motives, and their unspeakable darkness and superstition, and is not likely to be either too suspicious or too confiding. He presents Christianity without the Western flavour. It is in the earnest enthusiasm of the Chinese converts for the propagation of the faith that the great hope for China lies.

Until now Christianity has made very slow progress. Among the special obstacles are: First, the national vanity, and the contempt for anything introduced by the foreign barbarians. Second, the posthumous influence of Confucius, whose moral teaching, negative and defective as it is on some points, is regarded as final, and his maxims as perfect in their adaptation to the needs of society and government for all time. Third, the Chinese language itself, with its absence of an alphabet, the peculiar inflections and tones, the guttural and aspirated modulations which must be carefully observed, and the necessity of creating a vocabulary which shall rationally express the Christian ideas, and yet not be offensive to a critical and literary people. Fourth, the carefulness and universality of home education in superstitious and idolatrous beliefs and practices, children being taught from early infancy that reverence for the divinities of the Chinese Pantheon, shown according to established forms, is necessary to success in life.

Fifth, greater than all these special obstacles combined, is that of ancestor-worship, the actual and universal cult of the Empire. To abandon idolatrous worship and practices is easy, but withdrawal from the worship of the ancestral tablets, with its rites and sacrifices, brands a man as a reprobate and a brute. These rites represent reverence, sacredness, and filial piety; they have the sanction of immemorial usage and of the earliest memories of home, and the first act of worship recorded is the worship of ancestors by the Emperor Shun on his accession, in the dawn of Chinese history.

The practice probably took its rise in a tender and beautiful filial feeling, but apparently it has come to be largely inspired by fear. A Chinese truly " passes the time of his sojourning here in fear," and is in slavery not only to the terror of a dim and demon-haunted future, but to the present dread of the evils wherewith he may be afflicted in this life by the malevolence of the dissatisfied spirits of his ancestors. Dr. Yates, a very careful student of things Chinese, in an able paper on ancestor-worship, states that, including the cost of the festivals for the destitute dead, the enormous sum of 151,752,000 dollars is annually expended by the Chinese in quieting the spirits of the departed, and securing the living from their malignant action. If this worship ever dies, it will die hard.

Islam is absolutely intolerant of every form of ancestor-worship. The Roman Catholic missions, as my readers are aware, were agitated by a controversy as to concessions on this subject from 1610 to 1758, when Pope Benedict XIV. rejected all compromise. Protestant missions take the same course.

While making careful inquiries into mission work, both from the workers and from outsiders, and comparing the present status and conduct of Chinese converts with what they were when I was in China twenty years ago, I formed certain opinions on Protestant missions in China, which I now place briefly before my readers. At this time missions constitute so important a factor in the awakening of the empire, that no sensible or thoughtful person can ignore them without sacrificing his reputation for both sense and thoughtfulness. If I venture to write of myself at all in connection with the subject, it is but to say that I am not an enthusiast regarding foreign missions, but soberly believe that to " teach all nations " is the path of duty and of hope.

During the earlier period of my eight years of Asiatic travel the subject was of little or no interest to me. I may even have enjoyed the cheap sneers at missions and missionaries which often pass for wit in Anglo-Asiatic communities, among persons who have never given the work and its methods one half-hour of serious attention and investigation, and in travelling, wherever possible, I gave mission stations a wide berth.

On my later journeys, however, which brought me often for months at a time into touch with the daily life of the peoples, their condition even at the best impressed me as being so deplorable all round, that I became a convert to the duty of using the great means by which it can be elevated. To pass on to these nations the blessings which we owe to Christianity—our eternal hope, our knowledge of the Divine Fatherhood, our Christian ideals of manhood and womanhood, our best conceptions of the sanctities of domestic life and of the duties involved in social relationships, our political liberties, the position of women, the incorruptible majesty of our equal laws, the reformatory nature of our punishments, the public opinion permeated by Christianity which sustains right and condemns wrong, and a thousand things besides, which have come to us through centuries of the " Jesus Religion "—is undoubtedly our bounden duty. It is surely the height of unchristian selfishness to sit down contentedly among our own good things, and practically to regard China merely as an area for trade. Is it not also the height of disloyalty and disobedience to our nominal Master, whose last command, ringing down through centuries of selfishness, we have been satisfied to leave unfulfilled ?

I was influenced not so much by seeing the good work done by missionaries, as the tremendous need for it and the hopelessness of the religious systems of Asia. Several of the Asiatic faiths, and notably Buddhism, started with noble conceptions and a morality far in advance of their age. But the good has been mainly lost out of them in their passage down the centuries, and Buddhism in China, aiming at eclecticism, absorbed so much of the dæmonism, nature-worship, and heathenism of the country, that in the number and puerility of its superstitions, its alliance with sorcery, its temples crowded with monstrous and grotesque idols, the immorality of its priests, and the absence of the teaching of righteousness, it is now much on a level with the idolatries of barbarous nations. There is nothing to arrest the further downward descent of these systems, so effete, and yet so powerful as interwoven with the whole social life of the nation. *There is no resurrection power in any one of them*, and to the men who here and there are athirst for righteousness, and are groping after Him " who is not far from every one of us," they offer neither guidance nor help.

That there are such seekers is certain. Among the many " secret societies " of China, a " good few " are mainly religious, and a great number of the Christian converts in North China have been in their membership. An attempt to attain righteousness is their characteristic, and something may be learned from them of self-denial and aspiration. Their efforts all take more or less of an ascetic direction.

Among them are "Vegetarians," who abstain from meat with the object of "rectifying the heart, accumulating merit, and thus avoiding calamities in this world and retributive pains in the next." Several others are pledged to abstain from gambling and the use of opium, wine, and tobacco. The chief teaching of another is the duty of maintaining a patient spirit under injuries.

The books of the religious secret societies contain the best maxims and the highest moral teaching of "The Three Religions." They exhort to chastity, benevolence, carefulness in speech, self-denial, good works, the *conservation of the mental energies by rest and reflection*, the cultivation of the heart, and to much besides which is good. In alliance with the good are idolatrous rites, incantations, divination, and many grossly superstitious and puerile practices. It is believed that even the best among these societies are not altogether free from seditious tendencies, *i.e.*, the accomplishment of reform by destruction. But after making due allowance for what is foolish and evil, it is evident that in these unsatisfied spiritual instincts and cravings after righteousness, and above all in the substitution of a dissatisfied and earnest spirit for the self-satisfied complacency of the Confucianist, and the stolid materialism of the average Chinese, Christianity has allies not to be despised.

Up to this time (1899) the slow success which has been won has been almost entirely among the lower classes, and it has not been possible, by the methods hitherto pursued, to reach the *literati*, who in China are the leaders of a people whose reverence for letters is phenomenal.

Of the 2458 Protestant missionaries, including wives (many of whom are incapacitated for work by maternal duties), accredited to China, a large number are always at home "on furlough." Promising Christian work is often broken up by the departure of the missionary. A substitute may or may not be appointed, but the "personal equation" counts for much in China as elsewhere. The force available for actual work ought not to include the large number of new missionaries, who must inevitably spend the first year or two in learning to speak Chinese, during which period they are useful chiefly by lives of consistent righteousness. Throughout my long journeys I never saw a mission station, except perhaps Paoning Fu, which was not undermanned, *i.e.*, in which mission work was not seriously crippled and denied its natural expansion by lack of men.

In this time of inquiry into Western religion and science it becomes more and more important that missionaries, both men and *women*, should study the difficult language carefully, so as to fit themselves for conversation with the *literati*, and not be content with a limited command of the colloquial speech of coolies. It is being recognised in most influential quarters that if our trade is to expand, clerks and others going into mercantile life in China must begin the study of Chinese here under competent Chinese teachers. It might possibly be desirable for intending missionaries to do the same, and it would have the advantage of testing in each case the capacity for learning a difficult language, the incapacity being under present methods only discovered when it is too late to draw back. It appears very important that medical missionaries should have an undisturbed year after arriving in China for the study of the language.

Women's work has grown, and is growing so rapidly in China that its regulation needs serious consideration. Admirable as much of it is, and might be, it is beset with special difficulties. The fact of a young unmarried woman living anywhere but under her father's roof, exposes her character to the grossest imputations, which are hurled at her in the streets, and which can only be lived down by scrupulous carefulness. The Chinese etiquette, which prescribes the conduct seemly for women, and limits the freedom of social intercourse between the sexes, certainly tends to propriety, and though to our thinking tiresome, no young foreign woman attempting to teach a foreign religion can violate its leading rules without injury to her work.

For instance, it is improper for a woman to " ride " in an open chair, to receive men visitors at her house, or to shake hands with men, or to walk through the street of a town or village or to visit at native houses unattended by a middle-aged Chinese woman. It is not only improper but scandalous for a woman to be seen in a tight bodice, or any other fashion which shows her figure, and a foreign girl lays herself open to remarks which I scarcely think she would like to hear, when she appears in a fly-away hat, bent up and bent down, on which birds, insects, feathers, grasses, and flowers have been dumped down indiscriminately! The Mission Board of one large and successful Mission has found it desirable to issue rules for missionaries regarding dress and etiquette, and the China Inland Mission everywhere, and the Church Missionary Society missionaries in SZE CHUAN have solved the difficulty by adopting Chinese costume, the only Oriental dress which Europeans can wear with seemliness and dignity. I think it would add much to the safety of female missionaries, and to the respect in which they are held, if those missionary societies which object to Chinese costume would agree upon neat, simple uniforms for summer and winter, fulfilling the Chinese demand for propriety, and the European demand for tastefulness, and which should indicate at once that the wearer belongs to a large and important international union, and cannot be insulted with impunity.

Again it is necessary for young women to remember that a yellow skin makes no difference, and that any familiarity of manner or carelessness in deportment, which would be unsuitable here, is ten times more unsuitable in the case of Chinese men, such as servants, teachers, and "native helpers." In one province in which lady missionaries are specially numerous the violations of etiquette by some of them have been regarded as so likely to lead to outbreaks that the attention of our Foreign Office has been called to the subject. The openings for the work of sensible "godly" women are very great, but as a large proportion of those who go out are young and inexperienced, and the number is increasing, it is desirable that the whole subject should be reconsidered, and that women's work and general conduct should have the advantage of experienced and effectual supervision for the protection of the workers, and the prevention of those hindrances to the work which arise out of ignorance and inexperience, and in a few cases out of self-conceit and self-will.

Having ventured on these criticisms and suggestions, I must add that much of the wisest, most loving, most self-denying, and most successful work that I saw done in China was done by women.

My earliest ideas of missionary work were taken from a picture which represented a white man standing under a tree, preaching to an earnest, quiet, and dark-visaged crowd. Crowds gather round the foreign preacher in China, but this is often a temporary phase, with curiosity for its leading motive. His appearance, mistakes in speech, and attitudes are satirised, jeered at, and mimicked. One of the most popular theatrical performances in Shanghai a few years ago was a clever farce, representing a foreign missionary preaching to a crowd of Chinese.

Preaching is not a Chinese mode of instruction. Confucianism, still the great force in China, never had a preacher, and was propagated solely by books. It is said that there is not a lecture-hall in the empire. The Chinese methods of influencing are chiefly literary, catechetical, and conversational. The results of preaching have not been what was once hoped for, nor what they have been in some other countries. Many missionaries have told me that even the Chinese preaching in the "street chapels" is not fruitful in results.

It is possible that the introduction of Western modes of evangelising, not applicable to China, was at least premature, and has been the cause of much failure and disappointment. The foreign element, whether in methods, church architecture, house building, or the ignoring of Chinese custom, though partly inevitable, must always tend to represent Christianity as a "foreign religion," and to perpetuate it but as a sickly exotic. It is, I think, of great importance that Christianity should ally itself with all that is not evil in the national life, that it should uphold Chinese nationality, that it should incorporate Chinese methods of instruction with our own, and conserve all customs which are not contrary to its spirit. The teachings of experience have not been thrown away, and many missionaries have come to see that these are the lines of progress.

Those competent to judge have no doubt that Christianity is about to make great progress in China. With this, many questions already emerging will come to the front, and among the foremost is that of native agency in foreign pay. There is on one side the certainty that China can only be Christianised by the Chinese, and on the other the risks connected with the worldly or mercenary element, which have been fatal to many such persons whose sincerity had not been suspected. Here again experience is teaching useful lessons, one being that Christianity is never so extensively and rapidly propagated as by the spontaneous efforts and renovated lives of private Christians.

Among other questions are: How far the differences between Western churches are to be perpetuated in China; the place of the Chinese classics and of English in missionary schools; the obligation of the Sabbath; the attitude of Christianity to certain Chinese customs, and to any modified form of ancestor-worship; social intercourse between foreigners and Chinese; the social and pecuniary position of a native pastorate; the self-government of churches; and in Anglican missions the retention of the Prayer Book, as it at present stands, as the sole manual for public worship.

In conclusion I think that there is now an "open door" for the gospel in China, and that the prospect for Christianity is fairer than at any former period, but that if the Christian nations fail to realise their obligations to enter that door promptly and in force, with an army of earnest and well-equipped teachers, China may follow the example of Japan, and accept Western civilisation, while rejecting the Christian religion.

"Talk," said Mr. Gladstone on one occasion, "about the question of the day; there is but one question, and that is the gospel. It can and will correct everything needing correction."

It may be that the gospel will yet bring about the regeneration of China.

CONCLUDING REMARKS

THE subjects of our political and trade relations with China have been so ably and exhaustively treated by Lord Charles Beresford, M.P., and Mr. Colquhoun, and have been threshed out by so many other writers, that in these brief remarks I shall chiefly confine myself to the Chinese people and to my impressions of them, received in fifteen months of journeyings in three of the most important years in modern Chinese history.*

I doubt very much whether China is "breaking up." *If* she breaks up it will be owing to the policy of the great European nations in making her "lose face," and thereby weakening the authority of the Central Government over the provinces, local risings and possible disintegrations being the result. The "sphere of influence" policy, if pursued in earnest, would undoubtedly break up the empire.

In the three years in which I was travelling, off and on, in China, the Dragon Throne reeled, but righted itself, and the Government survived the Japanese war, the heavy indemnity, the loss of the suzerainty of Korea, and the aggressions of Russia. It extinguished, in blood, the serious Mohammedan rebellion in KANSUH, and has lately brought about the collapse of the rebellion in SZE CHUAN. The bond of union which connects the provinces with each other and with Peking has survived all these mishaps, and if it is broken, I believe it will be by foreign interference, and by the shifting and opportunist policy, enormous ambitions, and ill-concealed rivalries of certain foreign powers.

Nor do I believe that China is "in decay." I have travelled more than 8000 miles in the empire, and have seen, in some

---

* If I seem to pronounce opinions *ex cathedrâ* on very insufficient bases, it is owing to the avoidance of the constant repetition of the modest phrase "I think," which in nearly all cases must be understood.

regions, roads, canals, temples,* and some ancient public works, falling into disrepair. The Oriental throughout Asia prefers construction to renovation, and alongside of these decaying works there are new temples, new pagodas, new and handsome bridges, new *pai-fangs*, new bunds, and new works, rather of private than public origin.

The reader who has followed the foregoing chapters with any degree of interest can scarcely think that SZE CHUAN, at least, is in decay. Commercial and industrial energy is not decaying, the vast fleets of junks are not rotting in harbours and reaches; industry, thrift, resourcefulness, and the complete organisation both of labour and commerce, meet the traveller at every turn. Mercantile credit stands high, contracts are kept, labour is docile, teachable, and intelligent, its earnings are secure, and, on the whole, law and order prevail.

Nor is it like "decay" that in 1898—in spite of a political situation full of menace, of sporadic rebellions which largely checked business in their localities, of the serious news from Peking in September, which disorganised the trade of the northern ports, and of the disasters in connection with the Yellow River—the elasticity was such that the value of the import trade exceeded all previous records, while that of the export trade exceeded that of every previous year except 1897, the total volume of trade being the highest on record.

There was no export of silver, but a net import of Hk. Tls. 4,722,025, and there was no scarcity of it in any part of the country. China met the whole of her obligations without any depletion of her currency, and imported nothing that she did not obtain in exchange for exports.† The importance of stimulating the Chinese export trade is apt to be overlooked. China will only purchase from foreign countries that for which she can pay with her own products. The verdict of the Inspector-General of Maritime Customs in China on the commercial situation for 1898 is, "No doubt the Government is hard pressed for funds, but *the country grows wealthier every year.*" ‡

* Hundreds of temples, however, had undergone recent and thorough repair.

† See Appendix B.

‡ *Imperial Maritime Customs. Report on the Trade of China for 1898.* King & Son. London.

Among the reasons given for the alleged "decay" of China is its "over-population." It is true that there are seriously congested areas, even in SZE CHUAN, but if we take 400,000,000, the extreme estimate of the population, it is but ten times that of Great Britain, while the area of the empire is from sixteen to eighteen times as great.

What is "in decay" is the administration of government. The people are straight, but officialism is corrupt.*

The subject has been fully dwelt upon in other books, with which I suppose my readers to be acquainted. The theory of the Chinese Government is one of the best ever devised by the wit of man. Against every possible abuse apparent safeguards were provided. The enjoyment of property and life was secured to the people. The laws in the main were just, concise, and of equal pressure. The right of rising against a corrupt and oppressive official was guaranteed. Literary examinations were made the entrance to official life. Inferior birth was no bar to the attainment of high position. The laws of the country embodied the highest teaching of political ethics which it had received. The patriarchal theory of government was never so systematised, or acted upon for so long, and with so much consistency. The ethical teaching and the laws based upon it remain, and the strongest power in China to-day is Confucius; but the admirable theory of government has proved weak in presence of the neglected factor of the downward tendency of human nature in a pagan nation. The infamies of Chinese administration to-day have been riveted upon China by centuries of political retrogression, and the gradual lowering of the standard of public virtue in the absence of a wholesome public opinion. Certain forms of bribery, corruption, and peculation have obtained the force of custom, seven-tenths of the revenue is arrested by the "three hands" of officials, all sums allotted for public works, repairs, and military and naval equipment, suffer enormous depletion *en route* to their destinations, so that in the Japanese

---

* A couplet from a well-known anonymous lampoon, largely current as an expression of popular opinion, is translated thus:—

> "Three hands has every magistrate,
> And every officer three feet."

(The hands to clutch at bribes, the feet to run away from the enemy!)

war "a straight people with a corrupt Government" were easily subdued by "a corrupt people with a straight Government."*

One of the heaviest indictments against the system is, that under it it is hardly possible for a good man to be rigidly honest, and there are good men: and there are mandarins who, after a long and laborious period of office, actually live and die poor. A well-meaning man, finding himself entangled in the meshes of this system, is greatly to be pitied. Custom is all in favour of peculation, and however much such men would welcome a way of escape, to break with custom is as hard as to break off the opium habit. Another difficulty besets the well-intentioned man—his knowledge that his best efforts will certainly be frustrated by the unscrupulous clerks and retainers of his *yamen.*

In Chapter XXIII. I just touched on the very laborious life of a mandarin, who has to perform the work of six men, and rarely gets a holiday. For this amount of work he is virtually unpaid, far more than his wretchedly insufficient salary being expended on the necessary state of his office. These nominal salaries are the deadly upas tree, which has cast its fatal shadow over Chinese official life. They are the *crux* of the situation. They make peculation and corruption all but an absolute necessity. Short periods of office, paying for appointments, the evil custom of making presents to official superiors, the practice that, after paying into the Imperial Exchequer the fixed quota of taxation for his district, the magistrate can appropriate all that he can squeeze beyond it, subject to liberal gifts to the high officials of his province, are only a few of the evils of the Chinese administrative system. It is chiefly out of this margin squeezed

---

* In Mukden, early in that war, I saw Chinese regiments of remarkably fine physique marching to their doom, armed with matchlock and "Tower" guns, and pikes, the money which should have provided them with modern rifles having enriched the officials who had the spending of it. The modern rifles with which some of the rank and file were armed were of all patterns, so cartridges of a dozen different makes and sizes were dumped down on the ground in a vacant space in the city, without any attempt at classification, and the soldiers fitted them to their arms, sometimes throwing eight or ten back on the heap before finding one to suit the weapon. The commissariat officials were grossly dishonest, and where stores had accumulated, sold them for their own benefit. It is a common practice for a military mandarin to draw pay for 800 men, having only 400 with the colours, and, on an inspection day, to impress 400 coolies of the city, put them into uniforms, and parade them with the soldiers.

out of the people that the fortunes of the higher officials are made.*

Every writer on China exposes the iniquities of the system, and they come more or less to the ears and under the observation of every traveller. They affect a fourth of the human race, and have brought the most ancient of existing empires into the position of a "sick man"—helpless, appealing, with voracious Western nations gnawing at his extremities, and prepared to prey upon his vitals.

But China bristles with contradictions. The "sick man" ought to be "in decay," but he is not. His innate cheeriness is scarcely clouded by our repeated assertions that he ought to be dead, and he faces the future which we prophesy for him without misgiving! On the whole, peace, order, and a fair amount of prosperity prevail throughout the empire. The gains of labour are secure, taxation, even with the squeezes attending it, is rarely oppressive in the country, and in the towns is extremely light. The phrase "ground down" does not apply to the Chinese peasant. There is complete religious toleration. Guilds, trades unions, and other combinations carry out their systems unimpeded, and the Chinese genius for association is absolutely unfettered. The Chinese practically in actual life are one of the freest peoples on earth!

The reader may be staggered by what appears a monstrous paradox, in face of the opinions regarding the infamies of administration previously expressed, but if a single statement is applicable to the whole empire it is this, that freedom is the birthright of the people, that they possess "inalienable rights to life, liberty, and the pursuit of happiness," and that China is one of the most democratic countries on earth. The Government, feeble and evasive in its dealings with foreigners, when it sets its mind on something among its own people, is quite capable of carrying out its will, and is not nearly so impotent as many suppose. Yet it habitually plays only a most minute part in the economy of national life, and a Chinese may live and die without any other contact with it than the payment of land-tax. He is free in all trades and industries: to make money and to keep it: to emigrate and to return with his gains: free to rise from the peasant's hut to place and dignity:

---

* Mr. Meadows states that the highest mandarins get about ten times and the lowest about fifty times the amount of their legal incomes by means of "squeezes."

to become a millionaire, and confer princely gifts upon his province: free in his religion and his amusements: and in his social and commercial life.

I have not space, knowledge, or ability to enter into the inwardness of these extraordinary contradictions, and would only remark that we have to deal in China not with a mass of downtrodden serfs, but with a nation of free men.

I may be permitted, however, very diffidently to point out a few of the reasons which, in my opinion, militate against the evils of administration, and tend to the stability of the country. First among these is the village system. In China the unit is not the individual but the family, indivisible and sacred, the members of which are bound to each other in life and death by indissoluble ties, of the strength of which we cannot form a conception. Villages consist of groups of such families, with their headmen and elders, who are responsible for each individual, the step above them being the *hsien*, or district magistrate, who may be regarded as the administrative unit. The Chinese have a genius for self-government, and are by no means the "dumb, driven cattle" which some suppose them to be. The villages are self-governing, and no official dares to trench on their hereditary privileges. Every successive dynasty has found itself bound to protect them in these, and no "Son of Heaven" who called them in question could occupy the Dragon Throne for six months.

These privileges, which by established custom have become actual rights, consist primarily in the complete control of local affairs, the possession of lands, and absolute freedom for trade and industry. Among the many advantages of the village system is, that it enables villagers in countless civil cases to avoid the serious evils of litigation in the *yamens* by the simple method of referring them to arbitration before their headmen and elders.

Among other causes which tend to counterbalance the evils of the administration, is the system of strict surveillance and mutual responsibility, under which no man stands alone, and which as a vast network holds China together. This has its own evils, one of which is *mutual distrust*, which has, however, the good result of preventing men from combining intelligently against the Government. The system makes government easy, and certainly does not tend to disintegration.

Besides these there are the recognised right of rebellion when grievances become intolerable; the execution of a species of lynch law on culpable officials, which often takes the place of memorials to the Throne, and courts of appeal; a certain dread on the part of magistrates of being reported for corruption or inefficiency by the many spies of the Central Government, or by the Censors, who, though said not to be altogether free from venality, can, on occasion, be most remarkably outspoken; the general education of the people in the principles on which government is based; the genius for association which gives strength to the weak; and the universal training both at home and school in " The Five Duties of Man," which are : (1) Loyalty to the Sovereign, (2) piety to parents, (3) submissiveness to elders, (4) harmony between husband and wife, (5) fidelity to friends.*

This is the empire which we speak of "partitioning" and "breaking up," with as little emotion as if it were an ant's nest, with all its singular contradictions, and emphatic antagonisms of good and evil.

There is a wide difference between bullying, in diplomatic language "applying strong pressure," and making righteous and politic demands upon China. Nothing could be better for herself than the drastic reforms suggested by Lord C. Beresford, but some of them involve what I think would be an unwarrantable interference with her internal organisation. Among righteous demands may certainly be placed the fulfilment of treaty obligations—the giving security to the lives and property of foreigners throughout the empire, which can only be attained by the formation of an efficient army, or *gendarmerie*, well disciplined, drilled, armed, and paid, and *mobile*—giving foreigners the right

---

* Since writing the above pages I have read Mr. A. R. COLQUHOUN's chapters on "Government and Administration," "The Chinese People," and "Chinese Democracy," in which I find views similar to my own stated with great force, breadth, and intimate knowledge. The last chapter concludes with these important words : " It is only fitful glimpses which strangers are able to obtain of the inner working of Chinese national life—quite insufficient to form a coherent theory of the whole . . . but the data ascertained seem sufficient to warrant the inference of a vast, self-governed, law-abiding society, costing practically nothing to maintain, and having nothing to apprehend save natural calamities and national upheavals."

to live for trade purposes in the interior (a right only conceded by Japan in July, 1899), and an equable rearrangement of *likin* and *loti-shui.**

Likin and *loti-shui* are obnoxious taxes, and hamper trade effectively, and the abuses of the system are very great, but abrupt and sweeping changes would be very dangerous. It must be remembered that the provincial governments have lost seriously through the operations of the Imperial Maritime Customs (see p. 155), and rely mainly on *likin* for their revenue, that its abolition would involve a resort to direct taxation, which would be intolerable to a people accustomed to indirect, and would certainly lead to very serious risings in the West River and Yangtze valleys. Official needs, established custom, and the relations of the masses to custom, render the forcing of abrupt fiscal changes of this nature upon the Chinese most impolitic, risking the disorganisation and break up of China.

By bullying the Central Government it is made to "lose face" with its subjects, and its authority is by so much weakened. The value of our treaties absolutely depends on the power of the Government to give effect to them. The sole security of the Chinese bondholder, and for the sums invested, or to be invested in the railroads of the future, is the integrity and cohesion of the Chinese Empire. Touch this integrity, whether by active claims for "spheres of influence," with consequent disintegration, the enforced abolition of *likin*, or any policy of pressure, and our treaties will be but waste paper. With regard to most arrangements, however desirable in the way of reform they may be, the word "insist," pointing to coercion, should be blotted out of the vocabulary of discussion.

I am still a believer in the justice and expediency of the "Open Door" policy, as opposed to what I think is the fatal alternative policy of "spheres of influence." Many who would "rush" reforms in China, and are impatient of delay, and are perhaps bitten by the "lust of domination," assert that it is too

---

* Many people think that *likin*, an inland tax, levied by the provincial authorities on foreign goods in transit (*loti-shui* being a terminal tax), is an illegal blackmail, but it rests on precisely the same foundation as every other Chinese ordinance—an Imperial Decree—and its legality was certainly recognised by the British and German Governments when they accepted seven *likin* collectorates as collateral security for the last Anglo-German loan.

late for it, but I fail to see the reasons for such a "counsel of despair." The Marquess of Salisbury, at the end of June, 1898, said: "If I am asked what our policy in China is, my answer is very simple. It is to maintain the Chinese Empire, to prevent it falling into ruins, to invite it into paths of reform, and to give it every assistance which we are able to give it, to perfect its defence or to increase its commercial prosperity. *By so doing we shall be aiding its cause and our own.*" * This announcement of policy has not been recalled.

In the meantime it is impossible for China, pressed on every side, and vaguely conscious that she stands at the "parting of the ways," that "the old order" is changing, and that she is in the grip of new forces, to collect herself with a view to the reforms from which she cannot hope to escape, and she falls back on her old idea of statesmanship—the playing off one foreign country against another. After a career of empire of two thousand years, in which she has increased in wealth and population up to the present time, she finds herself at the dawn of a new century, confronted by problems of which her classics and her experience offer no solution, and the greatest of these is the FOREIGNER.

In concluding this chapter, it is worth while to consider whether there are any indications of reform from within, and whether the phrase, "The awakening of China," represents fact or not.

Our mechanical inventions, steamers, railroads, gas, telegraphs, electric light, steam machinery, dredgers, artillery, torpedoes, arms of precision, submarine telegraphy, steam printing, photography— our surgery, the beauty and "up-keep" of our foreign settlements, and their admirable municipal government, and our obvious wealth, have all been emissaries knocking the conceit out of those who come in contact with them. Chinese now work telegraph lines, own and run steam launches in large numbers, enter our hospitals as medical students, and take admirable photographs, nearly perfect in *technique*, only lacking in artistic feeling. Factories owned and run by Chinese are springing up here and there, and may eventually be successful. One of the great passenger lines on the Lower Yangtze belongs to the "Chinese Merchants' Company."

* The italics are my own.—I. L. B.

Inland, for many years, foreign families have been living lives elsewhere described—of different nationalities, but all worshippers of one invisible God. Such persons have introduced into remote regions kerosene lamps—which are doing much to alter social life in China, soap, lucifer matches and vesta lights, condensed milk and tinned provisions, sewing machines—enormously adopted by tailors, and much else, the utility of all of which has been recognised, and which have compelled the Chinese to admit the ability of the "barbarians."

It is known, at least to the Chinese within fifty miles of the coast, and up the Yangtze, on which Japanese steam lines are now running, that the Japanese, who received from themselves the Chinese classics centuries ago, have adopted the political and legal systems, industries, and naval and military methods of foreigners; that they have a straight Government, which no foreign power dares to bully; that they have been received on equal terms into the family of nations, and that their methods of warfare, before which China collapsed, were foreign methods. The fact that a yellow people, venerating and teaching their own classics, with a social order founded on Confucian principles, and with Chinese as its official language, has adopted, to a great extent, Western civilisation, and with manifest advantage, has produced a remarkable effect since the war.

Last, but very far from being least, as it affects the brain of the country and its natural leaders, is the circulation of the scientific, historical, and Christian literature of the West. This is the Western ferment which may "leaven the whole lump." This circulation received an enormous impulse when the reform edicts of the Emperor were promulgated, making a knowledge of Western learning imperative on students, and has not been greatly affected by the subsequent retrograde movement. It cannot be doubted that those edicts, premature and unwise as some of them were, were the direct result of the foreign literature which the Emperor had previously been reading with avidity.

The larger portion of this literature, which I believe is destined to reform and transform China, has been published by a society founded twelve years ago by some of the leading men in China, and named the "Society for the Diffusion of Christian and

General Knowledge." Sir Robert Hart, G.C.M.G., is its president in China, and Mr. Timothy Richards, an enthusiast about the language and people, and an optimist about the future of the empire, is its secretary and inspiring spirit.

The literature for which the demand is now greater than the supply, consists of distinctly Christian books, such as *Butler's Analogy ;* a *Life of Christ; Christianity, and the Progress of Nations ;* scientific books, as on *Agricultural Chemistry* and *Astronomy ;* books on economic subjects, such as *Productive and Non - Productive Labour, The Relation of Education to National Progress*, etc., and some of our best standard books are now in circulation, together with such special literature as *Essays for the Times, The Renaissance of China, Progress of China's Neighbours*, a periodical called *A Review of the Times*, and various others. The drift of the desire for knowledge is shown by the very large sale of Mackenzie's *History of the Nineteenth Century*, and of a *History of the Japanese War; Sixty Years of Queen Victoria's Reign* being also much in demand.

These books and many others, circulating largely among the *literati*, at once creating and expressing aspirations, all present in some form or other that higher ideal which produced those reformers, greatly led by Kang Yen-Wei, who advocated political, commercial, educational, and religious reform in 1898, rendering it memorable in Chinese history as a year in which men showed that the welfare of their country was dearer to them than life itself.

A few instances taken at random show how the Western leaven is working. Large sums have been subscribed by the Chinese for the object of teaching Western languages and learning, specially in the ports. Two wealthy Chinese offered to raise 10,000 dollars for the enlargement of the Women's Hospital in Shanghai, if Dr. Reifsnyder, the lady medical missionary, would consent to teach, Western medicine to Chinese girls. A Cantonese, one of the managers of the China Merchants' Co., was so impressed by Mr. Richards' translation of Mackenzie's *History of the Nineteenth Century*, that he bought a hundred copies, and sent them to the leading mandarins in Peking.

A HUNAN gentleman, visiting Shanghai two years ago, met

with the "C.L.S." magazine, *Review of the Times*, and was so impressed with its helpfulness to China, that he ordered two hundred copies, and distributed them monthly in HUNAN to those who had specially opposed foreigners and Christianity. These men, in their turn, ordered a complete set of the "C.L.S." books, and read them for two years in order to be sure of their contents.   Recently the Literary Chancellor of the province wrote to the "C.L.S." to the effect that China must reform, and on the lines indicated in the Society's publications, and in the name of the governor and gentry of HUNAN invited the Chinese editor to become a professor in the college of the provincial capital.*

The volume on *Agricultural Chemistry* has been very largely read.   Early in 1899 the Viceroy of Nanking and others raised £50,000 for an agricultural college, and invited Mr. Bentley, the author of the book, an American missionary, to be its head. The Viceroy in Central China, Chang-Chih-Tung, whose views on the use of opium I have previously quoted, actually sympathised with the Yangtze anti-foreign riots in 1891, but by 1894 had been so profoundly influenced by the study of Western literature that he sent a large donation to the "C.L.S.," and has lately published a book in which he strongly advocates the immediate adoption of a modern system of education.

It is not alone among the older men that our literature is producing marked effects here and there, but the literary students in considerable numbers are fired with the desire for Western learning.   Fifteen hundred applied for entrance to the new Peking University, of which the learned Rev. W. Martin, author of *A Cycle of Cathay*, is principal.   Occasionally foreign literature produces almost grotesque effects.   A *Hsien* magistrate, having read Dr. Faber's *Civilization, East and West*, was much impressed by the chapter on our Western treatment of prisoners, and at once set his own to work at spinning, weaving, and basket-making, to the intense amusement of the retainers of the *yamen*.

In SZE CHUAN I saw few, if any, indications of the awakening

---

* It was what are known as the "Hunan Tracts," an infamous literature circulated throughout the Empire, which accuses Christians of the vilest crimes, and urges the populace to expel them, which have been the cause of several of the anti-foreign riots. Now HUNAN is welcoming Western learning and Christian teachers.

which undoubtedly exists. A foreign traveller, whether he speak Chinese or not, does not see below the surface, and the province is far away from the centres in which the Western leaven is working most energetically, but in several places where I halted the mandarin sent to inquire if I had any "foreign books?" Kuei-chow is one of the most anti-foreign of the provinces, and it is noteworthy that lately her governor has sent to the "C.L.S." for 1000 dollars' worth of Western literature.

I think that there is no doubt that the leaven of Western thought is working surely though slowly among the literary class, and that the reform movement, scotched, but not killed, by the strong measures of the Empress Dowager, grew out of it.

Two causes favour the spread of Western literature; first that the four hundred millions of the empire possess one written language, and second, that there are 200 examination centres in China, and that at each, from 5000 to 10,000 students, the mandarins, lawyers, and leaders of the future, a million in all, are under examination every year. Our best literature, and our Christian literature, supplied to these centres reaches the most influential homes in the country. Mr. Archibald Little, the pioneer of steam navigation on the Upper Yangtze, and himself a Chinese scholar, strongly urges the supply of "C.L.S." literature to all these centres. He considers that the mental revolution now proceeding, and the reform movement, are largely due to the influence of books, and even says that in the circulation of Western literature he sees the great hope for the "Open Door!"

That irresistible forces are beginning to drive China out of her conceit and seclusion is evident. Ten years ago there were only two or three papers in the vernacular besides the official *Peking Gazette*. To-day there are over seventy, and native journalism is actively developing. Through the press the Young China Party—the creation of Anglo-Chinese schools and foreign influence, chiefly in the ports—gives expression to those feelings of unrest and discontent which its wider outlook on affairs produces. Through it the younger *literati*, awakened to a new conception of patriotism by contact with Western thought, denounce the ignorance and corruption of the magistracy, and urge as a remedy the introduction of mathematics and political economy into the provincial examinations! The Viceroy, Chang-

Chih-Tung, not only founded a paper "which was to engage the sympathies of the literary class in the work of progress and reform, and to interest its readers in questions of international and general importance,"* but made its support compulsory in all the *yamens* and libraries in the *Hu* provinces. Its staff is said to be composed of men who combine broad views with classical scholarship, and it is reputed to have great influence with the upper classes, even though the reforming Viceroy has had to withdraw his official support from it.

It is too early to write of the probable influence of the coming railroads. It is easy to take an exaggerated view, but undoubtedly rapid communication is a great foe to darkness and ignorance. Everywhere there are indications of a change in the "classes" which lead the "masses." There is a Chinese saying, that "if you wish to irrigate a piece of land you must first carry the water to the highest level, so, if you wish to enlighten a nation, you must begin with its leaders." Very important and valuable inquiries have been made into all subjects connected with trade; but this mental change, which will probably exercise an enormous influence on trade and our relations with China, has been singularly overlooked.

It is perhaps best that there should be no abrupt rupture with the past. The reform edicts, though abrogated, have kindled a flame; and though there may be suspended progress, China can never really go back any more, for the forces which have been set in motion have never yet suffered defeat. "The mills of God grind slowly," but they grind inexorably. Let us be patient with our ancient ally, and "invite" rather than bully her into "paths of reform." I fear much that the desperate determination of the European nations to secure her potentialities of trade by fair means or foul, may be driving her to her doom, and that in the clash and turmoil the symptoms of an increasing desire for reform from within—a reform which would slowly give us all we can righteously ask—are being overlooked or ignored.

Into her archaic and unreformed Orientalism the Western leaven has fallen for good or evil. Rudely awakened by the Japanese victories out of her long sleep, China, half dismayed

* *Times'* Shanghai correspondent.

and wholly dazed, with much loss of "face," and shaken confidence in the methods of diplomacy which have served her so well in the past, finds herself confronted by an array of powerful, grasping, ambitious, and not always over-scrupulous powers, bent, it may be, on over-reaching her and each other, ringing with barbarian hands the knell of the customs and polity which are the legacy of Confucius, clamouring for ports and concessions, and bewildering her with reforms, suggestions, and demands, of which she sees neither the expediency nor the necessity.

In this turmoil, and with the European nations thundering at her gates, it is impossible for China to attempt any reforms which would not from the nature of the case be piecemeal and superficial. The reform of an administration like hers needs the prolonged and careful consideration of the best minds in the empire, with such skilled and disinterested foreign advice as was given by Sir Harry Parkes to Japan when she embarked on her new career.

It must be remembered that the remodelling of the administrative system of China is beset with difficulties which have not existed in any other country, and which are accentuated by the vast population and area of the empire. Chinese statesmen (if there be such) have to consider what reforms could be carried out with the approval of the masses, *i.e.*, without bringing about a revolution. The very abuses of administration have gained something of the sanctity which attends on custom among this singular people. It is most important that those who have to deal with Chinese affairs should be able to obtain such information as would enable them to make a just estimate of the strength and probable diffusion of the desire for reform among the *literati*, at whose feet the masses lie with a genuine reverence.

China is certainly at the dawn of a new era. Whether the twentieth century shall place her where she ought to be, in the van of Oriental nations, or whether it shall witness her disintegration and decay, depends very largely on the statesmanship and influence of Great Britain.

ITINERARY

Cheng-tu Fu to Shanghai, by water, 2000 miles.

* The Chinese *li* is 1814 English feet, but the mountain and the plain *li* differ in length.

APPENDICES

APPENDIX A.

THE Rules of the Chinese Guilds are too long and elaborate for insertion in this appendix, and condensation would do them an injustice.

APPENDIX B.*

I. NET VALUE OF TOTAL TRADE OF PORTS IN THE YANGTZE BASIN, 1898.

	£
Shanghai	13,296,643
Chungking	2,614,031
Ichang	194,359
Sha-shih	25,666
Hankow	8,065,717
Kiukiang	2,625,083
Wuhu	1,527,079
Chinkiang	3,471,532
Soochow	229,113
Hangchow	1,199,022
	£33,248,245

* These tables were kindly prepared for this volume by W. H. Wilkinson, Esq., H.B.M. Consul at Ningpo, from the Trade Report for 1898 of the Chinese Imperial Maritime Customs. The Haikwan tael, in which the Customs accounts are kept, has been taken at 3s., as a fairer current equivalent than the 2/10⅝ average, by the advice of Mr. Jamieson, C.M.G., late Consul-General at Shanghai.

2. TRADE OF SHANGHAI, 1898.

	£	£
Foreign Goods—		
Total import		19,073,534
Less re-exported —		
(*a*) To foreign countries and Hongkong	745,000	
(*b*) To Chinese ports (chiefly to northern and Yangtze ports)	13,914,558	
	14,659,558	
Making net total foreign imports	4,413,976	

Native Produce—

Imported (chiefly from northern and Yangtze ports, Ningpo, Swatow, Canton, and Hangchow)		11,413,637
Less re-exported to foreign countries and Chinese ports	9,724,673	
Making net total Native imports	1,688,964	
Native produce of local origin exported to foreign countries	4,676,674 ⎫	7,193,704
Ditto to Chinese ports	2,517,029 ⎭	
Gross value of trade of Shanghai		£37,680,875
Net „ „ „	£13,296,643	

3. TOTAL NET IMPORT OF OPIUM INTO CHINA FOR 1898.

Quantity		6,638,333 lbs.
Value		£4,388,365

4. TOTAL VALUE OF FOREIGN TRADE OF CHINA IN 1898

= Hk. Taels 368,616,483 = £55,292,472.

5. SHARE OF ENGLAND IN CHINA'S TRADE FOR 1898.*

I. *Shipping.*

Flag.	Entries and Clearances.	Tonnage.	Percentages of Tonnage.	
			(A.) Including Chinese.	(B.) Excluding Chinese.
British	22,609	21,265,966	62·12	81·65
Chinese	23,547	8,187,572	23·92	—
Other nationalities	6,505	4,780,042	13·96	18·35
	52,661	34,253,580	100	100

* Note that these figures include trade conducted by Chinese, or under the Chinese flag, passing through the Maritime Customs.

II. *Trade.*

Flag.	Total Values Foreign & Coast Trade.	Transit Trade.	Total.	Percentages of Value.	
	£	£	£	(A.)	(B)
British . .	76,236,290	2,695,437	78,931,727	51·88	79·40
Chinese . .	50,163,445	2,410,663	52,574,108	34·56	—
Other nationalities	19,385,235	1,217,343	20,602,578	13·56	20·60
	145,784,970	6,323,443	152,108,413	100	100

6. PRINCIPAL IMPORTS INTO CHINA FROM FOREIGN COUNTRIES, 1898.*

	Quantity.	Value.
Opium . . .	6,638,000 lbs. . .	£4,388,385
Cotton goods . . .	.	11,642,824
Raw cotton . .	30,534,000 lbs. . .	425,959
Woollen Goods . .	.	478,525
Metals . . .	.	1,468,061
Matches (mainly Japanese)	11,352,304 gross .	389,561
Oil (Kerosene) . .	96,882,126 gallons .	1,787,205
Sugar . . .	10,793 tons . .	2,029,267
Other imports . .	.	8,827,113
Total . . .	. . .	. £31,436,900

7. PRINCIPAL EXPORTS FROM CHINA TO FOREIGN COUNTRIES, 1898.*

	Quantity.	Value.
Silk, of all kinds .	. 35,651,333 lbs. . .	. £8,415,584
Tea „ „ .	. 205,146,667 lbs. . .	. 4,331,922
Other Exports . .	.	. 11,108,066
Total . . .	. . .	. £23,855,572

* These tables, giving an excess of imports over exports, will be seen not to tally with my statement in the final chapter. In other years similar tables have given rise to the belief that China is being denuded of silver to pay for the balance, and is drifting towards bankruptcy. But the Inspector-General, in the Customs Report for 1898, from which these figures are taken, points out that, taking into account the value of the gold exported from China, of the tea sent to Siberia and Russia *viâ* the Han River, of the twenty million pounds of tea exported annually to Tibet, of the junk traffic to Korea and the South, and of other exports of which the Customs take no cognizance, there is an actual excess of exports over imports, as was shown by careful statistics in 1897. He also points out as a positive proof that the nation is well able to pay its way, that the Government remittances to Europe for the service of loans, amounting in 1898 to about Hk. Tls. 18,000,000, were made through foreign banks by the medium of bills of exchange against exports.—I. L. B.

INDEX

A.

Aconite, Trade in, 339.
Agricultural Chemistry, Circulation of the vol. on, 541.
Albumen factories, 65.
Allen, Consul Clement, his report on mission hospitals, 47.
Altar of Incense, An, 418.
American Baptists, The, 471.
Ancestor-worship, 522.
An Hui, North, 6.
An-shun Bridge, The, 460.

B.

Baber, Mr., 3, 265, 451; his papers on Western China, 156; on rock-dwellings, 467.
Baggage coolies, 196.
Baian Kara range, The, 2.
Baker, Mr., 416.
Bamboo suspension bridges, 378.
"Barbarians," Villages of the, 376, 377, 382–385.
Barbers, Itinerant, 80.
Be-dien, The author's interpreter, 55, 155; his character, 207.
Beggars, Treatment of, 187.
"Bellows" gorge. See Feng Hsiang.
Benevolent guilds, 182.
Benjamin, Bishop, 99, 100, 102.
Beresford, M.P., Lord Charles, 530; his suggested reforms, 536.
Blakiston, Captain, his description of the "Pillar of Heaven," 106; of trackers, 142.
Bourne, Consul, 140, 142, 149 (note), 496 (note), 499; on opium smoking, 515.
Brick-tea factories, 65.
Bridges, 231, 232, 252.

British Merchant, Dependence of the, upon the Chinese compradore, 20, 21 ; decrease of his trade, 64.
Buffalo, The water, 232, 235.
Bullock, Mr. and Mrs., 15.

C.

Callum, Mr., 348.
Canadian Mission, The, 519.
Canons of Filial Duty, The, 277.
"Canton opium," 512.
Carles, Consul, 188 (note); on missionaries helping trade, 47.
Cassels, Bishop, 281, 286.
Census, The taking of a, 270.
Century of Surnames, The, 277.
Chai-jen, 211, 390, 393, 396.
Chair-travelling, 202.
Chang, 423.
Chang Chih-tung, H. E., on opium smoking, 516; on education, 541; influence of Western literature on, 541.
Chang-fei, The temple of, 166, 167, 168 (note).
Chang-wo, The s.s., 83.
Chapel of Meditations, The, 358.
Che, 145.
Che-kiang, Province of, 1 ; use of *pahs* or haulovers in, 32; Christian converts in, 521.
Chengtu, 2, 8, 351, 352, 458, 463; musk trade of, 339; canals and bridges of, 355; population of, 343; temples of, 357; wall of, 355.
Chengtu plain, The, 194, 324, 329, 334, 347, 458 ; products of, 343, 348.
Chia-ling Fu, 3, 464, 477.
Chia-ling river, The, 3, 273, 280, 281, 314 ; affluents of, 4 ; walls on, 86.
Chiang-Ku, 463.

APPEAL of One Half of the Human Race, WOMEN, Against the Pretensions of the Other Half, MEN, to Retain them in Political, and Hence in Civil and Domestic, Slavery

William Thompson

With a new Introduction by Richard Pankhurst

This passionate summons to 'Women . . . wherever ye breathe degraded—awake!' was written in 1825. William Thompson described the *Appeal* as 'the joint property' of himself and Anna Wheeler, and parts of it as the exclusive product of her 'mind and pen' for, as he wrote, although he had thought much about 'the inequalities of the sexual laws', it was she who suffered from them.

The *Appeal* was provoked by James Mill's cryptic dismissal of political representation for women. Thompson, in responding, decried woman's reduction to 'involuntary breeding machine and household slave', and called upon men to throw off the 'tattered cloak' of male despotism. Today, more than a century and a half after its original publication the *Appeal* remains a landmark in the history of both the women's movement and of socialist thought.

'Key nineteenth-century text . . . at last made available in a popular edition, expressing the roots of English feminism'—*City Limits*

THE SUBJECTION OF WOMEN
John Stuart Mill

&

ENFRANCHISEMENT OF WOMEN
Harriet Taylor Mill

These two extraordinary landmarks in the struggle for women's equality came out of the passionate commitment of John Stuart Mill (1806-1873) and Harriet Taylor (1807-1858) to liberty and egalitarianism, and to each other through their partnership of almost thirty years. *Enfranchisement of Women* was first published in 1851, and *The Subjection of Women* in 1869, both powerfully arguing for women's full equality to alleviate the 'great amount of unhappiness even now produced by the feeling of a wasted life'.

'Has an assured welcome among women's studies courses, researchers into the history of the women's movement and feminists everywhere'— *Mary Stott, Guardian*